Law, Governance and Technology Series

Volume 21

The *Law-Governance and Technology Series* is intended to attract manuscripts arising from an interdisciplinary approach in law, artificial intelligence and information technologies. The idea is to bridge the gap between research in IT law and IT-applications for lawyers developing a unifying techno-legal perspective. The series will welcome proposals that have a fairly specific focus on problems or projects that will lead to innovative research charting the course for new interdisciplinary developments in law, legal theory, and law and society research as well as in computer technologies, artificial intelligence and cognitive sciences. In broad strokes, manuscripts for this series may be mainly located in the fields of the Internet law (data protection, intellectual property, Internet rights, etc.), Computational models of the legal contents and legal reasoning, Legal Information Retrieval, Electronic Data Discovery, Collaborative Tools (e.g. Online Dispute Resolution platforms), Metadata and XML Technologies (for Semantic Web Services), Technologies in Courtrooms and Judicial Offices (E-Court), Technologies for Governments and Administrations (E-Government), Legal Multimedia, and Legal Electronic Institutions (Multi-Agent Systems and Artificial Societies).

More information about this series at http://www.springer.com/series/8808

Joan-Josep Vallbé

Frameworks for Modeling Cognition and Decisions in Institutional Environments

A Data-Driven Approach

Springer

Joan-Josep Vallbé
Constitutional Law and Political Science
University of Barcelona
Barcelona
Spain

ISSN 2352-1902 ISSN 2352-1910 (electronic)
ISBN 978-94-017-9426-8 ISBN 978-94-017-9427-5 (eBook)
DOI 10.1007/978-94-017-9427-5
Springer Dordrecht Heidelberg New York London

Library of Congress Control Number: 2014951834

Printed on acid-free paper

Springer is part of Springer Science+Business Media (www.springer.com)

A la meva mare.
A la memòria dels meus avis materns.

Foreword

Certainly it is worthwhile to read this volume on the organizational side of judicial decision-making. It is a pleasure to introduce this sound analysis of junior judges' behavior in on-call services at Spanish lower courts. However, we think that this book means a lot more than that.

The author, Joan-Josep Vallbé, carries out his study at least within three interrelated dimensions—cognitive, behavioral and institutional. Starting from the general framework of bounded rationality and institutional analysis, he identifies the mechanisms at work and the conditions of uncertainty under which junior judges face a difficult decision-making environment. In this sense, as he states, it is also a study on processes that junior judges go through in order to achieve expertise in an institutionalized domain. The challenge that Vallbé takes up implies a thorough description of judges' cognitive skills and the way in which they develop a specific practical knowledge to overcome the actual situations they come to face. But, in documenting these skills and processes, the author displays as well a rich array of methods that are required to successfully tackle the problems raised by the social and political analysis of linked and shared data.

Moreover, "this book combines standard multivariate statistical methods such as ordinary least squares and logistic regression models with advanced machine learning techniques such as hierarchical clustering, multidimensional scaling, and topic models, thus treating text as data". This is right. Data analysis for contemporary political science is at the core of this work.

The result constitutes an elegant and updated development of the institutional perspective on human and artificial information processing in the AI tradition advanced by Herbert Simon, Alan Newell, James March, Paul DiMaggio and Walter Powell. This is not surprising. Actually, Joan-Josep Vallbé contributed significantly to the Spanish translation of *The Sciences of the Artificial*,[1] and developed the theoretical

---

Human rational behavior (and the rational behavior of all physical symbol systems) is shaped by a scissors whose two blades are the structure of task environments and the computational capabilities of the actor.

Herbert A. Simon

---

[1] H. A. Simon, *Las ciencias de lo artificial*, translation by Pablo Noriega and J.-J. Vallbé, Ed. Comares, Granada, 2006.

and methodological framework presented in this volume within successive research projects that furnished him with an ethnographic insight of courts and judicial behavior,[2] and with a firsthand knowledge of semantic technologies.[3] In the end, this book develops data analysis processing to open up a new space for a political science perspective on courts and legal settings as socio-cognitive institutions.

"Decision-making" is the cognitive action that shaped the notion of rationality in the second half of the XXth century. Inheritor of that tradition, Vallbé explores rationality in a rather particular social context that reveals the interplay between formal structured knowledge, unwritten social norms and practical problem solving under pressing moral circumstances. His subjects are junior judges whose hesitant decision-making is crunched between the weight of an institutional role recently invested on them and the pungent urgency of real life situations. At the fringe of institutional power and armed only with rote theoretical learning they are compelled to act.

Such rationality in the fringe of institutions is the problem-domain that the author defines and allows us to glimpse its epistemic, erotetic and ethnographic richness. Vallbé is guided in the exploration of this form of socio-cognitive rationality by the objective of constructing artifacts that support decision-making towards a more comfortable and effective performance and, as we have mentioned, he moves towards this objective through the application of a wise mixture of tools and methodologies.

In reading this text one is left with the pleasant realisation that Vallbé's wise choice of problem domain and approach will open paradigmatic research questions. Perhaps, on the shoulders of classic examples like Simon's work in the Bureau of Public Administration, Joan-Josep Vallbe's work on the Spanish judiciary behavior will help us shape a new type of bounded socio-cognitive rationality from decision-making in the fringe of institutions.

If *schools are for fish, not for scientists*, as Simon used to say, his is a genuine personal research journey. We wish the reader to learn as much as we have done from his endeavor.

IDT-IIA CSIC, Barcelona — Pompeu Casanovas
July 2014 — Pablo Noriega

[2] *Observatorio de Cultura Judicial Observatorio de Cultura Judicial del CGPJ. Estudio de datos cuantitativos y cualitativos; diseño y construcción de una red telemática de soporte para los jóvenes jueces en su primer destino, dependiente de la Escuela Judicial Española*, SEC2001-2581-C02-01, 2001–2004.

[3] *Semantically Enabled Knowledge Technologies*. EU-IST 2003-506826 (2003–2006) http://www.se-kt-project.com/.

Acknowledgements

A book is not the result of what one has learned from oneself, but rather a work about what one learns from others. Citing the work of others is the standard way to acknowledge their help, but all of us know that a great amount of help and inspiration comes in other ways.

Some of this help is formal such as funding and travel grants. In this sense, part of this book was developed under the projects *Observatorio de Cultura Judicial* [Observatory of Judicial Culture, OJC] (SEC2001-2581-C02-01, Ministry of Science and Technology), SEKT (Semantically Enabled Knowledge Technologies, EU-IST Project IST-2003-506826 SEKT),[4] and SEJ (2006-10695, Ministry of Education and Science). I would like to thank the Spanish General Council of the Judiciary and the Judicial School.

The Iuriservice application, which shall be referred to along the work, was firstly developed by the Institute of Law and Technology at the Autonomous University of Barcelona (UAB), and the company Intelligent Software Components (iSOCO), with the collaboration of the Spanish Judicial School and the General Council of the Judiciary (CGPJ). This research was also funded by the Agència de Gestió d'Ajuts Universitaris i de Recerca (AGAUR) from the Catalan Government (2006 BE-2 10242). I am also enormously grateful to Daniela Tiscornia from the Istituto di Teoria e Tecniche dell'Informazione Giuridica (ITTIG, Florence) for her invitation that made possible a stay in Italy to make research and give a push to critical parts of the research for the book.[5]

This book draws on my doctoral work, and obviously first-hand, priviledged help and direction was received from Pompeu Casanovas, former PhD advisor and yet now my friend. *Gràcies!* Pablo Noriega let me steal hist time and knowledge on many occasions, and presented me with Herbert Simon's *Reason in Human Affairs*.

Moreover, I would like to express my gratitude to all junior judges who participated in our survey, and in particular to those whom I interviewed for their kindness and absolute collaboration when I showed up in their courts. Logically this work

[4] www.sekt-project.org.

[5] Funded by AGAUR (BE-DGR 2008).

would have never been possible without their participation. Mr. Pascual Ortuo deserves special mention in this work for providing me with the opportunity to finish up my field work. And thanks to all those researchers who participated as interviewers in the survey on junior judges throughout Spain.

Mercedes Ayuso (UB) and Mónica Bécue-Bertaut (UPC) have been really important in this work, since they gave me access to the first database ever on Spanish junior judges. Thank you very much for that and for understanding my latish demands. Warmest thanks also to M. Antònia Martí for her guidance in Computational Linguistics and to all the CLiC and THERA staff (especially to Montse Nofre) for their help regarding the work on textual corpora. Granting me access to the morphological analyzer has been essential for this work. The R developers and user community will have my eternal gratitude.

The book was finished during my postdoctoral stage, first as visiting researcher at the Chair of Multilevel Governance of the Vrije Universiteit Amsterdam, and currently at the Institute for Information Law (IViR), Universiteit van Amsterdam. My thanks to Gary Marks and Liesbet Hooghe (VU), and to my new colleagues at UvA.

I would like to thank the two anonymous reviewers of this book, whose comments helped to improve my work, and Diana Nijenhuijzen and Neil Olivier at Springer for their assistance and help during the publishing process. Thanks also to my old colleagues and friends Aleks Jakulin, Enrico Francesconi, and Albert Meroño.

Special thanks to Esther Pano for all her kindness, wit, warmth, and for having read a draft of the first chapters in due time. And millions of thanks to Jaume Magre, such a combination of energy and wisdom, such a crossing between Ismael and Ahab.

Much other help, though, comes in rather informal ways, and it includes comments to drafts, coffee chats, wine chats, *pa-amb-tomàquet* chats, and various forms of giving and receiving feedback, affect, and love: thanks to Àlex, Oriol, Jose, Albert, Luis Marcos, Jesús, David, Francesc.

Thanks Johann Sebastian, Bob, John, Miles, Lee, Van, Johnny, Ben, and Chris for making me aware of so many different aspects of beauty.

The dedication of this book goes to my mother, for being the best example I know of rational adaptation to uncertain environments. My grandparents, I miss them every day. I would also like to thank the (little) rest of my family, especially to my sisters M. Àngels and Marta, of whom I am the proudest brother.

Contents

About the Author

Joan-Josep Vallbé is a political scientist. He works with social and computer scientists, urban designers, and legal professionals, on how to model, measure, and analyze the interaction between citizens and variation in their environment. Change may occur in micro-level contexts such as problem spaces in choice situations or in macro-level phenomena such as metropolitan growth or the regulatory environment. His recent affiliations include the University of Barcelona, and the Institute for Information Law (IViR) at the University of Amsterdam.

List of Figures

List of Tables

Chapter 1
Introduction

Abstract The work of the book that follows began because of a problem: a group of professionals (Spanish junior judges) needed to improve the conditions under which they had to make their decisions. So far a great deal of research effort (Casanovas et al. 2003; Benjamins et al. 2004a, 2005; Casanovas et al. 2005a, 2006a; Casellas et al. 2007) has been devoted to show and test that a solution to this problem might come through the design and application of an artificial intelligent device that helped in their decision-making process.

However, the aim of the present work is not to focus upon the process of building a system designed to support decision-making, but to explore whether and why such a decisional, organizational problem existed, and how it could be detected and represented. In other words, our objective is to explore what makes specially problematic this decision-making process by Spanish junior judges, and eventually why should an intelligent device may help them. This way we expect to better understand the role of organizations in making decisions.

In this introduction we shall start contextualizing our work. We then proceed briefly outlining the empirical background that surrounds our research. Thirdly we will introduce the artificial decision-support system we mentioned: its main features and the kind of research it implied. Fourthly we give a brief account of the theoretical scope of this book within the general field of decision-making within organizations. Finally, the work to be carried out in this book is presented. First, we introduce its basic hypotheses and assumptions. Second, its structure is outlined.

1.1 Decision-Making in Spanish Courts

The Spanish legal system belongs to the mainstream of the European civil law traditions. The civil law model, as opposed to the common law systems, refers to the legal orders that have developed in continental Europe—e.g., France, Spain, Portugal, Italy, and Germany—as well as in those nations of the world that have been under the rule of those continental, European countries—such as Brazil or Perú.

J.-J. Vallbé, *Frameworks for Modeling Cognition and Decisions in Institutional Environments*, Law, Governance and Technology Series 21, DOI 10.1007/978-94-017-9427-5_1

A distinct feature of civil law judicial systems is their bureaucratic component, which means that civil law judges are to be regarded as a branch of a bigger bureaucratic organization (the State). In this sense Merryman (2007, p. 38) comments that in civil law systems the "judicial service is a bureaucratic career; the judge is a functionary, a civil servant; the judicial function is narrow, mechanical, and uncreative".

In Spain, the administration of justice is in effect a large bureaucratic organization filled with different kinds of civil servants who usually develop lifelong careers within it. Other distinctive features of the Spanish judicial system are centralization, hierarchy, and unity of jurisdiction, though it has a high degree of complexity due to the existence of specialized jurisdictions. Moreover, courts are organized in different levels, whence decisions in lower courts may be challenged and appeals filed to higher courts. The Supreme Court [*Tribunal Supremo*] is the apex of the system, and below a number of instances—either general (such as the provincial audiences) or specialized (like the National Audience)—structure a complex, multilevel legal and judicial system.

Courts of First Instance and Magistrate [*Juzgados de Primera Instancia e Instrucción*], or simply lower courts, constitute the lower end of the judicial system proper.[1] These courts are the actual entry into Spain's judicial system, and these are the courts filled with junior judges (except those located in large cities, which are occupied by senior judges). Courts of First Instance and Magistrate handle most civil cases and decide on minor criminal offenses, but are also responsible for starting preliminary proceedings in any type of criminal offense.

1.1.1 On Call

One of the main organizational principles governing the Spanish legal and judicial system is the on-call service. Regularly lower courts remain on call for full eight-days periods, though the regular recurrence of on-call periods depends on the number of courts within a given judicial district. Should there only be one single court in a judicial district—which happens in 20 percent of the judicial districts—that judge and the court office would be almost *always* on call.

While on call, the court office is responsible for handling all incoming cases reported by the police, the public prosecution or by citizens at large. When an offense takes place within the boundaries of a judicial district, the judge on call will be in

[1] Justices of the Peace exist also at the local level. In fact, they are in municipalities without Courts of First Instance and Magistrate, and are filled with lay judges or magistrates who do not belong to the same administrative civil service as regular judges. Actually, these magistrates of the Peace are appointed by local governments themselves, and unlike judges a law degree is not required for them. In a sense, they are thought of as a first instance for citizen conflict resolution for minor civil issues.

charge of supervising all enquiries related to the facts of the case. Since the Spanish criminal procedure, like in any other civil law system, is based on the "inquisitorial" principle (as opposed to the "adversarial" or "accusatorial" principle of the common law system), judges on call are to lead the judicial police in all criminal enquiries (Merryman 2007).

The different activities the judge has to endure while on call may entail paying attention over a number of parallel issues (raised by the police, lawyers, prosecutors, citizens), and obviously the need for quick decisions seriously handicaps (or impedes) reviewing jurisprudence or precedents. At the best of times inexperienced judges have to rely on uncertain consultation with peers or senior judges, although crises may easily break in the wee hours, thus making consultation with peers quite unfeasible.

Thus when on-call, the decision-making processes are very likely to take place in a context of ambiguity, in sharp contrast with other routine and rule-based decisions that bind most legal proceedings in ordinary judicial decision-making.

1.2 Related Work

The few number of studies about this particular issue so far tell us that the on-call period is perceived by most Spanish junior judges as a stressful period that continually challenges their training as judges. For instance, Ayuso et al. (2002, 2003) gathered several data about the Spanish junior judges' needs, concerns, and problems, concluding that this should be a relevant topic to consider in future research (Ayuso et al. 2002, 2003) since the on-call service "raises many problems and doubts" among judges (Benjamins et al. 2004b).

In order to determine this account, Ayuso et al. (2003) used textual statistics techniques to analyze the judges' answers to a group of open-ended questions regarding their problems and difficulties in their workplaces. These data were gathered in the first large-scale survey campaign ever carried out in Spain on this particular matter (i.e., junior judges).[2] The main objective of this analysis was to "extract the domains in which the young judges face difficulties" and "to find problem areas of young judges", revealing that the on-call service received a major focus of attention among younger and more inexperienced judges. Yet, beyond that little work has been carried

[2] Judicial statistics in Spain have a qualified tradition that began with the end of Franco's authoritarian regime (1975) and the approval of a democratic constitution in 1978. Since 1984, the General Council of the Judiciary (the agency that rules the Spanish judges) has been carrying out nine in-depth opinion surveys among the Spanish population about the administration of justice, and seven internal surveys among Spanish judges. See Toharia Cortés and García de la Cruz Herrero (2005) for a quick review.

out so far in the direction of understanding the precise terms in which the on-call service influences junior judges' decision making.[3]

1.3 A Decision-Support System

Due to the fact that the on-call service in lower courts was perceived as a special factor of ambiguity and instability among junior judges regarding their institutional integration within the Spanish judicial system, a number of research and technology projects were carried out in order to deal with this problem. Indeed, since 2000, the Institute of Law and Technology (at the Universitat Autònoma de Barcelona) has been leading many research projects and case studies related to Spanish junior judges with the aim of

- identifying and assessing their features and needs, in order to
- build an intelligent decision-support system—called IURISERVICE—to help solving decision-making problems raised in lower courts when on-call.

Briefly stated, IURISERVICE is an intelligent FAQ system to provide assistance to young judges at their first appointment.[4] It is important to notice that this intelligent system shall not replace the legal databases that currently are a key piece in the everyday work of Spanish judges. They usually store judgements and legal doctrine, and enable an easy and quick access to this information (Rodrigo et al. 2004).

Instead, IURISERVICE is a web-based application that retrieves answers to questions raised by Spanish junior judges. This system offers access to a frequently asked questions (FAQ) database through a natural language interface—using semantically enriched technologies—where the judge describes the problem at hand and the application responds with a list of relevant question-answer pairs that offer solutions to that particular problem (Benjamins et al. 2005; Casanovas et al. 2006a).

Yet building a knowledge-based system to be used by actual users puts forth a set of methodological challenges that must be addressed in due time. An important one refers to the data available from which knowledge has to be acquired.

From data gathered through an extensive survey carried out in its most part during 2004–2005 (Casanovas et al. 2005b), a bulk of 800 questions referring to judges' practical problems was extracted. Then, with the participation and collaboration of the General Council of the Judiciary (GCPJ), the questions containing dilemmas (mostly regarding best-practices during on-call hours or staff management), were answered by senior judges—at the time teachers of the Spanish Judicial School).

[3] Rodrigo et al. (2004), Casanovas et al. (2005b), and Casanovas et al. (2006b) offer analyses on the technological implications of such a situation among judges, but a study on the decision process itself is still lacking.

[4] See Rodrigo et al. (2004) and Casanovas et al. (2005b) for a first contextualization.

The decision-support system was a milestone in the wider Observatory of Judicial Culture (*Observatorio de Cultura Judicial*, OCJ],[5] born out of a national-funded project in 2001 in order to carry out research on judicial behavior, reasoning, and professional profiles of judges, junior and senior. Its main objectives were to identify how the judges were currently working, which were their difficulties, and to provide the Spanish judicial system with useful tools to improve the performance of its judiciary (Poblet et al. 2008). In 2003, the European Comission-funded project SEKT offered the necessary framework within which IURISERVICE could be built and later implemented,[6] and a wonderful environment within which the present work began to walk.

1.4 Expert Decision-Making Within Organizations

Many general ideas underlie this work. One of them has been in the agenda of the cognitive and behavioral political sciences during the last 50 years—that "there is an intimate connection between organizational structure and the learning of frames of reference and roles by members of organizations" (Simon 1996, p. 161). This hypothesis was foreshadowed in Herbert A. Simon's *Administrative Behavior* as early as the 1940s (Simon 1947),[7] and was further elaborated in that milestone of analytical thinking that is March and Simon's *Organizations* (March and Simon 1958). Since then, a great deal of work has been done in bringing together different kinds of empirical findings in order to build theory on the implications of organizational constraints in human behavior, including decision making under ambiguity and uncertainty , thus populating a varied range of research fields:

[5] The Observatory of Judicial Culture (SEC2001-2581-C02-01, Ministry of Science and Technology) results from a coordinate project between the Autonomous University of Barcelona (UAB), the University of Barcelona (UB), the Polytechnic University of Catalonia (UPC), Intelligent Software Components (iSOCO) and the board of directors of the Spanish Judicial School.

[6] Semantically Enabled Knowledge Technologies, EU-IST Project IST-2003-506826 SEKT, www.sekt-project.org.

[7] Herbert Simon revised and published four editions of *Administrative Behavior*, of which only the third and fourth ones implied major changes to the original work (the second edition of 1957 may be considered a reprint). In the third edition Simon (1976) kept intact the first 11 chapters of the original edition (grouping them as part I of the new book) and added a second part which included 6 new chapters based on the author's previously published work on the theory of administration. Eleven years afterwards, Simon revised the book and produced a fourth and last edition (Simon 1997). For this new edition the author kept the original 11 chapters intact again, but changed the structure of the book compared to the third edition. Instead of adding more updated material to the third edition's second part, Simon opted for removing that entire part and producing a commentary for each of the original 11 chapters of *Administrative Behavior*, which implied a considerable updating effort (each commentary includes completely updated references). In order to stress out the historical moment in which several ideas where firstly pointed out, we shall cite the three editions distinctly throughout the book.

- *Organization theory*, which offers a general context upon which this research is to be founded.
- *Decision-making in organizational settings*, which makes decisions the central unit in analyzing human behavior in maze-like environments.
- *Decision-support systems in organizations*, which try to make more effective the steps along the paths of the maze.
- *Studies on rationality*, which are the bases upon which the study of human behavior may be supported.
- *Organizational learning*, which tries to explain how people become experts in certain organizational environments, and also how organizations learn from experience.
- *User-centered AI systems construction*, which shows that unless knowledge-based systems are based upon empirical data about users needs, and are tested by experts or users, they are very unlikely to be neither used nor useful.

The work that follows inhabits the boundary region between all of these fields, and it intends to benefit from each of them with the aim of understanding how people's behavior is influenced by their organizational environment, at the same time that reflects on how technology can help reducing uncertainty in particular scenarios. Thus I adopt a descriptive approach to decision-making (how decisions *are* made) keeping an eye on its prescriptive dimension (how decisions *might be* improved).

1.5 The Book

As a general framework, this book shows the results of a research about the implications—theoretical, methodological, and practical—of bounded rationality in the operation of a legal (political) institution. In particular, the work focuses on decisions made under uncertainty, and thus it emphasizes the role of decision-making in the analysis of organizations. This approach implies the distinction between two different kinds of mechanisms that take place in a decision-making environment.

On one hand, the first group of mechanisms regard the inner, cognitive mechanisms at work when actors—as information-processing systems and problem-solvers—make decisions, which impels us to take into account the limitations of knowledge and computing capabilities of the decision-maker. In order to do that, empirical work is needed to identify goals, problem perception and problem-solving strategies.

On the other hand, there are general political mechanisms among and within organizations, which "are intended to explain how the interests of the participants get balanced, compromised, suppressed, or are met to varying degrees" (Sylvan et al. 1990), and "provide a stable environment [. . .] that makes at least a modicum of rationality possible" (Simon 1983). These upper-level mechanisms provide in principle a general framework and a pattern of events in which decisions are possible and—more important—where its consequences may be somehow predicted or calculated (at least to a degree human beings can survive with).

While a great amount of literature and research has been devoted to analyze organizations as reliable patterns of events for (boundedly) rational decision-making, less effort has been consecrated to study when and under which circumstances these organizations cease to be such a reliable pattern of events for their members, in which case decision-makers face a number of particular problems.

1.5.1 Hypotheses and Basic Assumptions

A general formulation of our hypothesis is that the on-call service in Spanish lower courts challenges this organization's role as a reliable pattern of events from the judges' point of view.

In other words, the on-call service in the Spanish judicial system acts as a well defined organizational constraint in junior judges' decision-making process to the point of challenging both the predictability of their decisions, and their training as legal professionals. A key feature to understand this claim is that this books defends that this challenge is so due to the exclusively practical nature of the problems which take place during the on-call service, which contrasts with the theory-based content of both the standard Spanish legal education and regular judicial procedures.

Therefore the work presented in this book is based upon at least three important assumptions about human rationality and decision making according to its descriptive aim and therefore to the results of empirical research in this field.

1. First, that when judges try to find solutions to specific, practical problems, what they basically do—as all human beings—is to process information.
2. Secondly, the information that is processed is not specifically *legal* but information about the environment that shapes the decision to be made.
3. Thirdly, judges act rationally—i.e. they pursuit their goals by rational means—but as all human beings they are also constrained both by their cognitive capacities and by their institutional environment.

In order to give a clear idea of what are the potential and intended contributions of the book, these assumptions are further explained, qualified, and discussed in the first part of the book, while the second part is devoted to put our hypotheses to test against data.

The book has two main general goals. The first one is to explore the limits of "institutional rationality" from an information-processing standpoint, using for that the institution of the on-call service in Spanish lower courts.

Our second aim is to outline this decision-making "situation" in order to achieve a better understanding of the features, constraints and cognitive stress that constitute the conditions of uncertainty under which junior judges usually work, especially when on call. This second goal will imply an exploration of the demands imposed by the decision problems and the kind of knowledge needed to solve them. Thus in a sense it is also a study on processes to achieve expertise in an institutionalized domain.

In doing so, we expect to contribute at least to a rethinking of some basic notions of political science while presenting a "more cognitively plausible" (Mallery 1988) framework for modeling political cognition and decision-making, and for building expert knowledge-based systems.

1.5.2 Structure

Part I of this work sets forth the theoretical background of the work. Chapter 2 presents a review of how decision-making problems within organizations have been dealt with in political science, paying attention to the differences between rational choice theories and behavioral organization decision analysis.

In Chap. 3, the implications of bounded rationality for organizational decision analysis will be outlined, including a full discussion on the separation between the inner and outer environments of decisions.

Once the general framework has been put forth, Part II contains the empirical work, the data analysis. In particular, Chap. 4 will be focused on presenting two main blocks of relevant information to contextualize our case. First, it offers a description of the essential features of the Spanish judicial system, focusing on lower courts and on the main features of the on-call service.

Second, the survey data to be used in the rest of the book will be presented, and some of these data will be used in this chapter to draw a picture of the main agents in this book: junior judges. This description will focus on who these judges are, and how they perceive their institutional and professional environment. At the end of the chapter we will discuss to what extent decision problems when on-call can be explained by variation within judges' individual features or within higher-level factors.

The main conclusions arrived at in this chapter will lead to Chap. 5, that will begin with a clear presentation of the hypotheses of the work. Using textual data from judges' responses to open-ended survey questions and a varied toolkit for the statistical analysis of text, this chapter explores the kind of uncertainty that surrounds judges' decision making, and the kind of knowledge they use to overcome these situations.

To test our hypotheses, this book combines standard multivariate statistical methods such as ordinary least squares and logistic regression models with advanced machine learning techniques such as hierarchical clustering, multidimensional scaling, and topic models, thus treating text as data. In doing so, the book intends to contribute to the necessary collaboration between empirical social scientific approaches and the community of scientists that provide an incredible collection of tools and methods to make sense of and deal with the fastest growing resource of our time: data.

1.5.3 Replication Materials

All the data analyses carried out in this book have been made with the open-source and free statistical programming language R (R Core Team 2013). A companion to this book can be found in my GitHub repository,[8] where all the R scripts necessary to replicate the statistical analyses and visualizations presented in this book will be available. R can be freely downloaded in http://cran.r-project.org/ and installed in all common operating systems.

References

Ayuso, M., M. Bécue-Bertaut, R. Álvarez, O. Valencia, M. Álvarez, M. Hernández, and M. Santolino. (2002). Jueces jóvenes en España, 2002. Análisis estadístico de las encuestas a los jueces en su primer destino (promociones 48/49 y 50). Internal report (project sec-2001-2581-c02-01/02), Consejo General del Poder Judicial [General Council of the Judiciary].

Ayuso, M., M. Bécue-Bertaut, R. Álvarez, O. Valencia, M. Álvarez, and M. Santolino. (2003). Análisis estadístico de las encuestas a los jueces en su primer destino. Internal Report SEC-2001-2581-C02-01/02, Consejo General del Poder Judicial [General Council of the Judiciary], Escuela Judicial, Barcelona.

Benjamins, V. R., J. Contreras, M. Blázquez, L. Rodrigo, P. Casanovas, and M. Poblet. (2004a). The sekt use legal case components: Ontology and architecture. In *Legal knowledge and information systems. Jurix 2004*, ed. T. B. Gordon, 69–77. Amsterdam: IOS.

Benjamins, V. R., J. Contreras, P. Casanovas, M. Ayuso, M. Bécue-Bertaut, M. Lemus, and C. Urios. (2004b). Ontologies of professional legal knowledge as the basis for intelligent IT support for judges. *Artificial Intelligence and Law* 12 (4): 359–378.

Benjamins, V. R., P. Casanovas, J. Contreras, J. López-Cobo, and M. Lemus. (2005). Iuriservice: An intelligent frequent asked questions system to assist newly appointed judges. In *Law and the semantic web: Legal ontologies, methodologies, legal information retrieval, and applications*. Lecture notes in computer science, ed. V. Benjamins, P. Casanovas, J. Breuker, and A. Gangemi, vol. 3369, 205–222. Berlin: Springer.

Casanovas, P., V. R. Benjamins, J. Contreras, M. Lemus, and C. Urios. (2003). Iuriservice: un FAQ inteligente para los jueces en su primer destino. In *Internet y pluralismo jurídico: formas emergentes de regulación*, ed. P. Casanovas. Comares: Albolote.

Casanovas, P., M. Poblet, N. Casellas, J. Contreras, V. R. Benjamins, and M. Blázquez. (2005a). Supporting newly-appointed judges: A legal knowledge management case study. *Journal of Knowledge Management* 9 (5): 7–27.

Casanovas, P., M. Poblet, N. Casellas, J.-J. Vallbé, F. Ramos, V. R. Benjamins, M. Blázquez, L. Rodrigo, J. Contreras, and J. Gorroñogoitia. (2005b). Legal case study legal scenario D10.2.1. Case study: Intelligent integrated decision support for legal professionals. Technical Report D10.2.1, SEKT Project (EU-IST Project IST-2003-506826 SEKT), Barcelona.

Casanovas, P., N. Casellas, J.-J. Vallbé, M. Poblet, V. R. Benjamins, M. Blázquez, R. Peña-Ortiz, and J. Contreras. (2006a). Semantic web: A legal case study. In *Semantic web technologies: Trends and research in ontology-based systems*, ed. J. Davies, R. Studer, and P. Warren, 259–280. Chichester: Wiley. (Chap. 12)

[8] https://github.com/pepvallbe/FrameworksModelingCognition

Casanovas, P., J.-J. Vallbé, N. Casellas, M. Poblet, M. Blázquez, J. Contreras, V. R. Benjamins, and J. López-Cobo. (2006b). Legal case study after analysis D10.4.1. Case study: Intelligent integrated decision suppot for legal professionals. Technical Report D10.4.1, SEKT Project (EU-IST Project IST-2003-506826 SEKT), Barcelona.

Casellas, N., P. Casanovas, J.-J. Vallbé, M. Poblet, M. Blázquez, J. Contreras, J. López-Cobo, and V. R. Benjamins. (2007). Semantic enhancement for legal information retrieval: IURISERVICE performance. In *Proceedings of the 11th International Conference on Artificial Intelligence and Law (ICAIL)*, 49–57. Stanford: ACM.

Mallery, J. C. (1988). Thinking about foreign policy: Finding an appropriate role for artificially intelligent computers. Master's thesis, Department of Political Science and Artificial Intelligence Laboratory, MIT, Cambridge, MA. (Paper also presented to the panel "Analytical Frameworks for the Analysis of Conflict", at the 1988 Annual Meeting of the International Studies Association. St. Louis, Missouri).

March, J. G., and H. A. Simon. (1958). *Organizations*. New York: Wiley.

Merryman, J. H. (2007). *The civil law tradition: An introduction to the legal systems of Europe and Latin America*. 3rd ed. Palo Alto: Stanford University Press.

Poblet, M., J.-J. Vallbé, N. Casellas, and P. Casanovas. (2008). Judges as IT USERS: THE IURISERVICE EXAMPLE. In *E-justice, using information communication in the court system*, ed. A. Cerrillo and P. Fabra. Hershey: IGI Books.

R Core Team. (2013). *R: A language and environment for statistical computing*. Vienna: R Foundation for Statistical Computing.

Rodrigo, L., M. Blázquez, P. Casanovas, and M. Poblet. (2004). D10.1.1 legal case study before analysis, semantically enabled knowledge technologies. Technical report, EU-IST Project IST-2003-506826 SEKT.

Simon, H. A. (1947). *Administrative behavior: A study of decision-making processes in administrative organizations*. 1st ed. New York: Macmillan.

Simon, H. A. (1976). *Administrative behavior: A study of decision-making processes in administrative organizations*. 3rd ed. New York: The Free Press.

Simon, H. A. (1983). *Reason in human affairs*. Stanford: Stanford University Press.

Simon, H. A. (1996). *The sciences of the artificial*. 3rd ed. Cambridge: The MIT Press.

Simon, H. A. (1997). Allen Newell, 1927-1992. *National Academy of Sciences Biographical Memoirs*. vol. 71. Washington, DC: National Academies.

Sylvan, D., A. Goel, and G. Chandrasekaran. (1990). Analyzing political decision making from an information-processing perspective: JESSE. *American Journal of Political Science* 34 (1): 74–123.

Toharia Cortés, J. J., and J. J. García de la Cruz Herrero (2005). *La Justicia ante el espejo: 25 años de estudios de opinión del CGPJ*. Consejo General del Poder Judicial, Madrid, Spain.

Part I
Foundations

Chapter 2
Decisions and Organizations

Abstract This chapter explores the study of decision-making within organizations in the political science literature as part of institutional performance. The chapter builds upon a simple analytical model that combines the theory of human rationality underlying each approach to organizational decision-making, and the way institutions are perceived to influence human decisions.

2.1 Introduction

It is widely agreed that World War II marks a boundary between at least two different ways of analyzing and interpreting institutions and organizations. Despite a major methodological change was already challenging the whole social and behavioral sciences since the 1930s—specially at the University of Chicago—, the war implied also a further change in its scope and objects. In particular, it implied a rapid refining and deepening of the application of statistical methods to social phenomena (cf. Almond 1998). This change included the way institutions and organizations were viewed, studied, and analyzed.

From a pre-war organization theory that focused on "orderliness in organizations, for example, a clear division of labor and departmentalization based upon it" (Simon 1996b, p. 73), the "new" theory called attention to the actual processes which led members of organizations to make their decisions. These processes included, among others, emotions, motivation, cognition, and organizational structure. Herbert Simon's doctoral dissertation about decision-making processes in administration—first published as *Administrative Behavior* (Simon 1947)—had a lead role to play in this change.

His was not though the first attempt to deal with organizations as decision-making processes,[1] but it certainly was a foundational work that enabled the explosion of studies regarding decision-making within organizations after World War II, amidst the behavioral revolution in social sciences such as economics and political science.

[1] Simon himself pointed out this fact in his dissertation citing Barnard's *The Functions of the Executive* (Barnard 1938) as one of the first *deviations* from the mainstream theory of administration. Elsewhere (March and Simon 1958; Simon 1996a) the influence of John R. Commons' *Institutional Economics* (1934) in his theory of rationality is also acknowledged.

J.-J. Vallbé, *Frameworks for Modeling Cognition and Decisions in Institutional Environments*, Law, Governance and Technology Series 21, DOI 10.1007/978-94-017-9427-5_2

Table 2.1 Contrast between political theories neglecting the role of institutions and the behavioral approach. (Source: March and Olsen 1984)

Approach	Basic principles	Behavioral view
Contextual	Politics is an integral part of society; the polity is not differentiated from the society	A separated analysis of organizations is both possible and necessary
Reductionist	Political phenomena are aggregate consequences of individual behavior	The outcomes of the political process are ascribed to organizational structures and rules of appropriate behavior
Utilitarian	Action is the product of calculated self-interest	Political actors also respond to duties and obligations
Functionalist	History is an efficient mechanism for reaching uniquely appropriate equilibria	Possibilities for maladaptation and non-uniqueness in historical development
Instrumentalist	Decision making and the allocation of resources are the central concerns of political life	Political life is organized in more ways, namely around the development of meaning through symbols, rituals, and ceremonies

Whilst this approach served as an incipient but solid source for several and relevant works on organizational behavior that founded the currently spread theories of organization and firm behavior (e.g., Cyert and March 1955; Cyert and Simon 1956; March 1955, 1956; March and Simon 1958; Simon 1957), its impact in the political science or economics during the second half of the twentieth century should not be overweighed (Rubinstein 1998). In point of fact, some commentators contend that there was a time when institutions and organizations were forgotten by dominant *coteries* in political science (March and Olsen 1984). Reflecting on this question, Rothstein (1998, p. 139) claims that in approaches such as "structural-functionalism, system analysis, group theory (whether pluralist or élitist)—and, later, economic approaches such as neo-marxism—formal political institutions played little or no role".

This neglect of institutions has been approached in various ways. As an example, March and Olsen (1984) described at least five ways in which institutions were diminished in their relevance for political phenomena analysis. Table 2.1 summarizes their statement opposing the basic principles of these approaches regarding human political and social action to those elaborated by behavioral theories of human action.

During the immediate post-war period, three basic factors favored neglecting institutions and organizations from political analysis. First, in the context of (neo)Marxist analyses of some cataclysmic events in recent human history—war, fascism, communism, Nazism, etc.—political theories tended to focus upon isolated features of the political process such as "authoritarian personality" or "State capitalism". This bias is quite apparent in the work of some of the leading authors of the so-called Frankfurt School, such as Franz L. Neumann, Arkadiji Gurland, Otto Kirchheimer, and Max Horkheimer (Jay 1996).

The second factor was the development of a number of theories of political behavior within the behaviorist revolution in political science. In effect, classical behaviorist contributions were hardly focused on the decision-making processes that lead to political behavior. For instance, Easton (1965) centers his analysis on "political life as a system of behavior"—building on Talcott Parsons' "system" frameworks (Almond 1998, p. 73)—rather than on the individual as such system. Moreover, while Verba (1965, p. 513) affirms that "the political culture of a society consists of the system of empirical beliefs, expressive symbols, and values which defines the situation in which political action takes place", behaviorist analyses of political culture (Pye and Verba 1965) tended to approach the phenomenon in such a way that it enabled systematic and comparative analyses—responding to the behaviorist emphasis on the need for comparison for the achievement of a science of politics (Easton 1953)—thus leaving aside the study of the processes by which people create those empirical beliefs, symbols, and values.[2] Other classical examples of this approach were the studies on different aspects of democracy, whether focusing on its strict political conditions (Dahl 1956), its social and economic requirements (Lipset 1959, 1983), or the conditions under which it can be destroyed (Linz 1978). As a consequence, a reduced number of studies on the relation between organizational structure and individual decision making may be found in this literature.[3]

The third and last factor was promoted by new developments in game theory (von Neumann and Morgenstern 1944) and statistical decision analysis (Friedman and Savage 1952; Savage 1954). The application of their techniques definitely contributed to an important branch of political science—generally referred to as Rational Choice Theory —that assumed individuals were independent actors that tried to maximize their preferences behaving strategically in a world free from institutions (Rothstein 1998, p. 140) and abstracted to the extent that it was virtually considered to be only furnished with other people's utility functions.

As a matter of course, these two last approaches provided political science with a set of powerful analytic tools. As to the analysis of decision making, game theory and statistical decision analysis provided those tools mostly through an advanced use of statistics and mathematical models.[4] Their models were good and sophisticated predictors of what an ideal rational agent would do in an ideal organization-free situation. Nevertheless, doubts have been cast regarding their ability to work as predictors of actual political decisions (Blais 2000), which are inevitably made in institution-mediated environments. The reasoning is that they do not work as predictors of actual

---

[2] Reflecting on the origins of political culture studies, Almond and Verba (1989, p. 15) state that "[t]he development of statistical analysis made it increasingly possible to establish the patterns of interaction among attitudes, the relations of social-structural and demographic variables to attitude variables, and the relations of attitude variables to social and political behavior."

[3] Yet efforts were devoted to the study of the operation of particular organizations (e.g., Lipset 1983, pp. 387–438).

[4] As an assessment of this fact, see, for instance, Oskar Morgenstern's foreword to the first edition of Davis (1997).

decision situations in so far they do not search about the decision-maker's goals, motives, and capabilities, as they are considered to be already "given" (Allison and Zelikow 1999).

Yet a new interest in institutions has been announced and cheered in profusion (March and Olsen 1984; Powell and DiMaggio 1991; Olsen 2001; March and Olsen 2006).[5] A number of compilations reveal that this institutional revival has brought a great deal of different research programs not only in political science, but also in sociology (Scott 1995) and economics, the latter redefining the role of institutions on exchange (Williamson 1981, 1985; North 1990), the role of the state in the development of capitalism (Barzel 2002), and developing a new theory of the firm (Coase 1937, 1998; Williamson 2002). We also learn, though, that the authors who fit in this "movement" do not share a unique approach to institutions (Peters 1999), and that this discord has produced a number of "schools" dwelling in this so-called "new institutionalism" (Hall and Taylor 1996).

New institutionalism has been usually interpreted as a more realistic account of organizations, in reaction to an atomistic approach to "action as the product of goal-oriented, rational individuals" (Simon 1997), and to an "abstract, asocial conception of the contexts in which these goals are pursued" (DiMaggio and Powell 1991).

In the social sciences, this approach implied (a) the clear aim to construct theory and use quantitative data, (b) the analysis of "actual behavior rather than only [. . .] the formal, structural aspects of institutions" (Peters 1998), and (c) the concern with outcomes and decisions. To give a longer cite, March and Olsen (2006) argue that new institutionalism

> connotes a general approach to the study of political institutions, a set of theoretical ideals and hypotheses concerning the relations between institutional characteristics and political agency, performance, and change. Institutionalism emphasizes the endogenous nature and social construction of political institutions. [. . .] [Institutions] are collections of structures, rules, and standard operating procedures that have a partly autonomous role in political life.

Furthermore, these authors consider that this new approach is more realistic in the way it "tries to avoid unfeasible assumptions that require too much of political actors, in terms of normative commitments (virtue), cognitive abilities (bounded rationality), and social control (capabilities)" (March and Olsen 2006). Yet this chapter is aimed at showing that this assertion is rather optimistic in the sense that not all new institutionalist approaches try to overcome these "unfeasible assumptions".

Actually, some excellent reviews of the work done under the label *new institutionalism* tend to focus either on the differences between the new and old institutionalism (DiMaggio and Powell 1991), or on the different research programs and alternatives this approach lends to fields such as political science (March and Olsen 1984, 2006) or sociology. However, less effort has been devoted to study and compare the different

---

[5] See also Heclo (2006) for an excellent account of the American academic atmosphere that surrounded the fall and rise of institutions in the social sciences.

basic assumptions that underlie a varied number of approaches to decision-making in an organizational environment.[6]

In reality, while it is naturally assumed that each approach implies (a) a particular theory of human rationality, and (b) a particular interpretation of the way organizations affect human behavior, a thorough review of the literature according to these two variables is, as far as we know, still lacking.

Therefore, our aim in this chapter is *not* to give an accurate account of the historical development of new institutionalism, notably because this work has already been mastered by others—e.g., Thoenig (2000), plus the already cited March and Olsen (1984); DiMaggio and Powell (1991) and March and Olsen (2006). *Nor* shall we review all the different approaches to institutional analysis in current political science, since such an accurate analysis would lead us far beyond our scope.

Instead, we shall focus on the treatment of decision-making in political science literature as part of institutional performance, and this analysis will take into account both the theory of human rationality underlying each approach to organizational decision-making, and the way institutions are perceived to influence human decisions.

Yet before starting our work, a couple of comments ought to be made. First, this study is not concerned with the problem (if any) of discussing the meaning of the term *organization*. Instead, we will set out an operational definition from the beginning. Since our approach to organizations emphasizes the central role played by decision-making, the definition of *organization* that will be used also contemplates decision-making as a central point. *Organization*, therefore, might be now stated as "the pattern of communications and relations among a group of human beings, including the processes for making and implementing decisions" (Simon 1997, p. 19). The idea behind this definition has been embraced by authors from both behavioral and rational-choice theories. For instance, the idea that organizations provide order and predictability may be found in March and Olsen (2006) and Downs (1957) alike. In addition, March and Olsen (2006) defend that "[t]hey fashion, enable, and constrain political actors as they act within a logic of appropriate action", and that they "simplify political life by ensuring that some things are taken as given".

On the other hand, it is also important to point out that *organization* and *institution* should not be confused, adopting operationally the distinction usually accepted in institutional economics. According to North (1990), organizations may be viewed as "groups of individuals bound by some common purpose to achieve objectives", while institutions can be defined as "the rules of the game", so that it is the institutional framework in a society what influences "both what organizations come into existence and how they evolve" (North 1990). And inversely, organizations do cause changes in institutional framework.

In these terms, the Spanish judicial system can be viewed as an organization or group of organizations (including the Ministry of Justice and the General Council of

[6] But see Rothstein (1998).

the Judiciary), while the on-call service in lower courts may be seen as an institution. This knowingly contrasts with the rooted use of the term *institution* to refer to public organizations that is widely spread in most civil law countries and their legal and social sciences communities. Nevertheless, the distinction is in itself not entirely relevant for the development and understanding of the arguments in this book. Therefore, confusion is not expected if readers relax this "demarcation criterion" and think of these terms as quasi synonyms.

2.2 Decisions and Organizations: A Classification

Among the different ways to analyze organizational and institutional performance, one of them has been the way institutions affect and shape actors' preferences and which strategies organization members follow to reach their goals. For instance, Rothstein (1998, 146–152) draws a theoretical line along which he situates different scholars' theories. According to this line, one extreme would be occupied by William Riker's theoretical individualism, which denies any role to institutions in shaping individuals' preferences (e.g., Riker 1976). The other extreme would be populated by authors such as March, Olsen, DiMaggio, and Powell who have developed ideas such as "organizational culture" in order to explain the ways in which the preferences of organization members are influenced by the organization structure.

Although Rothstein (1998) does not further elaborate his approach populating the whole line with non-extreme approaches to the issue, the idea of the theoretical line happens to be a useful tool.

The question of how the organization structure influences agent's preferences is directly related to the question of how agents decide to make certain decisions within their organizations. For, if actors decide according to their preferences, the way institutions affect actors' preferences will be of utmost interest. Moreover, in each analysis of the way humans perform decisions underlies a theory of human abilities to gain the knowledge necessary to create the preferences that lead to decisions—i.e. rationality. Therefore, these two intertwined issues—organization influence and theory of rationality—should in our opinion be considered—along with the data that supports each proposal—in order to assess the contribution of both our own and others' analyses to organizational decision-making.

A simple way to broadly classify different approaches to organizational decision-making according to both variables may be creating four basic categories that define broad, extreme values of these variables (Model 1), as shown in Table 2.2. According to it, OI− means that organizational influence in decision-making is either ignored or denied; OI+ means that organizational influence is either implicitly assessed or explicitly analyzed; and TR+ means that the theory assumes that human beings are utility maximizers (*olympic rationality* (Simon 1983)), while TR− means that the theory assumes that individuals are only capable of a limited rationality.

Table 2.2 Model 1 classifying decision-making analysis according to organizational influence and theory of rationality

		Organizational influence	
		OI−	OI+
Theory of rationality	TR+	*A*	*B*
	TR−	*C*	*D*

Table 2.3 Model 2 classifying decision-making analysis according to organizational influence and rationality theory

		Organizational influence		
		OI−	OI+	
			OI+(+)	**OI+(−)**
Theory of rationality	TR+	*A*	*B*	*E*
	TR−	*C*	*D*	*F*

Certainly, this classification is simple, perhaps too simple. In effect, given that our interest here is to perform an analysis of the relation between rationality and organizational influence in decisions, OI− approaches (*A* and *C*) should be excluded. Notice that while the binary form of facing the problem of human rationality in the classification is rather neat and clear, the distinction between approaches acknowledging organizational influence (*B* and *D*) is rather poor. In actuality, the "organizational dimension" would require not only to acknowledge whether organizational factors must be accounted for in decision analysis (this is the criterium already proposed), but also the nature of this influence of the organizational factors in cases when it is affirmed. While the first dimension is clearly (though simply) represented in the model, the second one is not.

This nature of organization influence upon actors' preferences and, ultimately, upon decisions might be viewed from at least two very different perspectives. First, it could be viewed *negatively* in the sense that organizations normally shape preferences (a) selecting what alternatives are presented and discussed, and (b) setting the order in which these alternatives are presented and discussed. *Negative* influence, then, is not to be interpreted as though authors from this group make (negative) value judgments on the way organizations affect preferences (though they sometimes do). Instead, it means that institutions somehow limit the span of alternatives available in a decision situation, and thus they *constrain* human rational decision-making. The second view could *positively* assess the role of organizations by saying that organizations are tools made by humans in order to cope with a complex reality, and that they offer humans stable patterns of events that help strengthen human rationality. Again, this does not imply that authors in this group necessarily consider this situation desirable (though they sometimes do), but that organizations somehow *expand* human rational decision-making.

Taking these distinctions into account, a new classification might be created that incorporates the nature of organizational influence. Model 2—shown in Table 2.3—makes the distinction according to the direction of the organizational influence in decision-making. Thus OI+(+) is to be interpreted as a *positive* influence in the terms specified above, and OI+(−) is its *negative* counterpart.

Table 2.4 Model 3 classifying decision-making analysis according to the nature of organizational influence and rationality theory

		Organizational influence	
		OI+(+)	OI+(−)
Theory of rationality	TR+	Maximum rationality/ organization enhances decisions	Maximum rationality/ organization limits decisions
	TR−	Bounded rationality/ organization enhances decisions	Bounded rationality/ organization limits decisions

According to this model, approaches belonging to the group *A* and *C* would either ignore or deny any organizational influence in actors' premises (preferences, knowledge, etc.) before deciding. As already noted, they shall not be reviewed here. Group *B* would be populated with authors that, though considering human beings capable of a maximum of rationality, also consider that the organizational environment somehow enhances their ability to make decisions.

Group *D* is constituted by theories of organizational decision-making that consider organizational influences as enhancers of human rational capacity, and at the same time affirm that humans are capable of only a limited rational behavior. Group *E* is formed by authors who defend that while humans are perfectly rational, organizations/institutions limit their span of alternatives in various ways, thus altering the possibility to reach optimal options. Finally, group *F* is populated with authors who think that while humans are only capable of a bounded rationality, institutions limit even more such a capacity by limiting the span of alternatives they may choose upon (see Table 2.4).

In this chapter the further theoretical background around decision-making in political science shall be set forth according to this distinction (Model 3). First, we will review the rational choice theorists' approach to decisions and institutional performance, which assume maximum rationality (*B*, *E*). Second, we will deal with different views of bounded rationality in political analysis (*D*, *F*).

2.3 Rational Choice Theories

In this section those approaches that assume perfect rationality in humans are reviewed regarding their assessment of institutional or organizational factors in decision making. Under the common label *Rational Choice Theory* we include similar approaches that have received names such as public choice (Mueller 1997, 2003), positive political theory (Riker and Ordeshook 1973), and applications of social choice theory and game theory (Austen-Smith and Banks 1998). First, the theory of rationality underlying those approaches will be briefly presented as a set of basic principles and assumptions on human beings. The two last subsections are devoted to review two different views of the role of organizations in decisions.

2.3.1 Foundations

The origins of the application of the notion of perfect rationality in political science may be found at the roots of the so-called rational choice theory. According to a couple of well-known proponents of this approach, the role of rational choice theorists is "to build models that predict how individuals' self-oriented actions combine to yield collective outcomes" (Amadae and Bueno de Mesquita 1999, p. 270).

Nevertheless, in a deeper sense, two different sources—both just after World War II—may be found that explain this general aim of rational choice theories. On the one hand, a first source was the realization that computers were capable of symbolic processing (Simon 1996b), and thus computer programs could be created that "would properly model those mental processes involved in intelligent human behavior whatever they may be: information search, problem solving, learning, invention or creativity" (Casanovas and Noriega 2007, p. 16).

On the other hand, a different (though related) source was game theory, developed after World War II by John von Neumann and Oskar Morgenstern.

In effect, the application of game-theoretical approaches to political science and, in particular, to international relations is one of the keys to interpret the popularity of this theory of rational decision among political scientists until our days. The other is the elegance of their theory of decision.

Most models in this stream of political analysis start with a set of prior assumptions (Bennett 1995):

- Players: there must be two or more, whether they are individuals, groups, or nations.
- Strategies: each player of the game has a set of strategies that represent possible courses of action.
- Outcomes: a set of possible outcomes or solutions of the game.
- Preference functions: each player has a preference function that links a possible outcome with the player's utility.

Some early formulations of the rational-choice approach in political science felt strongly attracted to this view of human rationality, following the basic scope and methods of their leading counterparts in economics. But a particular elaboration of this set of assumptions for political science was not fully developed until the end of the 1950s, Anthony Downs and William H. Riker perhaps being the most prominent and cited representative authors of this shift.[7] In different ways, both authors set up

[7] A comprehensive account of the origins and theoretical or historical development of this approach to political phenomena is not attempted in this book. See Riker (1961) for an early bibliographical

the theoretical framework (Downs 1957) and most of the analytic tools (Riker 1958, 1962) upon which mainstream rational choice theories were and still are built and developed.

A foundational approach in modern political science such as Downs' *An Economic Theory of Democracy* (Downs 1957) combined a "neoclassical" approach to rationality with an account of how both individuals and organizations behaved in the political process. But while Downs' contribution to the theory of rationality is very modest (the basic neoclassical assumptions remain untouched in his *An Economic Theory of Democracy* (1957)), it certainly implied a momentum in the analysis of democratic societies, thus embodying a new and fresh look at political behavior.

Downs' notion of rationality draws directly on Kenneth Arrow's view of economic rationality (Downs 1957, p. 6): "A rational man is one who behaves as follows:

1. he can always make a decision when confronted with a range of alternatives;
2. he ranks all the alternatives facing him in order of his preference in such a way that each is either preferred to, indifferent to, or inferior to each other;
3. his preference ranking is transitive;
4. he always chooses from among the possible alternatives which ranks highest in his preference ordering; and
5. he always makes the same decision each time he is confronted with the same alternatives."[8]

As to institutions, Downs argues that "the government provides the framework of order upon which the rest of society is built" (Downs 1957), which is a close formulation to that of Herbert A. Simon (1983) who—as we saw in the Introduction—views organizations as providing "a stable environment [. . .] that makes at least a modicum of rationality possible".[9] In particular, Downs sees political order as a guarantee to reduce uncertainty in choice, in the sense that a stable political order—i.e., a stable institutional or organizational environment—provides the individual with an acceptable degree of prediction regarding other people's actions. Yet Downs does not go beyond this point as far as institutional analysis is concerned. Instead, such organizations as political parties or governments are presented in his model as rational, power-seeking agents, thus obviating any reference to organizational or institutional factors affecting decision-making in some way.

Downs' model contains a number of relevant methodological assumptions. First, it assumes a radical methodological individualism according to which collective behavior must be viewed as aggregate individual actions. In order to account for

review of some aspects of it (elections and aggregating of preferences), and see Amadae and Bueno de Mesquita (1999) for a historical review. General discussion may be found in Elster (1986).

[8] Arrow (1963) [1951] had broadly defined *rationality* as the behavior that satisfies his axioms I and II, i.e., the principles of connection (comparability) and transitivity between alternatives. See Arrow (1963, p. 11–21) for a full explanation.

[9] Yet as we shall see later on Simon linked the organizational structure to rationality.

these actions, both humans and organizations such as governments are viewed as goal-oriented, self-interested agents. Furthermore, their goals are represented by preferences, which agents try to maximize.[10] Since information is costly and incomplete, Downs' model must account for uncertainty, i.e., "any lack of sure knowledge about the course of past, present, future, or hypothetical events" (Downs 1957, p. 77), which the author concedes can be reduced by devoting certain amount of resources to information.

Therefore, Downs assumes a model which is partially based on the traditional neoclassical view of individual decision-making (utility maximization) but introducing uncertainty (or information cost) as a correction factor to the model, which is especially relevant for his account of *persuasion* and, in fact, for the mere existence of political parties in the political process. Put in a simple way (Downs 1957, Chap. 6), since people lack knowledge and complete information, both government and the opposition party—assuming a two-party system—use persuasion in order to provide voters with the information they need to decide their vote, i.e., in order to gain the voters' vote.[11] Although Downs' book contains numerous assertions about the world (factual assertions), no evidence is provided.

Thus Downs' is a deduced model,[12] one that presents politics as a market where voters' preferences are sold and bought, where parties (and governments) are sellers and voters are buyers, and where persuasion and ideology are explained by the mere existence of uncertainty.

Downs' work has been also considered—both by its critics (Simon 1985) and supporters (Riker 1961)—as one of the first contemporary attempts to articulate a coherent model of politics bringing the mathematical and game-theoretical apparatus from economics to political science. Reading his *Economic Theory of Democracy*, one can certainly conclude that the author applies the maximizing utility principle to politics, but in actuality his application is rather verbal, not extremely formalized. This might mean that Downs offered a general model in partial concordance with the main objective of his famous work, namely "to provide [...] a behavior rule for democratic government and to trace its implications" (Downs 1957, p. 3). He undoubtedly provides the model, but obviously its implications for political science were far from foreseeable at that moment.

On the other hand, a first systematic application of this general model—and of game theory and social choice theory, with the subsequent powerful analytic apparatus—to particular political phenomena was Riker's early work on voting (Riker

---

[10] In Downs' model of electoral process the government "seeks to maximize political support" (Downs 1957, p. 11), i.e., to be reelected, while voters try to minimize their information costs.

[11] Obviously, both parties seek to maximize votes. See Downs (1957, Chaps. 7 and 8) for the role of ideologies in this model.

[12] Almond (1998 p. 52) contends that in *An Economic Theory of Democracy* we have "inference without evidence". Moreover, referring to rational choice models in general he argues that "[t]he theory is parsimonious, logically consistent, mathematical and prefer experimental methods to observational and inductive ones for the testing of hypotheses" (Almond 1998, p. 86).

1958). This was a first hint of one of the most influential authors in what shall be known as positive political theory (Riker and Ordeshook 1973) or, more generally, rational choice theory.[13] Yet the actual benchmark of this approach will be Riker's *Theory of Political Coalitions* (Riker 1962), an application of the theory of n-person games to political coalitions, and a canonical text in rational choice literature.[14]

As noted above (in agreement with Rothstein 1998), Riker's radical methodological individualism and his turn in the mid-1950s to game-theoretical explanations of political phenomena represents an extreme view in our human-organization interaction model. Regarding his theory of rationality, its basic principles are—like Downs'—borrowed from neoclassical economics and game theory[15] and they may be seen as a set of principles and assumptions to be shared and accepted as foundational by future rational choice theory practitioners.

As stated above, Riker's work has usually been described as a radical individualistic approach to politics. Methodological individualism is apparent throughout his work after his first relevant contribution to election theory (Riker 1958) and it is maintained along later works. As a result, Riker and Ordeshook (1973, p. 1) contended in their *Introduction to Positive Political Theory* that "[people] are bundles of opinions about nature and of preferences about the alternatives nature offers them".

As to rationality in particular, it is assumed that "people behave as if they sort out and logically arrange the preferences in their bundles". Besides, the authors further assume that these people "are able to use the sorted bundles for decisions so that, when faced with a choice, they can choose as directed by their preferences". In conclusion, "[s]uch behavior we describe as *rational*" (Riker and Ordeshook 1973, p. 8).

Riker's first broad definition of rationality runs as follows (Riker 1962, p. 22):[16]

---

[13] Amadae and Bueno de Mesquita (1999) explain Riker's early introduction to "a new vein of literature that addressed political processes in the language of mathematics, including the work of John von Neumann and Oskar Morgenstern, Duncan Black, Kenneth Arrow, and Anthony Downs". We would rather say that while Neumann and Morgenstern's contribution to formalization and mathematical applications to political science is as powerful as uncontested, Downs' influence is of another kind, as noted above. Riker's very work shows that Downs' influence in future formal models of political behavior is hardly controversial. Besides, Riker (1961) himself assessed his intellectual roots acknowledging, among others, the influence of Arrow (1963) who in 1951 had put forth the difficulty to find or even conceive of a set of rules for collective decision over a number of alternatives under a number of acceptable normative requirements.

[14] See Robinson (1963) for a contemporary review of this book. Amadae and Bueno de Mesquita (1999) add Buchanan and Tullock (1962) and Olson (1965) to this canon.

[15] In his first description of the assumptions of his model of rationality Riker (1962, p. 16) acknowledges his sources: Von Neumann and Morgenstern, McKinsey, and Luce and Raiffa. However, Amadae and Bueno de Mesquita (1999) have noted—correctly in my opinion—that there are substantial differences between Riker's notion of rationality and the one from traditional economists in the sense that "the rationality of economic agents was thought of as mechanical rather than deliberate and conscious". Accordingly, Riker emphasized consciousness and purpose in political decision making in contrast with market decisions.

[16] Actually, as far as we know Riker's first attempt to define rationality was given in Riker (1958). However, according to the objective of that essay, the definition tended to be limited exclusively

> Given social situations within certain kinds of decision-making institutions (of which parlor games, the market, elections, and warfare are notable examples) and in which exist two alternative courses of action with differing outcomes in money or power or success, some participants will choose the alternative leading to the larger payoff. Such choice is rational behavior and it will be accepted as definitive while the behavior of participants who do not so choose will not necessarily be so accepted.

Austen-Smith and Banks (1998, pp. 263–264) offer a formal account of the very same assumptions or premisses:

> The primitives of any rational choice-theoretic formal model of politics include a specification of a set of the relevant individuals, denoted N; a set of feasible alternatives or outcomes, X, and, for each individual in N, a description of her preferences over the set X. [...]
> To formalize the idea of individual preferences, each individual in N is assumed to possess a binary preference relation on X, denoted R_i, where, for any two alternatives x and y, "$x R_i y$" is shorthand for the statement "according to individual i, x is at least as good as y". From R_i one can define i's strict preference relation, P_i (where "$x P_i y$" reads "according to individual i, x is strictly better than y") and i's indifference relation, I_i (where "$x I_i y$" reads "according to individual i, x and y are equally good"). [...]

A number of restrictions are established for this model, though, most of them being aimed at assuring that "individual-level decision problems are well defined" (Austen-Smith and Banks, 1998, p. 264), namely that possible flaws of collective rationality are never to be ascribed to individual irrational behavior but to collective choice paradoxes and problems. These restrictions refer to individual preferences regarding their completeness, consistency, continuity, and convexity (Austen-Smith and Banks 1998).

Taking this theoretical framework into account, the essence of politics is then "the selection of the preference of some person (or the potential preference of some person) to be the choice of society" (Riker and Ordeshook 1973, p. 2).[17] It refers to three different processes or problems that in my opinion synthesize Riker's research program:

1. the problem of preference selection (in society)—which may be summarized in Riker's interest in voting (Riker 1958, 1961; Riker and Ordeshook 1968);
2. the enforcement of the choices expressed in this selection—which refers to Riker's work regarding coalition building (Riker 1962);
3. the production of results or outputs coherent with those choices—which brings us to Riker's concern about the realm of *possibilia* and the normative aspects of politics.[18]

to the transitivity principle and the problems posed by Arrow and Black for collective rationality (Condorcet paradox), thus leaving other aspects aside.

[17] Let us recall here that according to Amadae and Bueno de Mesquita (1999, p. 270) the goal of positive political theory is to "build models that predict how individuals' self-oriented actions combine to yield collective outcomes".

[18] These three processes are referred to as the "mystery of politics" (Riker and Ordeshook 1973, p. 2).

This third problem—outcome production from choices—appears in Riker's work more general than the others in the sense that it has not deserved an as thorough treatment as the other two. Yet at the same time it is recognizable throughout all his work, though in my opinion is best represented by his notion of *heresthetics*, or the art of winning in politics either referred to as political manipulation (Riker 1986), or simply rhetoric (Riker 1996).

Nonetheless, it is precisely this factor what enables us to introduce Riker's notion of the role of institutions in the game of politics. Briefly stated, Riker's theory of political behavior requires a self-interested, rational agent who acts in a strategic, game-shaped environment. Riker's argument would be that so long as the output of politics refers both to the results that *can* be arrived at and those that *ought to* be obtained in social choice (Riker and Ordeshook 1973), institutions may have a role in setting the agenda of what is possible and desirable as game outputs. Like Downs, the basic assumption is that institutions are the rules of the game of politics, and that as rules they can be changed favoring particular actors.

This idea is apparent in the first of Riker's relevant papers pertaining to the rational choice approach (Riker 1958), in which the author explored the risk of irrational collective behavior (voting paradoxes) in the US Senate. Riker concludes that "[w]ith the consequences exposed, it may be that the Congress will wish to change its Rules in order to avoid the risk of behaving irrationally" (Riker 1958, p. 362). But the author immediately warns that these rules may also enable perverse behavior and results, in the sense that "the present Rules allow a skilled minority to defeat an unsophisticated majority; or, to put it differently, a committee chairman to control House action" (Riker 1958, p. 362).

On one hand, Riker focuses the function of agenda control on particular actors that "guide the operation of the body" within which collective decision-making takes place (Riker 1982).[19] This refers to different strategies these actors may carry out in order to seize the power of the decision-making body by taking control of some aspects of the voting procedure, i.e., establishing the order in which alternatives are presented, or generating themselves other alternatives to be voted upon.[20]

On the other hand, Riker's acknowledgement of this "institutional" fact does not mean that the author takes on an institutionalist analysis of the political process at all in the sense of carrying out a thorough analysis of the institutional mechanisms that take place in agenda setting or manipulation. Instead, this phenomenon is coherently

---

[19] In this same work Riker refers to a central problem to political enquiry as "the problem of explaining why some issues are politically salient and others not" (Riker 1982, p. ix).

[20] The idea of power as control over alternatives may be traced back to James March's notion of influence (March 1955, 1957). Indeed Riker himself, in a 1964 paper comparing formal definitions of *power* by Shapley and Shubik, March, Dahl, Cartwright, and Karlsson, referred to March's notion of *influence*—which Riker equalled to a definition of *power*—as "the ability to restrict outcomes" (Riker 1964, p. 342). However, we do not mean that Riker agreed with March's definition of *power*. See Riker (1964) for an explanation.

analyzed from a strategical, game-theoretical perspective in which a number of self-interested, strategical-behaving agents seek to alter voting procedures in such a way that they can take profit of such phenomena as majority cycling.[21]

Although Riker's work on this particular issue does not seem to reach the systematic treatment as the other two dimensions of politics as he saw it, most of his later works are devoted to this phenomenon (Riker 1986, 1996), and his view of the potential role of institutions in political output was to be highly influential in rational choice-based, new institutionalist approaches.

In conclusion, this brief review of the first attempts to present rational choice models of political behavior shows that these models tended to overweigh individual decision making as the result of the application of preference maximizing strategies in different political contexts. In these models, rationality is defined drawing upon Arrow's development of neoclassical economic concept of rational action.

These principles imply that rational decision making has at least the following features:

- The whole set of alternatives from which the decision maker has to choose is given and apparent before him/her.
- According to this set of alternatives, the decision-maker constructs a set of well-defined (and ordered) preferences.
- The set of preferences can be represented in a utility function for each individual.
- The decision for an individual consists on maximizing his/her utility function.

The influence of Riker's contributions is apparent in numerous examples of this kind of analysis that may be found throughout the early work of a group of his students, who were to become the flagship of the rational choice theory in political science.[22] These authors, and others, elaborated on the model to focus on party behavior (Ordeshook 1970), Pareto optimality in elections (Ordeshook 1971), game-theoretical rationality in elections (Riker and Zavoina 1970; Riker 1976; McKelvey 1976), spatial models of party competition (Hinich and Ordeshook 1970; McKelvey 1975; McKelvey and Ordeshook 1976; Aldrich and McKelvey, 1977), various aspects of collective choice in legislatures or similar bodies (Riker 1958; Schwartz 1977; McKelvey 1979; Weingast 1979; Ordeshook and Winer 1980), explorations on the (im)possibility of social choice functions under particular requirements (Ferejohn et al. 1982; Ferejohn and McKelvey 1983), and the relation between information and the aggregation of preferences (McKelvey and Ordeshook 1985a, b; McKelvey and Page 1986; McKelvey 1986; McKelvey and Ordeshook 1986; McKelvey 1987; McKelvey and Page 1990; Nielsen et al. 1990; McKelvey and Patty 2006).

As to organizations or institutions, these models do not explicitly deny that decisions are actually made within institutional environments, but the game-theoretical

[21] See a couple of examples in Riker (1982, pp. 173–181).

[22] This main corpus of authors is generally known as the Rochester school (at Rochester University), which is considered to have pioneered the rational choice revolution in political science. See Amadae and Bueno de Mesquita (1999) for an excellent account of this theme.

framework used to analyze political phenomena implies that "the variation among institutional, psychological, and ideological components of behavior are minimized" (Riker 1967, p. 642). Therefore, no institutional arrangements are explicitly taken into account that shape these individuals' preferences or their very ability to perform decisions.

This account of institutions might be interpreted as to be some kind of "rules of the game" (Downs) in the logical sense that decisions are not made in an empty world. These rules might also be interpreted as outlining the available alternatives in a decision situation (Riker), thus foregoing future rational choice-based institutional analyses that shall be commented on in the next two subsections.

The interest in institutions by rational choice theorists originated with the intention of bridging the gulf between abstract models of collective choice (in an empty and ahistorical world) and "more specialized formalizations which incorporate institutional specifics" (Shepsle 1985, p. 7).[23] In particular, the main claim made to traditional social choice models was that "[n]early thirty years of research on social choice has produced a large body of theoretical results. [. . .] While attention has been devoted to the mechanisms by which individual revealed preferences are aggregated into a social choice, rarely are other aspects of institutional arrangements treated endogenously" (Shepsle 1979, p. 27).

Therefore, it might be said that current rational choice theory has changed some of its foundational premises regarding the role of institutions in decision-making. Or otherwise stated, this approach to political phenomena has enriched its analysis by introducing institutions and their operation into its analysis. For, while it is still founded upon the idea of an individual or set of individuals with a well-defined set of preferences, institutions appear—following Riker's statements about it—either as the main source of available alternatives, their order, and the shape in which the information available is presented (Shepsle 2006a), or as *equilibrium institutions* (Shepsle 2006b).

Therefore, in the next subsection we will deal with those rational-choice theories that assume a *negative* view of institutions (*E*, in Table 2.3), highlighting the discussion that led to the introduction of institutions. Then, Sect. 2.3.3 will outline rational-choice theories that assume a *positive* view (*B*).

2.3.2 *Institutions Constrain Perfectly Rational Decisions*

The general idea of this branch of rational choice theory regarding institutions—coherently with their foundational premises—is that they are the "rules of the game"

[23] It is worth noticing that among the arguments for incorporating these institutional factors into models of strategic behavior one can find that "the appropriateness of models is not independent of the substantive phenomena they purport to explain", and that "characteristics of phenomena should inform models and, more importantly, constrain choices among alternative modeling forms", to further conclude that "models should be consistent with known facts and features of the situation under examination" (Shepsle 1985, pp. 7–8).

(North and Weingast 2000) or "game forms" (Shepsle 2006b) that act as a constraint to agents' action. In other words, these rules establish "the set of players, what actions players may take (must take, may not take, etc.), informational conditions under which they make their choices, the timing of moves, the role and timing of exogenous events, and the outcome that results from a distribution of choices and the realization of all random factors" (Shepsle 2006b, pp. 1031–1032). These rules may be formal (e.g., contracts) or informal (e.g., social taboos) (North 1990).

Shepsle's paper on institutional arrangements and equilibrium in social choice models (Shepsle 1979) was one of the first attempts to make explicit the role of institutions in rational choice models. Therein the author focuses on structure-induced equilibria, i.e., "the play of the game" itself (Shepsle 2006b), in the sense that a number of institutional mechanisms such as rules of jurisdiction or amendment control have "an important independent impact on the existence of equilibrium and, together with the distribution of preferences, [. . .] [they co-determinate] the characteristics of the equilibrium state(s) of collective choice processes" (Shepsle 1979, p. 29). Thus institutional arrangements affect outcomes.[24]

A year later Riker conceded that "we cannot leave out the force of institutions" (Riker 1980a, p. 432) because they can "affect social outcomes". In this work institutions are understood as the embodiment of a set of conventions, namely "rules of behavior, especially about making decision" in the sense that "decisions are customarily made within the framework of known rules, which are what we commonly call institutions" (Riker 1980a, p. 443). These institutions—Riker argues—affect somehow the content of decisions,[25] and therefore produce biases in decisions, social and individual.

Then the author concludes that since decisions are affected both by preferences and by institutional arrangements, institutions are worth studying, appreciating Shepsle's effort to include these factors—institutions as structure-induced equilibria—in rational choice models. Yet Riker objects that since institutions are mere sets of rules and that actors in social choice may want to change them in order to induce particular equilibria or outcomes in the future, institutions may be seen simply as "more alternatives in the policy space and the status quo of one set of rules can be supplanted with another set of rules" (Riker 1980a, p. 445).[26] Thence—Riker goes on—institutions are to be interpreted as "congealed" preferences, and if preferences lack equilibrium, "then also do institutions". Therefore, institutions are not to be considered "fixed exogenous constraints [but] changeable [and endogenous] features of the political landscape" (Shepsle 2006b).

---

[24] Shepsle's reference to the *equilibrium state* of a choice process is rather symptomatic of his early turn to a positive account of institutional influence in decision making. This approach is explained in Sect. 2.3.3.

[25] "[T]he ways the tastes and values [i.e., preferences] are brought forward for consideration, elminated, and finally selected are controlled by the institutions" (Riker 1980a, p. 443).

[26] "[T]he distinction between constitutional questions and policy questions is at most one of degree of longevity" (Riker 1980a, p. 445).

Later, Shepsle (2006b) revisited Riker's objection to the static treatment of institutions. Shepsle's counterargument to Riker's is that institutions may well still be considered as structurally inducing equilibria since, as it is usually the case in democratic legislatures, the same kind of majority is not sufficient for both policy decisions and institutional change decisions. In the latter case, numerous constitutions require special majorities in order to make collective decisions upon particular issues (such as the very structure of the state, or to remove a monarch). Then, from this standpoint institutions can be viewed as something more than Riker's "changeable features of the political landscape".[27]

Shepsle's response to Riker's objection reveals a central tension between the study of institutions and rational choice theories, one that focuses on the importance of considering what is the object of research at any given time and, most importantly, what are the units of analysis. On the one hand, Riker's endogenous consideration of institutions is critical to the study of the origins of institutions, institutional change, and evolution. If institutions are endogenous to the political process understood from the strategic model of politics, then they cannot strictly *matter* (Przeworski 2007). Yet, on the other hand, even if institutions are seen as endogenous to the political process, comparative, micro-level analyses on how agents "exploit their institutional environment" (Shepsle 2006b) may still be in need to account for variation in institutional settings as game forms. This partly explains the interest on how critical institutional arrangements such as electoral systems (Benoit 2004; Boix 1999; Helmke and Meguid 2008), democratic regimes (Acemoglu and Robinson 2005; Boix 2003) and the law (Hadfield and Weingast 2011) were adopted, as "primal settings" (Shepsle 2006b) or rules of the game that respond to their creators' preferences (Greif and Kingston 2011).

The micro-level analysis of institutional arrangements as constrains has led numerous rational choice theorists to elaborate on the traditional view of institutions as settings for agenda manipulation. Indeed, the renewed consciousness on the role of institutions led to an important change in rational choice theories "moving from models of voting—especially models of pure majority rule with their attendant emphasis on voting cycles and system instability—to an understanding of how institutional rules can shape collective choice" (Moe 1987, p. 476), focusing on both the rules themselves and the mechanisms set up to enforce them as separate instances.

Coherently, Weingast (1998, p. 169) has called this agenda-centered approach the "setter model". According to it, institutions set the agenda of alternatives among which a decision is to be made. In simple setter models, a single individual, group, or organization holds the exclusive power to set the defined set of alternatives according to which voters, other organization members or any particular group of decision-makers will construct their utility function. This general framework, though, permits a variety of approaches and applications including the study of constitutions (Riker

[27] See also Ordeshook (1980) for a comment on Riker's objection, and the latter's response (Riker 1980b), both centered on the notion of equilibrium.

1984; Acemoglu 2005; Weingast 2005; Colomer 2006; Shane 2006), executives (Rhodes 2006a), jury decisions (Guarnaschelli et al. 2000), judicial behavior (Epstein and Knight 2000), and international relations (Niou and Ordeshook 1987, 1990, 1991, 1994a, b, c; Schultz and Weingast 2003).

Yet the basic setter model has privileged legislative bodies as the main object for the application of rational choice models, since they constitute interesting and typical collective choice scenarios.[28]

In the 1980s, during the first institutionalist wave of rational choice theory, a typical institution—or set of institutions—for collective choice such as the US Congress deserved most attention by rational theorists.[29] These legislative studies show a varied number of objects, ranging from internal legislative rules to the relations between legislative bodies and other actors.[30]

For instance, Shepsle and Weingast (1981) offer an explanation of the way institutional arrangements—among other features—can produce biases to expected rational behavior in legislative settings. In effect, the authors explain the "empirical regularity of universalism in the realm of distributive policies", which means that in numerous legislative bodies rational legislators tend to support "coalitions well in excess of minimal wining size".[31]

Moreover, Shepsle and Weingast (1982, 1984b) generalize this model exploring the institutional arrangements that underpin "the operation of majority rule legislatures".[32] Following this vein, Denzau et al. (1985) offer a model of legislators' sophisticated voting, and Krehbiel (1985, 1986a, c) has showed other intricacies of legislative voting and has explored methods to better outline legislative decision-making from a rational choice perspective (Krehbiel 1986b).[33]

Shepsle and Weingast (1987), Krehbiel et al. (1987), and Krehbiel (1990) focus on the legislative process (proposing, amending, and vetoing) in order to model

---

[28] Hall and Taylor (1996) comment indeed that "rational choice institutionalism arose from the study of American congressional behaviour".

[29] According to Green and Shapiro (1994) at the end of the 1960s 5 % of articles in the *American Political Science Review* pertained to rational choice theory, while at the end of the 1970s they were over 20 %, and at the end of the 1980s they were reaching 40 % of total articles published in that journal. In other journals such as *Legislative Studies Quarterly*, its position might be even more dominant.

[30] Nowadays attention has been also focused on other legislative bodies, fostering the spread of rational choice models to comparative politics. See Bates (1997) for a brief review of rational choice models in comparative politics.

[31] See Weingast et al. (1981) for a complement on the same theme. Cox and Tutt (1984) elaborated case application on resource allocation in distributive politics, Niou and Ordeshook (1985) gave a different explanation of universalism in Congress. Other approaches in a "pork barrel" (i.e., distributive) setting are Ferejohn et al. (1987) and Weingast (1994).

[32] Shepsle and Weingast (1984a) use the same framework to cast doubts on the widespread belief that market failures need political (namely institutional) solutions.

[33] See Krehbiel (1988) for an excellent and thorough review on spatial models of legislative choice until 1988, and Krehbiel (2004) for a current overview of rational choice models of legislative organization.

and explain legislative committee power—Krehbiel (1988) present a case study on Senate voting—, while Ordeshook and Schwartz (1987) and Ordeshook and Palfrey (1988) produced a couple of influential studies on the precise process of agenda formation and control. Furthermore, Ferejohn and Krehbiel (1987) advanced the study of budget decisions by members of Congress. Austen-Smith and Riker (1987, 1990), and Ordeshook and Palfrey (1988) pay attention on information distribution in a legislative, agenda-setting scenario, and Gilligan and Krehbiel (1988, 1989, 1990, 1994) have devoted much attention to the relation between information and legislative rules.

In this vein, Weingast (1989) explores the impact of the open rule in the US Congress and uses it to predict legislative behavior, and Cox (2000) reflects generally on the way legislative rules affect the outcome of legislation. Also, McKelvey and Riezman (1992) treat seniority as an endogenous rule that legislative institutions enforce in order to procure the legislators' reelection, and Krehbiel (1993, 1999a, b, 2000) explores political parties' strategic behavior to control legislative outcomes.[34] Finally, other studies (Lupia and McCubbins 1994) incorporate learning processes to enrich legislative behavior models.[35]

Variations on the same theme assume that the setter that determines the content of the agenda is not always clear, and that influence may be rather obscure. This fact has recently favored rational choice approaches to bureaucracy. For example, Moran and Weingast (1982) offer an explanation of the way the U.S. Congress influences decisions made by (supposedly) independent regulatory agencies. In the same line, Weingast and Moran (1983) expand the model to explore bureaucracy and its influence on the agenda, while McCubbins and Schwartz (1984) and Calvert et al. (1989) build theory and apply it to particular cases in order to outline bureaucratic discretion, and to explain political motivations in congressional political behavior regarding regulatory decisions (see also McCubbins 1985). Indeed, further attempts to include the role of bureaucracy in decision making models have been interpreted as to "hold the promise of moving toward a well-integrated perspective on the larger institutional system", implying "a pioneering move toward a coherent general theory of political institutions" (Moe 1987, p. 476).[36]

In conclusion, so far we have seen that while the first records of rational choice models tended to be unidimensional by neglecting the influence of institutional arrangements in collective decision making, this assertion does not hold since the mid 1970s and 1980s. At that moment a new institutionalism pervaded political science including the most influential rational choice theories. Secondly, we have showed that a dominant branch of this approach adopts Riker's basic agenda-setting model.

---

[34] See Cox and McCubbins (1994) for a further treatment of party behavior in a legislative setting.

[35] See Shepsle and Weingast (1994) for a thorough review of positive theories of legislative behavior from rational choice perspective.

[36] Yet Terry Moe (1987) is not fully content of rational choice approaches to the relation between bureaucracy and legislative institutions in so far they tend to neglect the role of bureaucracy.

Despite the variety of approaches to institutional operation turns to be evident, a number of features seem to remain constant in almost all institutionalist rational-choice approaches reviewed so far. This model holds on a number of assumptions, namely:

- Decision makers are perfectly rational actors and behave as rational actors (in a neoclassical Arrovian sense).
- Collective decisions are made within an institutional environment, and can be modeled as non-cooperative games.
- Institutions may be seen as the rules of the game, or structural factors that constrain the number and content of alternatives in collective choice.
- Actors behave strategically in this environment in order to achieve their goals—namely, to maximize their utility functions.
- Actors may want to change the rules of the game (i.e., institutions) in order to manipulate present of future outcomes of collective decisions—namely, to eventually achieve their goals.

Consequently, since authors have focused mostly on how decision outcomes may be manipulated, given both fixed assumptions on human rationality and fixed (though changeable) institutional environments, actual decision processes are hardly approached or studied in detail. Therefore, scant attention has been paid to show evidence of the actual processes that enable decision makers make their decisions, namely, the actual interaction (if any) between humans and the organizations within which they act.

However, this view on institutions as a constraint, being dominant in rational choice theory, is not unique. Next section is devoted to briefly outline an alternate view of institutions within rational choice theory, a perspective that departs from the traditional view of institutions to embrace an account of their influence in decision processes that we may consider as rather positive.

2.3.3 Institutions Enhance Perfectly Rational Decisions

The first question one must ask when attempting a review of rational-choice approaches with a positive view of organizational factors to decision making is whether it makes any actual sense to defend such a position around organizational influence on decisions if at the same time one assumes humans are perfectly rational.

At a philosophical level, for instance, it could fit a Hobbesian view of the political process, in the sense that institutions at least enable human decision-making under certain reasonable conditions (security, peace, etc.). In the case of Hobbes himself, the part "Of Man" in his *Leviathan* (Hobbes 1651) contains an important auxiliary assumption about the human condition according to which humans, in order to achieve their goals, can be at least as naturally aggressive as rational.[37] In such a case, then, it is hard to think that, though aggression is rational, it is possible to make other (perfectly) rational decisions in an environment of permanent mutual aggression. Therefore, organizations, if not enhance human decision making, at least enable it.

A positive account of institutions (in our sense) for collective choice from a rational choice perspective may only be found in what has been generally understood as one of the two standard ways rational choice theorists have interpreted institutions, i.e., institutions as *equilibria* (Shepsle 2006b) or endogenous institutions (Calvert 1995; Shepsle 2006a), in opposition to institutions as exogenous constraints, as were the ones presented in the previous section. This does not mean that all endogenous interpretations of institutions are to be interpreted as positive accounts of institutions in our sense, but we shall see that it is reasonable to think that all such positive accounts in rational choice theory are developed under this perspective.

In principle, the approach that views institutions as *equilibria* does not imply a radical departure from the traditional—we might say Downsonian—view of institutions as "rules of the game". But these rules or institutions are not observed as external objects or factors to be accounted for in the analysis of decisions made in the political arena. An example of institutional analysis of the external type would be seeing market behavior as a cooperative game in which some exogenous elements exist (property rights, legal principles, etc.) in order to enforce agreements between agents (e.g., contracts). Yet as we have seen in the previous section, political processes (such as legislature choice) are not usually analyzed as cooperative but as non-cooperative games, because doing otherwise would pose the problem of lacking "any exogenous enforcement mechanisms" (Shepsle 1985, p. 8).[38] Thence the internalization of institutions as inner, not explicit rules for modeling collective choice in the political field. In effect, these rules are assumed to be provided by the actors themselves in their interactions and, even more, "[they] reflect the willingness of (nearly) everyone to engage with one another according to particular patterns and procedures (nearly all the time)" (Shepsle 2006a, p. 25). This view, then, "focuses on how interactions among purposeful agents create the structure that gives each of them the motivation to act in a manner perpetuating this structure" (Greif and Kingston 2011).

[37] Then, it follows that humans are rationally aggressive, by aggression meaning the unlimited—i.e., not bound by moral laws—use of power by men to achieve their desires. After the famous statement that "out of civil states, there is always war of every one against every one", and that "nothing is unjust" in that state of war, Hobbes states his notion of the right of nature: "The right of nature, which writers commonly call *jus naturale*, is the liberty each man hath, to use his own power, as he will himself, for the preservation of his own nature; that is to say, of his own life; and consequently, of doing any thing, which in his own judgment, and reason, he shall conceive to be the aptest means thereunto" (Hobbes 1651, § 14).

[38] Nonetheless, Weingast and Marshall (1988) attempted such an explanation of legislative behavior. In the model the authors show the limits of explicit market forms of exchange as bargaining enforcing systems in legislative settings. As a consequence, legislators seek alternate (non-market, organizational) institutions that guarantee durable exchange.

This focus on willingness, perpetuity, and ultimately on equilibrium are the main reasons why we count this perspective on the "positive" side of rational choice institutionalism. For, institutional arrangements here are not viewed as constraints to action or decision but rather as mechanisms that enable collective choice where action is based upon the expectations agents have regarding the behavior of others.

This approach is still recent and to our knowledge only a few examples or applications of this notion of institutions from a rational choice perspective may be found in the main literature. Shepsle (2006a, p. 25) calls Calvert (1995) "one of the intellectual architects of this perspective", though Weingast (1998) includes this approach in a broader branch of rational choice studies on institutional stability and, in particular, links it to the concept of self-enforcement, thus focusing on Douglas North's contributions to institutional evolution and stability.[39] As Engerman and Sokoloff (2008, p. 129) point out, these institutional arrangements "might be written or unwritten, formally spelled out or informally known, but, in any case, they come to be accepted by the relevant members of society".

This path leads to a major change in the focus of research. The previous view focused on how the institutional framework shaped behavioral outcomes—variation may be observed both in outcomes and in institutional constrains, but players abide by the rules. In institutions as equilibria, two different scenarios may be envisaged. First, when an institution is in equilibrium with its environment and it is resistant to exogenous shocks, it can be viewed as a constraint, since "the behaviors it fosters appear to be equilibrium resopnses to the opportunities provided by this (equilibium) arrangement" (Shepsle 2006b). If, on the other hand, variations in the environment shake the foundations of the institution so that departures from the rules may be observed among agents that create an entirely new strategic scenario, the institution-as-constrain model is no longer adequate to account for institutional change. The view of institutions as equilibria, then, ultimately leads to the study of how agents "are motivated to follow institutionalized patterns of behavior" (Greif and Kingston 2011) and how these motivations change—how the parameters that characterize the "primal strategic settings" can change in response to exogenous shocks (Shepsle 2006b).[40]

Be that as it may, the main literature on the endogenous approach to institutions from rational choice theory assumes that it has two main differences with respect to the exogenous perspective. The first one regards the level of analysis. The second, the nature of institutions.

[39] Furthermore, Weingast (2002, p. 661) asserts that in the endogenous approach "analysts study why institutions take particular forms, why they are needed, and why they survive".

[40] Notice that the focus on the exogenous change in the parameters is needed so that theoretical accounts of institution-as-equilibrium and institutional change are not an oxymoron. Otherwise, the necessarily self-enforcing nature of institutions as "equilibria" would not provide any room for institutional change. See Greif and Laitin (2004) for a full explanation.

As to the first question, in comparison to the view of institutions as exogenous constraints to action, the endogenous perspective is considered to constitute a different level of analysis, namely, it "takes the study of institutions to a deeper level" (Weingast 2002, p. 661). This means that while the perspective on institutions presented in the previous section tended to treat institutions as a given set of rules (of the game), or as a given or fixed environment, the endogenous perspective sets forth the need for institutions, i.e., why do humans need such environments to perform certain decisions. This is the main reason why most reviews of this perspective turn to Douglas North's (and colleagues) literature on institutional history, change, and stability, thus providing "microfoundations for macro-political phenomena" (Weingast 2002, p. 661).

Regarding the second question, from this perspective institutions can be viewed either as structured bodies of rules and arrangements, or rather as unstructured patterns of behavior (Shepsle 2006a). Therefore, rules may be formal or informal, though the focus on self-enforcement may promote studies on the latter. In our opinion this is one of the reasons that may explain the less success of this approach in rational choice theories, in comparison to its (negative) alternative.[41] In effect, endogenous institutions are seen as "equilibrium ways of doing things" (Shepsle 2006a, p. 26), or "as an equilibrium of behavior in an underlying game" (Calvert 1995, p. 58). Calvert further elaborates that "there are no institutional 'constraints' or 'preferences' aside from those arising out of the mutual expectations of individuals and their intentions to react in specific ways to the actions of others, all in an attempt to maximize their utility in a setting of interdependency. *Institution* is just a name we give to certain parts of certain kinds of equilibria" (Calvert 1995, p. 74).

This approach from rational choice institutionalism has different instances in recent political science production. First of all, and following North's contribution to the origins and evolution of economic institutions, the endogenous perspective has given rise to new historical accounts of political institutions. Secondly, it has promoted the study of unstructured patterns of behavior as endogenous institutions that lead to different kinds of equilibria.

As to the first group of studies, North and Weingast (1989) explore how certain institutional arrangements in seventeenth-century England allowed for a government commitment to property rights and thus to economic growth. Yet while traditional approaches to institutional change had usually focused on the establishment of a set of rules that enforced the king's obligation and action, this new perspective tries to set up a model to show that the institutional changes implemented after the Glorious revolution "altered the incentives of governmental actors in a manner desired by the winners of the Revolution" (North and Weingast 1989, p. 804).

Summing up, "[t]hese changes reflected an explicit attempt to make credible the government's ability to honor its commitments", securing private rights in the mid-long run and thus promoting economic growth. Therefore, the authors show an

---

[41] Indeed, Shepsle (2006a, p. 30) comments that "[t]he Archimedian lever of rational choice institutionalism is provided by the *structure* of structured institutions".

alternate model of historical institutional analysis to that of rules as a constraint or control to power; instead, they promote a positive view of institutional change in the sense that the new arrangements enabled the king's commitment to be credible and in consequence that private rights such as property rights were guaranteed.

A second example is given by Weingast (1998) who applies this model to explain American political stability before the Civil War, in the sense that a set of rules such as "the balance rule were necessary to implement and maintain American federalism during the antebellum era" (Weingast 1998, p. 178).

More recently, Bueno de Mesquita (2000) delivers an alternate endogenous interpretation of the origins of sovereignty. In his model, the origins of the modern territorial state model are to be found in the Concordat of Worms rather that in the Treaty of Westphalia. In a few words, the "Concordat of Worms created a property right over territory (specifically, bishoprics) [...] [that] created competition between kings and thepope over political control. The contest for control manifested itself, in part, through the erection of new political institutions" (Bueno de Mesquita 2000). Moreover, while the church promoted institutions that tended to demote economic growth (in order to maintain its influence and dominance over monarchies), kings tended to design institutions that promoted economic growth as a way to take the church's weight off their shoulders. This change had further institutional consequences, namely, "[t]he competition that was institutionalized at Worms fomented the construction of new executive, judicial, taxing, and legislative apparatus that eventually emerged as the state as we know it" (Bueno de Mesquita 2000). However, not all endogenous approaches have a historical perspective. As noted above, a set of authors have rather focused on the informal way rules are institutionalized, delivering studies on unstructured institutions. An example of equilibrium pattern of behavior from this perspective is senatorial courtesy. It refers to an American practice by which a presidential appointment might be revoked if either the senior senator of the president's party, or the senators from the state to which the appointment applies raise objections to it.[42]

A further example explores the self-enforcement of some endogenous institutions that in the long run lead to social cooperation. In this sense, the studies by Axelrod (1980a, b), Axelrod and Hamilton (1981), Axelrod and Dion (1988), and Axelrod (2006) on the application of the prisoner's dilemma (in an artificially created computer tournament) show that an institution such as tit-for-tat[43] can lead to stable cooperation on successive repetitions of the same game.[44] Weingast (2002) observes

[42] Cited in Shepsle (2006a), referring to Maltzman and Binder (2005) and Jacobi (2005).

[43] The program TIT-FOR-TAT in the computer tournament embodied such a strategy: "cooperate initially, and thereafter cooperate if the other side cooperated last time and defect if the other side defected last time" (Axelrod 1980a, p. 4).

[44] Axelrod (1980a) further acknowledges that, to the bewilderment of some game theorists, when the game is applied repeated times, "at least in this first tournament, it paid to be nice", thus not being aggressive. But see Vlaev and Chater (2007) for further findings on the role of context in cooperative and uncooperative choices in the same game.

that it shows that "in some contexts, the incentives of repeated play are sufficient to enforce long-term social cooperation", to conclude that "a fundamental aspect of institutions is that they provide the means for the enforcement of cooperation".

In conclusion, though a precise description of institutions from this perspective is sometimes perceived as difficult, it is assumed that they "structure human actions by providing incentives that shape economic and political behavior" (Engerman and Sokoloff 2008, p. 122). In particular, these endogenous analyses tend to conclude that these institutional arrangements are both (a) self-enforced (thus avoiding the problem of exogenous enforcement, or *Quit custodiet ipsos custodes?*) and (b) as sustainable in time as other more structured or formalized forms of institutional organization (Calvert 1995).

2.3.4 Discussion

In this section rational-choice institutionalism has been presented taking into account the (unique) theory of rationality underlying the whole approach, and two different approaches to institutions.

Regarding the theory of rationality, its foundational principles may be found in Riker's development of Arrow's notion of rational action (focusing on transitive preferences), that might be summarized as the neoclassical economic principles regarding human action plus the notion of purpose, that allows for a picture of political self-interested and strategic-behaving agents acting in a game-shaped environment. According to this picture, any rational action implies (a) a given set of alternatives upon which a decision-maker must choose; (b) that the decision-maker has a well-defined an ordered set of preferences; (c) that these preferences are represented in a utility function; (d) that the decision-maker will (rationally) act so as to maximize his/her utility function.

Regarding the way institutions affect human decision making, two different approaches have been presented. The first one is dominant among rational choice theorists and views institutions as the rules that constrain what alternatives can be discussed and in what order they are decided upon. Therefore, institutions are viewed as exogenous factors that control the agenda. However, this is not a unique perspective regarding institutions, and an alternate approach proposes studying institutions as endogenous factors that enable both a deeper analysis of the role of institutions in decision-making and the avoiding the problem of the enforcement of the rules of the game.

While the first approach, then, views institutions as a constraint to decisions, namely negatively in our sense, the second one tends to analyze institutions as an environment that promotes equilibrium situations, thus focusing on their enhancing, positive role for decision making.

Finally, we have reviewed different instances of these two approaches in the literature. Regarding the negative view of institutions, rational choice theorists have privileged legislative choice studies as they represent an ideal setting for testing the models. A common pattern in almost all this production is, first, to consider institutional factors as fixed and given, and then, to analyze how different strategic actors behave so as they can benefit from collective choice outcomes by manipulating the agenda in various ways. As to the positive view of institutions, historic accounts of institutional change and evolution still dominate this approach, leaving aside traditional analyses that focused on the view of institutions as control over the power of particular actors (e.g., monarchs or the church).

Rational choice theory has not been uncontested in political science. Two different kinds of criticism might be expected: one devoted to the empirical soundness of the applications of rational choice theories to political phenomena; the other to the empirical soundness and adequacy of its basic assumptions on human rationality.

Regarding the first set of criticism, to date several critiques have have been put forth to the actual capabilities of the theories and also to the accomplishment of its promises or objectives. Perhaps the most structured and systematic criticism was Green and Shapiro's *Pathologies of Rational Choice Theory* (Green and Shapiro 1994). At least it is the one that has attracted most attention (Cox 1999), to the extent that it has produced numerous and lasting secondary production (e.g., Monroe 1997; Levesque 2004), including a whole *Critical Review* double issue dedicated to it.[45]

Green and Shapiro (1994) based their argument against rational choice on the general assertion that while its theoretical models are sophisticated and have been impressively improved since its foundations, its empirical contributions have been, to say the least, modest or scarce.[46] Thus their attention is on "the empirical focus of rational choice theory" (Green and Shapiro 1994, p. 6)—if the theory is to be viewed as scientific—and therefore most part of the critique deals with its alleged methodological failures (namely pathologies).

These critics argue, first, that since rational choice theory founders wrote their canonical works (Arrow 1963; Downs 1957; Olson 1965), "few theoretical insights derived from rational choice theory have been subjected to serious empirical scrutiny" (Green and Shapiro 1994, p. 9). It follows that when these empirical tests have been carried out, they show that most rational choice theories do not hold on acceptable methodological standards applicable to other allegedly scientific social science theories.

These methodological shortcomings refer to two distinct phenomena (Green and Shapiro 1994, pp. 33–46). First, scrutinized rational choice works show problems related to a generalized lack of strictness in the application of statistical techniques (sampling, inference, etc.). Second, there are methodological flaws directly related to the universalist claims of rational choice. Green and Shapiro (1994, p. 33) assert that

> these concern the way hypotheses are conceptualized, the manner in which they are transformed into testable propositions, and the interpretation of empirical results when tests are conducted. We contend that these [...] mistakes stem from a method-driven rather than problem-driven approach to research, in which practitioners are more eager to vindicate one or another universalist model than to understand and explain actual political outcomes.

---

[45] *Critical Review* 9: 1/2 (1995: Winter/Spring): pp. 1–300.

[46] The authors speak of a "relative dearth of sound empirical work" (Green and Shapiro 1994, p. ix).

This leads, according to Green and Shapiro, (a) to ill-tested post hoc explanations of known political phenomena (Green and Shapiro 1994, pp. 34–38), (b) to a kind of theory and prediction formulation that inevitably escapes standard empirical validity testing, and (c) to dubious methods for selecting and interpreting evidence when hypotheses are tested (Green and Shapiro 1994, pp. 42–46).

Their conclusion is that therefore some of the identity marks of rational choice theories such as universalism and its predictive power should be rethought and, in fact, abandoned.

In response to this criticism several papers have flourished, even 10 years after the first wave (Levesque 2004). Expectedly, the discussion has tended to focus on problems pertaining more to philosophy of science than to strict science practice. Therefore, a great deal of discussion has been devoted to the nature of scientific explanation (Chong 1995; Lane 1995; MacDonald 2003), the nature of empirical research and the role of theory in it (Fiorina 1995; Diermeier 1995; Lohman 1995; Shepsle 1995; McCubbins and Thies 1996), and the necessity of universalism in science (Ferejohn and Satz 1995),[47] together with some reassessments of rational choice theory as such (Ordeshook 1995; Schofield 1995; Levesque 2004; Hay 2004) and scattered references to the discussion on the notion of rationality in the theory. Yet the latter point refers more to rational choice theorists' internal debate about whether a 'thin' or 'thick' rationality is best suited for their models (Elster 1986; Friedman 1995; Yee 1997; Grafstein 1997) than to an actual discussion on the real capabilities of human reason.[48]

At this point one might think that given the two different accounts of institutional influence in human decision making within a unique notion of rationality, no relation should be established between a theory of rationality and the direction and nature of institutional influence on decisions. Nonetheless, our opinion is (a) that both exogenous and endogenous interpretations of institutions in rational choice theory fit in what Hall and Taylor (1996) call the 'calculus approach' to the way institutions affect the behavior of individuals, and (b) that there is a natural relation between the account of rationality and the account of institutions.

However different they may seem, both exogenous and endogenous approaches to institutions actually "focus on those aspects of human behaviour that are instrumental and based on strategic calculation" (Hall and Taylor 1996, p. 939). Given a theory of rationality that assumes that a decision maker seeks to maximize a utility function based on a well-defined set of preferences, both exogenous and endogenous accounts view institutions as outlining the game, yet they do that in different manners and, most importantly at different levels. While the former approach assumes that institutions embody the (exogenously set) rules of that game, the latter assumes institutions are (endogenously set and self-enforcing) patterns of behavior that allow for equilibria in the interaction among different political agents.

---

[47] See Moe (1979) for an early discussion on rational choice positivist criteria.

[48] But see Hay (2004) and Levesque (2004) for an attempt to discuss the validity of rational choice theories' assumptions on rationality.

Engerman and Sokoloff (2008) put it rather clearly:

> Institutions influence the beliefs and behaviors of individuals and groups, and thus the preferences and priorities expressed through both private and public decisions. Another important role of institutions is providing for efficient property rights, trust, and effective incentives, thus facilitating the organization and conduct of appropriate and constructive transactions and interactions among individuals and firms.

Either by limiting the possible alternatives or by enabling equilibrium situations, both accounts indeed assume that "[i]nstitutions affect behaviour primarily by providing actors with greater or lesser degrees of certainty about the present and future behaviour of other actors" (Hall and Taylor 1996, p. 939).[49] This means that in fact both perspectives see institutions as providing the environment for the natural strategical interaction among perfectly rational political actors, though they propose distinct theories on the nature of that environment and its impact on political outcome. Yet, they do not "capture fully the complexity of the interrelationship between individuals and the institutions influencing their behavior" (Greif and Laitin 2004).

This conclusion, in our opinion, has to do with two distinctive features of rational choice institutionalism. The first one is its micro-foundational objective, in the sense that whatever the role of institutions, rational choice theorists' analyses are always actor-centered (Thelen 1999, p. 377) (or even preference-centered) and thus try to provide models on an exclusively individual basis. This means that once the institutional arrangements are known, the individual unit is sufficient to explain his/her behavior. The second feature stems from the former and refers to the consequent functional view of institutions found in rational choice theories. Certainly, "rational choice institutionalists start with individuals and ask where institutions came from" (Thelen 1999, p. 379).[50]

Therefore, the debate on assumptions about human rationality is paramount to understand human behavior, because there is a natural analogy between a theory that assumes perfect rationality in strategical decision-makers and the explanation of the way the rules of the game or the patterns of behavior are enforced by or over these agents in order to produce different kinds of equilibria.

Nonetheless, the discussion over rational choice basic assumptions (i.e., on rationality) has been relatively absent from the mainstream discussion on its fruitfulness and general validity for political science.[51] However, a thorough discussion took place in economics on the utility-maximization model, which we saw was the one adopted by early rational choice theorists.

---

[49] Hall and Taylor (1996, p. 940) further point out that "institutions persist because they embody something like a Nash equilibrium, [. . .] individuals adhere to these patterns of behaviour because deviation will make the individual worse off than will adherence".

[50] Here Thelen is citing Zysman's comments at Conference of Europeanists, Chicago. No further reference is given.

[51] Weingast (2002) cites Knight and North (1997) as an example of the revision of such assumptions. Yet the paper focuses on economics, not on political science. Satz and Ferejohn (1994) pose a general discussion on whether rational choice theories are to be regarded as psychological theories.

The basic contention of these critics was that a more realistic and empirically sound account of human (indeed, limited) rationality was seriously needed in order to give an adequate explanation of both economic and political processes, namely an account of human decisions within organizational environments. This new model gave rise to behavioral analyses of decisions and organizations, challenging both rational choice and behaviorist models of political phenomena. This model we present in the next section.

2.4 Political Theories of Bounded Rationality

2.4.1 Foundations

The early formulation of the idea that "human beings are able to achieve only a very bounded rationality" was set forth in the context of Herbert Simon's assessment—in *Administrative Behavior* (Simon 1947)—of the level of efficiency an administrative organization was able to achieve. To this end, the author exposed the limits that should be taken into account regarding the decision-maker.

These limits to rationality included (a) limits regarding physiology (skills, habits and reflexes); (b) limits regarding the decision-maker's values and conceptions of purpose; and (c) limits regarding the knowledge the decision-maker is able to accumulate, process, and channel. "These are the 'limits' to rationality—Simon (1947, pp. 39–40) claims—with which the principles of administration must deal", thus uttering the closest form of the key notion of bounded rationality for the first time.

In his autobiography, Herbert Simon reflects on the nature and impact of his first work. Regarding its nature, he affirms that the book "examines administration as a decision-making process, introducing that framework with the help of a maze metaphor" (Simon 1996a, p. 85). Regarding its impact, the author assumes that the work "challenged [...] much of the received administrative theory of its day, and provided a new conceptual framework (decision making) for the analysis and description of organizational phenomena" (Simon 1996a, p. 86).

From this standpoint, then, it would be rare in principle to defend a position in which one assumed that human rationality is limited without assuming at the same time that humans need some institutional environment in order to make decisions, regardless of the specific influence these institutional arrangements may have on decision outcomes.[52] However, some approaches to decision making from the field of political psychology tend to diminish institutional factors in decision-making while assuming an empirically-based theory of human rationality, thus acknowledging limits to reason.

[52] Otherwise it would be difficult to defend that humans are capable of making good decisions at all.

As an example, Hermann and Kegley (1995) argue—correctly, in our opinion—that some students of international relations tend to see "states as unitary actors with motives and images similar to particular types of people". As they identify this methodological flaw in studies on democracy and international peace, they intend to look inside the "black box" (the leaders' inner environment) provided that "knowledge about leaders' perceptions may help to clarify the currently rather inconclusive results in attempts to differentiate between the cultural and the institutional explanations of the democratic peace". In centering on very particular crisis situations, their focus is almost exclusively on the personal, psychological level, but not on the organizational one: "it is the leader—his or her ways of processing information, beliefs about the world, personal needs—who may make a critical difference in the decision to initiate a war" (Hermann and Kegley 1995). But it appears that while solving one reductionism by taking psychological constraints into account, they fall into another reductionism themselves by neglecting any institutional constraints or simply influence to the leaders' decision, i.e., by neglecting organizational factors in shaping the information processing, beliefs, and personal needs of these leaders.[53]

Nevertheless, this approach is minority among those political scientists who try to base the study of political phenomena upon realistic assumptions regarding the human condition. The intention of the rest of this chapter is to show a number of approaches of other kind.

2.4.2 *Institutions Constrain Boundedly Rational Decisions*

A few years after both the behaviorist and the game-theoretical waves in political science, a reaction took place against both (1) the view held in behaviorist theories according to which institutions were to be interpreted only as the arena in which the political process took place (e.g., Easton 1965), and (2) the rational-choice/game-theoretic approaches that interpreted institutions only as agenda-setters but neglected other organizational factors in shaping actors' preferences (e.g., Riker and Ordeshook 1973).

This reaction, however, did not imply the existence of a leading group of political scientists defending a particular program, nor a great deal of literature on the questions that concern us. Instead, we'd rather speak of a set of rather isolated reactions against different aspects of early behaviorism and rational choice. The main caveat

[53] A further methodological comment might arise from their claim that "in situations that potentially serve as preludes to war, what leaders *are like* becomes *very important*, as do their perceptions of the nature of the crisis. Indeed, given the degree of support that this proposition has garnered, it—like the proposition that democratic governments *do not* wage war against one another—has gained the status of an empirical law in the study of foreign policy decision making" (Hermann and Kegley 1995). The words in italics (that are mine) denote the very different nature of the two allegedly empirical assertions, which does not make them worth equalling. While the second is empirically testable, the first one is not.

of this approach, though, is that while most of attention has been placed on the way institutional arrangements influence political decision making, the discussion on the assumptions on rationality has been rather scarce. Therefore, since no explicit discussion on rationality is identified, our review becomes difficult, although a few examples can be presented.

For instance, Bachrach and Baratz (1962) set forth a severe critique of the way both pluralists and elitists viewed the exercise of power. In their analysis the authors focused on the effects of organization (power) on decision-making: "power may be, and often is, exercised by confining the scope of decision-making to relatively 'safe' issues" (Bachrach and Baratz 1962, p. 948). This discussion led them to further consider the central point of what issues enter or not in the political agenda (or "political arena", as they called it).

Regarding the direction of organizational influence on decision-making, the central point of their model is that exercising power basically means to "devote [one's] energies to creating or reinforcing social and political values and institutional practices that limit the scope of the political process to public consideration of only those issues which are comparatively innocuous to [one]" (Bachrach and Baratz 1962, p. 948). This is quite clear when they assume that "organization is the organization of bias" in the sense that power is shaped both by the issues that *are* discussed and those which *are not*.

Although their model does not explicitly state any theory of human rationality, it would be almost impossible to include them in any branch of rational choice theory. It would also be hardly possible to assume that the authors accept rational choice assumptions on rationality. Yet no discussion on this issue is put forth. However, the flow of studies that descends from their seminal work allows us to situate this branch of analysis within a vision that at least does not assume that humans are capable of a perfect rationality.

In effect, this critical vein has had an important number of followers, especially in policy analysis. It has produced a number of good analyses on agenda-setting (Baumgartner and Jones 1991; Soroka 1999) that in different manners elaborate on this *negative* view of organizational influence, fostering the consolidation of the 'bounded rationality' model in public policy analysis (Jones 2003; Baumgartner et al. 2009).

Furthermore, works on issue-salience and issue-attention (Downs 1998; Henry and Gordon 2001; Howlett 1997; Peters and Hogwood 1985; Weissert 1991; Jones and Baumgartner 2005) take account of the role of (allocation of) attention and emotions in decision-making.[54] And Schneider and Ingram (1990) make an interesting point in reviewing behavioral assumptions underlying five general types of policy

[54] It is worth noting here that Anthony Downs (1998) has abandoned the main assumptions regarding his "rational man" (Downs 1957), a model upon which the rational choice approach was in part built.

instruments. Nevertheless, among these "behavioral assumptions" they do not count suppositions about human rationality.[55]

Moreover, while broadening its substantial scope, this approach to policy analysis has also widened its methodological range of possibilities in order to assess the way the agenda is set—i.e., the process by which a decision is made about what decisions will be able to be made within the political process. Methods such as network analysis (cf. Rhodes 2006b), classic content analysis (Baumgartner et al. 2011), and automated document classification, scaling, and topic identification (Hillard et al. 2007) are now being increasingly used.

Regarding the particular issue of the limits of rationality, as we said, it has received scant attention with a few exceptions (Jones 2003), and most of them within policy analysis literature. For instance, Goodin et al. (2006) explicitly speak of "the illusion of instrumental rationality completely governing the policy process", referring to the illusion that "policy makers begin with a full set of ends (values, goals) that are to be pursued, full information about the means available for pursuing them, and full information about the constraints (material, social, and political resources) available for pursuing them". Based upon the limits on human rationality, then, the authors propose considering policy making as a process of discovery, in which human limits are overcome through deliberation and eventually persuasion among different political actors (Goodin et al. 2006). In the same vein, Freeman (2006) sees public policy making as a learning process that begins with uncertainty, and Rein (2006) explores the ways through which policy makers deal with "reframing ends so as better to cope with the unavoidable problems of vagueness and conflict".[56]

Moreover, even some rational choice theorists seem to have relaxed some of the strongest assumptions on rationality. For instance, Denzau and North (1994) put forth some empirical problems with the classical view of rationality stating that "it is impossible to make sense out of the diverse performance of economies and polities if one confines one's behavioral assumptions to that of substantive rationality in which agents know what is in their self-interest and act accordingly".[57] Moreover, though in a different manner, Frank (1987) revised some assumptions of the neoclassical model of rationality by including anger and conscience (in a word, emotions) in his utility-maximization model.

In conclusion, while most students of organizational factors in decisions make assumptions on human rationality that somehow would commit them to bounded rationality, they rarely devote discussion to this particular issue. Instead they tend to assume that institutions are mainly tools that channel the exercise of power interpreted as an agenda-setting mechanism. Nevertheless from this scant work it is not possible to establish a clear linkage between bounded rationality and organizational

---

[55] See March and Olsen (1983) for the implications of political attention in huge administrative reorganization programs.

[56] A similar motivation may be found in Winship (2006).

[57] Substantive rationality refers to the previously presented theory of maximizing rationality. Section 2.4.3 and Chap. 3 shall clarify and discuss this notion.

factors in decision-making. Next section is devoted to show how a link may be established between the notion of bounded rationality and a particular analysis of organizations.

2.4.3 *Institutions Enhance Boundedly Rational Decisions*

In their analytical and innovative approach to organizations, March and Simon (1958) stated the differences between their *new* "administrative man" as opposed to the rational man of economics and statistical decision theory, and the "administrative man" of classical organization theory.[58]

This approach had already been presented in some economic subfields, such as the theory of the firm. In effect, two widely cited critiques of the neoclassical approach focused on the theory of firm behavior in oligopolistic markets. In a first joint paper Cyert and March (1955) introduced two major changes in measuring the influence of organizational structure in price fixing with respect to the classical view. They referred to (1) the real-world source of the value of the variables at work in actual price establishing policies within firms, and to (2) the fact that the decision-maker's identification with the goals of the firm was paramount in pricing decisions.

In a further elaboration of their argument, Cyert and Simon (1956) added other organizational factors that influenced the firm's behavior.[59] In particular, they affirmed that "[a] general theory of the firm will have to contain variables related both to the external environment and the internal organization".

This program implied changing four basic assumptions that challenged neoclassical economics. First, profit maximization as the motivational basis for firm's decision-making was to be substituted by the notion of "acceptable level of profits". This change—the authors claimed—was based upon the fact that the neoclassical view of a profit-maximizer entrepreneur was not empirically tested. The second change referred to the role of operational norms (planning procedures) in the evaluation of a firm's behavior. Third, the organizational structure (departmentalization) was to be accounted for, mainly because the subunits within the organization were likely to produce their own goals, and the policy deciding allocation of resources to these subunits might produce unwanted results in pursuing the firm's main goals. Finally, the authors challenged the (non-empirical, thus mainly deduced) way the neoclassical theories of the firm presented their models of decision rules.

This approach to decision-making, then, challenges from the outset a simpler consideration of human decision-making within organizations, especially in business firms, but also in typical bureaucratic organizations, that has been and still is quite popular among economists and political scientists.

---

[58] Simon himself had already posited this idea a little bit earlier (Simon 1955, p. 114).

[59] Other developments around a behavioral approach to the firm by the same authors may be found in March (1962), Cyert and March (1963), Cyert et al. (1959).

As to the theory of rationality, whereas the neoclassical model of rationality deals with a complete set of well-defined and ordered preferences before a utility maximizer, this other approach presents a boundedly rational human being in front of a very simplified model of the world that enables her to cope with its otherwise overwhelming complexity (March 1978). Thus it also challenges a game-theoretical approach to decision-making.

This idea refers, then, to the way humans are able to cope with the complexity of the world and with their own limitations, thus emphasizing the necessity to separate the inner and the outer environment of a decision situation. One of the most cited formulations of the notion of bounded rationality is that "the apparent complexity of our behavior over time is largely a reflection of the complexity of the environment in which we find ourselves" (Simon 1996b, p. 53).

More recent approaches—in political science—present the same flavor while emphasizing the role of organizations in decision making (Rothstein 1998, p. 147):

> Without denying that individual action is purposive, this approach assumes that individuals cannot be considered to have the computational or cognitive ability necessary to be fully rational [...]. Instead, they tend to follow "scripts" or "templates" given to them by the institutions in which they are acting. In a sense, in this cultural understanding of institutions, institutions not only determine actors' preferences but also to some extent create them.

The connection between this notion of rationality and organizational behavior was already present in Simon (1947, p. 241), where the author concludes that what in actuality molds human behavior is not rationality:

> Instead, behavior is determined by the irrational and nonrational elements that bound the area of rationality. The area of rationality is the area of adaptability to these nonrational elements. Two persons, given the same possible alternatives, the same values, the same knowledge, can rationally reach only the same decision. Hence, administrative theory must be concerned with the limits of rationality, and the manner in which organization affects these limits for the person making a decision. [...] The theory must determine [...] how institutionalized decision can be made to conform to values developed within a broader organizational structure. The theory must be a critique of the effect (judged from the point of view of the whole organization) of the organizational structure upon the decisions of its component parts and its individual members.

The approach that combines bounded rationality with a *positive* influence of organizational factors in decision-making has had many different applications in political science, including bureaucratic organizations, group decision-making, judicial settings, elections, and international relations. Obviously, public institutions are privileged settings upon which political science has focused its efforts to understand decision processes.

2.4.3.1 Bureaucracy

As to bureaucratic organizations, the keystone of public power enforcement, Kettl (2006) refers to the role of institutional factors that link decisions and actions in this particular environment. He claims that "to a powerful degree, bureaucratic power depends on decisions" (Kettl 2006, p. 369), and in this sense, the coordination within bureaucracies (the link between decisions and actions) turns to be a major issue.

Regarding bureaucracy analysis, Bendor and Moe (1985) present an in-depth critique of some neoclassical approaches to bureaucracy.[60] In particular, their critique targets some formal neoclassical models that attempt to explain regulatory behavior (Peltzman), and a "theory of budgets and bureaucratic supply" (Niskanen), which appears to have some connections with that of Cyert and Simon (1956). The authors posit a general methodological critique that targets the unit of analysis: Bendor and Moe (1985) claim that neoclassical approaches "make no real attempt to disaggregate institutional decision makers", meaning that their basic unit of analysis is not the individual but "bureaus, legislatures, and interest groups". Regarding the theory of rationality of neoclassical approaches, the authors' object that these models oversimplify human capabilities (both assume that decision makers are preference maximizers), and the amount of information available in a decision situation (both authors assume perfect information for decision makers, at least for some of them).

As a response, Bendor and Moe (1985) propose a model of the interaction among bureaucrats, politicians and interest groups, which is "a dynamic model of adaptive behavior that is very much in the spirit of the behavioral tradition", explicitly referring to authors such as Simon, March, Cyert, Cohen, and Axelrod. At the core of this model lie two critical notions (Bendor and Moe 1985, p. 756):

- Decisions made by individuals are ways by which they adapt themselves to their environment, "moving in directions that appear to promise them greater utility", and assuming sub-optimal solutions.
- Individuals are "only minimally informed about their environments and about each other, basing their adaptive decisions on feedback about the success of their prior decisions".

2.4.3.2 Group Decision-Making

Another perspective of organizational factors in decision which has taken place within political science is group decision-making, the legislature being one particular public institution of great relevance in this field. Carey (2006) faces the problem of decision-making within legislative organizations. Yet his objective is not exactly to explain *how* decisions are actually made, and thus he does not need to explicitly defend neither an olympic nor a bounded notion of rationality.

Nevertheless, organization structure has a role in his approach in the *positive* direction in that legislatures often promote specialization of their members in order

[60] However, Miller and Moe (1983) had adopted many neoclassical assumptions in earlier accounts of the bureaucratic phenomenon.

to achieve better decisions, given the wide range of subjects to be decided upon. He even refers to "expertise" (Carey 2006, p. 441) among legislature members.[61]

Carey's argument brings him to the point of agenda setting and the role of parties in legislatures—as gatekeepers—, which is the keystone of decision making in those institutions. The argument affirms that parties produce "privileged agenda setters who determine which proposals are debated and voted on, and in which order" (Carey 2006, p. 444).

So far, this argument would seem identical to the one defended by authors from the previous section in the sense that institutions delimit the range of possible alternatives to be decided upon. Yet the author states that these organizational factors are precisely what "make[s] it possible for legislators to realize gains unrealizable in unorganized, state-of-nature assemblies" (Carey 2006, p. 445).[62]

The same spirit seems to appear in Stoker (2006) about how institutions influence local governance in terms of its actors' decision-making.

2.4.3.3 Judicial Settings

Judicial settings have been also a field where to study decision-making. In this case the relation between organizational factors and bounded rationality has been mostly treated in terms of adaptive, rule-based behavior (in low, trial courts), and also in terms of the role of values and information in decisions around hard cases (high courts). Accordingly the models showed in the literature (e.g., Gibson 2006), these studies tend to focus their attention generally either on the weight judges' values and ideologies have in their decision-making, or on the role of routines or other responses to environmental stimuli in low-level courts.

Regarding judges' beliefs and their impact to their decisions, Walker (1972) offered a brief research note on the partisan influences on judicial decision making at trial-level. In this regard, racial matters have received major attention (e.g., Carroll and Mondrick 1976), though in other cases general individual policy preferences (e.g., Johnson 1987; Hausegger and Haynie 2003) and judges' personal characteristics (e.g., van Koppen and Kate 1984) have been used to operationalize variables indicating judges' belief structures.

As regards the study of adaptive responses to environmental stimuli in trial courts, seminal contribution by Schubert (1968) and Mohr (1976) introduced the organizational perspective pioneered by Simon, March, Olsen and others into the study of courts as organizations. In particular, Schubert (1968) emphasized the importance of focusing on people's actual behavior in the context of judicial literature, linking

[61] Other authors on legislatures have faced the problem of allocation of attention (March 1990, p. 3) focusing on the solutions organizational structure may imply to the problem of the bottleneck of attention and time. Cox (2006) is an example though from the rational choice approach.

[62] See Uslaner and Zittel (2006) for a more macro approach on institutional and behavioral factors in parliamentary and congressional legislative behavior.

the new approaches both to Oliver Wendell Holmes' jurisprudential tradition, and to Charles S. Pierce's philosophical pragmatism. Regarding the new approach he asserted that "[it] seeks to relate what we think we know, and what we can learn, about how persons behave in adjudicatory roles and institutional relationships, to a general body of theory about human decision-making behavior" (Schubert 1968, p. 409).

As for Lawrence B. Mohr, his was one of the first attempts to state a general theoretical framework for the study of courts as organizations according to the behavioral organization and decision-making analysis. Contrasting the differences between classical organization approaches such as Weber's and Gulick and Urwick's, and Simon and March's, Mohr's contribution is to be seen as a crucial reflection on the role of the outer environment in decision-making when applied to courts, asserting that "decision-making groups—even a single decision-making group—within an organization may well be subject to different contexts at different times and may shift, with changes of context, into different modes of choice" (Mohr 1976, p. 627).

Following this theoretical framework, Heydebrand (1977) offered an empirical assessment of the role of environmental elements in determining the nature of tasks and the allocation of resources in courts as public bureaucracies, while Saks and Kidd (1981) approach human information processing issues in order to focus on heuristic biases in decision-making. Besides, Albonetti (1987) explores a behavioral model of prosecutor's decision-making. In particular, the author attempts an explanation of how "uncertainty emerging from stereotypical perceptions of cause and effect relationships between successful case prosecution and containments thereof does affect the prosecutor's initial decision to 'go forward' with a charge" (Albonetti 1987, p. 311).

A different approach to the judicial world within political science is that of McGuire (2006), who views the judicial process as a public policy, and thus the approach does not focus directly on the judge's decision making process, or at least on the way these decisions are actually made. In actuality, the central point is on the way decisions are made *by* courts, and not *in* courts.

On the other hand, a vast majority of literature about judicial decision-making comes from Common Law systems, mainly the US and Great Britain. In turn, these studies tend to focus on decisions of High Courts—or how decisions by High Courts affect low-courts decisions (e.g., Johnson 1987)—where hard cases arise and are discussed. This makes these approaches of limited interest to us because we will focus our research on daily decisions made in particular organizational environments. Moreover, we will consider judicial decision-making as a kind of organizational decision-making process that is not essentially different from other decision-making processes that imply expert knowledge, e.g., medical decision-making.

2.4.3.4 Elections

The analysis of the relation between electoral systems and decision-making (Bowler 2006) is also important in our review: according to Duverger's Law, the shape of the electoral system affects the number of parties in a political system. Following this argument, the shape of the electoral system will generate particular winners or losers in a political process, and thus choosing a electoral system may be a critical issue. This leads to the institutional factors that may determine collective decision-making under a particular amount of uncertainty.

In contrast to the dominant rational-choice approach to this issue, Bowler (2006, p. 584) recognizes that a change in an electoral system—in the context of a stable democracy—might have impact on voters' preferences, though it is not clear to what extent this impact can be measured (or has been measured). Marginally, this reflection leads also to a more broad discussion on the relation between types of democracy (direct or indirect) and decision-makers' (citizens) preferences (see Budge 2006), namely the impact of the way democracy is organized on the citizens' preferences and thus in their decisions.

But it has also led to investigations on the role of bounded rationality in voters' behavior, i.e., on the heuristics voters use in order to process limited political information and produce reasonable political judgments.

The study of the cognitive and mental processes that underlie and (partly) explain political behavior has a tradition that would lead us to the remote origins of political science and political philosophy. In the beginnings of the twentieth century (1908) Graham Wallas attempted in *Human Nature in Politics* to recover this tradition bewildered by the fact that "nearly all students of politics analyse institutions and avoid the analysis of man", and triggered by the belief that "the student of politics must, consciously or unconsciously, form a conception of human nature, and the less conscious he is of his conception the more likely he is to be dominated by it" (Wallas 2004).

More recently, the advances of the cognitive sciences have enabled a thorough and more systematic—though not fully consensual—study of the cognitive processes underlying political behavior, that includes features such as emotions, evocation, heuristics, mental models, conceptual structures, and belief systems (e.g., Marcus 1988, 2000; Druckman 2004).[63]

In this direction, Lau and Redlawsk (2001) provide an excellent review of five different cognitive heuristics employed by voters, and present empirical results for studying both the context of heuristic usage, and the quality of political decision making. Their approach links political sophistication to the efficiency of heuristics usage in political behavior in the sense that heuristics turn to be more efficient tools—i.e., helping make accurate political judgments—when used by experts than when employed by non-experts.

2.4.3.5 International Relations

Finally, a field particularly well-treated by decision analysis is international relations (IR). In it there are many different approaches altogether. For instance,

[63] Herbert Simon explicitly referred to—and acknowledged—Wallas' contributions in his article "Human nature in politics" (Simon 1985).

the analysis of international organizations as tools for decision-making (for states, basically) (Duffield 2006), although their efficiency in this role is still under discussion (Keohane and Martin 2003).

In this vein, March and Olsen (1998) established a theoretical framework for international relations from a standpoint that committed both to an institutionalist approach and to bounded rationality, emphasizing "the substantial role of identities, rules, and institutions in shaping human behavior" (March and Olsen 1998, p. 951). Their critique to game-theoretic/rational-choice approaches to international relations covers the following issues:

- The consequential logic of explanations of human and nation behavior ("history is seen as the consequence of the interaction of willful actors").
- The assumption that individuals and organizations drive their action according to calculation of its consequences "as measured against prior preferences" implies a set of problems that refer to both (a) the actual capacity of humans to perform such calculations, and to (b) the problem of inconsistent preferences observed in empirical studies on humans.
- The problem of exogenous uncertainty is usually tackled with reference to "some variation on an assumption of rational expectations", which involves (a) unreal assumptions on the ability of actors to predict the future, and (b) a simplification of "problems of preference complexity and endogeneity by seeing politics as decomposing complex systems into relatively autonomous subsystems, most commonly by linking them hierarchically".

Other authors in the IR field have also been highly sensitive to the limits of human computing capabilities in proposing computerized models of international decision-making. In effect, Schrodt (1990, 1998) builds on theory on bounded rationality (Kahneman et al. 1982) and pattern recognition—as a basis for human problem-solving and expert knowledge generation (Newell and Simon 1972)—in order to model the way foreign policy experts make decisions. His approach, then, combines empirical behavioral data about human decision-making with advanced methodologies for modeling and representing knowledge, namely, event data analysis (Gerner et al. 1994; Schrodt and Gerner 2001; Gerner et al. 2002).

Still others have explored the role of perceptions in predicting foreign policy decision making. Herrmann (1988, p. 844), for instance, employs the notion of *schemata* as a tool that "organizes knowledge about the Soviet Union and American foreign policy", connecting this notion with information processing based problem-solving models as the one provided by Simon and Newell (1971), and Newell and Simon (1972).

This approach has been further developed and applied to an image-based theory of international relations (Herrmann and Fischerkeller 1995; Herrmann et al. 1997), to "mass public decisions to go to war" (Herrmann et al. 1999), to cognitive-based explanations of international norms (Herrmann and Shannon 2001), and to elite's decision making in foreign policy (Herrmann and Keller 2004).[64]

It differs from classical models of decision-making (decision trees, etc.) both in the core assumptions upon which they are based, and in the perspective of analysis they apply. As to the first issue, standard theory of decisions is based on a number of (at least) controversial assumptions: that goals can be isolated, that context does not affect utilities, that humans can produce accurate probabilities calculi, that the definition of goals, choices, and evidence is possible, and that each outcome produces a set of utilities that are independent of other outcomes. This leads to the second issue: all these assumptions being "given" in the classical decision approach, the natural unit of analysis is the "choice situation".

Evidence has been presented which shows that actual decisions rarely occur that way, that these assumptions are rather unrealistic, and that they hardly allow for accurate explanations of the processes that lead to real decisions. Klein and Calderwood (1991), for instance, show the results of field research on decision-making of fireground commanders. Their main conclusion is that in actual decision processes, almost no decisions are preceded by a process of considering alternatives or—even less—assessing probabilities.

Instead, the authors present a model implying that decision makers understand "a situation in terms or its familiarity to previous experiences" (Klein and Calderwood 1991, p. 1021), which in turn involves serial processing of options (instead of generating a set of options to be compared to each other), the establishment of satisficing expected results (instead of optimizing), the use of imagination in order to place possible options in context (instead of multiattributive utility analysis). As to the question of the unit of analysis, in the authors' own words: "It emphasizes the way the situation is understood more than the decision event of choosing between several alternatives".

2.4.4 Discussion

In conclusion, then, there are at least three elements from this conceptual framework that are central to our discussion on the interaction between organizational factors and bounded rationality in decision analysis.

The first one is the influence of organizational structure in shaping preferences and knowledge of the organization members. This implies linking the individual's choice structure to the organization's structure with the general aim to unfold the "the process of choice which leads to action" (Simon 1947, p. 1) as a central aspect in the study of organizations.

---

[64] See also Herrmann (1988) for a methodological discussion about the use of cognitive-based approaches in international relations.

The second element is the distinction between goals and subgoals. Summarizing the approach, in the heart of decision-making is choice, which implies selection—whether conscious or unconscious—of alternatives out of the ones that are both objectively possible and subjectively apparent. The notion of selection leads to a multitude of alternative possible actions that present themselves to the choice-maker and among which he has to finally select.

This approach is based on the observed fact—early discovered by students of organizations, e.g., Selznick (1943, 1948) and Simon (1947)—that organization members' behavior is rarely guided by the same goals that, in principle, guide the organization's behavior as a whole (its final objectives).

This question led Selznick (1943, 1948) to the distinction between professed (final, original) and operational goals, arguing that "the actual procedures of every organization tend to be molded by action toward those goals which provide operationally relevant solutions for the daily problems of the organization as such".

This process refers also to what the author calls the "organization paradox": the very same organization structure makes their members pursuit a set of goals (operational) that are not the main ones by which the organization is (in principle) guided. In other words, what Selznick was affirming is that the *actual* behavior of an organization was to be found in these operational goals and not in the professed, final goals, and that this dominance of operational goals was possible through routinization and specialization (departmentalization).[65]

This very same question also led Simon (1947) to the distinction between 'value judgments'—the ones that lead toward the selection of final goals—and 'factual judgments'—the ones that refer to the implementation of the final goals (Simon 1947). Yet he also realized that both kinds of judgments do never appear clearly separated to the administrator, so in order to make some decisions the administrator will have to be able to identify some mediate goals that permit some grade of achievement of at least one final goal.

Selznick's approach seems to emphasize routinization as an instance of a kind of Weberian "instrumental rationality" (as opposed to "value rationality") that covers all the relevant aspects of organizational behavior (cf. Weber 1978, pp. 3–63). In a sense, though, this approach may lead to a role-based theory of human behavior within organizations that, ultimately, leads to a kind of round argument that has been already identified and criticized (Simon 1997, pp. 17–28).

In a nutshell, role-based explanations may be useful when they identify stable patterns of behavior within organizations that help explain, for instance, organization stability. Certainly, "not only is the role defined for the individual who occupies it, but it is known in considerable detail to others in the organization who have occasion to deal with him" (March and Simon 1958, p. 4). Thence the stability and predictability of the environment of other persons that typically surrounds a decision-maker, which enables high degrees of coordination in organizational behavior.

[65] See March and Simon (1958, pp. 40–47) for a general critique of Selznick's model of bureaucracy and his general theory of organization.

However, analyzing organizational behavior in a role-theoretical manner has many problems. On one hand, "it does not leave any room for rationality" (Simon 1997) because while the agent who plays the role is functional from a social standpoint, there is not evidence of the premises of his decisions, his calculations, knowledge, or motivations. Hence, the agent cannot be a rational actor; he is simply a role player. Certainly, it challenges the very notion of rational behavior (a particular action defined by the *choice* of adequate means) by diminishing the role of choice in rational action. On the other hand, such a perspective would ignore some basic behavioral features of organizations. For instance, early works (Cyert and Simon 1956) showed that search for better alternatives in firms was triggered by the realization that its aspiration level of profits had not been achieved. Tummolini and Castelfranchi (2006) have used the notion of roles as "coordination artifacts" that enable action within institutions by assigning conventional power to particular agents and allowing other agents know the former *have* this power. This approach has been applied in fields such as multi-agent systems and electronic institutions.

Finally, the third element is the notion of bounded rationality. It was firstly referred to as a *compromise* the decision-maker must have with the fact that when one selects a particular path, "the alternative that is finally selected never permits a complete or perfect achievement of objectives, but is merely the best solution that is available under the circumstances" (Simon 1997).

In conclusion, Herbert Simon's pathbreaking work served as an important basis upon which several further work was to stand. We already noted that he himself and James March further developed in *Organizations* (March and Simon 1958, pp. 137–142) the core idea that decisions are surrounded by a specifiable environment, and that this environment can and must be analyzed in order to grasp the actual way decisions are made.

2.5 Conclusions

In this chapter a simple model has been presented in order to classify and briefly review different approaches to decision-making within organizations in political science. To this end, two variables have guided the critical account: the theory of rationality underlying each perspective, and the organizational influence on decision-making, dividing this last factor into two sub-variables (nature of influence and direction of influence). Table 2.5 summarizes the four approaches presented in the chapter outlining the main authors reviewed for each approach.[66]

One of the many critiques this model may have to face is that in its simplicity the picture represents a world of research programs that are neatly separated and that seldom communicate or debate with each other. Certainly, we have already noted

[66] Some authors appear in more than one table cell due to changes in their approaches. Years between parentheses point out the approximate moment of these changes.

Table 2.5 Summary of each perspective in our classification according to their main authors

	Organizations enhance decisions	Organizations limit decisions
Maximum rationality	R. Axelrod, B. Bueno de Mesquita (2000), R. L. Calvert (1995), D. Dion, S. L. Engerman, W. D. Hamilton, W. J. Marshall, D. North (1989), K. A. Shepsle (2006), K. L. Sokoloff, B. R. Weingast (1988, 2002)	D. Acemoglu, D. Austen-Smith, J. S. Banks, R. L. Calvert (1989), J. M. Colomer, G. W. Cox, A. T. Denzau, A. Downs (1957), L. Epstein, J. Ferejohn, T. W. Gilligan, S. Guarnaschelli, C. Johnsen, J. Knight, K. Krehbiel, A. Lupia, M. D. McCubbins, R. D. McKelvey, T. Moe (1987), M. J. Moran, E. M. S. Niou, P. C. Ordeshook, T. R. Palfrey, R. A. W. Rhodes, R. Riezman, W. H. Riker (1980), K. A. Schultz, P. M. Shane, K. A. Shepsle (1979), B. R. Weingast
Bounded rationality	C. A. Albonetti, R. Abu-Jabr, J. Bendor (1985), S. Bowler, R. Calderwood, J. M. Carey, J. Ciarrochi, R. Cyert, M. D. Cohen, J. N. Druckman, J. S. Duffield, M. P. Fischerkeller, D. J. Gerner, J. L. Gibson, R. Herrmann, W. V. Heydebrand, D. Kahneman, R. O. Keohane, D. F. Kettl, G. Klein, R. R. Lau, J. G. March, G. E. Marcus, L. Martin, K. T. McGuire, T. Moe (1985), L. B. Mohr, A. Newell, J. P. Olsen, D. P. Redlawsk, T. Y. E. Schooler, Ph. A. Schrodt, G. Schubert, V. P. Shannon, H. A. Simon, P. Slovic, P. E. Tetlock, A. Tversky, E. M. Uslaner, P. S. Visser, J. F. Voss, T. J. Walker, G. Wallas, Ö. Yilmaz, T. Zittel	P. Bachrach, M. Baratz, F. R. Baumgartner, A. Downs (1998), A. T. Denzau (1994), R. H. Frank, R. Freeman, C. S. Gordon, G. T. Henry, B. W. Hogwood, M. Howlett, H. Ingram, B. D. Jones, D. North (1994), G. Peters, A. Schneider, S. Soroka, C. S. Weissert

that debate has taken place around a number of issues, though the impression is that interventions from one perspective into the other's matters are rather sparse. Though it is not within our scope to go through the detailed terms of the debate, the identification of its main points seems worth presenting. In our opinion there are at least three basic (and intertwined) dimensions along which (almost always implicit) such criticism takes place:

- The first refers to the assumptions made by each perspective. The main target of behavioralists (e.g., Simon 1978) is the simplified and empirically ungrounded models of rationality and general human behavior contained in rational-choice and game-theoretical approaches to political and economic processes. Rational choice theorists tend to defend their approach referring to the argument of the relative relevance of the actuality of these assumptions for building useful predictive models (Friedman 1953).

- The second dimension refers to the methodology used for building the models. Rational-choice proponents (e.g., Shepsle 2006a) argue that behavioralists' excessive concern and emphasis on every single detail about these assumptions seriously raises the difficulty of the construction of operative theories that enable scientific progress. Among the arguments one may emphasize that behavioral models are too case-specific (which does not allow them to build general models of decision-making), behavioral proponents arguing that rational choice models, in pursuing universal laws, are too general to give real accounts of actual situations. Behavioralists tend to add that unless theories are able to face empirical tests, scientific progress will not occur anyway.
- The third dimension refers to the research agenda within both approaches. Behavioralists usually claim that while they intend to build descriptive theories of decision—how decisions happen—, game-theoretical or rational-choice approaches, since they are committed to the existence of optimal solutions and to viewing human beings as preference maximizers, build normative theories—i.e., they are concerned on how decisions ought to happen.[67] This might explain, for instance, why rational choice theorists are so concerned in finding reasons to an apparent paradox, namely that the interaction among rational actors often produce "suboptimal or inefficient collective outcomes" (Thelen 1999). In conclusion, a set of strong assumptions on the nature of human rationality such as that rational human actors should produce optimal and efficient outcomes produces a bias on the account of the role of institutions in decision making. It implies, then, a normative bias in rational choice theory in the sense that theorists establish an ideal point from which they think rational decision makers should depart in their political behavior (i.e., perfect rationality), and then try to explain why in actuality this point is almost never reached.

Whatever the exact terms of this quasi-debate may be,[68] the research put forth in this book imposes a number of requirements that are hard to meet from a rational-choice approach. Either if we treat institutions as rules of the game or as equilibria, the main concern of rational choice theories rests on *outcomes*. We have seen that in both

[67] In some contexts, applicants of the non-behavioral approach do acknowledge that "decision theory is not proposed as a *descriptive* theory; it does not purport to provide a good description of how people actually behave when making choices under uncertainty" (Henrion et al. 1991, p. 67).

[68] Bennett (1995, pp. 28–30) makes an excellent example of the non-debating nature of the controversies, in the sense that some potential arguments are reduced to trivial issues. While claiming to respond to the main criticisms the game-theoretical approach has received during more than 40 years, it turns that, according to him, the main arguments of the critics have been based upon a set of woeful misunderstandings or dislikes, namely: (a) the mathematical guise of game-theoretical approach ("some critics appear to have an inbuilt aversion to anything containing numbers"); (b) the misunderstanding of the word *game*, which turns to be "deeply offensive" to someone; (c) the also misunderstood attachment (by some critics) of game-theoretical approaches to free-market economics; (d) and, finally, confusing rationality with selfishness.

rational choice approaches to institutions, although usually individuals (or individual decisions) are the units of analysis, essentially the same logic of explanation holds for these theories' main purpose: "to explain collective outcomes by reference to the maximizing actions of individuals" (Green and Shapiro 1994). These outcomes are *explained* differently, but given that all (or most) individual courses of action within a particular institutional "game" are equilibrium responses to an institutional script (Shepsle 2006a)[69] by nature rational choice institutionalism is more interested in exploring what motivated the set up of primary institutional arrangements and how individuals exploit institutions to pursue their interests rather than concerned with the actual processes that shape the relationship between individuals and institutions.

And yet, this book is concerned with such *processes*, or at least with the identification of the main institutional elements that populate the environment of the decisions made by a group of individuals. Therefore, we need a theoretical framework to understand and represent the actual link between the structure of organizations and the way people perceive problems to make rational decisions. This very problem is at the core of theories of bounded rationality, and the next chapter will explore the implications of adopting this behavioral model to analyze organizational decision making.

References

Acemoglu, D. 2005. Constitutions, politics, and economics: A review essay on Persson and Tabellini's *the economic effects of constitutions*. *Journal of Economic Literature* 43 (4):1025–1048.

Acemoglu, D., and J. A. Robinson. 2005. *Economic origins of dictatorship and democracy*. New York: Cambridge University Press.

Albonetti, C. A. 1987. Prosecutorial discretion: The effects of uncertainty. *Law and Society Review* 21 (2): 291–313.

Aldrich, J. H., and R. D. McKelvey. 1977. A method of scaling with applications to the 1968 and 1972 Presidential elections. *The American Political Science Review* 71 (1): 111–130.

Allison, G., and P. Zelikow. 1999. *Essence of decision. Explaining the cuban missile crisis*. 2nd ed. New York: Addison Wesley Longman.

Almond, G. 1998. Political science: the history of the discipline. In *A new handbook of political science*, ed. R. E. Goodin and H.-D. Klingemann, 50–96. Oxford: Oxford University Press.

Almond, G., and S. Verba, eds. 1989. *The civic culture revisited*. Newbury Park: Sage.

Amadae, S. M., and B. Bueno de Mesquita. 1999. The Rochester School: The origins of positive political theory. *Annual Review of Political Science* 2:269–295.

Arrow, K. J. 1963. *Social choice and individual values*. 2nd ed. New York: Cowles Foundation.

Austen-Smith, D., and J. S. Banks. 1998. Social choice theory, game theory, and positive political theory. *Annual Review of Political Science* 1:259–287.

Austen-Smith, D., and W. H. Riker. 1987. Asymmetric information and the coherence of legislation. *The American Political Science Review* 81 (3): 897–918.

Austen-Smith, D., and W. H. Riker. 1990. Asymmetric information and the coherence of legislation: A correction. *The American Political Science Review* 84 (1): 243–245.

[69] Institutions are "equilibrium ways of doing things" (Shepsle 2006a, p. 26).

Axelrod, R. 1980a. Effective choice in the prisoner's dilemma. *Journal of Conflict Resolution*, 24:13–25.
Axelrod, R. 1980b. More effective choice in the prisoner's dilemma. *Journal of Conflict Resolution* 24 (3): 379–403.
Axelrod, R. 2006. *The evolution of cooperation*. New York: Basic Books (revised edition).
Axelrod, R., and D. Dion. 1988. The further evolution of cooperation. *Science* 242 (4884): 1385–1390.
Axelrod, R., and W. D. Hamilton. 1981. The evolution of cooperation. *Science* 211:1390–1396.
Bachrach, P., and M. Baratz. 1962. Two faces of power. *The American Political Science Review* 56 (2): 947–952.
Barnard, C. I. 1938. *The functions of the executive*. Cambridge: Harvard University Press.
Barzel, Y. 2002. *A theory of the state. Economic rights, legal rights, and the scope of the state*. Cambridge: Cambridge University Press.
Bates, R. H. 1997. Comparative politics and rational choice: A review essay. *The American Political Science Review* 91 (3): 699–704.
Baumgartner, F. R., and B. D. Jones. 1991. Agenda dynamics and policy subsystems. *The Journal of Politics* 53:1044–1074.
Baumgartner, F. R., J. M. Berry, M. Hojnacki, D. C. Kimball, and B. L. Leech. 2009. *Lobbying and policy change. Who wins, who loses, and why*. Chicago: The University of Chicago Press.
Baumgartner, F. R., S. Brouard, C. Green-Pedersen, B. D. Jones, and S. Walgrave. 2011. The dynamics of policy change in comparative perspective. *Comparative Political Studies* 44 (special issue): 947–1119.
Bendor, J., and T. Moe. 1985. An adaptive model of bureaucratic politics. *The American Political Science Review* 79 (3): 755–774.
Bennett, P. G. 1995. Modelling decisions in interantional relations: Game theory and beyond. *Mershon International Studies Review* 39 (1): 19–52.
Benoit, K. 2004. Models of electoral system change. *Electoral Studies* 23 (3): 363–389.
Blais, A. 2000. *To vote or not to vote: The merits and limits of rational choice theory*. Pittsburgh: University of Pittsburgh Press.
Boix, C. 1999. Setting up the rules of the game: The choice of electoral systems in advanced democracies. *American Political Science Review* 93 (3): 609–624.
Boix, C. 2003. *Democracy and redistribution*. New York: Cambridge University Press.
Bowler, S. 2006. Electoral systems. In *The Oxford handbook of political institutions*, ed. R. A. W. Rhodes, S. A. Binder, and B. A. Rockman, 577–594. Oxford: Oxford University Press.
Buchanan, J. M., and G. Tullock. 1962. *The calculus of consent: Logical foundations of constitutional democracy*. Ann Arbor: University of Michigan Press.
Budge, I. 2006. Direct democracy. In *The Oxford handbook of political institutions*, ed. R. A. W. Rhodes, S. A. Binder, and B. A. Rockman, 595–610. Oxford: Oxford University Press.
Bueno de Mesquita, B. 2000. Popes, kings, and endogenous institutions: The Concordat of Worms and the origins of sovereignty. *International Studies Review* 2 (2):93–118.
Calvert, R.L. 1995. Rational actors, equilibrium, and social institutions. In *Explaining social institutions*, ed. J. Knight and I. Sened, 57–95. Ann Arbor: University of Michigan Press.
Calvert, R. L., M. D. McCubbins, and B. R. Weingast. 1989. A theory of political control and agenda discretion. *American Journal of Political Science* 33 (3): 588–611.
Carey, J.M. 2006. Legislative organization. In *The Oxford handbook of political institutions*, ed. R. A. W. Rhodes, S. A. Binder, and B. A. Rockman, 431–454. Oxford: Oxford University Press.
Carroll, L., and M. E. Mondrick. 1976. Racial bias in the decision to grant parole. *Law and Society Review* 11 (1): 93–107.
Casanovas, P., and P. Noriega 2007. Introduction: Legal knowledge, electronic agents, and the semantic web. In *Trends in llegal knowledge—the semantic web and the regulation of electronic social systems*, ed. P. Casanovas, P. Noriega, D. Bourcier, and F. Galindo, 15–40. Florence: European Press Academic Publishing.
Chong, D. 1995. Rational choice theory's mysterious rivals. *Critical Review* 9 (1/2): 37–57.

Coase, R.H. 1937. The nature of the firm. *Economica* 4 (16): 386–405.
Coase, R. 1998. The new institutional economics. *The American Economic Review* 88 (2): 72–74.
Colomer, J. M. 2006. Comparative constitutions. In *The Oxford handbook of political institutions*, ed. R. A. W. Rhodes, S. A. Binder, and B. A. Rockman, 217–238. Oxford: Oxford University Press.
Cox, G. W. 1999. Electoral rules and the calculus of mobilization. *Legislative Studies Quarterly* 24 (3): 387–419.
Cox, G. W. 2000. On the effects of legislative rules. *Legislative Studies Quarterly* 25 (2): 169–192.
Cox, G. W. 2006. The organization of democratic legislatures. In *The Oxford handbook of political economy*, ed. B. R. Weingast and D. A. Wittman, 141–161. New York: Oxford University Press.
Cox, G. W., and M. D. McCubbins. 1994. Bonding, structure, and the stability of political parties: Party government in the house. *Legislative Studies Quarterly* 19 (2): 215–231.
Cox, G. W., and T. N. Tutt. 1984. Universalism and allocative decision making in the Los Angeles County Board of Supervisors. *The Journal of Politics* 46 (2):546–555.
Cyert, R., and J. G. March. 1955. Organizational structure and pricing behavior in an oligopolistic market. *American Economic Review* 45: 129–139.
Cyert, R., and J. G. March. 1963. *A behavioral theory of the firm*. Englewood Cliffs: Prentice-Hall.
Cyert, R. M., and H. A. Simon. 1956. Observation of a business decision. *The Journal of Business* 29 (4): 237–248.
Cyert, R. M., E. A. Feigenbaum, and J. G. March. 1959. Models in a behavioral theory of the firm. *Behavioral Science* 4 (2): 81–95.
Dahl, R. A. 1956. *A preface to democratic theory*. Chicago: The University of Chicago Press.
Davis, M. 1997. *Game theory. A nontechnical introduction*. Mineola: Dover
Denzau, A. T., and D. C. North. 1994. Shared mental models: Ideologies and institutions. *Kyklos* 47:3–31.
Denzau, A. T., W. H. Riker, and K. A. Shepsle. 1985. Farquharson and fenno: Sophisticated voting and home style. *The American Political Science Review* 79 (4): 1117–1134.
Diermeier, D. 1995. Rational choice and the role of theory in political science. *Critical Review* 9 (1/2): 59–70.
DiMaggio, P. J., and W. W. Powell. 1991. Introduction. In *The new institutionalism: Organizational factors in political life*, ed. W. W. Powell and P. J. DiMaggio, 1–38. Chicago: The University of Chicago Press.
Downs, A. 1957. *An economic theory of democracy*. New York: Harper and Row.
Downs, A. 1998. Up and down with ecology: The "issue-attention cycle". In *Political theory and public choice*, 100–112. Northhampton: Edward Elgar.
Druckman, J. N. 2004. Political preference formation: Competition, deliberation, and the (ir)relevance of framing effects. *American Political Science Review* 98:671–681.
Duffield, J. S. 2006. International security institutions: Rules, tools, schools, or fools? In *The Oxford handbook of political institutions*, ed. R. A. W. Rhodes, S. A. Binder, and B. A. Rockman, 633–653. Oxford: Oxford University Press.
Easton, D. 1953. *The political system. An inquiry into the state of political science*. New York: Knowff.
Easton, D. 1965. *A systems analysis of political life*. New York: Wiley.
Elster, J., ed. (1986). *Rational choice*. Oxford: Basil Blackwell.
Engerman, S. L., and K. L. Sokoloff. 2008. Debating the role of institutions in political and economic development: Theory, history, and findings. *Annual Review of Political Science* 11:119–135.
Epstein, L., and J. Knight. 2000. Toward a strategic revolution in judicial politics: A look back, a look ahead. *Political Research Quarterly* 53 (3): 625–661.
Ferejohn, J., and K. Krehbiel. 1987. The budget process and the size of the budget. *American Journal of Political Science* 31 (2):296–320.
Ferejohn, J., and R. D. McKelvey. 1983. Von Neumann-Morgenstern solution social choice functions: An impossibility theorem. *Journal of Economic Theory* 29:109–119.

Ferejohn, J., and D. Satz. 1995. Unification, universalism, and rational choice theory. *Critical Review* 9 (1/2): 71–84.

Ferejohn, J., D. M. Grether, and R. D. McKelvey. 1982. Implementation of democratic social choice functions. *The Review of Economic Studies* 49 (3): 439–446.

Ferejohn, J., M. Fiorina, and R. D. McKelvey. 1987. Sophisticated voting and agenda independence in the distributive politics setting. *American Journal of Political Science* 31 (1): 169–193.

Fiorina, M. 1995. Rational choice, empirical contributions, and the scientific enterprise. *Critical Review* 9 (1/2): 85–94.

Frank, R. H. 1987. If *Homo economicus* could choose his own utility function, would he want one with a conscience? *The American Economic Review* 77 (4): 593–604.

Freeman, R. 2006. Learning in public policy. In *The Oxford handbook of public policy*, eds. M. Moran, M. Rein, and R. E. Goodin, 367–388. New York: Oxford University Press.

Friedman, M. 1953. The methodology of positive economics. In *Essays in positive economics*, 3–43. Chicago: The University of Chicago Press.

Friedman, J. 1995. Economic approaches to politics. *Critical Review* 9 (1/2): 1–24.

Friedman, M., and L. J. Savage. 1952. The expected-utility hypothesis and the measurability of utility. *The Journal of Political Economy* 60 (6): 463–474.

Gerner, D. J., P. A. Schrodt, R. A. Francisco, and J. L. Weddle. 1994. Machine coding of event data using regional and international sourcess. *International Studies Quarterly* 38 (1): 91–119.

Gerner, D. J., R. Abu-Jabr, P. A. Schrodt, and Ö. Yilmaz. 2002. Conflict and mediation event observations (CAMEO): A new event data framework for the analysis of foreign policy interactions. Paper prepared for delivery at the Annual Meeting of the International Studies Association, NewOrleans.

Gibson, J. L. 2006. Judicial institutions. In *The Oxford handbook of political institutions*, eds. R. A. W. Rhodes, S. A. Binder, and B. A. Rockman, 514–534. Oxford: Oxford University Press.

Gilligan, T. W., and K. Krehbiel. 1988. Complex rules and congressional outcomes: An event study of energy tax legislation. *The Journal of Politics* 50 (3): 625–654.

Gilligan, T. W., and K. Krehbiel. 1989. Asymmetric information and legislative rules with a heterogeneus committee. *American Journal of Political Science*, 33 (2): 459–490.

Gilligan, T. W., and K. Krehbiel. 1990. Organization of informative committees by a rational legislature. *American Journal of Political Science* 34 (2): 531–564.

Gilligan, T. W., and K. Krehbiel. 1994. The gains from exchange hypothesis of legislative organization. *Legislative Studies Quarterly* 19 (2): 181–214.

Goodin, R. E., M. Rein, and M. Moran 2006. The public and its policies. In *The Oxford handbook of public policy*, ed. M. Moran, M. Rein, and R. E. Goodin, 3–38. New York: Oxford University Press.

Grafstein, R. 1997. Thick rationality and the missing 'brute fact': The limits of rationalist incorporations of norms and ideas: Comment. *The Journal of Politics* 59 (4): 1040–1047.

Green, D. P., and I. Shapiro. 1994. *Pathologies of rational choice theory: A critique of applications in political science*. New Haven: Yale University Press.

Greif, A., and C. Kingston. 2011. Institutions: Rules or equilibria? In *Political economy of institutions, democracy and voting*, ed. N. Schofield and G. Caballero, 13–43. Berlin: Springer.

Greif, A., and Laitin, D.D. 2004. A theory of endogenous institutional change. *American Political Science Review* 98 (4): 633–652.

Guarnaschelli, S., R. D. McKelvey, and T. R. Palfrey. 2000. An experimental study of jury decision rules. *The American Political Science Review* 94 (2): 407–423.

Hadfield, G. K., and B. Weingast 2011. Endogenous institutions: Law as a coordinating device. USC Center in Law, Economics and Organization Research Paper 11-20, USC Center in Law, Economics and Organization, Los Angeles, CA.

Hall, P. A., and R. C. R. Taylor. 1996. Political science and the three institutionalisms. *Political Studies* XLIV:936–957.

Hausegger, L., and Haynie, S. 2003. Judicial decisionmaking and the use of panels in the Canadian Supreme Court and the South African Appellate Division. *Law and Society Review* 37 (3): 635–657.

Hay, C. 2004. Theory, stylized heuristic or self-fulfilling prophecy? The status of rational choice theory in public administration. *Public Administration* 82 (1): 39–62.

Heclo, H. 2006. Thinking institutionally. In *The Oxford handbook of political institutions*, ed. R. A. W. Rhodes, S. A. Binder, and B. A. Rockman, 731–742. Oxford: Oxford University Press.

Helmke, G., and B. M. Meguid. 2008. Endogenous institutions: The origins of compulsory voting laws. Paper presented at the annual meeting of the MPSA Annual National Conference, MPSA, Chicago, IL.

Henrion, M., J. S. Breese, and E. J. Horvitz. 1991. Decision analysis and expert systems. *AI Magazine* 12 (4): 64–91.

Henry, G. T., and Gordon, C. S. 2001. Tracking issue attention: Specifying the dynamics of the public agenda. *The Public Opinion Quarterly* 65 (2): 157–177.

Herrmann, R. 1988. The empirical challenge of the cognitive revolution: A strategy for drawing inferences about perceptions. *International Studies Quarterly* 32 (2): 175–203.

Hermann, M. G., and C. W. Kegley. 1995. Rethinking democracy and international peace: Perspectives from political psychology. *International Studies Quarterly* 39 (4): 511–533.

Herrmann, R. K., and M. P. Fischerkeller. 1995. Beyond the enemy image and spiral model: cognitive-strategic research after the cold war. *International Organization* 49 (3): 415–450.

Herrmann, R. K., and J. W. Keller. 2004. Beliefs, values, and strategic choice: U.S. leaders' decisions to engage, contain, and use force in an era of globalization. *The Journal of Politics* 66 (2): 557–580.

Herrmann, R. K., and V. P. Shannon. 2001. Defending international norms: The role of obligation, material interest, and perception in decision making. *International Organization* 55 (3): 621–654.

Herrmann, R., J. F. Voss, T. Y. E. Schooler, and J. Ciarrochi 1997. Images in international relations: An experimental test of cognitive schemata. *International Studies Quarterly*, 41 (3): 403–433.

Herrmann, R., P. E. Tetlock, and P. S. Visser 1999. Mass public decisions to go to war: A cognitive-interactionist framework. *The American Political Science Review* 93 (3): 553–573.

Heydebrand, W. V. 1977. The context of public bureaucracies: an organizational analysis of federal district courts. *Law and Society Review* 11 (5): 759–821.

Hillard, D., S. Purpura, and J. Wilkerson. 2007. An active learning framework for classifying political text. Paper presented at the 2007 annual meeting of the Midwest Political Science Association.

Hinich, M. J., and P. C. Ordeshook. 1970. Plurality maximization vs. vote maximization: A spatial analysis with variable participation. *The American Political Science Review* 64 (3): 772–791.

Hobbes, T. 1997 [1651]. *Leviathan, or the matter, forme and power of a commonwealth ecclesiasticall and civil*. New York: Simon and Schuster.

Howlett, M. 1997. Issue-attention and punctuated equilibria models reconsidered: An empirical examination of the dynamics of agenda-setting in Canada. *Canadian Journal of Political Science* 30 (1): 3–29.

Jacobi, T. 2005. The senatorial courtesy game: Explaining the norm of informal vetoes in 'advise and consent' nominaions. *Legislative Studies Quarterly* 30 (2): 193–217.

Jay, M. 1996. *The dialectical imagination: A history of the Frankfurt School and the Institute for Social Research 1923-1950*. Berkeley: University of California Press.

Johnson, C. A. 1987. Law, politics, and judicial decision making: Lower federal court uses of Supreme Court decisions. *Law and Society Review* 21 (2): 325–340.

Jones, B. D. 2003. Bounded rationality and political science: Lessons from public administration and public policy. *Journal of Public Adminsitration Research and Theory* 13 (4): 395–412.

Jones, B. D., and F. R. Baumgartner. 2005. *The politics of attention. How government prioritizes problems*. Chicago: The University of Chicago Press.

Kahneman, D., Slovic, P., and Tversky, A., eds. 1982. *Judgment under uncertainty: Heuristics and biases*. Cambridge: Cambridge University Press.

Keohane, R.O., and L. Martin. 2003. Institutional theory as a research paradigm. In *Progress in international relations: Appraising the field*, ed. C. Elman and M. F. Elman, 71–107. Cambridge: MIT Press.

Kettl, D.F. 2006. Public bureaucracies. In *The Oxford handbook of political institutions*, ed. R. A. W. Rhodes, S. A. Binder, and B. A. Rockman, 366–384. Oxford: Oxford University Press.

Klein, G. A., and R. Calderwood. 1991. Decision models: Some lessons from the field. *IEEE Transactions on Systems, Man, and Cybernetics* 21 (5): 1018–1026.

Knight, J., and D. C. North. 1997. Explaining economic change: The interplay between cognition and institutions. *Legal Theory* 3: 221–226.

Krehbiel, K. 1985. Obstruction and representativeness in legislatures. *American Journal of Political Science* 29 (3): 643–659.

Krehbiel, K. 1986a. Sophisticated and myopic behavior in legislative committees: An experimental study. *American Journal of Political Science* 30 (3): 542–561.

Krehbiel, K. 1986b. A technique for estimating congressmen's ideal points. *The Journal of Politics* 48 (1): 97–115.

Krehbiel, K. 1986c. Unanimous consent agreements: Going along in the Senate. *The Journal of Politics* 48 (3): 541–564.

Krehbiel, K. 1988. Spatial models of legislative choice. *Legislative Studies Quarterly* 13 (3): 259–319.

Krehbiel, K. 1990. Are Congressional committees composed of preference outliers? *The American Political Science Review* 84 (1): 149–163.

Krehbiel, K. 1993. Where's the party? *British Journal of Political Science* 23 (2): 235–266.

Krehbiel, K. 1999a. Paradoxes of parties in Congress. *Legislative Studies Quarterly* 24 (1): 31–64.

Krehbiel, K. 1999b. The party effect from A to Z and beyond. *The Journal of Politics* 61 (3): 832–840.

Krehbiel, K. 2000. Party discipline and measures of partisanship. *American Journal of Political Science* 44 (2): 212–227.

Krehbiel, K. 2004. Legislative organization. *The Journal of Economic Perspectives* 18 (1): 113–128.

Krehbiel, K., K. A. Shepsle, and B. R. Weingast. 1987. Why are Congressional committees powerful? *The American Political Science Review* 81 (3):929–945.

Lane, R. 1995. What rational choice explains. *Critical Review* 9 (1/2): 107–126.

Lau, R. R., and D. P. Redlawsk. 2001. Advantages and disadvantages of cognitive heuristics in political decision making. *American Journal of Political Science* 45 (4): 951–971.

Levesque, R. 2004. Pathologies of rational choice theories, a mistaken diagnosis? Paper presented at the Annual Meeting of the Canadian Political Science Association.

Linz, J. J. 1978. *The breakdown of democratic regimes: Crisis, breakdown, and reequilibration*. Baltimore: The Johns Hopkins University Press.

Lipset, S. M. 1959. Some social requisites of democracy: Economic development and political legitimacy. *The American Political Science Review* 53 (1): 69–105.

Lipset, S. M. 1983. *Political man: The social bases of politics*. 2nd ed. London: Heinemann.

Lohman, S. 1995. The poverty of Green and Shapiro. *Critical Review* 9 (1/2):127–154.

Lupia, A., and M. D. McCubbins. 1994. Who controls? Information and the structure of legislative decision making. *Legislative Studies Quarterly* 19 (3): 361–384.

MacDonald, C. 2003. The value of discourse analysis as a methodological tool for understanding a land reform program. *Policy Sciences* 36: 151–173.

Maltzman, F., and S. A. Binder. 2005. Congress and the politics of judicial appointments. In *Congress reconsidered*, ed. L. Dodd and B. Oppenheimer. Washington: CQ.

March, J. G. 1955. An introduction to the theory and measurement of influence. *The American Political Science Review* 49 (2): 431–451.

March, J. G. 1956. Influence measurement in experimental and semi-experimental groups. *Sociometry* 19 (4): 260–271.

March, J. G. 1957. Measurement concepts in the theory of influence. *The Journal of Politics* 19 (2): 202–226.
March, J. G. 1962. The business firm as a political coalition. *The Journal of Politics* 24 (4): 662–678.
March, J. G. 1978. Bounded rationality, ambiguity, and the engineering of choice. *The Bell Journal of Economics* 9 (2): 587–608.
March, J. G. 1990. *Decisions and organizations*. Oxford: Basil Blackwell.
March, J. G., and J. P. Olsen. 1983. Organizing political life: What administrative reorganization tells us about government. *The American Political Science Review* 77 (2): 281–296.
March, J. G., and J. P. Olsen. 1984. The new institutionalism: Organizational factors in political life. *The American Political Science Review* 78 (3): 734–749.
March, J. G., and J. P. Olsen. 1998. The institutional dynamics of international political orders. *International Organization* 52 (4): 943–969.
March, J.G., and J. P. Olsen. 2006. Elaborating the "new institutionalism". In *The Oxford handbook of political institutions*, ed. R. A. W. Rhodes, S. A. Binder, and B. A. Rockman, 3–20. Oxford: Oxford University Press.
March, J. G., and H. A. Simon. 1958. *Organizations*. New York: Wiley.
Marcus, G. E. 1988. The structure of emotional response: 1984 presidential elections. *The American Political Science Review* 82 (3): 737–761.
Marcus, G. E. 2000. Emotions in politics. *Annual Review of Political Science* 3: 221–250.
McCubbins, M. D. 1985. The legislative design of regulatory structure. *American Journal of Political Science* 29 (4): 721–748.
McCubbins, M. D., and T. Schwartz 1984. Congressional oversight overlooked: Police patrols versus fire alarms. *American Journal of Political Science* 28 (1): 165–179.
McCubbins, M. D., and M. F. Thies. 1996. Rationality and the foundations of positive political theory (or, rational choice without apology) [Gourisei to jisshou shugi seiji riron no kiso]. *Rebaiasan [Leviathan]* 9: 7–32.
McGuire, K. T. 2006. The judicial process and public policy. In *The Oxford handbook of political institutions*, ed. R. A. W. Rhodes, S. A. Binder, and B. A. Rockman, 535–554. Oxford: Oxford University Press.
McKelvey, R. D. 1975. Policy related voting and electoral equilibrium. *Econometrica* 43 (5): 815–843.
McKelvey, R. D. 1976. Intransitivities in multidimensional voting models and some implications for agenda control. *Journal of Economic Theory* 12: 472–482.
McKelvey, R. D. 1979. General conditions for global intransitivities in formal voting models. *Econometrica* 47 (5): 1085–1112.
McKelvey, R. D. 1986. Covering, dominance, and institution-free properties of social choice. *American Journal of Political Science* 30 (2): 283–314.
McKelvey, R. D. 1987. Elections with limited information: A multidimensional model. *Mathematical Social Sciences* 14:77–99.
McKelvey, R. D., and P. C. Ordeshook. 1976. Symmetric spatial games without majority rule equilibria. *The American Political Science Review* 70 (4): 1172–1184.
McKelvey, R. D., and P. C. Ordeshook. 1985a. Elections with limited information: A fulfilled expectations model using contemporaneous poll and endorsement data as information sources. *Journal of Economic Theory* 36: 55–85.
McKelvey, R. D., and P. C. Ordeshook. 1985b. Sequential elections with limited information. *American Journal of Political Science* 29 (3): 480–512.
McKelvey, R. D., and P. C. Ordeshook. 1986. Information, electoral equilibria, and the democratic ideal. *The Journal of Politics* 48 (4): 909–937.
McKelvey, R. D., and T. Page. 1986. Common knowledge, consensus, and aggregate information. *Econometrica* 54 (1): 109–127.
McKelvey, R. D., and T. Page. 1990. Public and private information: An experimental study of information pooling. *Econometrica* 58 (6): 1321–1339.

McKelvey, R. D., and J. W. Patty. 2006. A theory of voting in large elections. *Games and Economic Behavior* 57:155–180.
McKelvey, R. D., and R. Riezman. 1992. Seniority in legislatures. *The American Political Science Review* 86(4): 951–965.
Miller, G. A., and T. M. Moe. 1983. Bureaucrats, legislators, and the size of government. *The American Political Science Review* 77 (2): 297–322.
Moe, T. M. 1979. On the scientific status of rational models. *American Journal of Political Science* 23 (1): 215–243.
Moe, T. 1987. An assessment of the positive theory of 'congressional dominance'. *Legislative Studies Quarterly* 12 (4): 475–520.
Mohr, L. B. 1976. Organizations, decisions, and courts. *Law and Society Review* 10 (4): 621–642.
Monroe, K. R. 1997. Review of "Pathologies of Rational Choice Theory: A Critique of Applications in Political Science" by D. P. Green and I. Shapiro. *Political Theory* 25 (2): 289–295.
Moran, M. J., and B. R. Weingast 1982. Congress as the source of regulatory decisions: The case of the Federal Trade Commission. *The American Economic Review* 72 (2): 109–113 (Papers and Proceedings of the 94th Annual Meeting of the American Economic Association).
Mueller, D. C., ed. 1997. *Perspectives on public choice. A handbook*. Cambridge: Cambridge University Press.
Mueller, D. C. 2003. *Public Choice III*. Cambridge: Cambridge University Press.
Newell, A., and H. A. Simon. 1972. *Human problem solving*. Englewood Cliffs: Prentice-Hall.
Nielsen, L. T., A. Brandenburger, J. Geanakoplos, R. D. McKelvey, and T. Page. 1990. Common knowledge of an aggregate of expectations. *Econometrica* 58 (5): 1235–1239.
Niou, E. M. S., and P. C. Ordeshook. 1985. Universalism in Congress. *American Journal of Political Science* 29 (2): 246–258.
Niou, E. M. S., and P. C. Ordeshook. 1987. Preventive war and the balance of power. *The Journal of Conflict Resolution* 31 (3): 387–419.
Niou, E. M. S., and P. C. Ordeshook. 1990. Stability in anarchic international systems. *The American Political Science Review* 84 (4): 1207–1234.
Niou, E. M. S., and P. C. Ordeshook. 1991. Realism versus neoliberalism: A formulation. *American Journal of Political Science* 35 (2): 481–511.
Niou, E. M. S., and P. C. Ordeshook. 1994a. Alliances in anarchic international systems. *International Studies Quarterly* 38 (2): 167–191.
Niou, E. M. S., and P. C. Ordeshook. 1994b. A game-theoretic interpretation of Sun Tzu's "The Art of War". *Journal of Peace Research* 31 (2): 161–174.
Niou, E. M. S., and P. C. Ordeshook. 1994c. "Less filling, tastes great". The realist-neoliberal debate. *World Politics* 46 (2): 209–234.
North, D. C. 1990. *Institutions, institutional change and economic performance*. New York: Cambridge University Press.
North, D. C., and B. R. Weingast. 1989. Constitutions and commitment: The evolution of institutions governing public choice in seventeenth-century England. *The Journal of Economic History* 49 (4): 803–832.
North, D. C., and B. R. Weingast. 2000. Introduction: Institutional analysis and economic history. *The Journal of Economic History* 60 (2): 414–417.
Olsen, J. P. 2001. Garbage cans, new institutionalism, and the study of politics. *American Political Science Review* 95 (1): 191–198.
Olson, M. 1965. *The logic of collective action: Public goods and the theory of groups*. Cambridge: Harvard University Press.
Ordeshook, P. C. 1970. Extensions to a model of the electoral process and implications for the theory of responsible parties. *Midwest Journal of Political Science* 14 (1): 43–70.
Ordeshook, P. C. 1971. Pareto optimality in electoral competition. *The American Political Science Review* 65 (4): 1141–1145.

Ordeshook, P. C. 1980. Political disequilibrium and scientific inquiry: A comment on William Riker's "Implications from the disequilibrium of majority rule for the study of politics". *The American Political Science Review* 74 (2): 447–450.

Ordeshook, P. C. 1995. Engineering or science: What is the study of politics? *Critical Review* 9 (1/2): 175–188.

Ordeshook, P. C., and T. R. Palfrey. 1988. Agendas, strategic voting, and signaling with incomplete information. *American Journal of Political Science* 32 (2): 441–466.

Ordeshook, P. C., and T. Schwartz. 1987. Agendas and the control of political outcomes. *The American Political Science Review* 81 (1): 179–199.

Ordeshook, P. C., and M. Winer. 1980. Coalitions and spatial policy outcomes in parliamentary systems: Some experimental results. *American Journal of Political Science* 24 (4): 730–752.

Peters, B. G. 1999. *Institutional theory in political science. The 'new institutionalism'.* London: Pinter.

Peters, G. B. 1998. Political institutions: Old and new. In *A new handbook of political science*, ed. R. E. Goodin and H.-D. Klingemann, 205–220. Oxford: Oxford University Press.

Peters, B. G., and B. W. Hogwood. 1985. In search of the issue-attention cycle. *The Journal of Politics* 47 (1): 238–253.

Powell, W. W., and P. J. DiMaggio, eds. 1991. *The new institutionalism: Organizational factors in political life*. Chicago: The University of Chicago Press.

Przeworski, A. 2007. *Capitalism, Democracy, Science*, 456–503. Baltimore: Johns Hopkins University Press.

Pye, L. W., and S. Verba, eds. 1965. *Political culture and political development*. Princeton: Princeton University Press.

Rein, M. 2006. Reframing problematic policies. In *The Oxford handbook of public policy*, M. Moran, M. Rein, and R. E. Goodin, 389–405. New York: Oxford University Press.

Rhodes, R. A. W. 2006a. Executives in parliamentary government. In *The Oxford handbook of political institutions*. R. A. W. Rhodes, S. A. Binder, and B. A. Rockman, 323–343. Oxford: Oxford University Press.

Rhodes, R. A. W. 2006b. Policy network analysis. In *The Oxford handbook of public policy*, eds. M. Moran, M. Rein, and R. E. Goodin, 425–447. New York: Oxford University Press.

Riker, W. H. 1958. The paradox of voting and Congressional rules for voting on amendments. *The American Political Science Review* 52 (2): 349–366.

Riker, W. H. 1961. Voting and the summation fo preferences: An interpretive bibliographical review of selected developments during the last decade. *The American Political Science Review* 55 (4): 900–911.

Riker, W. H. 1962. *The theory of political coalitions*. New York: Yale University Press.

Riker, W. H. 1964. Some ambiguities in the notion of power. *The American Political Science Review* 58 (2): 341–349.

Riker, W. H. 1967. Bargaining in a three-person game. *The American Political Science Review* 61 (3): 642–656.

Riker, W. H. 1976. The number of political parties. *Comparative Politics* 9 (1): 93–106.

Riker, W. H. 1980a. Implications from the disequilibrium of majority rule for the study of institutions. *The American Political Science Review* 74 (2): 432–446.

Riker, W. H. 1980b. A reply to Ordeshook and Rae. *The American Political Science Review* 74 (2): 456–458.

Riker, W.H. 1982. *Liberalism against populism. A confrontation between the theory of democracy and the theory of social choice*. San Francisco: Freeman.

Riker, W.H. 1984. The heresthetics of constitution-making: The presidency in 1787, with comments on determinism and rational choice. *The American Political Science Review* 78 (1): 1–16.

Riker, W. H. 1986. *The art of political manipulation*. London: Yale University Press.

Riker, W. H. 1996. *The strategy of rhetoric*. New Haven: Yale University Press.

Riker, W. H., and P. C. Ordeshook 1968. A theory of the calculus of voting. *The American Political Science Review* 62 (1): 25–42.

Riker, W. H., and P. C. Ordeshook. 1973. *An introduction to positive political theory*. Englewood Cliffs: Prentice-Hall.

Riker, W. H., and W. J. Zavoina. 1970. Rational behavior in politics: Evidence from a three person game. *The American Political Science Review* 64 (1): 48–60.

Robinson, J. A. 1963. Decision-making and coalition building: A review. *The Journal of Conflict Resolution* 7 (4): 763–768.

Rothstein, B. 1998. Political institutions: An overview. In *A new handbook of political science*, ed. R. E. Goodin and H.-D. Klingemann, 133–166. Oxford: Oxford University Press.

Rubinstein, A. 1998. *Modeling bounded rationality*. Cambridge: MIT Press.

Saks, M. J., and R. F. Kidd. 1980/1981. Human information processing and adjudication: Trial by heuristics. *Law and Society Review* 15 (1): 123–160.

Satz, D., and J. Ferejohn. 1994. Rational choice and social theory. *The Journal of Philosophy* 91 (2): 71–87.

Savage, L. J. 1954. *The foundations of statistics*. New York: Wiley.

Schneider, A., and H. Ingram. 1990. Behavioral assumptions of policy tools. *The Journal of Politics* 52 (2): 510–529.

Schofield, N. 1995. Rational choice and political economy. *Critical Review* 9 (1/2): 189–211.

Schrodt, P. A. 1990. Parallel event sequences in international crises. *Political Behavior* 12 (2): 97–123 (Cognition and Political Action).

Schrodt, P. A. 1998. Pattern recognition of international crises using hidden Markov models. In *Non-linear models and methods in political science*, ed. D. Richards. Ann Arbor: University of Michigan Press.

Schrodt, P. A., and D. J. Gerner. 2001. Analyzing the dynamics of international mediation processes. Paper prepared for 18th Annual Political Methodology Summer Conference, Emory University.

Schubert, G. 1968. Behavioral jurisprudence. *Law and Society Review* 2 (3): 407–428.

Schultz, K. A., and B. R. Weingast. 2003. The democratic advantage: Institutional foundations of financial power in international competition. *International Organization* 57 (1): 3–42.

Schwartz, T. 1977. Collective choice, separation of issues and vote trading. *The American Political Science Review* 71 (3): 999–1010.

Scott, W. R. 1995. *Institutions and organizations*. Thousand Oaks: Sage.

Selznick, P. 1943. An approach to a theory of bureaucracy. *American Sociological Review* 8 (1): 47–54.

Selznick, P. 1948. Foundations of the theory of organization. *American Sociological Review* 13 (1): 25–35.

Shane, P. M. 2006. Analyzing constitutions. In *The Oxford handbook of political institutions*, ed. R. A. W. Rhodes, S. A. Binder, and B. A. Rockman, 191–216. Oxford: Oxford University Press.

Shepsle, K. 1985. Prospects for formal models of legislatures. *Legislative Studies Quarterly* 10 (1): 5–19.

Shepsle, K. 2006a. Rational choice institutionalism. In *The Oxford handbook of political institutions*, ed. R. A. W. Rhodes, S. A. Binder, and B. A. Rockman, 23–38. Oxford: Oxford University Press.

Shepsle, K., and B. Weingast. 1982. Institutionalizing majority rule: A social choice theory with policy implications. *The American Economic Review*, 72 (2): 367–371.

Shepsle, K. A. 1979. Institutional arrangements and equilibrium in multidimensional voting models. *American Journal of Political Science* 23 (1): 27–59.

Shepsle, K. A. 1995. Statistical political philosophy and positive political theory. *Critical Review* 9 (1/2): 213–222.

Shepsle, K. A. 2006b. Old questions and new answers about institutions: The Riker objection revisited. In *The Oxford handbook of political economy*, ed. B. R. Weingast and D. A. Wittman, 1031–1049. New York: Oxford University Press.

Shepsle, K. A., and B. R. Weingast. 1981. Political preferences for the pork barrel: A generalization. *American Journal of Political Science* 25 (1): 96–111.

Shepsle, K. A., and B. R. Weingast. 1984a. Political solutions to market problems. *The American Political Science Review* 78 (2): 417–434.

Shepsle, K. A., and B. R. Weingast. 1984b. Uncovered sets and sophisticated voting outcomes with implications for agenda institutions. *American Journal of Political Science* 28 (1): 49–74.
Shepsle, K. A., and B. R. Weingast. 1987. The institutional foundations of committee power. *The American Political Science Review* 81 (1): 85–104.
Shepsle, K. A., and B. Weingast. 1994. Positive theories of congressional institutions. *Legislative Studies Quarterly* 19 (2): 149–179.
Simon, H. A. 1947. *Administrative behavior: A study of decision-making processes in administrative organizations*. 1st ed. New York: Macmillan.
Simon, H. A. 1955. A behavioral model of rational choice. *The Quarterly Journal of Economics*, 69 (1): 99–118.
Simon, H. A. 1957. The compensation of executives. *Sociometry* 20 (1): 32–35.
Simon, H. A. 1978. Rationality as process and as product of thought. *The American Economic Review* 68 (2): 1–16 (Papers and proceedings of the 90th annual meeting of the American Economic Association).
Simon, H. A. 1983. *Reason in human affairs*. Stanford: Stanford University Press.
Simon, H. A. 1985. Human nature in politics: The dialogue of psychology with political science. *The American Political Science Review* 79 (2): 293–304.
Simon, H. A. 1996a. *Models of my life*. Cambridge: MIT Press.
Simon, H. A. 1996b. *The sciences of the artificial*. 3rd ed. Cambridge: MIT Press.
Simon, H. A. 1997. *Administrative behavior: A study of decision-making processes in administrative organizations*. 4th ed. New York: Free Press.
Simon, H. A., and A. Newell. 1971. Human problem solving: The state of the theory in 1970. *American Psychologist* 26 (2): 145–159.
Soroka, S. 1999. Policy agenda-setting theory revisited: a critique of Howlett on Downs, Baumgartner and Jones, and Kingdon. *Canadian Journal of Political Science*, 32 (4): 763–772.
Stoker, G. 2006. Comparative local governance. In *The Oxford handbook of political institutions*, ed. R. A. W. Rhodes, S. A. Binder, and B. A. Rockman, 495–513. Oxford: Oxford University Press.
Thelen, K. 1999. Historical institutionalism in comparative politics. *Annual Review of Political Science* 2: 369–404.
Thoenig, J.-C. 2000. New institutionalism and organizational theory: A review article. *Public Administration*, 78 (2): 455–460.
Tummolini, L., and C. Castelfranchi. 2006. The cognitive and behavioral mediation of institutions: Towards an account of institutional actions. *Cognitive Systems Research* 7 (2–3): 307–323.
Uslaner, E. M., and T. Zittel. 2006. Comparative legislative behavior. In *The Oxford handbook of political institutions*, ed. R. A. W. Rhodes, S. A. Binder, and B. A. Rockman, 455–473. Oxford: Oxford University Press.
van Koppen, P. J., and J. T. Kate. 1984. Individual differences in judicial behavior: Personal characteristics and private law decision-making. *Law and Society Review* 18 (2): 225–247.
Verba, S. 1965. Comparative political culture. In *Political culture and political development*, ed. L. W. Pye and S. Verba, 512–560. Princeton: Princeton University Press.
Vlaev, I., and N. Chater. 2007. Context effects in games:Local versus global sequential effects on choice in the prisoner's dilemma game. *Judgment and Decision Making* 2 (5): 380–389.
von Neumann, J., and O. Morgenstern. 1944. *The theory of games and economic behavior*. Princeton: Princeton University Press.
Walker, T. G. 1972. A note concerning partisan influences on trial-judge decision making. *Law and Society Review* 6 (4): 645–649.
Wallas, G. [1920] 2004. *Human nature in politics*. 3rd ed. Whitefish: Kessinger.
Weber, M. 1978. *Economy and society: An outline of interpretive sociology*, vol. 2. Berkeley: University of California Press.
Weingast, B. R. 1979. A rational choice perspective on Congressional norms. *American Journal of Political Science* 23 (2): 245–262.

Weingast, B.R. 1989. Floor behavior in the U.S. Congress: Committee power under the open rule. *The American Political Science Review* 83 (3): 795–815.

Weingast, B. 1994. Reflections on distributive politics and universalism. *Political Research Quarterly* 47 (2): 319–327.

Weingast, B. 1998. Political institutions: Rational choice perspectives. In *A new handbook of political science*, ed. R. E. Goodin, and H.-D. Klingemann, 167–190. Oxford: Oxford University Press.

Weingast, B. R. 2002. Rational-choice institutionalism. In *Political science: State of the discipline*, ed. I. Katznelson and H. V. Milner, 660–692. New York: Norton.

Weingast, B. R. 2005. The constitutional dilemma of economic liberty. *The Journal of Economic Perspectives* 19 (3): 89–108.

Weingast, B. R., and W. J. Marshall. 1988. The industrial organization of Congress; or why legislatures, like firms, are not organized as markets. *The Journal of Political Economy* 96 (1): 132–163.

Weingast, B. R., and M. J. Moran. 1983. Bureaucratic discretion or Congressional control? Regulatory policymaking by the Federal Trade Commission. *The Journal of Political Economy* 91 (5): 765–800.

Weingast, B. R., Shepsle, K. A., and Johnsen, C. 1981. The political economy of benefits and costs: A neoclassical approach to distributive politics. *The Journal of Political Economy* 89 (4): 642–664.

Weissert, C. S. 1991. Issue salience and state legislative effectiveness. *Legislative Studies Quarterly* 16 (4): 509–520.

Williamson, O. E. 1981. The economics of organization: the transaction cost approach. *The American Journal of Sociology* 87 (3): 548–577.

Williamson, O. E. 1985. *The economic institutions of capitalism: Firms, markets, relational contracting*. New York: Free Press.

Williamson, O. E. 2002. The theory of the firm as governance structure: From choice to contract. *The Journal of Economic Perspectives* 16 (3): 171–195.

Winship, C. 2006. Policy analysis as puzzle solving. In *The Oxford handbook of public policy*, ed. M. Moran, M. Rein, and R. E. Goodin, 109–123. New York: Oxford University Press.

Yee, A. S. 1997. Thick rationality and the missing 'brute fact': The limits of rationalist incorporations of norms and ideas. *The Journal of Politics* 59 (4): 1001–1039.

Chapter 3
Bounded Rationality and Organizations

Abstract From a behavioral standpoint, a decision is the result of the adaptation of an individual to the constraints imposed by both the external environment and the limits of rationality (inner environment). This chapter presents the theoretical framework for our behavioral analysis of rational decisions within organizations. This framework will be outlined through two different levels of analysis. First, the general features of the inner environment of a decision—i.e., the psychological aspects regarding rationality in human mind. Second, the external environment of a decision—i.e., the outer shape of means and ends, provided generally by the organization.

3.1 Introduction

Decisions are not made in a vacuum. Human beings have always had a persistent tendency to create organizations and institutions (markets, hospitals, and so forth) in order to make stable, better rational decisions than they would have been able to do otherwise. Sometimes these organizations are purposely created—e.g. the United Nations, the Bolshevik Party—, sometimes institutions are not the result of a conscious planning—e.g., the price system in markets Hayek (1945) or markets themselves (Popper 1961).[1]

In effect, humans act (and therefore decide) within a net of organizations and people from which they neither can nor want to escape. This net includes our social or external environment, furnished with markets, factories, stores, public administrations, universities, and other people.

This work deals with *organizational* decision-making, not in the sense of decisions made *by* organizations, but in that of decisions made *within* them. This implies that our observation of the process of making a decision is dependent not only upon

[1] DiMaggio and Powell (1991, p. 8) make their point on this particular issue by distinguishing economic and public choice approaches to institutions to those that come from more sociological fields. From their standpoint, the former consider that "institutions are the products of human design, the outcomes of purposive actions by instrumentally oriented individuals". On the contrary, the latter defend that "while institutions are certainly the result of human activity, they are not necessarily the products of conscious design". Interestingly, two of the most relevant and earliest contributions against the "conscious design" argument come from the economic field—namely Hayek (1945) and Simon (1955). See also Simon (1996b, Chap. 2).

J.-J. Vallbé, *Frameworks for Modeling Cognition and Decisions in Institutional Environments*, Law, Governance and Technology Series 21, DOI 10.1007/978-94-017-9427-5_3

human capabilities to deal with reality, but also on the environment into which these decisions are made. For, we presume that organizations (and institutions) "have an ordering effect on how authority and power is constituted, exercised, legitimated, controlled, and redistributed" (March and Olsen 2006a). Our organizational approach also implies the distinction between two different kinds of mechanisms that take place in a decision-making situation (Simon 1955).

On one hand, there are general political mechanisms among and within organizations, which (a) show the interaction among agents, and (b) in principle provide a stable framework that enables rational action. Therefore, these upper-level mechanisms offer a pattern of events according to which decisions are possible and where its consequences may be more or less predicted or calculated. In other words (March and Simon 1958, p. 139), "the organizational and social environment in which the decision maker finds himself determines what consequences he will anticipate, what ones he will not; what alternatives he will consider, what ones he will ignore".

On the other hand we account for a set of inner, cognitive mechanisms at work when political actors make decisions. We assume that human beings act rationally, though they are not able to be perfectly rational. This refers to the limitations of knowledge and computing capabilities of the decision-maker in order to make a reasonable choice among the different possibilities at hand. March and Simon (1958, p. 138) claimed that "we can only speak of rationality relative to a frame of reference; and this frame of reference will be determined by the limitations on the rational man's knowledge".

Since this work assumes that these mechanisms are equally relevant in the analysis of decision-making, we shall refer to both of them. In fact, the aim of this work is to explore the interaction between both environments, focusing upon the decision-maker (judges) facing particular decision problems. Referring to the separation of both environments, Simon (1957, p. 261) affirmed that

> a great deal can be learned about rational decision making by taking into account, at the outset, the limitations upon the capacities and complexity of the organism, and by taking account of the fact that the environments to which it must adapt possess properties that permit further simplification of its choice mechanisms.

Summing up, from our standpoint a decision would be the result of the adaptation of an individual to the constraints imposed by both the general mechanisms (external environment) and the limits of rationality (inner environment) (Simon 1955, 1957; March and Simon 1958; Simon 1996b), as shown in Fig. 3.1.

Furthermore, a rational decision is that which leads to select the appropriate means to reach particular ends. (This is to say that a rational decision is that which leads to a goal in a most effective way.) Thus a rational decision-maker is he or she who selects the means that lead to this effective decision (Simon 1947, p. 61).

This chapter presents the theoretical framework for our analysis of rational decisions within organizations. This framework will be outlined through the study of two different levels of analysis. First, the general features of the inner environment of a decision—i.e., the psychological aspects regarding rationality in human mind—will be presented according to standard theories in cognitive science. Second, the external

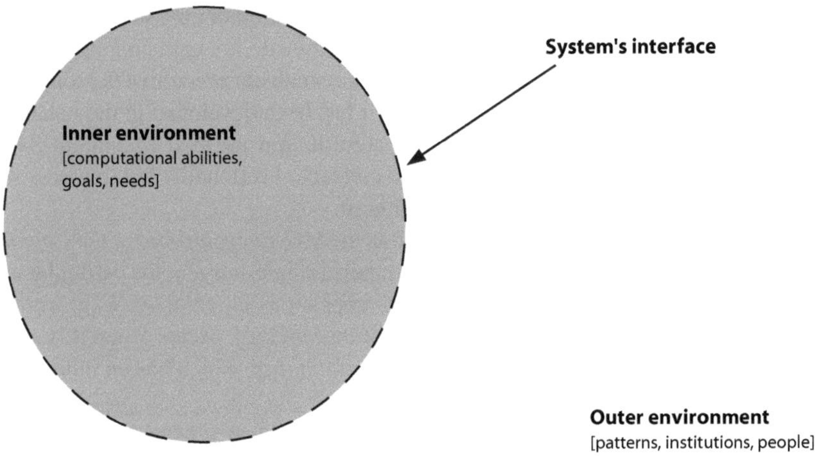

Fig. 3.1 Distinction between inner and outer environment in decision-making

environment of a decision—i.e., the outer shape of means and ends, provided generally by the organization—will be outlined according to major trends in organization theory such as organizational decision analysis and naturalistic decision making. In the next section we will focus on the first part of this issue, centering our analysis on the inner, cognitive level of decision analysis. Section 3.3 will be devoted to the role of organizations as patterns of events for rational decisions.

3.2 The Inner Environment of Decisions

Let us now recall the rational choice approach to decision-making in organizations briefly presented in the previous chapter. One of the main criticisms it has received claims it does not give a realistic account of how decisions are made in real situations, but that it delivers *idealized* visions of what a rational decision *ought to* be. In particular, some of its results are inaccurate because they cannot explain:

- The actual motivations that bind the decisions of all the agents implied in a (strategic-oriented, game-like) decision situation.
- The processes that lead to maximizing decisions (how the agents acquire the information needed, how they make the calculations, or whether they are capable of making the kinds of decisions they are supposed to perform).

Moreover, these theories do not give any account of how the decision-maker acquires knowledge about future events, or probability distributions of future events, knowledge about the available alternatives, knowledge about the consequences of these alternatives, and knowledge about his or her own ordered preferences. These theories do not even take account of the actual computational processes by which humans arrive at the conclusion that one option is better than another one. In a nutshell, they presume that humans maximize preferences, but they do not explain *how*.

Our objective in this section is to present a more realistic account of the role played by cognition in rational decision-making as it has been developed in the behavioral sciences, thus connecting cognition with goal formation and goal attainment. Therefore, our aim here is not to fully discuss the concept of rationality but to assess what level of rationality human beings are capable of.

In fact, even an authoritative source such as the *MIT Encyclopedia of the Cognitive Sciences* (Wilson and Keil 1999) does not contain a single entry for the particular noun *rationality*. Instead, *rational* almost always appears as an adjective (e.g., *rational agency, rational choice theory, rational decision-making*), except when it is a noun modified by another adjective, as in *bounded rationality*, which has an independent entry indeed.

With the aim of establishing a working definition, as a general basis, a rational decision is "choosing among alternatives in a way that 'properly' accords with the preferences and beliefs of an individual decision maker or those of a group making a joint decision" (Doyle 1999). Thus it includes (a) a decision-maker (individual or group), (b) a set of preferences and beliefs, (c) a set of alternatives before the decision-maker, and (d) a ("proper") choosing action.

In the classical economic theory of rational decision-making, preferences are shaped by a utility function, which implies a number of assumptions:

1. The whole set of alternatives from which the decision maker has to choose is given and appears before the decision maker. There is not an agreement among different theories of rational choice upon this issue, delivering different models for certainty, risk, and uncertainty.[2]
2. Each alternative has a complete set of consequences attached.
3. The decision maker chooses the alternative that best matches the most preferred set of consequences. In the case of certainty, there is not ambiguity in the choosing action. In the case of risk or uncertainty, the expression *expected utility* has been coined to define a rational decision in terms of the probabilities of occurrence of the utilities that would generate all possible consequences (Savage 1951; Friedman and Savage 1952; Savage 1954). In "risky" situations, the probabilities of the outcomes are supposed to be known (e.g., in gambling situations); in "uncertain" or "ambiguous" situations, their precise likelihood is ignored (Shafir 1999). Thus

[2] Certainty refers to the complete knowledge of the alternatives. Utility theory would fit in this set of theories (Wellman 1999; Weirich 2004). Utility theory is concerned with the measurement and representation of preferences, and it starts with a preference order, $\lesssim$, which is generally considered to be a complete pre-order over the outcome space, σ, and where $y \lesssim x$ means that y is weakly preferred to x. If $\neg(x \lesssim y)$, x is strictly preferred. Then, the preference order can be represented by a real-valued utility function, $U : \sigma \rightarrow R$, in the sense that $U(y) \leqslant U(x)$ if and only if $y \lesssim x$. If U represents $\lesssim$, then so does $\varphi \circ U$, for any monotone function φ on the real numbers [notation taken from Wellman (1999)]. Therefore, utility is an ordinal scale. A second group produces theories that "assume accurate knowledge of a probability distribution of the consequences of each alternative" (risk) (March and Simon 1958, p. 137). Finally, a third group assumes that the decision maker cannot assign definite probabilities to the occurrence of particular consequences (uncertainty).

in these cases the preference comparison is over prospects rather than outcomes (Wellman 1999), i.e., over expectations about possible outcomes (Friedman and Savage 1952). It is agreed that in case of uncertainty, rational decision is difficult, and some explanations and models of it have been delivered regarding both uncertainty and risk (Bell and Raiffa 1988; Bell 1988; Fishburn 1988). What has not reached a parallel degree of agreement is whether all actual human decisions are surrounded by a notable degree of uncertainty.

Considering the enumeration, it is apparent that the conditions under which a decision could be viewed as rational—from the classical point of view—are rather demanding to the decision-maker. Effectively, it assumes that (a) all the alternatives are given, (b) that the decision-maker knows all the consequences of each alternative, and (c) that the decision-maker has a utility-ordering function for all the consequences (and thus for all the alternatives). The behavioral approach to decision-making has produced a bulk of empirical research that challenges this rather optimistic view of human capabilities for knowing, ordering preferences, and making choices.

These features of classical economic theory led Herbert A. Simon to the first systematic attempt to present the alternate notion of bounded rationality and its consequences for economic, administrative, and political decision making. This early work was mainly done during the 1950s (e.g., Simon 1955, 1957),[3] the moment in which he turns to cognitive psychology and a primeval computer science in order to better study and describe the psychology of human problem solving and "discovering the symbolic processes that people use in thinking" (Simon 1996a, p. 189).[4] Noriega (2006, p. xxxiii) has identified three basic dimensions through which Simon covers the different problems produced by the classical theory of human rationality:

- The difference between an omniscient rationality and a rationality that must contend with restrictions on information, time, and analysis capacity.
- The difficulty to find an optimal solution for some decision problems, which is usually overcome by lowering the aspiration level from optimal to satisfactory or *satisficing* (Simon 1996b, Chaps. 2 and 5)—namely, both satisfying and sufficient.[5] It also refers to the problem of the uniqueness of solutions (Simon 1955).
- The difference between substantive rationality of "economic man" and procedural rationality (Simon 1976), which is twofold:
  - A process through which individuals explore a space (of possible solutions) searching for *satisficing* solutions.
  - A process through which organizations evolve in order to survive in a satisfactory manner within their environment.

[3] But not Simon (1951), which is a rare exception.

[4] Later on he retrospects his contributions on this notion in *The Sciences of the Artificial* (Simon 1996b, esp. Chap. 2).

[5] The term *to satisfice* was coined by Simon himself mixing up *satisfy* and *suffice*.

Table 3.1 Correspondence between Simon's different dimensions of rationality and their levels of a analysis

Dimensions of rationality	Levels of analysis
Bounded *vs.* Omniscient	Cognitive limits
Satisficing *vs.* Optimizing	Aspiration levels
Procedural *vs.* Substantive	Strategies for goal-attainment

These three dimensions refer, consecutively, to different levels of analysis (see Table 3.1). The first one accounts for the cognitive limitations all human beings have for contending with a complex environment. The second applies the knowledge about these limits on human cognition and draws a picture of what levels of satisfaction human beings are able to achieve in their goal-oriented action. Finally, the third dimension refers to the particular strategies human beings (or organizations) carry out in order to achieve those *satisficing* levels of goal-attainment in solving their problems.

The three dimensions are touched upon in this section in this particular order, presenting a view of human rationality that both challenges the major assumptions of the neoclassical approach to rational decision-making, and in our opinion helps understanding the mechanisms that, in spite of human natural limitations, allow for rational decisions.

Therefore, the rest of this section will be devoted to discuss the contrast between maximizing rationality and bounded rationality with respect to three different features: the cognitive limits that shape human rationality (Sect. 3.2.1), the problem of aspiration levels (Sect. 3.2.2), and finally, the strategies for goal attainment (Sect. 3.2.3).

3.2.1 Bounded vs. Omniscient Rationality

In behavioral theories of decision-making, *adaptation* is the key. The individual is seen as an adaptive system whose goals draw the interface between its inner and outer environments. This poses a problem that presents two different questions. The first one is where to put this interface—where to draw the line between both environments. The second one is what consequences should we expect from deciding where to draw this line.

To face this two-fold problem, Simon came up with the celebrated example of an ant making "his laborious way across a wind- and wave-molded beach" (Simon 1996b, p. 51), whose path from point A to point B is represented in Fig. 3.2.

As to the first question, the interface between the inner and the outer environment is defined by the goals the ant (decision-maker) wants to attain, and thus its behavior will depend (a) on what do it longs to do, and (b) in what environment it will be trying to do it. Some features of its behavior will be explained by the inner characteristics of the ant, but most of the behavior will be accounted for by its goals and the shape of the beach. In Sect. 2.4.3 we cited part of the formulation of the notion of bounded rationality delivered by Simon (1996b, p. 53). We may put it here in its complete form:

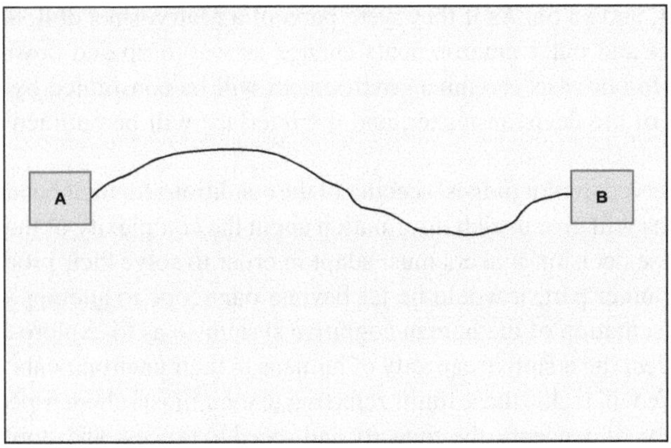

Fig. 3.2 Representation of the path followed from point A to B by an agent. Behavior (the path) is mostly explained by the complexity of the environment

> Human beings, viewed as behaving systems, are quite simple. The apparent complexity of our behavior over time is largely a reflection of the complexity of the environment in which we find ourselves.

The main advantage of this viewpoint is that few things about the inner environment need to be known or accounted for in order to get to understand an individual's behavior—e.g., in the form of her decisions. In a simplified form, we just need to know (a) some features regarding the individual's cognitive system, and (b) the individual's goals. For, these features bind the adaptation of the deciding individual to her environment, the rest being the strategies the individual will follow in order to solve a problem.[6]

It is important to note, though, that the decision on the boundary line between the inner and outer environments is subjected to high discretion: we shall decide to draw it depending on our units of analysis—individuals, organizations, states, communities, tribes.

In our case, the goal is to study the process by which individuals (junior judges) make decisions in a particular institutional environment (on-call situations). Then, the outer environment to which he or she must adapt will be constituted, first, by the space of the problem that must be solved,[7] and, then, the "space" represented by the on-call institution, *within* a more general external environment represented by the judicial organization, which at the same time is part of an even more general external

[6] In Simon's terms, these strategies in problem-solving behavior are not part of the inner environment yet, as long as they are *artificial*, i.e., "learned and […] subject to improvement through the invention of improved designs and their storage in memory" (Simon 1996b, p. 53).

[7] The notion of *problem space* is commonly used in explaining problem-solving processes in cognitive sciences. It refers to the typical situation of a problem solver confronted by a task. "The task is described objectively […] in terms of a *task environment*. It is defined by the problem solver, for purposes of attacking it, in terms of a *problem space*" (Simon and Newell 1971, p. 148). We will be back on it in Sect. 3.2.3.3.

environment, and so on. As if they were parts of a Matryoshka doll, the boundaries of both inner and outer environments change as we go up and down in our level of analysis. In our case, the inner environment will be constituted by the cognitive architecture of the decision-maker, and the interface will be outlined by his or her goals.

Thus observed, junior judges' account of the conditions for their behavior in particular situations will give us rich information about the complexity of the environment to which these decision-makers must adapt in order to solve their problems.

As to the inner part, it would be far beyond our scope to attempt a detailed and accurate presentation of the human cognitive system so as to explore the limits that somehow affect the adaptive capacity of humans to their environments when solving problems. We will tackle these limits referring to their most salient aspects, including the acquisition of concepts, the capacity and speed to process and store information, and our ability to process natural language. They are briefly presented in the following sections.

3.2.1.1 Concept Attainment and Categorization

Concepts are "the elements from which propositional thought is constructed, thus providing a means of understanding the world" (Hampton 1999, p. 176), including our own experiences, which in turn are related to our history. As foundational elements of knowledge, they have obviously received attention, both in studies related to the way concepts are attained and processed (studies with an explanatory aim, e.g., memory) and in research about the ways these concepts are to be represented (studies with a constructive aim, e.g., knowledge representation) (Gärdenfors 2004). This brief subsection refers to the former.

A great deal of research has been devoted to study the limits of human beings in processes of concept learning, concept attainment, and, in general, categorization, which is "the process by which distinct entities are treated as equivalent" and which "permits us to understand and make predictions about objects and events in our world" (Medin and Aguilar 1999, p. 104).[8]

Typical experiments for concept attainment are planned to test the ability to acquire a particular concept from the manipulation of artificially produced concepts—namely, concepts built only for the sake of the research. In this context, concept learning is thought of as involving "the processes of generalization and abstraction, so it is not sufficient to show simply that subjects can learn to discriminate the set of stimuli with which they are trained" (Eysenck 1990, p. 73).

In concept learning experiments, concept acquisition capacity is measured as the time needed by an individual to recognize concepts non-randomly, e.g., that the subjects are able to classify new stimuli according to the knowledge (concepts) previously acquired. These concepts are conceived of as a set of features or attributes applicable to an object.

[8] See Anderson and Matessa (1991) for a proposal of an algorithm for rational categorization.

In this context, a classical approach is that of Bruner et al. (1986) [1956], who gave account of a number of laboratory experiments on concept learning. They found that a number of strategies for concept learning could be identified and evaluated "in a relatively systematic way, both in terms of their objectives and in terms of the steps taken to achieve these" (Bruner et al. 1986, p. 235). They also reported, though, that there are a number of factors that can sensitively diminish the subjects' efficiency. In effect, when subjects are faced to time and information constraints, their results are less successful and accurate. However, the authors were "struck by the notable flexibility and intelligence of [the] subjects in adapting their strategies to the information, capacity, and risk requirements [. . .] imposed to them" (Bruner et al. 1986, p. 238).

In this sense, other evidence has been presented that suggest that humans have perceivable limitations on their speed in attaining concepts under particular (though common) situations (Lebowitz 1986; Michalski 1987; Simon 1996b, pp. 59–63), and also in their concept (symbol) processing activity, as shall be seen in the next section.

3.2.1.2 Storing and Processing Information

According to standard cognitive science (Anderson 1983; Newell 1990), memory is not a unitary system, but it is divided in a short-term memory (STM) and a long-term memory (LTM) in a way that information may be transferred from one memory to the other.

STM is seen as a working memory, a kind of "temporal" store for the information needed in a particular process.[9] It is functionally limited because it "is used to hold the coded knowledge that is to be processed for the current task [but then] it is necessary to replace that knowledge when the current task changes" (Newell 1990, p. 355). These functional limits have been measured and refer (a) to the speed in which STM removes the "old" data to be replaced, (b) to how long STM is able to last information-processing activity in a single problem space (Newell 1990, p. 355), (c) the time it needs in order to store new information to be processed (Simon 1996b, 63–66), and (d) to the amount of information it is able to hold (Miller 1956).[10]

As to our capacity for processing information, Miller (1956) reported in a classical study the "severe limitations on the amount of information that we are able to receive, process, and remember". Then he added that "by organizing the stimulus input simultaneously into several dimensions and successively into a sequence of chunks, we manage to break (or at least stretch) this information bottleneck". As to the measurement of that limit to process information at a given time, the author reports that in the experiments carried out "this span is usually somewhere in the neighborhood of seven" chunks of information, plus or minus two.

---

[9] STM processes information in form of *chunks* (Feigenbaum and Simon 1984), information units.

[10] But see Jones (2002).

On the other hand, the organization of long-term memory (LTM) and the way information is stored, retrieved, and indexed has also been a fruitful field for psychological research. Basically LTM is viewed as an infinite "library" of stored and indexed information. It seems to have no limits in its storing capacity and presents an associative structure (Newell and Simon 1972, p. 792). Here experiments with chess players and other kinds of experts have shown that information is stored in a relational form, and that memory shows an organization of list structures (lists that contain listed elements). It leads to pattern recognition and expertise.[11]

The main consequence of the limits of our memory system (the information bottleneck) is seriality in our information-processing activity—i.e., the necessity humans have to do things in a one-at-a-time manner (Simon 1980).[12] A mechanism of bounded rationality for dealing with these limits is attention (Simon 1983, p. 21), i.e., the need to focus attention on what we are doing at a time. Attention is usually filtered by emotions, which can either distract us or call our attention to something. Castelfranchi et al. (2006) thus refer to emotions as modifiers of knowledge accessibility.[13]

In fact, a notable amount of research shows an increasing interest in the role of emotions (and intuition) in traditionally "hard" fields as financial decision making (Lipshitz and Shulimovitz 2005). Emotions also have received a renewed attention in some behavioral accounts of political behavior and decision making (Marcus 1988, 2000).[14]

3.2.1.3 Natural Language Processing

Apart from the debates around the nature of language and discussions about linguistic universals, a great deal of research has focused on the way humans process, utter, and comprehend language.[15] A brief sample of what the leading journal of the field

[11] We shall come back to LTM in Sect. 3.2.3 for reasons that will be then properly explained.

[12] But see also Anderson et al. (2004) who softens the seriality condition.

[13] They refer to the classical work by Brower and Cohen (1982) on emotions and cognition. See Pfeifer (1982) for a computational model of emotions in cognition.

[14] Unfortunately we cannot devote more space and time to emotions, though it seems likely that this issue shall become more and more relevant in fields such as multi-agent systems or virtual institutions (Castelfranchi and Falcone 2004; Tummolini and Castelfranchi 2006; Castelfranchi et al. 2006; Castelfranchi and Paglieri 2007).

[15] The classical issue on linguistic universals arises from the belief that the diversity of languages is only apparent (superficial) and that there is a (deep) structure shared by all human languages. The role of linguistic theory is then to search these linguistic universals. Apart from the criticisms this program has received as for its empirical breadth (Sampson 2001), other critics have focused on its increasing abstraction and formalization of linguistics—a radical separation of the linguistic form out of its social context (Hymes 1977, p. 76)—, where each level of universality has been subverted by the anomalies found in language. Thus the universal features in human language are almost nothing but an open catalogue in the phonologic, grammatical, and semantic level. It is difficult to think of a comprehension process within a synchronic system of abstractions, for language is

Cognitive Science has published on this particular issue in the last 30 years will serve as a picture of such interest.

As for structural features of human performance in language processing, Christiansen and Chater (1999a) offer a connectionist explanation of human performance in processing recursive language structures that occur in speech, and Smolensky (1999) combines generative grammar and connectionist approach to language.[16] Gerken and Bever (1986) study the relation between particular linguistic features (such as intuition) and basic cognitive processes. Jurafsky (1996) explores disambiguation, Langacker (1986) introduces a cognitive grammar, and Schank (1980) reflects on meaning, conceptual representations, and memory.

As for linguistic comprehension, Carrithers and Bever (1984) observe eye-fixation patterns in readers in order to assess a comprehension-based model of reading and listening. Chaiklin (1984) considers the role of verbal rules in the use of procedural knowledge for problem-solving, while others (Chi et al. 1994) explore the role of self-explanations in improving text comprehension. Dascal (1989) and Gibbs (1989) explore the role of literal meaning and context in understanding.[17] Riesbeck (1980) studies the relative role of spatial reasoning in reading directions for the first time, and explore conversation comprehension. Winograd (1980) has focused on the relation of natural language understanding as a cognitive process to be applied to computers.[18]

As for language utterance, many studies have been devoted to the nature and use of metaphors (Lakoff and Johnson 1980; Indurkhya 1987; Gerrig 1989; Martin 1992; Clausner and Croft 1997; Fernández-Duque and Johnson 1999), discourse contribution (Clark and Schaefer 1989),[19] the use of referring expressions (Dale and Reiter 1995), the role of emotions in narratives (Dyer 1983a),[20] coreference processing (Gordon and Hendrick 1998), the pragmatics of locative expressions (Herskovits 1985), the relation between discourse processing and conceptual structure (Morrow 1986), and other variables such as interestingness in discourse (Hidi and Baird 1986).

---

diachronic. The Chomskyan view of language leaves aside its use. Simon (1996b, p. 76) refers to the debate among linguists around the nativist view of language, that refers partly to the problem of universals in language. He proposes an interpretation of the nativist question according to which "producing and understanding the utterances of others depend on some characteristics of the human central nervous system which are common in all languages but also essential to other aspects of human thinking besides speech and listening". This interpretation concords perfectly with the view of the human mind architecture shaped by the other parameters briefly presented above.

[16] See Christiansen and Chater (1999b) for a state of the art—as for 1999—of the connectionist approaches to human language processing. See also Miikkulainen and Dyer (1991) and Gupta and Touretzky (1994) for other connectionist applications.

[17] See Gibbs (1984) for a general reflection on the status of literal meaning in psychological theory.

[18] See also Winograd (1972) and Winograd and Flores (1986).

[19] Stone (2004) sketches "a direct computational role for the rules of language in planning contributions to collaborative conversation".

[20] See also Dyer (1983b).

3.2.2 *Satisficing Rationality vs. Optimizing Rationality*

Put in the simplest way, the main conclusion of the previous section could be that "what a person *cannot* do he or she *will not* do" (Simon 1996b, p. 28). This section goes a little farther in this argument by showing the features of a satisficing policy.

3.2.2.1 Preference Reversal

A principal requirement of an optimizing organism—as the theory of subjective expected utility (SEU) puts it (Friedman and Savage 1952; Savage 1954)—is that all alternatives must be measurable in terms of a utility function. As we saw in the introduction, that function expresses the individual's preferences in an ordinal scale, the principle of transitivity in preferences being a key assumption of maximizing rationality.[21]

Leaving aside the serious problem of majority cycling and agenda manipulation and its consequences on transitivity in voting (Arrow 1963),[22] one of the actual problems emphasized by several behavioral studies on the field is that while there is not evidence whatsoever of the existence of such a utility function in human beings, empirical research shows that human preferences under certain situations are far from consistent, in general, and hardly transitive, in particular, and thus that many strong assumptions of the SEU theory—such as variance, apart from transitivity—do not concord with actual human behavior.

Simon (1979) made a strong point on this lack of empirical validity of neoclassical accounts of rational behavior, focusing on the weaknesses of the latter explaining decision processes in business organizations which included varying levels of uncertainty and imperfect competition. At the same time, he made an equally strong point around the empirical basis of the bounded rationality model, supporting his arguments with a notable amount of empirical research (Simon 1979, pp. 501–502).

In this direction, Daniel Kahnmeman and Amos Tversky pioneered the research on the empirical basis of certain aspects of the neoclassical approach. For instance, checking SEU theory in decisions under risk (Kahneman and Tversky 1979) they uncovered phenomena that linked choice with risk aversion—e.g., the certainty effect and reflection effect—in the sense that "certainty increases the aversiveness of losses as well as the desirability of gains" (Kahneman and Tversky 1979, p. 269).[23] They

[21] Transitivity may be described as the following: if A is preferred to B, and B is preferred to C, then necessarily A is preferred to C.

[22] See Cox and Shepsle (2007) for a recent treatment of the issue.

[23] Or, "people overweight outcomes that are considered certain, relative to outcomes which are merely probable" (Kahneman and Tversky 1979, p. 265). The authors also identified a source of inconsistent preferences in a common pattern of behavior such as that people tend to "disregard

also proved that people were poor predictors of the future (Kahneman and Tversky 1979; Shapira 2008).[24]

But facts are also reported that describe preference reversal when choices are framed in different manners, in what is referred to as *framing effects* (Tversky and Kahneman 1981). Tversky and Kahneman (1981) deliver data that cast doubts on the adequacy of such criteria as coherence and consistency for evaluating rational behavior, proposing bounded rationality as a framework under which preference reversal can be explained. In this same direction, Tversky and Kahneman (1986) showed that strong assumptions of SEU theory such as cancellation and variance were not met in actual decision behavior and that framing effects were the main cause of preference inconsistency.

In a more recent study, Tversky et al. (1990) elaborate on the causes of preference reversal in gambling situations and seriously challenge those rational models that explain preference reversal simply as violations of specific axioms such as independence and transitivity.[25]

In the political science field, Druckman (2004) recently carried out a research on the impact of framing effects on changing citizens' preferences, incorporating elite competition on frames and citizens' conversations about frames as the key variables that diminish frame effects on political behavior. The main conclusion was that framing effects are not as pervasive as initially assumed, at least among citizens with a high level of expertise.

Yet he also concluded that among non-experts, "when framing effects persist, they can be even more pernicious than often thought—not only do they suggest incoherent preferences but they also stimulate increased confidence in those preferences". This view of a rather narrow role of framing effects contrasts with those of other political

---

components that the alternatives share, and focus on the components that distinguish them" (Kahneman and Tversky 1979, p. 271). A complete collection of papers on this issue may be found at Kahneman et al. (1982).

[24] See Shapira (2008) for a newest review of these phenomena applied to real-world managerial decision making situations, in contrast with the laboratory experiments carried out by Kahneman and Tversky and colleagues.

[25] Further empirical assessments of other aspects of SEU theory have been carried out by the same authors. See, for instance, Kahneman and Thaler (1991), Tversky and Kahneman (1991), and Kahneman et al. (1997). A retrospect view on this research program on the psychological foundations of rational models is given by Kahneman (2003a), and a sample of the idea that guided a life-time research activity may be found in the same author's 2002 lecture on occasion of receiving the Nobel Prize in Economic Sciences. Referring to his work in collaboration with Amos Tversky, he asserts that "[o]ur research attempted to obtain a map of bounded rationality, by exploring the systematic biases that separate the beliefs that people have and the choices they make from the optimal beliefs and choices assumed in rational-agent models" (Kahneman 2003b, p. 1449). Besides, he ascertains that "a particularly unrealistic assumption of the rational-agent model is that agents make their choices in a comprehensively inclusive context, which incorporates all the relevant details of the present situation, as well as expectations about all future opportunities and risks" (Kahneman 2003b, p. 1459). Kahneman has compiled and discussed some of this collective research program in a recent volume (Kahneman 2012).

scientists that assume a wider influence, even when conclusions are also arrived at through due empirical research. This is the case of Quattrone and Tversky (1988) who conclude that "errors [in choice and judgment] are common and systematic, rather than idiosyncratic or random, hence they cannot be dismissed as noise".

3.2.2.2 Satisficing as a Trigger for Search

Bounded rationality is not only related to preference reversal and framing of decisions, but also and above all to the simpler notion of relative achievement of goals, which implies choosing without examining all possible behavior alternatives and without ascertaining that these are in fact all the alternatives (March 1990a). Yet surely decision-makers, in absence of a utility function that leads their choice, must have some measure of aspiration in order to direct their action.

Briefly, the concept of *aspiration level* refers to a multidimensional measure for what people may or want to attain, and turns to be the mechanism humans use for *satisficing* in their goal-oriented action.[26] Research on decision-making in firms (Cyert and Simon 1956; Cyert and March 1963) explored the way in which organizations (firms) set levels of aspirations (but not maximizing functions).

In particular, Cyert and Simon (1956) pioneered the study of firm decision-making in oligopolistic markets through the change of general assumptions made by classical theories of firm decision-making, such as "the entrepreneurial imperative of profit maximization" (Cyert and Simon 1956, p. 45). Stemming from the framework given by previous work on goal-setting in organizations (March 1954), and on the empirical validity of the maximization principle (Simon 1955; March 1955), they showed that establishing an acceptable level of profits—plus taking other variables into account, such as the impact of planning procedures and the allocation of firm's resources—allowed for a new vision and analysis of planning processes.

In a nutshell, the main conclusion was that search behavior (for new alternatives) in organization was caused by the perception of a failure in meeting its (acceptable) goals, as other behavior such as slack in organizations—i.e., behavior that deviates from the main organizational goals, resulting in a misuse of limited resources—could also be explained by a perception that the acceptable levels had been already attained or surpassed (March and Simon 1958; Cyert et al. 1959).

The main idea here is that aspiration levels are mechanisms of bounded rationality for (a) allocating attention on particular matters (those that do not *satisfice* enough),

[26] As far as we know, the first application of the concept of *aspiration level*—widely used in psychological studies—to economic decision-making was made by Simon (1955), and March and Simon (1958) made use of it when studying individual conflict within organizations, and also in their analysis of innovation. As for *satisfice*, the word was coined by Simon himself mixing up *satisfy* and *suffice*.

and (b) triggering search for new alternatives (thus, re-allocating our attention in search activities).[27]

Application of satisfactory levels instead of optimal ones in game or competitive situations has also proved satisfactory in leading to stable situations that otherwise would be impossible (i.e., with the application of optimality). One example is given by the Prisoner's Dilemma, which shows that cooperative strategies can be rational when an optimizing policy is substituted for a *satisficing* one (Simon 1983, 1996b).[28]

The psychological foundation of this "trigger for search" is the notion of *generate-and-test*, which refers to the very capacity of humans to solve problems: "we have a problem if we know what we want to do (the test), and if we don't know immediately how to do it" (Newell and Simon 1976, p. 121) in which case we have the ability to *generate* (search for) possible solutions for the test.

Summing up, this draws a picture of rational human beings that turns to be rather different from the one drawn by theories that assume perfect rationality in human action, especially regarding two different features of bounded rationality. First, the idea of the very existence of a utility function is challenged by observations of preference reversal and inconsistency in choice situations. Second, the notion of *aspiration level* can be used both as a mechanism for attention allocation and as an induction to change situations of unsatisfactory levels of goal attainment.

We are thus left with a view of a human decision-maker who has perceivable limits on his computational abilities, who is not always able to maintain the coherence and consistency of his preferences, and who needs to focus his attention to search for alternatives when the ones tested are not sufficiently satisfactory. In the next section, a final step is made in exploring bounded rationality. In particular, it deals with the mechanisms for search.

3.2.3 Procedural Rationality vs. Substantive Rationality

Applied to decision-making, the difference between substantive and procedural rationality is the difference between the ability to choose *the* correct course of action and the ability to choose *a* good (enough) course of action.

The picture of the economic man given by neoclassical economic theory is that of a human being who purports to deal with the "real world" in all its complexity (and that may help her to achieve her goals using rationality). This view assumes a theory of human problem solving in which optimal solutions (decisions) are arrived at through

---

[27] Hence March's celebrated formula of aspiration level as "a trigger for search" (March 1990a, p. 3), or the previous assertion that the "recognition of the unacceptability of available alternatives triggers search activity" (March and Simon 1958, p. 116).

[28] See our comments on the repeated application of this game in Sect. 2.3.3. Cf. Axelrod and Hamilton (1981); Axelrod and Dion (1988); Axelrod (2006).

a chain of mental processes of the kind depicted in the first chapter (foundations of rational-choice theories, Sect. 2.3.1) and in our working definition of *rationality*.

The model of a boundedly rational human being, in contrast, draws a picture of an individual who cannot perceive the world in such a detailed manner. Instead, she makes it with a highly simplified image of it, in which one situation (problem) is only loosely connected with another situation (problem). Thus she can make decisions with relatively simple rules of thumb that do not make impossible demands upon her capacity for thought.

In particular, then, the problem of procedural *versus* substantive rationality is the problem of the way by which humans develop strategies to adapt to their environments—i.e., in order to achieve their goals (solve their problems). This question poses the further problem whether performing complex tasks requires a highly complex memory organization. Or, in other words, it puts forth our main problem: how problems that require huge amounts of expert knowledge (stored in memory) are actually worked out.

According to the viewpoint adopted in the previous sections, the search for solutions in rich domains will be determined by the complex structure of these problems rather than by the limits of human memory.

3.2.3.1 Procedural Rationality in Organizations

The study of the way humans develop search strategies in particularly complex problem spaces run parallel to the development of techniques and tools for helping organizations to achieve higher levels of efficiency in their decisions, that is, to achieve procedural rationality. A number of techniques have been proposed, operations research (OR) and artificial intelligence (AI) being among the most popular ones.

These developments are based upon simplified models of real-world problems, although they enable taking a huge number of different variables into account in order to find an optimal solution to a problem. Yet unless the model of the problem used in the analysis and the real-world problem have the very same properties, the solutions will hardly be optimal.

Typically OR works with simplified models of problems so that solutions can be worked out, but these solutions are only optimal *within* a simplified model of the problem that has been thus formalized, but in the real-world problem, the solution, at best, will be good enough (Simon 1996b). Even more, OR and techniques such as linear programming have limited application to ill-structured problems, compared to heuristic search enabled by symbolic AI-based applications, which ease working with less well-structured problem spaces.[29] The price is that with AI optima are rarely

[29] A well-structured problem is that which (1) "can be described in terms of numerical variables, scalar and vector quantities"; (2) have goals to be attained that "can be specified in terms of a well-defined objective function—for example, the maximization of profit or the minimization of

found. The trade-off lies between "satisficing in a near-realistic model (AI) against optimizing in a greatly simplified model (OR)" (Simon 1996b, p. 28).

3.2.3.2 A Computer Model of the Mind

The heuristic models developed under the label of *artificial intelligence* were applied bearing in mind the idea that these tools actually helped to better understand human heuristic processes precisely because they performed their processes *in the same way* humans actually performed them. Behind this idea resided the strong belief that human thinking could be reduced to a set of information or symbol manipulating (information-processing) processes, in such a way that computers (being symbol-processing systems themselves) would be able to simulate.[30]

This idea, that triggered the development of artificial intelligence jointly with cognitive science, was the result of work done at the RAND Corporation and the Carnegie Institute of Technology by Herbert A. Simon (at Carnegie Institute of Technology), Allen Newell and J. Cliff Shaw (at RAND's Systems Research Laboratory), and others, since the early 1950s. An early formulation of these ideas may be found in a report on the General Problem Solver (GPS)—a joint research project of RAND and Carnegie Tech—for the RAND Corporation (Newell et al. 1958b). The main objective of this research was to "understand the information processes that underlie human intellectual, adaptive, and creative abilities" by means of constructing "computer programs that can solve problems requiring intelligence and adaptation" (Newell et al. 1958b). The same ideas were soon publicly stated with notable optimism (Simon and Newell 1958; Newell et al. 1958a; Simon 1961).[31]

cost"; (3) and "there exist computational routines (*algorithms*) that permit the solution to be found and stated in actual numerical terms" (Simon and Newell 1958, pp. 4–5). An ill-structured problem, then, is the opposite, and most organizational decision problems of the kind we are dealing with are, therefore, ill-structured problems.

[30] The notions of *symbol* and of *physical symbol system* (or, *information-processing system*) were the bases upon which cognitive science and artificial intelligence built their powerful ability to both simulate human intelligence and produce intelligent behavior by computers. "Symbols lie at the root of intelligent action, which is, of course, the primary topic of artificial intelligence. [...] For all information is processed by computers in the service of ends, and we measure the intelligence of a system by its ability to achieve stated ends in the face of variations, difficulties and complexities posed by the task environment" (Newell and Simon 1976, p. 114). For the foundations of the symbolic approach, see Newell and Simon (1976); Newell (1980, 1981), and Newell (1990, pp. 72–80). For some applications and further research within this paradigm, see Anderson (2005); Brooks (1981); Ourusoff (1985). For the relation between the symbolic level and the system's functional architecture, see Pylyshyn (1984). For an introduction to the alternative connectionist approach the architecture of mind, see Rumelhart (1989).

[31] Simon and Newell (1958) made a set of predictions about the achievements of computers for the next 10-year period: (1) that a "digital computer will be the world's chess champion, unless the rules bar it from competition"; (2) that "a digital computer will discover and prove an important new mathematical theorem"; (3) that "a digital computer will write music that will be accepted by critics as possessing considerable aesthetic value"; and (4) that "most theories in psychology will take

It is also worth noting that the analogy was not made between the computer and the neurophysiological structure of human brain, but between two physical systems that process symbols in order to perform activities regarded as *thinking* or *intelligent*.

Finally, the computer was also viewed as a way to test theories on complex human thinking processes such as problem solving and learning, which gave a definite impulse to cognitive sciences as a meeting point between other disciplines such as computer science, economics, linguistics, and notably artificial intelligence (Simon 1980).

In effect, under all these developments—that involved research and development of information processing languages, production systems languages, and simulation of search in complex environments—underlied a brand-new information-based theory of human cognition and, in particular, a novel theory of human problem solving. The notion of *problem* soon led Allen Newell to the notion of *heuristics*, or "things that aid discovery" (Newell et al. 1958b, pp. 1–2),[32] in the sense that "a genuine problem-solving process involves the repeated use of available information to initiate *exploration*, which discloses, in turn, more information until a way to attain the solution is finally *discovered*" (Newell et al. 1958b, p. 1).[33] These informations are heuristics. A theory of human problem solving was thus set forth including a "space" in which the problem solver searched for a solution.

3.2.3.3 Task Environment and Problem Space

Regarding "space", Newell (1990, p. 98) describes *problem space* as "the space the agent has created within which to search for the solution to whatever problem it is currently attending. It is the agent's attempt to bound the problem so it can be worked on. Thus, the agent adopts some problem space in which to solve a problem. The agent is then located at some current state in the space". Therefore, while the task environment (the objective structure of the problem, also known as *problem environment*) molds the structure of the problem space, the problem space is the representation of that task environment in the information-processing system (the problem solver).[34]

The distinction of task environment and problem space leads, in fact, to two different representations of the same thing made by two different agents. The task environment itself may be represented by the observer. The problem space is the

the form of computer programs, or of qualitative statements about the characteristics of computer programs". See Noriega (2006, pp. LI–LIII) for an assessment of the results of these predictions.

[32] Allen Newell was introduced to the notion of *heuristics* by the mathematician George Polya, whose courses at Stanford University he attended to in the late 1940s (Simon 1996a, p. 199).

[33] Italics are ours.

[34] This is the keystone of the approach (in fact, a theory) presented in *Human Problem Solving* (Newell and Simon 1972). It founds upon the work briefly described above, and its main intuitions had already been presented in a number of publications (e.g., Newell et al. 1958a), but this constitutes the authors' definite attempt to summarize and systematize all these findings and analyses.

internal representation of the task environment by the behaving subject (the decision maker). Therefore, *the problem of analyzing a subject's decision process will mostly imply the problem of interpreting and representing the way in which the subject represents and interprets the objective environment of the problem to be solved.*

3.2.3.4 LTM and Information-rich Domains

Considering what has been explored so far, the notion of the decision-maker as an adaptive system turns to be clearer. On one hand, in the sense that the structure of the problem to be solved (within a particular problem space) is the essential constraint to which the system has to adapt in order to solve a problem. On the other hand, in that the actual behavior of this adaptive individual solving a problem will tell us (a) how complex the problem is, and (b) "what aspects of behavior are determined by the psychology of the problem solver" (Newell and Simon 1972, p. 79).

Given a problem, a problem space (providing the paths that may lead to a solution), and a problem solver (who is an adaptive system), Newell and Simon (1972, p. 83) proposed that the level of adaptivity (or intelligence, or expertise, we may add) is a measure of the success the problem solver shows with problems of a certain kind, thus exploring the relation between certain problems and the skill needed to solve them.

Solving the problem $3 + 3 =?$ does not require special skills for an adult person with a basic level of literacy. Solving the problems that professionals of any field (medicine, judiciary, fire departments) must solve every day require special skills. These skills are needed because the environment of the problems they face requires the availability, recovery, and management of huge amounts of information stored in these professionals' long-term memory (LTM).

Our simpler calculation problem did not require retrieving any amount of information from the LTM. Rather, its solution comes generally "as automatic, largely unconscious, and relatively undemanding of computational capacity" (Stanovich and West 2000).[35] The question is not whether expert professionals are inherently more intelligent than other adults but whether they possess a sufficient store of information related to their field and the ability to recover that information in a sufficiently efficient way so that problems may be solved. This is why some people are considered experts. While their basic cognitive system is invariant and the same as the average human being (Newell 1990), the difference between the layman and the expert lies (a) in the amount of information about a particular domain stored in his LTM, and

[35] In the dual-process theories of reasoning, this would be a canonical description of the so-called System 1 of the mind. While System 1 is mainly automatic and almost devoid of voluntary control, System 2 requires certain amount of attention resources to be allocated to solve complex problems. See (Stanovich and West 2000) and (Kahneman 2012).

(b) in his ability to search, recognize, associate, and retrieve this information in order to make certain decisions about that domain (Simon 1996b, p. 87).[36]

As long as the LTM is thus viewed as a "place" where the search occurs (in particular kinds of problems), it may be regarded as standing beyond the goals of the problem-solver, which mark the boundary between both environments. Therefore, the long-term memory is another part of the outer environment to which the subject has to adapt, especially when deciding over information-rich domains (Simon 1996b).

3.2.4 Concluding Remarks: The Limits that Shape Rationality

In this section the main features of the inner environment of a typical decision-maker have been put forth in order to assess what level of rationality is to be expected in human normal behavior. There is a notable amount of empirical research supporting the view of a (boundedly) rational human being in cognitive sciences, organization and management, and information processing psychology. Human thought processes in difficult problem-solving, concept-attainment, and decision-making tasks have been described successfully in terms of basic information-processing processes.

We have presented the main characteristics of the inner environment in different steps. First, we discussed the concept of rationality presenting an alternative to the one adopted by neoclassical economics and rational-choice approaches to political decision-making.

Second, this notion of rationality has led us to consider three different dimensions according to which these two different views of rationality may be analyzed. The first one has dealt with the difference between bounded and omniscient rationality, which refers to the cognitive limits all human beings share in our processing of information. The second one takes account of the difference between satisficing and optimizing as valid criteria for interpreting human behavior as goal-oriented action, introducing the notion of *aspiration level*. The third one accounts for the difference between procedural and substantive rationality. While the latter refers to the outcomes of rational choice, the former centers on the process through which a rational choice is arrived at (Simon 1978). In this last part a number of issues have been presented and discussed, such as technological means to reach procedural rationality in organizations, the historical and basic theoretical grounds of a computer model of the mind, and the relevant notions of *problem space* and *task environment*.

These issues provide the framework in which human problem solving can be understood as a process by which humans use certain methods (heuristics) within a problem space in order to attain a goal, namely the solution of a problem.

The purpose of this work required the presentation and explanation of a theory of human problem solving, although to give a detailed account of the theory of

[36] See Kolodner (1983) for a computer model of retrieval and search processes in long-term memory.

heuristic search would fall beyond our scope.[37] Moreover, we are aware that the theory presented here has been extended since the 1970s through a great deal of research in cognitive science, mainly on cognitive architectures.[38]

In this sense, three main cognitive architectures have been developed in order to incorporate and expand the theory of human problem solving. SOAR (Laird et al. 1987) was proposed as an architecture for general intelligence and as a candidate for a unified theory of cognition (Newell 1990, p. 38). Seen as an intelligent system, it performs small tasks (Tower of Hanoi, resolution theorem proving, means-ends analysis, etc.) as well as larger ones (algorithm discovery, production scheduling of replacement windshields, etc.). It also learns by chunking on all tasks it performs (Newell 1990, pp. 216–217).[39]

ACT-R (Adaptive Character of Thought) (Anderson 1996)—elaborating ACT* (Anderson 1983), which founded upon Newell's contributions on the role of production rules in procedural knowledge (Anderson 1996)—has centered upon complex cognition through decomposition of cognition (Anderson and Gluck 2001). It has received attention and has been applied in different research areas such as conflict resolution (Belavkin and Ritter 2004), linguistic metaphor analysis (Budiu and Anderson 2003), and theory of choice (Lovett 1998).

Finally, ICARUS (Langley et al. 2004) has been presented as an "extended theory of human problem solving" (Langley and Rogers 2005) which deals with many features regarding representation, performance, and learning in puzzle-like problem-solving situations (e.g., the Tower of Hanoi).

Although these advances are impressive, and the applications numerous, the core assumptions of Newell and Simon's theory of human problem solving seem to stand and are still referred to not only as seminal work but also as a still valid general framework (Anderson 1987).

In conclusion, then, these assumptions and the features of the inner environment have set forth the basic limits that shape human rationality, which might be summarized as:

- Limits on what we *can* know (cognitive limits)
- Limits on what we *can expect* to do (aspiration levels)
- Limits on what we *can* and *actually* do (task environment)

[37] We *assume* a theory of heuristic search according to the framework we have presented. See Newell and Simon (1972, Chap. 4).

[38] A cognitive architecture "specifies the infrastructure that remains constant across different domains and knowledge bases" (Langley et al. 2004).

[39] See Newell (1992, pp. 425–437) for an overview of *Unified Theories of Cognition* (Newell 1990) and Newell (1992, pp. 437–492) for a thorough discussion on the relevance and appropriateness of both the book and SOAR.

3.3 The External Environment of Decisions

3.3.1 Introduction

This section holds on two simple ideas that have been already presented in this chapter. The first one is that individuals are adaptive systems who act in an environment in order to solve their problems. In effect, at the beginning of this chapter we stated that placing the boundary between the inner and the outer environment of a deciding system was quite arbitrary since it depended upon whose decisions do we want to deal with. Many early students within the behavioral tradition (Cyert and Simon 1956; Cyert and March 1955) opted for setting that boundary at the fringes of the organization rather than placing it at the individual level. Such a decision has implied the systematic study of the mechanisms for organizational bounded rationality in a similar way that others have focused their efforts on studying the mechanisms of individual bounded rationality. Some of the latter have been already pointed out in previous sections. For instance, we saw how we humans deal with our poor ability to attend to different things at a time recurring to attention (and emotions). Similarly, organizations may have problems to attack a great amount of important matters at the same time and have to make use of allocation of attention (e.g., in the form of resources) in order to assure a particular problem is tackled in due time and by appropriate means (March 1990a).

This and other mechanisms—such as routinized behavior or departmentalization—make organizations adaptive systems that are able to achieve goals and make decisions in ways that single individuals would have never dreamt of. Building the "Big Mac" between Lake Michigan and Lake Huron, "discovering" America, and successfully carrying out the Brécourt Manor Assault are all instances of such achievements. These mechanisms are part of an organization's inner environment in the sense that they allow for adaptation to the external environment.[40]

As we have also pointed out, we decided to set the boundary at the individual level, so these organizational mechanisms that otherwise would be considered the inner environment, are viewed here as the most important portion of external environment within which the individual has to adapt and make choices—decisions.

[40] Considering the organization as an adaptive system to overcome the cognitive limits of its members is not new and has its roots in at least as far as Weber's vision of bureaucracy as the coordination mechanism for the achievement of the goals of a political authority (March and Simon 1958, pp. 36–37). Since Weber's, others followed that studied bureaucratic phenomena, e.g., Selznick (1943, 1948). However, Weber did never went into the micro aspects of the interaction between the individual and the bureaucratic organization, but remained interested in bureaucracy and bureaucratization and their integrative role in democratic society through particular rules of behavior and action (Lipset 1983, p. 10). Selznick represents a slight variation of this model when he focuses both on the anticipated responses and on the unanticipated ones of this "machine" model. See March and Simon (1958, pp. 34–81) for a review of these classical theories of bureaucracy, and cf. Weber (1978a, pp. 956–1005).

Thus in our case, the problems junior judges have to face when on-call will have to be understood as demands of this external environment rather than the judicial organization's mechanisms to deal with its bounded rationality.

So while in the account (in the rest of this chapter) of these demands we shall give a brief introduction to some general features to be taken into consideration, by no means they are to be considered fixed or given, for it will be our analysis of the individual's adaptive problem-solving behavior that will tell us the precise nature, characteristics, and complexity of this external environment and of the particular problems it puts forth. This is the second idea.

Therefore, at this point we should make a decision on what features of the external environment are to be most relevant to our analysis. In order to make that choice for this tentative presentation, we have used the conclusions sketched in the few earlier works on the matter (Rodrigo et al. 2004; Casanovas et al. 2005). In a preliminary overview on Spanish judges, Rodrigo et al. (2004, p. 15) stressed the characteristics of the on-call period arguing that judges' decision-making in these circumstances "may entail simultaneous decision making over a number of parallel issues (raised by the police, lawyers, prosecutors, etc.)", which points out the problem of allocation of attention, i.e., the problem of paying attention to a few things at a time.

Furthermore, it was detected that "the need for quick decisions makes it difficult to review jurisprudence or precedents, so inexperienced judges have to rely on uncertain consultation with peers or senior judges". This last point raises, first, the general problem of decision-making under uncertainty, particularly shaped by lack of complete information about the problem to be solved. Secondly, in this particular context it also refers to the lack of experience—i.e., knowledge gathered from past problem-solving activities, and expertise—, which in turn leads to the need of some kind of devices such as adaptive rules or routines—that are usually viewed as the quintessential mode of bureaucratic behavior—in order to deal with usual problems and situations.

In a further account, Casanovas et al. (2005, p. 20) analyzed samples of qualitative data on the conditions under which junior judges usually work and detected another potential problem regarding personnel at courts. In particular it was observed that:

> One of the perennial problems of the Spanish judicial system is that first instance courts in remote areas are plagued with vacancies of the judicial staff. [. . .] [I]n some Autonomous Communities members of the judicial staff still depend on the Ministry of Justice and they are organized at the national level. After a compulsory period of permanency in a judicial unit, judicial staff tends to move to another area, usually closer to their homeland. This also holds true for civil servants of the Autonomous Communities with competencies over judicial staff. As a result, in remote areas judges may occasionally find at their arrival either a deserted unit (i.e. the officials have moved to another area and the new ones have not yet arrived), a unit filled with substitute and poorly trained personnel, or a unit filled with newly recruited staff who aims to spend a short period of time there before moving to another area.

Furthermore, the assessment of these data also uncovered that "one of the main concerns of judges at the beginning of their service is how to manage judicial staff" as they are heads of the judicial office and thus sometimes they have to "establish some organizational ground rules". This point should make us aware of the potentiality of conflict in organizations, which usually refers to the existence of mutually inconsistent preferences within the same organizational unit.

Therefore our focus will purposely emphasize those aspects that are potentially most relevant for our further case-study analysis (such as decisions under uncertainty or allocation of attention); thus it shall necessarily de-emphasize other features. This in any case is to be understood as that these other features are not important in different analyses of an administrative organization.[41]

Bearing this in mind, this section deals with a number of features and mechanisms that structure organizations in general and their behavior as they have been studied in the tradition of behavioral organizational decision analysis.

Section 3.3.2 brings up allocation of attention and extends some ideas pointed out in previous sections. Section 3.3.3 explores organizational mechanisms for dealing with conflict within organizations. Section 3.3.4 we shall briefly tackle the role of adaptive responses (routines) as a necessary constituent of any administrative organization. Finally, Sects. 3.3.5 and 3.3.6 will relate the aforementioned features with the notions of uncertainty and expertise, respectively.[42]

3.3.2 The Bottleneck of Attention

In a certain point of the previous section it was concluded that, when faced to a problem situation, the decision-maker builds herself a definition of that situation that necessarily varies a great deal with respect to the "objective" situation. The main reason for that is the "objective" situation is too complex, too full of details to be completely attended by a human mind.

One way humans and organizations have traditionally found comfortable to deal with this shortcoming is to split complex tasks into smaller parts, or to specialize members of the organization with particular parts of the problem. These are observable phenomena in nearly all organizations with which we are familiar (universities, firms, NGOs, political parties, and so forth). In effect, various parts of a complex issue are dealt with by different individuals or groups of individuals, so that the problem is factored "into a number of nearly independent parts, so that each organizational unit handles one of these parts and can omit the others from its definition of the situation" (March and Simon 1958, p. 151).

This way, a task (goal) is broken down into small subtasks (subgoals) in order to (a) enable sufficiently simple models of the reality and (b) allow focusing attention to a few problems at once so that a human mind (or organization department) can handle them. As a consequence, when trying to achieve subgoals, the human or the

---

41 See Hodgkinson and Starbuck (2008) for an assessment of the variety of features analyzed in a most recent compilation in the field.

42 The order of the first three subsections of this section draws on March (1990b).

department tends to decide ignoring or omitting the upper, general goal(s), centering the focus of attention to a few particular issues at one time.

March and Simon (1958, pp. 152–153) identified three major cognitive mechanisms by which this tendency is reinforced in members of an organizational unit. The first one—at the individual level—is the reinforcement through selective perception and rationalization, in the sense that human beings—as we have seen in the previous section—tend to filter out those things that are discordant with their frame of reference, and therefore to see only those things that are consistent with their established frame of reference.

In this sense, March and Shapira (1987) explored how attention influences managers' decisions in risky and risk-taking situations. To this end, they reviewed the main sources of data and literature on managerial behavior and perceptions on risk situations and on risk-taking decisions. One of their conclusions was that risk-preference varies with changes "among a set of inconsistent and ambiguous preferences", and that the focus of attention tends to emphasize a few key aspects of a problem instead of attempting a rich picture of it.

In this direction, they found that risk-prone decisions happen in contexts when managers perceive their firm is under their target level of performance, and that when that happens, the prospect of gains receives more attention than the dangers of loss attached to that alternative. On the contrary, risk-averse decisions take place when the firm is above that level and in those cases "the dangers of falling below the target dominate attention".[43] They concluded that "understanding action in the face of incomplete information may depend more on ideas about attention than on ideas about decision".

The second mechanism—at an intraorganizational level—is the reinforcement through the content of in-group communication, which affects the focus of information. For example, March and Feigenbaum (1960) explored the way the evocation of alternatives served as one of the most "important modes of interpersonal influence" to the extent that they biased group decisions and post-discussion individual decisions.

The third one—at an organizational level—is the reinforcement through selective exposure to environmental stimuli, such as the division of labor in the organization, in such a way that perceptions of the environment are biased before they experience the filtering action of the frame of reference.

A classic approach on this issue was delivered by Cyert and March (1955), who advanced the study on attention as channeled through the intraorganizational communication patterns in the form of bias on information that led to pricing decisions in the context of an oligopolistic market. They showed that the intensity of attention

[43] It is noteworthy to comment that the authors add to the target level of performance a survival level as another critical focal value for attention in managerial decision-making. In this case, the focus of attention and therefore risk-taking decisions also vary when performance is well above the survival level or nearly at that level. However, this added value seems rather context-dependent and will not be taken into account here.

had consequences in the firm's price policy, which ultimately led to changes in the firm's relative market position.

Elsewhere, Cyert and Simon (1956) introduced the idea that the allocation of attention may be a double-edged sword. In their example, attention appears in the form of allocation of resources to particular firm subunits or departments. When these resources are allocated above the minimum required, organization members may perceive that the organization level of aspiration has been surpassed and the situation can lead to slack behavior, i.e., behavior that is perceived to be hardly justifiable in terms of the firm's explicit goals and subgoals.

On the contrary, when the level of aspiration is perceived still to be attained, attention is focused on the search for alternatives that may assure a satisfactory level of goal-attainment. The authors conclude that "these opportunities [for new alternatives] do not enter into the firm's perceptions until some form of shock (such as failing to meet its goals) forces a kind of search behavior on the organization" (Cyert and Simon 1956, p. 54).

In this same direction, Cyert et al. (1959) and Manns and March (1978) showed that energy spent in search for new alternatives is strongly related to the perceptions organizations have of their success or failure with respect to their expectations.

In particular, Cyert et al. (1959) concluded that search is triggered by failure perception and that organization goals "change as the organization observes its success (or lack of it) in the market".

On their part, Manns and March (1978) related financial conditions of university departments to changes of collegiate curricula, showing that the perception of an adverse financial situation of the departments triggered search activity with the aim of providing a more attractive collegiate offer that could ultimately lead to a better financial situation.[44]

In a recent paper Sutcliffe and Weick (2008, p. 59) argue that time pressure diminishes the ability to process information asserting that "capacity is also limited when time is short". Other scholars have focused on the consequences of time pressure in processing capacities. For instance, in a study on consumer information overload, Hahn et al. (1992, p. 376) concluded that "the most important finding that this study reveals is that the information overload effect depends on the factor of time pressure". Furthermore, Speier et al. (1999) explored the impact of interruptions—i.e., time fragmentation—on individual decision making, finding that "interruptions induce information overload", thus triggering attention narrowing processes. In particular, they concluded that while "interruptions facilitate performance on simple tasks [they hinder] performance on complex tasks".[45]

---

[44] The authors also noted that those departments with higher reputation were less prone to introduce changes in their curriculum. They hypothesized that reputation provided "alternative financial opportunities, alternative bases for attracting students, and alternative sources of power for bargaining with administrators" (Manns and March 1978). See also Levinthal and March (1981) for a further treatment of organizational search related to technological change.

[45] Kock (2000) has recently contributed to the study of information overload in individual decision making. Focusing on the relation between this phenomenon and worker performance, the author

Finally, in the section devoted to the description of our mechanisms for storing and processing information (Sect. 3.2.1.2), we saw that emotions may be seen as mechanisms for avoiding or solving bottlenecks of attention, and in this role they have received attention, though with less intensity than other organizational mechanisms for bounded rationality (Shapira 2008). The central idea is that emotions are "a force that helps direct actions toward particular goals by holding attention on them and the means of their realization" (Simon 1997, p. 91), and it has mainly led to the study of motivational aspects in decision making (Simon 1967, 1992; Shapira 1981), and the relation of affect on intuition and, ultimately, on decisions (Sadler-Smith and Sparrow 2008; Daniels 2008).

3.3.3 *Conflict in Organizations*

Another feature to be aware of is that organizations are potential *loci* for conflict. Conflict refers to the existence of "multiple actors with inconsistent preferences" (March 1990a, p. 5) in a single organization, and the analysis of conflict within organizations has had two main *foci* of interest:

- Preference inconsistency and explanatory models.
- Organizational mechanisms for dealing with inconsistency of preferences.

Regarding the first one, which is devoted to account for the existence of inconsistent preferences and to propose models (either descriptive or normative) that help explain the phenomenon, the neoclassical approach to decision-making tended to assume that a complete hierarchy of ends existed in organizations—as individuals—that served as the reference to which all choice alternatives must be weighed (Downs 1957). Yet, as we have already seen, the early students and observers of how decisions happened in organizations soon pointed out that there was scarce evidence that this hierarchy took place in its full completeness either in organizations or in individuals.

The existence of multiple and conflicting preferences and interests in organizations has called the attention of a varied number of students of organizations, and in particular it has received a special treatment in the study of bureaucracy (e.g., Crozier 1964; Downs 1967) and policy analysis (e.g., Mayntz 1976; Bardach 1977).

For instance, the issue of collective choice has led many political scientists to deal with the problem of aggregation of individual preferences (e.g., Arrow 1963; Buchanan and Tullock 1962) in order to propose prescriptive models of strategic

---

challenges some traditional assumptions (a) on the role of information overload in work performance, and (b) on the impact of individual factors (versus task factors) in work performance. As to the role of the time factor the author reports that "information overload is more generally seen as related to the pressure to perform tasks within a certain timeframe, than to the amount of information that has to be processed" (Kock 2000, p. 262).

and bargain-oriented behavior in organizational settings (e.g., Shepsle and Weingast 1982; Shepsle 1985; Weingast 1998; Shepsle 2006).[46]

A classic analysis of conflict processes within organizations has been attempted in terms of power relations between the parts in conflict, but this kind of analysis soon proved rather uncomfortable and problematic as regards the problem of measurement of influence (March 1955, 1956, 1957) and the general fruitfulness of carrying out empirical research based on the concept of power (March 1966).

Others have focused more attention on behavioral features of some particular organizations to propose descriptive models of how conflict in preferences takes place in these organizations. In a well-known approach, Cohen et al. (1972) concluded that choice in organizations such as universities fitted well in a garbage-can model in which goals where confused, already-made solutions sought for problems, and behavior was therefore inherently organizationally inconsistent.[47]

Within the same tradition, March (1962) proposed seeing the business firm as a political coalition based on the existence of organizational units defending mutually inconsistent preferences about the same resources. And, further, Baier et al. (1986) explored the difficulties in policy implementation due to "conflict of interest between policy makers and bureaucratic agents, and thus to deficiencies in organizational control".

The second focus on conflict in organizations has referred to the mechanisms organizations have developed in order to deal with the existence of inconsistent preferences. Empirical research on this issue shows not only that conflict exists (De Dreu and Gelfand 2007) but that efforts to extinguish it within organizations are rather modest. Instead, organizations seem to develop mechanisms that help avoiding that contradictory preferences and interests spring at the same time (March and Simon 1958, Chap. 3).

Students of organizations have identified at least three main mechanisms through which organizations try to attack this type of conflict. The first one refers to the very structure of the organization, through the creation of subunits (departments) and dividing labor between them. That way, "the total system of decisions that need to be made [are factorized] into relatively independent subsystems, each of which can be designed with only minimal concern for its interactions with the others (Simon 1997, p. 240).

The idea behind division of labor—from the standpoint of conflict management—is that reducing the interdependence among subunits, the organization reduces "the audience for any particular decision process" (March 1990a, p. 7), and therefore the likelihood of conflict arising across subunits diminishes.

A second mechanism refers to the limits of attention and sets fourth time as a scarce but key resource that imposes seriality in preventing the problem of parallel salience

[46] See Lang (2005) and Chevaleyre et al. (2006) for a computational approach to social choice.

[47] See Bendor et al. (2001) and Olsen (2001) for a discussion on the research fruits of the garbage-can model.

of contradictory issues. It lets up to Sect. 3.3.2 above, where we discussed the problems associated to the allocation of attention, and ultimately to Sect. 3.2.1.2, where focus of attention was analyzed as a cognitive mechanism for individual bounded rationality.

Finally, the third conflict buffer (March 1990a) refers to organizational slack in the sense that an unbalanced distribution of resources makes it difficult that multiple contradictory demands spring at the same time.

In conclusion, then, regarding the mechanisms organizations produce in order to attack this problem, they mainly seek to avoid parallel salience of contradictory interests by avoiding serious bottlenecks of attention and information that would impede decision-making and, ultimately, efficient problem-solving.

3.3.4 Routines and Programmed Responses

Bureaucracy (either in public or private organizations) has usually been identified with routine behavior, and this feature of almost all organizations has received attention since a systematic study of organizations started with Max Weber.

Although the Weberian account of routine behavior in bureaucratic organizations has eminently a positive flavor as far as the organizational outcomes is concerned—routines are seen as those necessary mechanisms through which organizational goals are reached (Weber 1978b, pp. 956–1005)—the study of the nature of routine behavior and its components has been outnumbered by other accounts of the relation between the individual and the organization that have highlighted routines in negative terms.[48]

Simon (1997, p. 89) defined routines as "embodiments of 'once and for all' decisions", which means that they are decisions themselves when applied in concrete situations.

As decisions, therefore, routines are understood as an individual's response to an environmental stimulus, but a response that "has been developed and learned at some previous time as an appropriate response for a stimulus of this class" (March and Simon 1958, p. 139).[49] Fifty years later, routines are still defined in a similar fashion: "*patterned processes* in the treatment of organizational issues regardless of whether these patterns derive from explicit policies and procedures or from implicit values and norms" (Royer and Langley 2008, p. 252).

Notice that focusing on these *processes* rather than on the ready-made *embodiments*, Royer and Langley (2008) defend a procedural view of routines in front of an content-based or substantive one, in the vein of Simon's distinction between

[48] See von Mises (1996) for a review of some views on bureaucracy.

[49] Routines have received many names such as programs (March and Simon 1958), rules (Zhou 1997), organizational processes (Bendor and Hammond 1992).

procedural and substantive rationality (Simon 1978).[50] In effect, March and Simon (1958) viewed this kind of response as occupying one extreme of a continuum that marked two different kinds of response from the individual facing an organizational stimulus. On the other extreme lay a typical problem-solving activity that involves search and discovery of alternatives (see Sects. 3.2.2 and 3.2.3). Others, though, propose observing them as "decision practices that channel the paths of organizational decision making" (Royer and Langley 2008, p. 252).[51]

However, the observation of everyday situations and the accounts of actual decision making situations (e.g., Klein and Calderwood 1991) makes reasonable to think that organization members usually do face situations that may lie between these two extreme situations described by March and Simon, in which cases they may search first in their "repertory of response programs" (March and Simon 1958, p. 140)—for which an analysis of ready-made solutions would seem most adequate—and then, if these programs are not adequate, they may search for other alternatives (March and Simon 1958; Cyert et al. 1959),[52] in which case the adoption of a *procedural* view of routines (Royer and Langley 2008) would be worth undertaking.

In effect, the interest in routines stems from behavioral data showing that a notable proportion of organizational behavior is based on following rules rather than on calculating consequences of that behavior (Cyert et al. 1959). In particular, March and Olsen (1998) argue that organizations' behavior—as individual's—is the product of the interrelation between "rational action based on expectations of consequences and rule-based action seeking to fulfill identities within environments that influence but do not uniquely dictate actions".[53]

Routine behavior, then, occurs when choice is simplified by de development of a script of a fixed response (March and Simon 1958, p. 143), by "the application of standard operating procedures or rules to appropriate situations" (March 1981), which in turn tends to increase the *predictability* of individual activities within an organization.[54]

In their early contribution, March and Simon (1958) observed that routines could generally be described in programs that contained details of the tasks an individual or group must accomplish for relatively stable activities. The reality and relevance of these programs has led many students of organizational behavior to focus their analysis upon many of its potential faces, including their content (March and Simon

[50] Cf. Sect. 3.2.3 above on this distinction.

[51] Royer and Langley (2008) conclude that decision routines are "a key component of organizational decision making and [...] an (albeit delicate) path to improving effectiveness". Yet Sutcliffe and McNamara (2001) warn that "decision makers may become complacent when they rely on prescribed decision practices, a tendency that can have untoward consequences for the organizations in which they are embedded".

[52] See also Sect. 3.2.2.2 above.

[53] See Harrison and March (1984) for a further discussion around the consequences of viewing decision-making as an estimate of the future values of the alternatives available.

[54] The issue of the appropriateness in rule-based behavior has received attention in the literature. See March and Olsen (2006b) on "the logic of appropriateness".

1958, pp. 144–147) and their influence in organizational learning, since "organizations [learn] by encoding inferences from history into routines that guide behavior" (Levinthal and March 1981, p. 320).

Indeed, this last feature of this kind of adaptive response by individuals in organizational settings are of our particular interest in so far these rules of behavior are thought to synthesize experience and reflect on typical problem-solving situations (March 1981; March and Olsen 1984; March 1990a).

As we saw in Sect. 3.2.3.4, memory plays a main role in human problem-solving. In the memory "are stored both repertories of possible solutions to classes of problems that have been encountered in the past and repertories of components of problem solutions" (March and Simon 1958, p. 177). We have also seen that the role of memory in problem-solving has received notable attention in some literature, especially in the computational approach to human problem-solving (Newell and Simon 1972; Newell 1990).

Problems with memory organization and retrieval affect the information processing about preferences and consequences (March 1978), both at the individual level (Newell and Simon 1972; Simon 1973) and at the organizational level (March and Simon 1958; Cyert and March 1963).

Routines are definitely relevant in our analysis so far they are not only devices for solving immediate problems, but, most importantly, they are devices for learning and for turning inexperienced professionals into experts. And so far they are, obviously, a mechanism for making better decisions. The relation between adaptive rules of behavior and learning from experience has been related to different aspects of organizational behavior, change, and evolution. For instance, it has led to explore the adaptive models of organizational search. In this sense Levinthal and March (1981) assume that "the success of an organization depends partly on its technology", technology meaning "any semi-stable specification of the way in which an organization deals with its environment, functions and prospers" (Levinthal and March 1981, p. 307). The authors connect this with organizational learning (the role of learning in finding optimal solutions in simple situations), explaining decision making as a result of experiential learning, that is, "as a consequence of an organization's successes and failures in meeting performance targets, or search expenditures made and their outcomes, and of the (sometimes mistaken) inferences made from experience" (Levinthal and March 1981, p. 308).

On the other hand, Levitt and March (1988) and March (1990a) view routines as containing (expert) knowledge from which inferences are made in order to guide both individual and organization behavior (i.e., in order to make decisions), but they also point out that although normally these routines are distributed among organizational members and that "[t]hey are recorded in a collective memory that is often coherent but is sometimes jumbled", sometimes this memory is lost (Levitt and March 1988, p. 320), contributing to uncertainty.

3.3.5 Uncertainty

Uncertainty is a highly voluble concept and puts forth serious problems of measurement and standardization (Lowe 2003). It has received attention from many fields, especially economics (e.g., Raiffa 1970; Shafer 1984; Tversky and Kahneman 1974; Tversky 1974; Hirshleifer and Riley 1979; Kahneman et al. 1982; Glimcher 2003). However, interest may be also found in other fields, from international relations (e.g., Heradstveit and Bonham 1986; Sanders 1998) to cognitive sciences and artificial intelligence (e.g., John and Langley 1995; Lang 2005; Langley and Sage 1994; Lebiere et al. 2003).

In organizational decision analysis, uncertainty is also a relevant notion. In their classic approach, March and Simon (1958, pp. 113–115) related uncertainty with conflict in organizations, affirming that uncertainty takes place when "the individual does not know the probability distributions connecting behavior choices and environmental outcomes". As we have already seen, in such a situation, the decision-maker is expected to increase his search activity in order to find new alternatives (see Sect. 3.2.2.2). In the same tradition, however, the phenomenon of uncertainty has been further elaborated and studied. A classical framework is given by Thompson and Tuden (1967),[55] who distinguished between uncertainty about goals—what March (1990a, p. 12) calls ambiguity about preferences (see also March 1978)—and uncertainty about means—ambiguity about relevance, in March's terms, which refers to an ambiguous account of the value of the terms of causal relation between actions or events.[56]

Elaborating on March's distinction, Heradstveit and Bonham (1986, p. 342) propose a different two-fold view of uncertainty: environmental uncertainty, which "stems from ambiguity that is inherent in the event", and outcome uncertainty, which "refers to disagreement about the existence and nature of cause-effect relationships". While the latter notion could be adopted here as it matches in an exact manner with Thompson and Tuden's uncertainty about means, the former notion of environmental uncertainty does not seem to add accuracy to the concept.[57] While uncertainty about goals might be interpreted as a problem of conflict within organizations as we have approached it (already touched in Sect. 3.3.3, and in consonance with March and

---

[55] Cited by Royer and Langley (2008, p. 253).

[56] Cf. Cohen et al. (1972) for the example about the garbage-can model. March (1990a) added two more ambiguities as complications in decision-making: ambiguity about history (interpretation of the past as a basis for predictions about the future), and ambiguity about interpretation (information misunderstandings). See also March (1978).

[57] In effect, it rather seems that Heradstveit and Bonham's concept of environmental uncertainty responds to a fusion between March's concepts of ambiguity about history and ambiguity about interpretation. It is uncertain whether this change would help to our own approach, so in principle it shall not be adopted here. However, Heradstveit and Bonham (1986, p. 344) give interesting methodological insights on cognitive mapping in relation to uncertainty.

Simon (1958)), uncertainty about means has been related to the "procedural" notion of routines (Royer and Langley 2008) that has been described in Sect. 3.3.4 above.

In this sense, uncertainty about means would imply lack of knowledge about the action—in the form of practices or processes—to be undertaken in order to solve a problem. According to the perspective on human problem solving already presented (see Sects. 3.2.3.4 and 3.2.2.2), both individuals and organizations process information in order to solve their problems. We have also seen that the process of solving the problem has at least two different moments. In the first one, the decision-maker will search for solutions in his long-term memory (LTM) in the form of patterns related to past problems and solutions attached to those problems. The second one is that when this search fails, the decision-maker will initiate the search for new alternatives or solutions.

We also saw that the extent to which an individual is able to recognize, associate, and retrieve information stored in his LTM and, thus, to propose a rapid solution makes the difference between a layman and an expert. In these terms, in conclusion, uncertainty about means is related to procedural rationality and to expertise.

3.3.6 Expertise

The analysis of the role of expertise in decision-making is not a novelty (e.g., de Groot 1978), and it received attention in artificial intelligence and cognitive science in the context of building expert systems (e.g., Kibler and Hall 1986; Carbonell 1986; Chandrasekaran 1986), exploring theories on discovery processes (e.g., Langley et al. 1987; Simon, 1993; Schunn and Anderson 1998; Langley 2001), proposing theories of learning (e.g., Winston 1982; Anderson 1989; Lebiere et al. 2003), as well as exploring the very nature of expertise in problem solving (e.g., Chi et al. 1982; Bédard and Chi 1992).[58]

In the late 1980s and early 1990s a number of students of decision making processes realized that behavioral and organizational explanations of decisions—such as the ones provided by Cyert and March (1963) and March and Simon (1958)—, despite being highly realistic and accurate in its whole approach, still failed when applied to actual and complex decision situations (Rosen et al. 2008).

To cite an early diagnosis for this situation, Klein and Calderwood (1991, p. 1018) asserted that

> the prevailing paradigms in decision research, based as they are in simplified and highly structured laboratory tasks, have limited utility in operational domains characterized by high time pressure, uncertainty, and ambiguity, continually changing conditions, ill-defined goals, and distributed decision responsibilities.

Since then, and elaborating on the pillars of organizational decision-making analysis, a slight variation of this approach has been producing a number of works that emphasize (a) the need for empirical observation of decision process in actual (naturalistic)

---

[58] See Feltovich et al. (2006) for a recent and thorough review of studies on expertise in psychology.

environments—hence they are referred to as naturalistic decision making (NDM) analysis; with the aim to (b) "understand how professionals are able to translate their experience into quality decisions within [those] 'real-world' environments" (Rosen et al. 2008, p. 212), thus pointing out the relevance of expertise in actual decision-making.[59] Therefore, organizational decision analysis and naturalistic decision analysis are to be seen as complementary, non exclusive, approaches.

In their early and seminal contribution to actual decisions with expertise, Klein and Calderwood (1991) proposed an empirical and realistic model of decision-making which emphasized the role of memory and pattern-recognition. Studying urban fire commanders' decision processes in time-pressure situations, they presented different models that explained ways in which people represented their understanding or recognition of the situation that preceded the decision. This process, then, is understood as a "matching process between situations and actions instead of the generation of, and choice from, the set of possible actions" (Rosen et al. 2008, p. 214).

This view is in clear contrast with other approaches that used models such as decision trees as an actual explanation of these processes, and emphasizes "the importance of understanding decision making in context" (Rosen et al. 2008, p. 213), namely in a real context. On the contrary, the naturalistic decision-making approach to expertise is coherent with other behavioral studies of this phenomenon. For instance, Michelene Chi and colleagues have produced an outstanding record of publications that relate expertise, knowledge organization, and problem representation.

In this line, Bédard and Chi (1992) assess that expert performance is not only a function of the amount of knowledge experts have with respect to novices, but that factors such as the organization of that knowledge are equally if not more relevant. Besides, the authors perform a very informative—and useful—overview of two relevant features in any account of expertise (comparing novices and experts). The first one, as we have already noted, is knowledge, not only focusing on the amount of domain knowledge but on its structure. The second one refers to problem-solving behavior, which includes problem representation, problem-solving strategies, and decision quality.

Rosen et al. (2008) review the two basic levels in which expertise has been approached. The first refers to expertise as "a function of extensive domain specific knowledge", represented by studies such as de Groot (1978) and Chase and Simon (1973). The second refers to the fact that the decision-maker's adaptation to the task demands enable expertise (Ericsson and Chi 1996), which in turns refers to the problem of uncertainty about means tacked in the previous section (see Sect. 3.3.5 above).

On the other hand, Chi (2006) makes another two-fold distinction in studies on expertise. One group of works are devoted to "study truly exceptional people with the goal of understanding how they perform in their domain of expertise", while a

[59] See, for instance, Currey and Botti (2003) for an application of naturalistic decision analysis in critical care nurses' decision making.

second perspective is devoted to "study experts in comparison ot novices [assuming] that expertise is a level of proficiency that novices can achieve".

According to this general framework, a number of studies have been devoted to different features of expertise, such as the development of cues that relate different tasks, the organization of the expert's knowledge base, pattern recognition, diagnostic feedback, problem representation and situation assessment, memory skills, automaticity in performance, and self-regulated processes. Moreover, a link has been established between expert performance, intuition, and the "dynamics of the problem and its context" (Sadler-Smith and Sparrow 2008, p. 315) in the sense that expert intuitive performance is not context-free but strongly context-dependent, for it will be the structure and the characteristics of the particular problem that will determine what particular path the expert will follow, i.e., the nature of the intuition (Klein and Calderwood 1991; Sadler-Smith and Sparrow 2008).[60]

3.4 Elements for an Organizational Decision Analysis

Wrapping up, in this chapter we have set forth the theoretical framework that is to background our attempt of a descriptive (i.e., neither normative nor prescriptive) decision analysis. We have explored the implications of separating the inner and outer environments in decision-making analysis. We have chosen the individual's skin as the boundary between the inner and the outer environment.

Regarding the inner environment, we saw that decisions are made with respect to a simplified model of the world (what March and Simon (1958, p. 139) call a "definition of the situation") required by the limits of human rationality.

In this direction, three different dimensions have been presented that explain the limits that shape human rationality. The first one refers to the cognitive limits humans have to process information, which are mostly viewed as limits in our capacity for attaining and learning concepts, storing and processing information, and processing natural language.

The second dimension accounts for the notion of *satisficing* as a mechanism of human bounded rationality. First, we have reviewed the critiques to those approaches that are based on unrealistic assumptions on human rationality such as preference consistency. Second, we have seen that a satisficing policy can also be seen as a trigger for search for better alternatives. In particular, satisficing is a way to decrease the complexity of problems by "weakening the requirements for solution" (Simon 1978, p. 12).

The third dimension tackles the difference between procedural rationality and substantive rationality and briefly presents a problem-solving theoretical framework

[60] Bédard and Chi (1992, p. 138) categorically assert that "[o]ne of the characteristics of expertise is that it is task specific. There appears to be little transfer from high-level proficiency in one domain to proficiency in other domains".

that helps understand the mechanisms individuals use in order to adapt to the constraints imposed by the outer environment. In particular, a theory of problem-solving has been presented that accounts for the way human beings selectively (heuristically) search for solutions in a 'space' provided by the problem to be solved.

Regarding the external environment, we started from the premise that the elements of this simplified model of the world are neither fixed nor given but are the outcomes of the interaction between the individual and his social and organizational environment (including his psychological outcomes) (Simon 1955; Cyert and Simon 1956). This is especially important in information-rich domains as the one we are interested in.

We argued that, as a consequence, only the analysis of the individual's adaptive problem-solving behavior would give us access to the characteristics and complexity of this external environment through the problems that spring from it (and that are perceived by the individual).

Nonetheless, we decided that a preliminary overview of the potential factors to be accounted for in our case study would be worth presenting. Our presentation was based upon our and others' previous observation of incomplete data pertaining to our case-study, and are to be understood as reasonable intuitions on a set of phenomena that shall be properly analyzed in the second part this book.

In our approach, we have started focusing on the organization as the most relevant part of the outer environment in the context of our work. First two major general factors have been identified that make rationality possible in an organizational environment:

- The organization's structure is a rather stable pattern of events enabling both predictability and stability of the behavior of the people that surrounds the decision-maker.
- The organizational frame reinforces the human tendency to split problems, tasks, and goals into smaller subparts, achieving a rather simplified model of the objective situation.

Later on, we have seen that there may be a number of problems that can challenge rationality in decision-making within organizations, and some mechanisms that typically counteract these phenomena have been briefly presented as they appear in the mainstream specialized literature on organizational decision analysis.

It has been concluded that our ulterior analysis should at least take into account three different potential phenomena, namely, (a) bottlenecks of attention—tasks and subtasks division, selective perception, and communication biases—that show that attention is a scarce resource; (b) mutually inconsistent preferences within the organization—departmentalization, time as a scarce resource, organizational slack; (c) the production and institutionalization of effective adaptive responses—routines, organizational memory—to particular situations.

Finally, two sections have been devoted to relate the former elements to two further phenomena that are potentially critical in our case. The first is uncertainty, mainly understood as lack of knowledge about the processes to be followed in order to solve a problem.

This notion of uncertainty has led us finally to our last section, devoted to expertise. This relation becomes clear when both uncertainty and expertise are understood as functions of procedural rationality, i.e., as functions of the process of search for alternatives by the decision-maker.

Globally, these features are seen as mechanisms that make organizations adaptive systems that are able to achieve goals and make decisions that otherwise (e.g. at an individual level) would have been very difficult, if possible, taking into consideration the picture we gave of human beings as boundedly rational, information-processing, problem-solving, adaptive organisms.

In conclusion, two final observations may be made at this point of research, one substantive and the other methodological.

First, we observe that behavioral literature on decision-making rarely presents decisions as made under conditions of absolute certainty, and in this respect we suggest that the amount of uncertainty surrounding a decision may be viewed as a function of the effectivity in which mechanisms for organizational bounded rationality succeed in that particular situation. In this sense, the relation between procedural rationality and uncertainty (Royer and Langley 2008), and then the relation of both with expertise seems critical in our empirical approach to decision-making in the interpretation phase.

Regarding the second observation, it is noteworthy that in our approach to the definition of the outer environment, we have pointed out the relevance of considering this environment's demands as they are perceived by the decision-maker. This commitment implies that our analysis will not be based upon 'objective' definitions of problems but rather on data gathering the decision-makers' perceptions of those problems.

The methodological and substantive implications of this approach will be apparent in the second part of the book.

References

Anderson, J. R. 1983. *The architecture of cognition*. Cambridge: Harvard University Press.

Anderson, J. R. 1987. Methodologies for studying human knowledge. *Behavioral and Brain Sciences* 10:467–505.

Anderson, J. R. 1989. A theory of the origins of human knowledge. *Artificial Intelligence* 40:313–351.

Anderson, J. R. 1996. ACT: A simple theory of complex cognition. *American Psychologist* 51 (4): 355–365.

Anderson, J. R. 2005. Human symbol manipulation within an integrated cognitive architecture. *Cognitive Science* 29 (3): 313–341.

Anderson, J. R., D. Bothell, M. D. Byrne, S. Douglass, C. Lebiere, and Y. Qin. 2004. An integrated theory of the mind. *Psychological Review* 111 (4): 1036–1060.

Anderson, J. R., and K. A. Gluck. 2001. What role do cognitive architectures play in intelligent tutoring systems? In *Cognition & instruction: Twenty-five years of progress*, ed. D., Klahr, and S. M. Carver, 227–262. Mahwah: Lawrence Erlbaum Associates.

Anderson, J. R., and M. Matessa. 1991. An iterative Bayesian algorithm for categorization. In *Concept formation: Knowledge and experience in unsupervised learning*, ed. D. Fisher, and M. Pazzani, 43–68. San Mateo: Morgan Kaufmann Publishers Inc.
Arrow, K. J. 1963. *Social choice and individual values*. 2nd ed. New York: Cowles Foundation.
Axelrod, R. 2006. *The evolution of cooperation*. Revised ed. New York: Basic Books.
Axelrod, R., and D. Dion. 1988. The further evolution of cooperation. *Science* 242 (4884): 1385–1390.
Axelrod, R., and W. D. Hamilton. 1981. The evolution of cooperation. *Science* 211:1390–1396.
Baier, V. E., J. G. March, and H. Sætren. 1986. Implementation and ambiguity. *Scandinavian Journal of Management Studies* 2:197–212.
Bardach, E. 1977. *The implementation game*. Cambridge: MIT Press.
Bédard, J., and M. T. H. Chi. 1992. Expertise. *Current Directions in Psychological Science* 1 (4): 135–139.
Belavkin, R. V., and F. E. Ritter. 2004. OPTIMIST: A new conflict resoution algorithm for ACT–R. http://citeseer.ist.psu.edu/698403.html. Accessed 10 July 2009.
Bell, D. E. 1988. Disappointment in decision making under uncertainty. In *Decision making: Descriptive, normative, and prescriptive interactions*, ed. D. E. Bell, H. Raiffa, and A. Tversky, 358–383. Cambridge: Cambridge University Press.
Bell, D. E., and H. Raiffa. 1988. Risky choice revisited. In *Decision making: Descriptive, normative, and prescriptive interactions*, ed. D. E. Bell, H. Raiffa, and A. Tversky, 99–112. Cambridge: Cambridge University Press.
Bendor, J., and T. H. Hammond. 1992. Rethinking Allison's models. *The American Political Science Review* 86 (2): 301–322.
Bendor, J., T. Moe, and K. Shotts. 2001. Recycling the garbage can: An assessment of the research program. *American Political Science Review* 95 (1): 169–190.
Brooks, R. A. 1981. Symbolic reasoning among 3-D models and 2-D images. *Artificial Intelligence* 17: 285–348.
Brower, G. H., and P. R. Cohen. 1982. Emotion influences in memory and thinking: Data and theory. In *Affect and cognition*, ed. M. S. Clark, and S. T. Fiske, 291–331. Hillsdale: Lawrence Erlbaum Associates.
Bruner, J. S., J. J. Goodnow, and G. A. Austin. 1986. *A study of thinking*. 2nd ed. New Brunswick: Transaction Books.
Buchanan, J. M., and G. Tullock. 1962. *The calculus of consent: Logical foundations of constitutional democracy*. Ann Arbor: University of Michigan Press.
Budiu, R., and J. R. Anderson. 2003. Verification of sentences containing anaphoric metaphors: An ACT-R computational model. In *Proceedings of the Fifth International Conference on Cognitive Modeling*, ed. D. Detje, D. Doerner, and H. Schaub, 39–44, Universitats-Verlag Bamberg, Bamberg, Germany.
Carbonell, J. G. 1986. Derivational analogy: A theory of reconstructive problem solving and expertise acquisition. In *Machine learning: An artificial intelligence approach*, vol. II, ed. R. S. Michalski, J. G. Carbonell, and T. M. Mitchell, 371–392. Los Altos: Morgan Kaufmann Publishers Inc.
Carrithers, C., and T. G. Bever. 1984. Eye-fixation patterns during reading confirm theories of language comprehension. *Cognitive Science* 8:157–172.
Casanovas, P., N. Casellas, J. -J. Vallbé, M. Poblet, F. Ramos, J. Gorroñogoitia, J. Contreras, M. Blázquez, and V. R. Benjamins 2005. Iuriservice II: Ontology development and architectural design. In *Proceedings of the International Conference on Artificial Intelligence and Law, ICAIL-05,AAAI-ACM*, 188–195, Bologna, Italy.
Castelfranchi, C., and R. Falcone. 2004. Founding autonomy: The dialectics between (social) environment and agent's architecture and powers. In *AUTONOMY 2003*, vol. LNAI 2969, M. Nickles, M. Rovatsos, and G. Weiss, 40–54, Berlin: Springer.

Castelfranchi, C., F. Guiardini, and F. Marzo. 2006. Symposium on 'Cognition and Rationality: Part I' Relationships between rational decisions, human motives, and emotions. *Mind & Society* 5:173–197.
Castelfranchi, C., and F. Paglieri. 2007. The role of beliefs in goal dynamics: prolegomena to a constructive theory of intentions. *Synthese* 155:237–263.
Chaiklin, S. 1984. On the nature of verbal rules and their role in problem solving. *Cognitive Science* 8:131–155.
Chandrasekaran, G. 1986. Generic tasks in knowledge-based reasoning. High-level building blocks for expert systems design. *IEEE Expert* 1 (3): 23–30.
Chase, W. G., and H. A. Simon. 1973. Perception in chess. *Cognitive Psychology* 4 (1): 55–81.
Chevaleyre, Y., U. Endriss, J. Lang, and N. Maudet. 2006. A short introduction to computational social choice. Research report, The Institute for Logic, Language and Computation, University of Amsterdam, Amsterdam, The Netherlands.
Chi, M. T. H. 2006. Laboratory methods for assessing experts' and novices' knowledge. In *Cambridge handbook of expertise and expert performance*, ed. K.A. Ericsson, N. Charness, P. Feltovich, and R. Hoffman, 167–184. New York: Cambridge University Press.
Chi, M. T. H., N. de Leeuw, M. -H. Chiu, and C. LaVancher. 1994. Eliciting self-explanations improves understanding. *Cognitive Science* 18:439–477.
Chi, M. T. H., R. Glaser, and E. Rees. 1982. Expertise in problem solving. In *Advances in the psychology of human intelligence*, vol. 1, ed. R. J. Sternberg, 7–75. Hillsdale: Erlbaum.
Christiansen, M. H., and N. Chater. 1999a. Connectionist natural language processing: The state of the art. *Cognitive Science* 23 (4): 417–437.
Christiansen, M. H., and N. Chater. 1999b. Toward a connectionist model of recursion in human linguistic performance. *Cognitive Science* 23 (2): 157–205.
Clark, H. H., and E. F. Schaefer. 1989. Contributing to discourse. *Cognitive Science* 13:259–294.
Clausner, T. C., and W. Croft. 1997. Productivity and schemacity in metaphors. *Cognitive Science* 21 (3): 247–282.
Cohen, M. D., J. G. March, and J. P. Olsen. 1972. A garbage can model of organizational choice. *Administrative Science Quarterly* 17 (1): 1–25.
Cox, G. W., and K. A. Shepsle. 2007. Majority cycling and agenda manipulation: Richard McKelvey's contributions and legacy. In *A positive change in political science: The legacy of Richard McKelvey's most influential writings*. Ann Arbor: University of Michigan Press.
Crozier, M. 1964. *The bureaucratic phenomenon*. Chicago: University of Chicago Press.
Currey, J., and M. Botti. 2003. Naturalistic decision making: A model to overcome methodological challenges in the study of critical care nurses' decision making about patients' hemodynamic status. *American Journal of Critical Care* 12 (3): 206–211.
Cyert, R., and J. G. March. 1955. Organizational structure and pricing behavior in an oligopolistic market. *American Economic Review* 45:129–139.
Cyert, R., and J. G. March. 1963. *A Behavioral Theory of the Firm*. Englewood Cliffs: Prentice-Hall.
Cyert, R. M., E. A. Feigenbaum, and J. G. March. 1959. Models in a behavioral theory of the firm. *Behavioral Science* 4 (2): 81–95.
Cyert, R. M., and H. A. Simon. 1956. Observation of a business decision. *The Journal of Business* 29 (4): 237–248.
Dale, R., and E. Reiter. 1995. Computational interpretations of the Gricean maxims in the generation of referring expressions. *Cognitive Science* 18:233–263.
Daniels, K. 2008. Affect and information processing. In *The Oxford handbook of organizational decision making*, ed. G. P. Hodgkinson, and W. H. Starbuck, 325–341. New York: Oxford University Press.
Dascal, M. 1989. On the roles of context and literal meaning in understanding. *Cognitive Science* 13:253–257.
De Dreu, C. K. W., and M. J., Gelfand, eds. 2007. *The psychology of conflict and conflict management in organizations*. London: Psychology Press.
de Groot, A. 1978. *Thought and choice in chess*, 2nd ed. The Hague: Mouton de Gruyter.

DiMaggio, P. J., and W. W. Powell. 1991. Introduction. In *The New Institutionalism: organizational factors in political life*, ed. W. W. Powell, and P. J. DiMaggio, 1–38. Chicago: University of Chicago Press.
Downs, A. 1957. *An economic theory of democracy*. New York: Harper and Row.
Downs, A. 1967. *Inside bureaucracy*. Brown: Little.
Doyle, J. 1999. Bounded rationality. In *The MIT encyclopedia of the cognitive sciences*, ed. R. A. Wilson, and F. C. Keil, 92–94. Cambridge: MIT Press.
Druckman, J. N. 2004. Political preference formation: Competition, deliberation, and the (ir)relevance of framing effects. *American Political Science Review* 98:671–681.
Dyer, M. G. 1983a. *In-depth understanding*. Cambridge: MIT Press.
Dyer, M. G. 1983b. The role of affect in narratives. *Cognitive Science* 7:211–242.
Ericsson, K. A., and M. T. H. Chi. 1996. Expert and exceptional performance: Evidence of maximal adaptation to task constraints. *Annual Review of Psychology* 47:273–305.
Eysenck, M. W., eds. 1990. *The Blackwell dictionary of cognitive psychology*. Oxford: Basil Blackwell.
Feigenbaum, E. A., and H. A. Simon. 1984. EPAM-like models of recognition and learning. *Cognitive Science* 8:305–336.
Feltovich, P., M. J. Prietula, and K. A. Ericsson. 2006. Studies of expertise from psychological perspectives. In *Cambridge handbook of expertise and expert performance*, ed. K. A. Ericsson, N. Charness, P. Feltovich, and R. Hoffman. New York: Cambridge University Press.
Fernández-Duque, D., and M. L. Johnson. 1999. Attention metaphors: How metaphors guide the cognitive psychology of attention. *Cognitive Science* 23 (1): 83–116.
Fishburn, P. C. 1988. Normative theories of decision making under risk and under uncertainty. In *Decision making: Descriptive, normative, and prescriptive interactions*, ed. D. E. Bell, H. Raiffa, and A. Tversky, 78–98. Cambridge: Cambridge University Press.
Friedman, M., and L. J. Savage. 1952. The expected-utility hypothesis and the measurability of utility. *The Journal of Political Economy* 60 (6): 463–474.
Gärdenfors, P. 2004. *Conceptual spaces. The geometry of thought*. Cambridge: MIT Press.
Gerken, L., and T. G. Bever. 1986. Linguistic intuitions are the result of interactions between perceptual processes and linguistic universals. *Cognitive Science* 10:457–476.
Gerrig, R. J. 1989. Empirical constraints on computational theories of metaphor: Comments on Indurkhya. *Cognitive Science* 13:235–241.
Gibbs, R. W. 1984. Literal meaning and psychological theory. *Cognitive Science* 8:275–304.
Gibbs, R. W. 1989. Understanding and literal meaning. *Cognitive Science* 13:243–251.
Glimcher, P. 2003. *Decisions, uncertainty, and the brain. The science of neuroeconomics*. Cambridge: MIT Press.
Gordon, P. C., and R. Hendrick. 1998. The representation and processing of coreference in discourse. *Cognitive Science* 22 (4): 389–424.
Gupta, P., and D. S. Touretzky. 1994. Connectionist models and linguistic theory: Investigations of stress systems in language. *Cognitive Science* 18:1–50.
Hahn, M., R. Lawson, and Y. G. Lee. 1992. The effects of time pressure and information load on decision quality. *Psychology & Marketing* 9 (5): 365–378.
Hampton, J. A. 1999. Concepts. In *The MIT encyclopedia of the cognitive sciences*, ed. R. A. Wilson, and F. C. Keil, 176–179. Cambridge: MIT Press.
Harrison, J. R., and J. G. March. 1984. Decision-making and post-decision surprises. *Administrative Science Quarterly* 29:26–42.
Hayek, F. A. 1945. The use of knowledge in society. *The American Economic Review* 35 (4): 519–530.
Heradstveit, D., and M. Bonham. 1986. Decision-making in the face of uncertainty: Attributions of Norwegian and American officials. *Journal of Peace Research* 23 (4): 339–356.
Herskovits, A. 1985. Semantics and pragmatics of locative expressions. *Cognitive Science* 9:341–378.

Hidi, S., and W. Baird. 1986. Interestingness—a neglected variable in discourse processing. *Cognitive Science* 10:179–194.
Hirshleifer, J., and J. Riley. 1979. The analytics of uncertainty and information—an expository survey. *Journal of Economic Literature* 17 (4): 1375–1421.
Hodgkinson, G. P., and W. H. Starbuck, eds. 2008. *The Oxford handbook of organizational decision making*. New York: Oxford University Press.
Hymes, D. 1977. *Foundations in sociolinguistics: An ethnographic approach*. London: Tavistock Publications Ltd.
Indurkhya, B. 1987. Approximate semantic transference: A computational theory of metaphors and analogies. *Cognitive Science* 11:445–480.
John, G. H., and P. Langley. 1995. Estimating continuous distributions in Bayesian classifiers. *Proceedings of the Eleventh Conference on Uncertainty in Artificial Intelligence*, 338–345, Morgan Kaufmann, Montreal, Canada.
Jones, D. M. 2002. The 7 plus minus 2 urban legend. In *MISRA C Conference*. Knowledge Software.
Jurafsky, D. 1996. A probabilistic model of lexical and syntactic access and disambiguation. *Cognitive Science* 20:137–194.
Kahneman, D. 2003a. Maps of bounded rationality: Psychology for behavioral economics. *The American Economic Review* 93 (5): 1449–1475.
Kahneman, D. 2003b. A psychological perspective on economics. *The American Economic Review (Papers and Proceedings of the One Hundred Fifteenth Annual Meeting of the American Economic Association)* 93 (2): 162–168.
Kahneman, D. 2012. *Thinking, fast and slow*. London: Penguin Books.
Kahneman, D., and R. Thaler. 1991. Economic analysis and the psychology of utility: Applications to compensantion policy. *The American Economic Review (Papers and Proceedings of the Hundred and Third Annual Meeting of the American Economic Association)* 81 (2): 341–346.
Kahneman, D., and A. Tversky. 1979. Prospect theory: An analysis of decision under risk. *Econometrica* 47 (2): 263–291.
Kahneman, D., P. Slovic, and A. Tversky, eds. 1982. *Judgment under uncertainty: Heuristics and biases*. Cambridge: Cambridge University Press.
Kahneman, D., P. Wakker, and R. Sarin. 1997. Back to bentham? Explorations of experienced utility. *The Quarterly Journal of Economics* 112 (2. In Memory of Amos Tversky (1937–1996)): 375–405.
Kibler, D., and R. P. Hall. 1986. A model of acquiring problem solving expertise. In *Machine learning: A guide to current research*, 137–140. Norwell: Kluwer Academic Publishers.
Klein, G. A., and R. Calderwood. 1991. Decision models: Some lessons from the field. *IEEE Transactions on Systems, Man, and Cybernetics* 21 (5): 1018–1026.
Kock, N. 2000. Information overload and worker performance: A process-centered view. *Knowledge and Process Management* 7 (4): 256–264.
Kolodner, J. L. 1983. Reconstructive memory: A computer model. *Cognitive Science* 7:280–328.
Laird, J. E., A. Newell, and P. S. Rosenbloom. 1987. SOAR: An architecture for general intelligence. *Artificial Intelligence* 33:1–64.
Lakoff, G., and M. Johnson. 1980. The metaphorical structure of the human conceptual system. *Cognitive Science* 4:195–208.
Lang, J. 2005. Some representation and computational issues in social choice. In *Proceedings of the Eighth European Conference on Symbolic and Quantitative Approaches to Reasoning with Uncertainty (ECSQARU)*, Barcelona.
Langacker, R. W. 1986. An introduction to cognitive grammar. *Cognitive Science* 10:1–40.
Langley, P. 2001. Heuristics for scientific discovery: The legacy of Herbert Simon. Presented at the Twenty-Third Annual Conference of the Cognitive Science Society.
Langley, P., D. Choi, and D. Shapiro. 2004. A cognitive architecture for physical agents. Technical report, Institute for the Study of Learning and Expertise, Palo Alto, CA.
Langley, P., and S. Rogers. 2005. An extended theory of human problem solving. *Proceedings of the Twenty-Seventh Annual Meeting of the Cognitive Science Society*, Stresa, Italy.

Langley, P., and S. Sage. 1994. Induction of selective Bayesian classifiers. In *Proceedings of the Tenth Conference on Uncertainty in Artificial Intelligence*, 399–406, Morgan Kaufmann, Seattle, WA.

Langley, P., H. A. Simon, G. L. Bradshaw, and J. M. Zytkow. 1987. *Scientific discovery: Computational explorations of the creative process*. Cambridge: MIT Press.

Lebiere, C., R. Gray, D. Salvucci, and R. West. 2003. Choice and learning under uncertainty: A case study in baseball batting. *Proceedings of the Annual Meeting of the Cognitive Science Society*, 704–709.

Lebowitz, M. 1986. Concept learning in a rich input domain: Generalization-based memory. In *Machine learning: An artificial intelligence approach*, vol. II, ed. R. S. Michalski, J. G. Carbonell, and T. M. Mitchell, 193–214, Morgan Kaufmann Publishers Inc., Los Altos, CA.

Levinthal, D., and J. G. March. 1981. A model of adaptive organizational search. *Journal of Economic Behavior and Organization* 2 (4): 307–333.

Levitt, B., and J. G. March. 1988. Organizational learning. *Annual Review of Sociology* 14:319–340.

Lipset, S. M. 1983. *Political man: The social bases of politics*. 2nd ed. London: Heinemann.

Lipshitz, R., and N. Shulimovitz. 2005. Intuition and emotion in bank loan officers' credit decisions. *Cognitive Engineering & Decision Making* 1 (2): 212–233.

Lovett, M. 1998. Choice: Elaborating ACT-R's theory of choice. In *The atomic components of thought*, ed. J. R. Anderson, and C. Lebiere, 255–296. Mahwah: Erlbaum.

Lowe, W. 2003. Uncertainty. In *Encyclopedia of social science research methods*. Thousand Oaks: Sage.

Manns, C. L., and J. G. March. 1978. Financial adversity, internal competition, and curriculum change in a university. *Administrative Science Quarterly* 23:541–552.

March J. G.. 1954. Group norms and the active minority. *American Sociological Review* 19 (6): 733–741.

March J. G. 1955. An introduction to the theory and measurement of influence. *The American Political Science Review* 49 (2): 431–451.

March J. G. 1956. Influence measurement in experimental and semi-experimental groups. *Sociometry* 19 (4): 260–271.

March J. G. 1957. Measurement concepts in the theory of influence. *The Journal of Politics* 19 (2): 202–226.

March J. G. 1962. The business firm as a political coalition. *The Journal of Politics* 24 (4): 662–678.

March J. G. 1966. The power of power. In *Varieties of political theory*, ed. D. Easton, 39–70. Englewood Cliffs: Prentice-Hall.

March J. G. 1978. Bounded rationality, ambiguity, and the engineering of choice. *The Bell Journal of Economics* 9 (2): 587–608.

March J. G. 1981. Footnotes to organizational change. *Administrative Science Quarterly* 26:563–577.

March J. G. 1990a. *Decisions and organizations*. Oxford: Basil Blackwell.

March J. G. 1990b. Introduction: a chronicle of speculations about decision-making in organizations. In *Decisions and organizations*, 1–21. Oxford: Basil Blackwell.

March J. G., and E. A. Feigenbaum. 1960. Latent motives, group discussion, and the "quality" of group decisions in a non-objective decision problem. *Sociometry* 23 (1): 50–56.

March J. G., and J. P. Olsen. 1984. The new institutionalism: Organizational factors in political life. *The American Political Science Review* 78 (3): 734–749.

March J. G., and J. P. Olsen. 1998. The institutional dynamics of international political orders. *International Organization* 52 (4): 943–969.

March J. G., and J. P. Olsen. 2006a. Elaborating the "new institutionalism". In *The Oxford handbook of political institutions*, ed. R. A. W. Rhodes, S. A. Binder, and B. A. Rockman, 3–20. Oxford: Oxford University Press.

March J. G., and J. P. Olsen. 2006b. The logic of appropriateness. In *The Oxford handbook of public policy*, ed. M. Moran, M. Rein, and R. E. Goodin, 689–708. New York: Oxford University Press.

March J. G., and Z. Shapira. 1987. Managerial perspectives on risk and risk-taking. *Management Science* 33 (11): 1404–1418.
March J. G., and H. A. Simon. 1958. *Organizations*. New York: Wiley.
Marcus, G. E. 1988. The structure of emotional response: 1984 presidential elections. *The American Political Science Review* 82 (3): 737–761.
Marcus, G. E. 2000. Emotions in politics. *Annual Review of Political Science* 3:221–250.
Martin, J. H. 1992. Computer understanding of conventional metaphoric language. *Cognitive Science* 16:233–270.
Mayntz, R. 1976. Environmental policy conflicts: The case of the German Federal Republic. *Policy Analysis* 2:577–588.
Medin, D. L., and C. Aguilar. 1999. Categorization. In *The MIT encyclopedia of the Cognitive Sciences*, ed. R. A. Wilson, and F. C. Keil, 104–106. Cambridge: MIT Press.
Michalski, R. S. 1987. Concept learning. In *The encyclopedia of artificial intelligence*, ed. S. C. Shapiro, 185–194. New York: Wiley.
Miikkulainen, R., and M. G. Dyer. 1991. Natural language processing with modular PDP networks and distributed lexicon. *Cognitive Science* 15:343–399.
Miller, G. A. 1956. The magical number seven, plus or minus two: Some limits on our capacity for processing information. *The Psychological Review* 63:81–97.
Morrow, D. G. 1986. Grammatical morphemes and conceptual structure in discourse processing. *Cognitive Science* 10:423–455.
Newell, A. 1980. Physical symbol systems. *Cognitive Science* 4:135–183.
Newell, A. 1981. Additional notes on physical symbol systems. Document from The Allen Newell Collection, Department of Computer Science, Carnegie Mellon University, Pittsburgh, PA.
Newell, A. 1990. *Unified theories of cognition*. Cambridge: Harvard University Press.
Newell, A. 1992. Précis of UNIFIED THEORIES OF COGNITION. *Behavioral and Brain Sciences* 15:425–492.
Newell, A., J. C. Shaw, and H. A. Simon. 1958a. Elements of a theory of human problem solving. *The Psychological Review* 65:151–166.
Newell, A., J. C. Shaw, and H. A. Simon. 1958b. Report on a General Problem Solving program. Technical Report P-1584, RAND Corporation, Santa Monica, CA.
Newell, A., and H. A. Simon. 1972. *Human problem solving*. Englewood Cliffs: Prentice-Hall.
Newell, A., and H. A. Simon. 1976. Computer science as empirical enquiry: Symbols and search. *Communications of the Association for Computing Machinery* 19 (3): 113–126.
Noriega, P. 2006. Introducción para la edición en castellano. In *Las ciencias de lo artificial*, ed. H. A. Simon. Granada: Ed. Comares.
Olsen, J. P. 2001. Garbage cans, new institutionalism, and the study of politics. *American Political Science Review* 95 (1): 191–198.
Ourusoff, N. 1985. The physical symbol system hypothesis of Newell and Simon: A classroom demonstration of artificial intelligence. *SIGCSE Bulletin* 17 (3): 19–23.
Pfeifer, R. 1982. Cognition and emotion: An information processing approach. CIP Working Paper 436, Carnegie Mellon University, Pittsburgh, PA.
Popper, K. R. 1961. *The poverty of historicism*. Kegal Paul: Routledge.
Pylyshyn, Z. 1984. *Computation and cognition, toward a foundation for cognitive science*. Cambridge: MIT Press.
Quattrone, G., and A. Tversky. 1988. Contrasting rational and psychological analyses of political choice. *The American Political Science Review* 82 (3): 719–736.
Raiffa, H. 1970. *Decision analysis: Introductory readings on choices under uncertainty*. 2nd ed. Reading: Addison Wesley.
Riesbeck, C. 1980. "you can't miss it!" Judging the clarity of directions. *Cognitive Science* 4:285–303.
Rodrigo, L., M. Blázquez, P. Casanovas, and M. Poblet. 2004. D10.1.1 Legal case study before analysis, semantically enabled knowledge technologies. Technical Report, EU-IST Project IST-2003-506826 SEKT.

Rosen, M. A., E. Salas, R. Lyons, and S. M. Fiore 2008. Experts and naturalistic decision making in organizations: Mechanisms of effective decision making. In *The Oxford handbook of organizational decision making*, ed. G. P. Hodgkinson, and W. H. Starbuck, 211–230. New York: Oxford University Press.

Royer, I., and A. Langley. 2008. Linking rationality, politics, and routines in organizational decision making. In *The Oxford handbook of organizational decision making*, ed. G. P. Hodgkinson, and W. H. Starbuck, 250–270. New York: Oxford University Press.

Rumelhart, D. E. 1989. The architecture of mind: A connectionist approach, Chap. 4. In *Foundations of cognitive science*, ed. M. Posner, 133–159. Cambridge: MIT Press.

Sadler-Smith, E., and P. R. Sparrow. 2008. Intuition in organizational decision making. In *The Oxford handbook of organizational decision making*, ed. G. P. Hodgkinson, and W. H. Starbuck, 305–324. New York: Oxford University Press.

Sampson, G. 2001. *Empirical linguistics*. London: Continuum International.

Sanders, D. 1998. International relations: Neo-realism and neo-liberalism. In *A new handbook of political science*, ed. R. E. Goodin, and H. -D. Klingemann, 428–445. Oxford: Oxford University Press.

Savage, L. J. 1951. The theory of statistical decision. *Journal of the American Statistical Association* XLVI:55–67.

Savage, L. J. 1954. *The foundations of statistics*. New York: Wiley.

Schank, R. C. 1980. Language and memory. *Cognitive Science* 4:243–284.

Schunn, C. D., and J. R. Anderson. 1998. Scientific discovery. In *The atomic components of thought*, ed. J. R. Anderson, and C. Lebiere, 385–428. Mahwah: Erlbaum.

Selznick, P. 1943. An approach to a theory of bureaucracy. *American Sociological Review* 8 (1): 47–54.

Selznick, P. 1948. Foundations of the theory of organization. *American Sociological Review* 13 (1): 25–35.

Shafer, G. 1984. Review of "Judgment under uncertainty: Heuristics and biases". *Journal of the American Statistical Association* 79 (385): 223–224.

Shafir, E. 1999. Decision making. In *The MIT encyclopedia of the cognitive sciences*, ed. R. A. Wilson, and F. C. Keil, 220–223. Cambridge: MIT Press.

Shapira, Z. 1981. Making trade-offs between job attributes. *Organizational Behavior and Human Performance* 28:331–355.

Shapira, Z. 2008. On the implications of behavioral decision theory for managerial decision making: Contributions and challenges. In *The Oxford handbook of organizational decision making*, ed. G. P. Hodgkinson, and W. H. Starbuck, 287–304. New York: Oxford University Press.

Shepsle, K. 1985. Prospects for formal models of legislatures. *Legislative Studies Quarterly* 10 (1): 5–19.

Shepsle, K. 2006. Rational choice institutionalism. In *The Oxford handbook of political institutions*, ed. R. A. W. Rhodes, S. A. Binder, and B. A. Rockman, 23–38. Oxford: Oxford University Press.

Shepsle, K., and B. Weingast. 1982. Institutionalizing majority rule: A social choice theory with policy implications. *The American Economic Review* 72 (2): 367–371.

Simon, H. A. 1947. *Administrative behavior: A study of decision-making processes in administrative organizations*. 1st ed. New York: Macmillan.

Simon, H. A. 1951. A formal theory of the employment relationship. *Econometrica* 19 (3): 293–305.

Simon, H. A. 1955. A behavioral model of rational choice. *The Quarterly Journal of Economics* 69 (1): 99–118.

Simon, H. A. 1957. Rational choice and the structure of the environment. In *Models of man, social and rational*, 261–273. New York: Wiley.

Simon, H. A. 1961. Human cognition and problem solving. The Voice of America Lectures, Control of the Mind Series 16, University of California Medical School.

Simon, H. A. 1967. Motivational and emotional controls of cognition. *Psychological Review* 74:29–39.

Simon, H. A. 1973. Does scientific discovery have a logic? *Philosophy of Science* 40 (4): 471–480.

Simon, H. A. 1976. From substantial to procedural rationality. In *Method and appraisal in economics*, ed. S. J. Latsis, 65–86. Cambridge: Cambridge University Press.

Simon, H. A. 1978. Rationality as process and as product of thought. *The American Economic Review (Papers and Proceedings of the Ninetieth Annual Meeting of the American Economic Association)* 68 (2): 1–16.

Simon, H. A. 1979. Rational decision making in business organizations. *The American Economic Review* 69 (4): 493–513.

Simon, H. A. 1980. Cognitive science: The newest science of the artificial. *Cognitive Science* 4 (1): 33–46.

Simon, H. A. 1983. *Reason in human affairs*. Stanford: Stanford University Press.

Simon, H. A. 1992. The bottleneck of attention: Connecting thought with motivation. Research report, Carnegie Mellon University/National Science Foundation/DARPA, Pittsburgh, PA.

Simon, H. A. 1993. *Adaptive Strategies in Thought and Processes*. Number 9 in Comunicazioni Scientifiche di Psicologia Generale. Università degli Studi di Roma 'La Sapienza', Facolta di Psicologia. Edizioni Scientifiche Italiane, Roma.

Simon, H. A. 1996a. *Models of my life*. Cambridge: MIT Press.

Simon, H. A. 1996b. *The sciences of the artificial*. 3rd ed. Cambridge: MIT Press.

Simon, H. A. 1997. *Administrative behavior: A study of decision-making processes in administrative organizations*. 4th ed. New York: The Free Press.

Simon, H. A., and A. Newell. 1958. Heuristic problem solving: The next advance in operations research. *Operations Research* 6 (1): 1–10.

Simon, H. A., and A. Newell. 1971. Human problem solving: The state of the theory in 1970. *American Psychologist* 26 (2): 145–159.

Smolensky, P. 1999. Grammar-based connectionist approaches to language. *Cognitive Science* 23 (4): 589–613.

Speier, C., J. S. Valacich, and I. Vessey. 1999. The influence of task interruption on individual decision making: An information overload perspective. *Decision Sciences* 30 (2): 337–360.

Stanovich, K. E., and R. F. West. 2000. Individual differences in reasoning: Implications for the rationality debate? *Behavioral and Brain Sciences* 23:645–726.

Stone, M. 2004. Intention, interpretation and the computational structure of language. *Cognitive Science* 28:781–809.

Sutcliffe, K. M., and G. McNamara. 2001. Controlling decision-making practice in organizations. *Organization Science* 12 (4): 484–501.

Sutcliffe, K. M., and K. E. Weick. 2008. Information overload revisited. In *The Oxford handbook of organizational decision making*, ed. G. P. Hodgkinson, and W. H. Starbuck, 56–75. New York: Oxford University Press.

Tummolini, L., and C. Castelfranchi. 2006. The cognitive and behavioral mediation of institutions: Towards an account of institutional actions. *Cognitive Systems Research* 7 (2–3): 307–323.

Tversky, A. 1974. Assessing uncertainty. *Journal of the Royal Statistical Society. Series B (Methodological)* 36 (2): 148–159.

Tversky, A., and D. Kahneman. 1974. Judgment under uncertainty: Heuristics and biases. *Science* 185:1124–1131.

Tversky, A., and D. Kahneman. 1981. The framing of decisions and the psychology of choice. *Science* 211:453–458.

Tversky, A., and D. Kahneman. 1986. Rational choice and the framing of decisions. *The Journal of Business* 59 (4. Part 2: The Behavioral Foundations of Economic Theory): S251–S278.

Tversky, A., and D. Kahneman. 1991. Loss aversion in riskless choice: A reference-dependent model. *The Quarterly Journal of Economics* 106 (4): 1039–1061.

Tversky, A., P. Slovic, and D. Kahneman. 1990. The causes of preferences reversal. *The American Economic Review* 80 (1): 204–217.

von Mises, L. 1996. *Bureaucracy*. Grove City: Libertarian Press, Inc.

Weber, M. 1978a. *Economy and society: An outline of interpretive sociology*, vol. 2. Berkeley: University of California Press.

Weber, M. 1978b. *Economy and society: An outline of interpretive sociology*, vol. 1. Berkeley: University of California Press.

Weingast, B. 1998. Political institutions: Rational choice perspectives. In *A new handbook of political science*, ed. R. E. Goodin, and H. -D. Klingemann, 167–190. Oxford: Oxford University Press.

Weirich, P. 2004. Economic rationality. In *The Oxford handbook of rationality*, Chap. 20, ed. A. R. Mele, and P. Rawling. New York: Oxford University Press.

Wellman, M. P. 1999. Utility theory. In *The MIT encyclopedia of the cognitive sciences*, ed. R. A. Wilson, and F. C. Keilpages, 859–861. Cambridge: MIT Press.

Wilson, R. A., and F. C. Keil, eds. 1999. *The MIT encyclopedia of the cognitive sciences*. Cambridge: MIT Press.

Winograd, T. 1972. *Understanding natural language*. New York: Academic.

Winograd, T. 1980. What does it mean to understand natural language? *Cognitive Science* 4:209–241.

Winograd, T., and F. Flores. 1986. *Understanding computers and cognition: A new foundation for design*. Norwood: Ablex Publishing Corporation.

Winston, P. H. 1982. Learning new principles from precedents and exercises. *Artificial Intelligence* 19:321–350.

Part II
Data Analysis

Chapter 4
Empirical Context

Abstract This chapter provides all the contextual information and data necessary to carry out the empirical analysis in this book. The main objectives of this chapter are, first, to familiarize the reader with both the organizational context under study (the Spanish judicial system) and with the main characteristics of Spanish junior judges as a professional body; second, to explore whether problems raised during judges' daily practice can be explained either by individual characteristics of junior judges (e.g., education) or by specific features of the locations in which they carry out their jobs.

4.1 Introduction

Spain's transition from an authoritarian regime to a democracy had an obvious impact on the possibility of carrying out research projects on institutions—whether political or not—and on social and political elites. In this direction, a great deal of research has been carried out on religion and religious communities (e.g., Hermet 1985; García Herrando 1993; Estruch 1993) voters (e.g., Linz and Montero 1986; Montero 1998; Gunther et al. 2004; Penella 2005; Muñoz-Mendoza 2012), associations (e.g., Montero et al. 2006), political parties (e.g., Linz and Montero 1999; Gunther et al. 2002), labor organizations (e.g., Cerviño Cuerva 2003), political elites (Capo 1981; Matas 1995; Magre 1999; Reniu 2001; Calvet 2005), and specific features of the performance of political institutions (e.g., Magre 2006), just to mention an excellent achievement). Finally, the recent and thorough approach to the Spanish army's NCOs (Martínez 2007) is to be seen as quite an achievement regarding one of the hitherto almost unexplored Spanish institutions.

José Juan Toharia's doctoral dissertation at Yale University in 1974 (Toharia Cortés 1975) was the first systematic approach to Spanish judiciary in the history of Spanish social sciences.[1] Since then, there has certainly been a great deal of social research on different aspects of Spanish legal culture, including the pragmatic study of certain

[1] (Toharia Cortés 1975) is the abridged Spanish version of that dissertation.

J.-J. Vallbé, *Frameworks for Modeling Cognition and Decisions in Institutional Environments*, Law, Governance and Technology Series 21, DOI 10.1007/978-94-017-9427-5_4

judicial decisions including jury (Casanovas 1997, 2000), [2] or the cost of litigation in Spain (Pastor-Prieto 1993).

Since 1984, the General Council of the Judiciary (the governing body for the Spanish judiciary) has carried out nine in-depth opinion surveys among the Spanish population about the administration of justice; besides, seven internal surveys among Spanish judges about numerous aspects of their professional activity have been also completed (Toharia Cortés and García de la Cruz Herrero 2005). This means that virtually all research done on Spanish judges in Spain has been either promoted and published by the Spanish General Council of the Judiciary (e.g., CIS 1984; Demoscopia 1999), or based on the Council's official data sets (e.g., Toharia Cortés 1987, 2006).

Yet regarding Spanish junior judges specifically, it was not until 2001 that a first wide survey on junior judges—out of official records from the Spanish Judicial School, though in collaboration with this institution—took place that focused upon their experiences in their first appointments, their opinions on their education, and the main problems they faced in their workplaces.[3]

Open-ended questions were placed throughout the questionnaire covering all of its parts. These questions enabled the interviewee to give more or less elaborated responses to particular questions. Ayuso et al. (2002) consider that this way "less stereotyped responses are thus obtained, which show the perception judges have about their professional problems in a much sharper way than it is the case when the same problems are dealt with closed questions". Therefore, open questions were to be seen as a complement to the main corpus of (closed) questions. A general conclusion from judges' responses to open-ended questions was that the on-call period was specially regarded as problematic by judges (Benjamins et al. 2004a)—specially junior judges—, and that this was an important topic worth considering for future research in the field (Ayuso et al. 2002, 2003).

This conclusion bound the design of a second questionnaire specifically addressed to junior judges who were still working at their first appointments and that might help gaining a better understanding of the specific problems junior judges encountered during their first two professional years as judges at court. The data from this second survey are the one we use in this book.

This chapter provides all the contextual information and data necessary to bring forth our analysis, and has two main objectives. On one hand, the chapter is designed to familiarize the reader with both the organizational context under study (the Spanish judicial system, Sect. 4.2) and with the main characteristics of Spanish junior judges

[2] Actually, Casanovas (1995) proposed a social scientific (and actually behavioral) research framework linking the study of Spanish legal institutions as decisions to some of Herbert Simon's insights about organizational decision making. See also Casanovas (2001).

[3] I would like to thank Drs. Mercedes Ayuso (UB) and Mónica Bécue (UPC) for their help and permission to have full access to their database for this work. The results of this survey were reported by Ayuso et al. (2003) and (2002) as internal reports for the Spanish General Council of the Judiciary, and by Álvarez et al. (2005) in a collection volume on law and technology.

as a professional body (Sect. 4.4). On the other hand, as explained in the introduction of this book, previous research (Ayuso et al. 2002, 2003) has provided some ground to support the idea that junior judges perceive the on-call service as the source of most of their professional problems. However, no research so far has explored whether doubts in decision-making among junior judges may be explained either by individual characteristics of junior judges (e.g., education) or by specific features of the locations in which they carry out their jobs (e.g., population density). To explore this issue is the second objective of this chapter (Sect. 4.5).

4.2 The Spanish Judicial System

4.2.1 The Spanish Legal System

Spain began its path to become a democracy at general Franco's death in the late 1975, and it was formally declared a parliamentary democracy with the official enactment of the 1978 Spanish Constitution. The transitional process from an authoritarian to a democratic regime in Spain implied major changes within the main social and political institutions of the country itself (see Tezanos et al. 1989). For instance, a strongly centralized political organization gave way to a progressive political decentralization originating the creation of 17 so-called autonomous communities, new political entities conceived of between the simple and highly dependent French regions and the more autonomous federal *länder*. Despite a similar model was very shortly applied during the 2nd Republic in the 1930s, and despite Spain's social, political, and cultural heterogeneity,[4] this "autonomous" organization was quite a new thing in modern Spanish political history.

All autonomous communities have both legislative ability—i.e., are able to pass bills on a number of matters—and executive autonomy on their own matters. Thus apart from the Spanish High Chamber [*Senado*] and the Low Chamber [*Congreso de los Diputados*]—which can only legislate on matters that are the State's exclusive competence—, 17 further legislative assemblies sprung up, every one of them being able to legislate—among other things—on the rules that govern their own organization and manner of work. All the 17 autonomous legislative bodies are unicameral. Finally, their basic organization is established in statutes of autonomy, which have a high rank in the Spanish legal system—at the level of *Ley Orgánica*—but they are not officially federal constitutions.[5]

Along with this organizational change, obviously the new democracy brought also deep changes in the operation of its main legislative and executive branches. Yet while law and lawmakers were rapidly changing, "the newly inaugurated democracy

[4] Lancaster (2002, p. 1513) comments that "given this heterogeneity, Spain is best described as a multinational state".

[5] Spanish Constitution, arts. 146 and 147.

did not bring about a substantial transformation of the judicial system" (Poblet and Casanovas 2005, p. 186). In effect, the main features of the Spanish judicial system have remained essentially untouched in the last two centuries (Toharia Cortés 1975, 2003).[6]

In a few words, Spain's legal system is part of the mainstream of European civil law systems, specially of the "napoleonic" kind (Toharia Cortés 2003, p. 307). Toharia Cortés (1989) gives a succinct description of this system:

> Justice emanates from the people and it is administered in the name of the king by a self-governing body of independent, responsible, and professional judges, in accordance with certain principles and criteria (such as absence of judicial creativity, subjection to a specific set of "sources of the law", appeals, written opinions expressing reasons, popular participation in some criminal cases, free access, publicity, and, in the criminal area, the inquisitorial system) within a system of courts comprising four specialized areas (civil, criminal, labor, and administrative) and subject to review in matters concerning basic individual rights by the *Tribunal Constitutional* (Constitutional Court).

Therefore, among the two distinct, modern legal traditions of the democratic world—civil law and common law—, Spanish judges are of the former kind. It means that, in contrast to the common law tradition, civil law judges are integrated in a bigger bureaucratic organization (the State) of which they are a branch. Particularly, it is a judge that may be defined as "a specialized civil servant [who] decides the cases brought to him by applying a body of written legal norms, which is assumed to provide a complete and coherent repertoire of solutions; his functional orientation is inquisitorial and conflict solving" (Toharia Cortés 2001, p. 8017).

In the first systematic approach to the figure of the Spanish judge, Toharia Cortés (1975); Toharia Cortés (2003) pointed out three basic features of the Spanish judge that, while amidst the civil law tradition, made him quite special.

In a few words, the first characteristic refers to the judges' bureaucratic tradition, in the sense that in contrast with other bureaucratic systems such as the French (which originated from the 1789 revolution), in Spain judges have *always* been public servants of the State administration. Secondly, the Spanish regular judge has in general a higher degree of powerlessness than other judges from other civil law systems due to "the existence of a plurality of specialized jurisdictions [which pulverize] social reality into a number of lots" (Toharia Cortés 1975, p. 33). Thirdly, despite being somehow powerless, Spanish judges do have a particular capacity for creativity in substantive legal matters. This means that despite judicial decisions (i.e., judgements) are not officially considered a source for law (in contrast to common law traditions), Spanish Supreme Court decisions may be considered as a *de facto* source for judicial decisions (Toharia Cortés 1975, p. 34).[7]

[6] As an illustration, the basic Spanish law organizing all judicial matters (*Ley Orgánica del Poder Judicial*, LOPJ) which was in force in 1974 had been enacted in 1870 (Toharia Cortés 1975, p. 192).

[7] In point of reality, this ability of the Supreme Court may be extended downward to other judging instances such as Provincial Audiences which also establish in a *de facto* manner orientations for law interpretation which may be taken into account by judges at courts of first instance and magistrate.

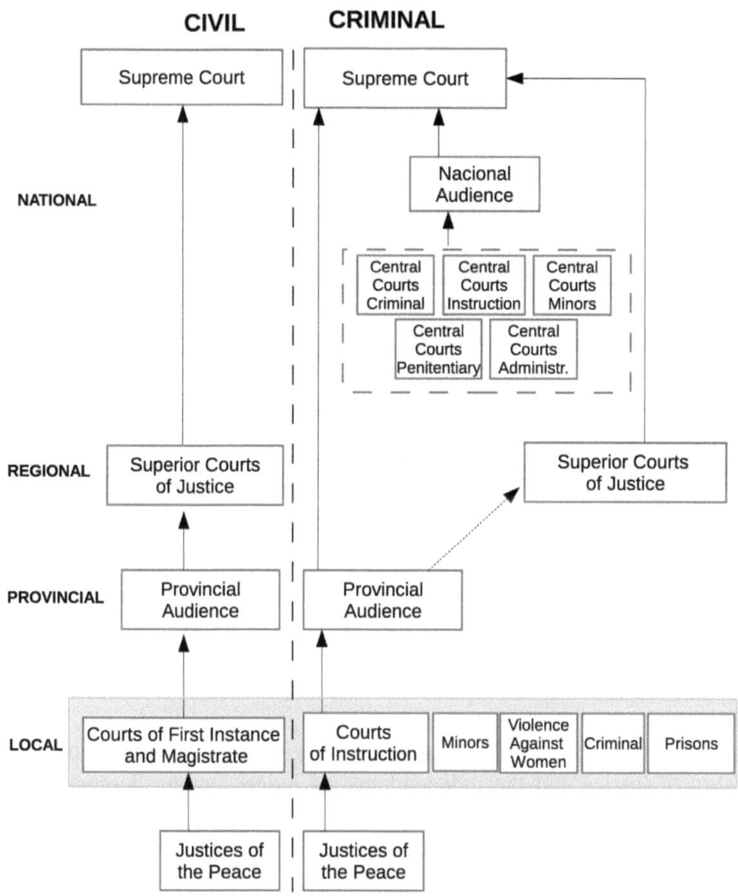

Fig. 4.1 The structure and hierarchy of the Spanish courts system. Courts of First Instance and Magistrate, or simply lower courts, are the entry point for junior judges in the judicial system

In conclusion, as the next section will show, the Spanish judge works in a highly complex judicial system pertaining to the civil law tradition but with some peculiarities which affect judges' labor status, power, and ability to "create" legal interpretations.

4.2.2 Organization of the Spanish Judicial System

4.2.2.1 Structure

As noted above, the Spanish judicial system is highly centralized and complex at the same time, due to the existence of a number of specialized jurisdictions. Figure 4.1 shows the structure of the Spanish courts system. The Supreme Court is the apex of the judicial system and its highest appeal instance, with jurisdiction throughout the Spanish territory. Just below the Supreme Court, and still at the national level we find the National Audience, which is the highest specialized jurisdiction court in Spain for criminal, administrative, and labor matters. It is a collegiate court and handles specially relevant criminal cases such as terrorism, drug trafficking, and crimes against the Spanish institutions.[8] Nevertheless, the most important specialized jurisdiction in Spain is the Constitutional Court, which indeed is not part of the judicial system but an instance for constitutional matters and resolution.

The Superior Courts of Justice are the highest appeal instance at the regional level (for civil matters), corresponding one Superior Court of Justice for every Autonomous Community. These courts hear appeals on civil matters from the Courts of First Instance and from the Provincial Audience, apart from civil cases involving members of either the parliament or the government of the Autonomous Community.

Finally, Courts of First Instance operate at the local level and constitute the entry to the Spanish judicial system (Lancaster 2002). Courts of First Instance deal with most civil cases and less serious criminal cases, though serve as on-call courts for all kind of criminal offenses. Finally, Justices of the Peace are nonprofessional judges located in municipalities which do not have Courts of First Instance and handle minor civil issues.

4.2.2.2 Access to the Judicial Professional Career

The research on judicial selection has been connected to discussions regarding both the quality of justice and the independence of judges among democratic regimes (Goldman 2001). In Spain the literature on judges selection regarding their independence has been usually carried out by legal experts (e.g., González-Granda 1993) who discuss either judges' legal and labor status (i.e., studies on the *función judicial*) or legal and formal aspects of the selection process itself (García-Valdés 1987). Besides, Jiménez-Asensio (2001) offers a view of Spanish judicial selection system from a comparative perspective.

On the other hand, a few studies in Spain have been devoted to study the judicial selection process as a measure of (different forms of) quality of justice. As in most aspects of the social approach to judges, the first achievement in this field was Toharia Cortés (1975, Chap. 2), who offered a discussion of judges selection process in terms of (a) judges' own evaluation of the process itself, (b) judges' socialization process—related to their social origins, and (c) their evaluation regarding the quality of the knowledge gathered during the selection process (i.e., the preparation of the entrance examination).

More recently, di Federico (2005) coordinated a state-of-the-art comparative volume which explored the recruitment and evaluation of judges' professional career in

[8] The two central courts below the National Audience serve this court as courts of first instance and have national jurisdiction.

several European countries. In this context, Poblet and Casanovas (2005) provided a discussion on both selection and evaluation mechanisms in the Spanish judicial system, within the context of a wide research program on the application and impact of information technologies and knowledge management systems in the Spanish legal—specially judicial—system (see also Casanovas et al. 2003; Benjamins et al. 2004b, 2005; Casanovas et al. 2005; Casellas et al. 2006; Poblet et al. 2008; Casellas 2008).

Regarding their recruitment, the basic selection system for Spanish judges is a public, competitive entrance examination [*oposición libre*] among law graduates, completed by successful conclusion of a course in the Judicial School and, currently, finally supported by a short period of practical work in a court.[9]

Being a Spanish citizen and 18 years old—apart from holding a law degree—are the only requirements to be candidate to the entrance examination.[10]

Although the original 1985 law provided that a set proportion of judges may be selected from clerks of the court and other legal professionals with some minimum experience, a controversial reform of the law in 2003 established that a competitive examination would be—as it actually was before 1985—the only way to become a judge in Spain.

Figure 4.2 outlines the whole process since a candidate takes the entrance examination until he or she is appointed to a Court of First Instance and Magistrate. We see that it is composed by three different exercises, one written and two oral. Two basic features may be emphasized about the examination. First, with the exception of constitutional law, which is only included as a topic in the first exercise (written), all three exercises are mainly on the same topics. And second, all three exercises, though specially both oral ones, demand a great mnemonic capacity from the candidate's part.

Poblet and Casanovas (2005, p. 193) give an essential description of this issue:

> The selection process [...] largely relies on the assessment of the candidate's ability to memorise things. Legal topics basically cover the same topics covered by the law school curricula: civil, criminal, constitutional, and general law [...]; civil and criminal procedure, administrative, commercial and labour law [...]. In oral examinations, candidates are required to "recite"—to "sing", in the judicial jargon—five different topics selected at random (out of 300) within a specific amount of time. According to data form the Judicial School, candidates have spent up to four years after graduation preparing for the competitive examination. To do so, they normally hire a "coach" or *preparador* (usually, a senior judge or prosecutor) who teaches them how to "sing" properly and provides useful tips for recitations that are carefully rehearsed once or twice a week.

---

[9] All matters regarding the judicial selection and organization are provided by the *Ley Orgánica 6/1985, de 1 de julio, del Poder Judicial* (i.e., Organic Law 6/1985, of 1 July, on the Judiciary) and a specific regulation about the development of the selection process (*Reglamento 1/1995, de 7 de junio, de la Carrera Judicial*). We take into account all reforms up to May 2007.

[10] Poblet and Casanovas (2005, p. 192) actually comment that "the only impediments to become a candidate are: physical or psychical impairment to perform the judicial task, and being found guilty of a crime".

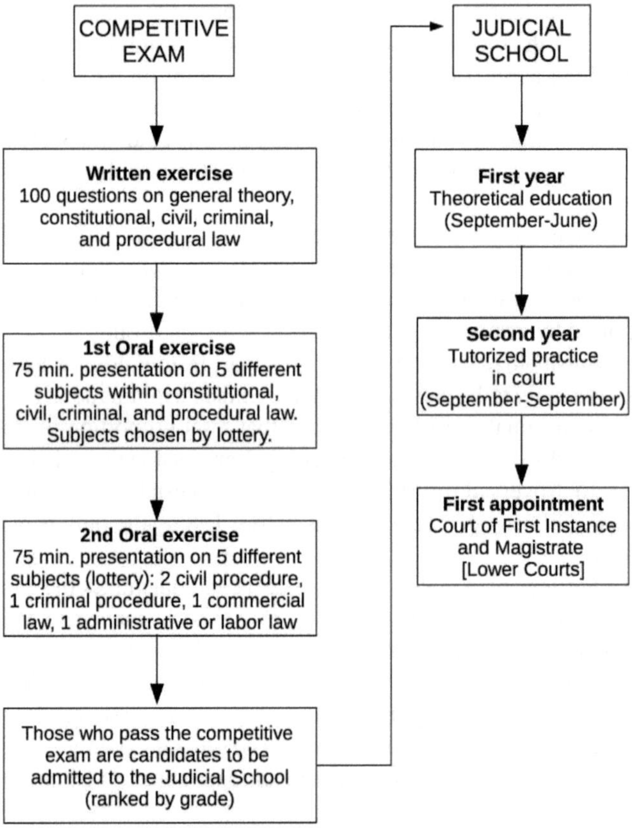

Fig. 4.2 The whole sequence of steps to become a judge in Spain (translated and adapted from the Spanish General Council of the Judiciay's official site: http://www.poderjudicial.es)

Regarding some of the consequences of this kind of selection process on judges themselves, (Jiménez-Asensio 2001, p. 3) comments that:

> Little wonder if, at the end, successful candidates will have developed a strong capacity for endurance. But, by the same token, some of them will also develop some kind of psychical alteration (generally, incidental and, exceptionally, more severe): anxiety, emotional imbalances, anguish, etc. It is a tough experience, even if judges tend to overcome it very quickly. Those hundreds or thousands who fail, in contrast, will have used years preparing for the examination with neither compensation nor guarantees to access the job market.

Therefore, Spain presents a selection process for judges which in principle is common—in general terms—among civil law countries. It thus implies that the judiciary is part of the governmental bureaucracy. The method of competitive entrance is shared by countries such as France, Portugal, Belgium, Italy, Perú, and Brazil, though the first two (and Spain) require a supplementary period in some kind of judicial school after passing the competitive exam (Goldman 2001, p. 8026). Nevertheless, the Spanish selection system is unique regarding the mnemonic demands of its competitive examination.

Candidates who pass the entrance examination are considered civil servants on practical training, and they do not acquire the category of judges until passing the further Judicial School examinations. After that, as said above, they spend at least six months in a guided, practical internship in a court with a senior judge. Judicial appointments are determined by judges' results in the entrance examination and the Judicial School, so that the best ones may choose their destination among the ones available.

The judicial career has three different categories (in rank order): judge, senior judge, and senior judge of the Supreme Court. Judges with at least 3 years of experience must promote to the following category, which implies a court change (i.e., being appointed to courts of larger cities or even more specialized courts). Thus professional promotion in the judicial hierarchy is compulsory and is based on seniority, after a minimum of 3 years in service.[11]

In conclusion, the first appointment locations of Spanish junior judges are Courts of First Instance and Magistrate scattered throughout the Spanish territory. They must remain 1 year in the specific location of their first appointment before they may apply for a transfer to another Court of First Instance and Magistrate (e.g., one closer to their homeland). However, they shall actually spend at least 3 years in this kind of courts before promoting.

4.2.3 Courts of First Instance and Magistrate

4.2.3.1 Distribution and Basic Functions

In Spain there are currently 4984 judges located over 3654 courts, a third of which are Courts of First Instance and Magistrate, or simply lower courts. Lower courts are located in all the province capitals and more populated cities according to the basic territorial unit for judicial organization which is the judicial district [*partido judicial*], a design implemented in the mid nineteenth century. Currently the Spanish judicial system has 432 judicial districts, each of them having one or more Courts of First Instance and Magistrate (see Table 4.1).

In Spain there are currently 1046 Courts of First Instance and Magistrate (CGPJ 2013), which are distributed according to a population criteria, having achieved an average of 10.6 judges per 100,000 citizens in 2012 (see Table 4.1).

As noted above, despite the existence of the Justice of the Peace, the Courts of First Instance and Magistrate are the actual entry of the whole Spanish judicial system. Besides, these are the kind of courts where junior judges start their professional

[11] However, the law also provides that "[a]ny Judge may waive promotion to the rank of Senior Judge expressly notifying the General Council of the Judiciary in the manner and within the term determined by the Council. This waiver shall require him/her to remain in the rank of Judge for 2 years and this waiver may be repeated up to a maximum of three times. Once the terms have elapsed, the Judge shall be promoted according to the corresponding rota".

Table 4.1 Number and distribution of the Spanish judicial districts, and number of members of the judiciary per 100,000 people. (Source: CGPJ 2013)

Autonomous community	No. of districts	Judicial density
Andalucía	85	10.3
Aragón	16	10.6
Asturias	18	14.0
Illes Balears	6	11.6
Islas Canarias	20	12.0
Cantabria	8	12.6
Castilla y León	41	11.7
Castilla-La Mancha	31	8.7
Catalunya	49	10.1
Comunitat Valenciana	36	10.0
Extremadura	21	10.0
Galicia	45	12.0
Madrid	21	10.6
Murcia	11	9.9
Navarra	5	10.1
Euskadi	14	10.4
La Rioja	3	11.4
Ceuta	1	–
Melilla	1	–
Total	432	10.9

career, though in large cities these courts cannot be filled with entering judges but with more experienced ones (thus subjected to a first promotion after as service). Therefore, junior judges are appointed to courts located in medium to small cities.

Courts of First Instance and Magistrate handle most civil cases and decide upon minor criminal offenses. Moreover, they are also responsible for opening preliminary proceedings in any type of criminal offense. Logically most criminal proceedings—e.g., resulting from violent situations—start during the on-call service.

4.2.3.2 The Court Office

Court office[12] is the official name given to "the organisation instrumental in supporting and assisting jurisdictional activity of Courts and Tribunals" (LOPJ article

[12] Matters related to the organization, functioning and staff of the court office are regulated in *Ley Orgánica 6/1985, de 1 de julio, del Poder Judicial*, volumes V and VI, articles 435–481. LOPJ hereafter.

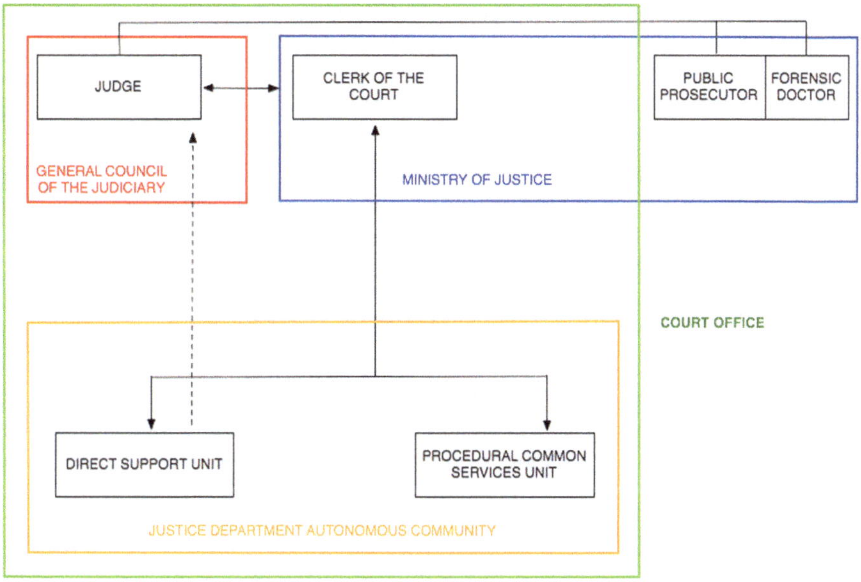

Fig. 4.3 The court office, its basic components, units, and administrative levels

435.1). The organic law establishes that the court office shall be based on the principles of hierarchy, division of functions, and coordination, though it shall be ruled by criteria such as agility, efficacy, efficiency, rationalization of work, responsibility of management, coordination and cooperation among administrations, with the general aim of ensuring a high quality of service deserved by citizens according to their rights and duties.

Figure 4.3 shows, first, the basic organization of the court office (within the green line). According to the law, the basic organizational element of this structure is the Unit "which includes appointments therein, linked functionally on the basis of their tasks" (article 436 LOPJ). There are two types of units, direct support units, and procedural common services units.

The direct support unit is the one that "assists judges in performing their duties, carrying out the necessary action for the precise and effective fulfilment of as many decisions as are issued" (article 437.1 LOPJ), while the common services unit, "without being integrated in a specific judicial body, assumes the centralised work of management and support in activities deriving from the application of procedural laws". Duties of the common services thus include general management activities such as "registration and distribution, acts of communication, judicial assistance, enforcement of judicial decisions and voluntary jurisdiction".

The posts corresponding to both units must be filled with low-rank civil servants—either with permanent or temporary contract—who may carry out a number of activities: procedural and administrative management, and judicial assistance. In most cases, these civil servants are selected by (and depend on) the Department of

Justice of the corresponding Autonomous Community, and a high educational degree (such as a law degree) is by no means required.

Both units function under the command of the clerk of the court. Clerks of the court are a national, professional body of high rank civil servants depending on the Ministry of Justice,[13] whose essential task is to authenticate court documents, for which they must "provide authentic records of the performance of proceedings at the Court and before thereof and of the facts occurred that are relevant from a procedural point of view through the appropriate acts and proceedings" (article 453 LOPJ).[14] Like judges, they are selected through public, competitive entrance examinations and must have a law degree.

In particular, clerks of the court have the power to manage and supervise the staff as regards procedural or technical aspects, including supervising the distribution of cases among civil servants and arranging their activity. They are also responsible for driving the legal procedure including giving orders for the conduct of the proceedings—except for those exclusively exercised by judges—which means proceedings such as order, certification, notification or enforcement (article 456 LOPJ).

Moreover, clerks of the court are responsible for the Judicial Management Records Office, and for "the deposit of goods and articles affected to the court files, as well as for the deposit of pieces of evidence in criminal cases at the premises assigned thereto" (article 459 LOPJ). Finally, clerks of the court are in charge of the official statistics regarding the court's activity, which they must make known by law to the National Court Statistics Commission for its approval (article 461 LOPJ).

Finally, the third essential component of the court office is obviously the judge. Judges in Spain do not depend on the Ministry of Justice but on the General Council of the Judiciary, the governing body of the Spanish judiciary. The Spanish constitution created this governing body in order to ensure the judiciary's independence. It is responsible for appointments, promotions, inspection, and discipline matters regarding Spanish judges (see Moreno Catena 2003, pp. 241–257).

Again in Fig. 4.3 we may see that one of the most salient features of the court office as it is currently set up is that three different administrations, which are not hierarchically related (i.e., General Council of the Judiciary, Ministry of Justice, and Autonomous Community) are responsible for its three essential components.

A first conclusion regarding this multilevel organization is that no clear hierarchical lines may be drawn among its members. Obviously the judge is the head of the court, but it is not clear whether he/she be also head of the court office, since he/she is not directly responsible for the clerk's work—who is part of an independent body, so

[13] Article 443 LOPJ establishes the requirements to become a clerk of the court. Public prosecutors and forensic doctors are also dependent of the Ministry of Justice, but they are not considered part of the court office.

[14] This task may also include authenticating and granting the integrity of recorded material such as court trials, issuing certifications or authenticated copies of court procedures, and granting the powers of attorney for litigation.

in a sense they are peer professionals—and has no direct control over the direction or management—even technically or procedurally—of the civil servants' work within the direct support and common services units (which is the clerk's duty).

This lack of clear hierarchical relationship is even more apparent among judges and public prosecutors and forensic doctors, the latter two being completely independent from the court office.

Yet judges seem to have actual authority, and we shall see later that they also affirm to have a high degree of satisfaction regarding their relationships with all the other members of the court office. However, interaction among bodies depending on distinct political and administrative levels may not enable rapid and efficient conflict resolution, thus providing potential instability foci at workplace.

4.2.4 The On-Call Service

One of the main organizational principles governing the Spanish jurisdiction resides on the on-call period of judicial settings, i.e., Courts of First Instance and Magistrate. The organization of on-call activities are stated in the Section II of a general regulation aimed at ordering accessory matters of the judicial activity.[15]

This regulation provides, first, that at least one of the Courts of First Instance and Magistrate within each judicial district will be on call, establishing a rotation system among all courts that ensures a continuous, non-stop service throughout the whole year. Regularly courts (i.e., judges and the court office) remain on call for full one-week periods. The law also provides that at least one public prosecutor and a forensic doctor will be available during on-call services.

While on call, the court office is responsible for handling all incoming cases reported by the police, the public prosecution or merely by citizens. This means that a judge who is on call must handle all reports drawn up by the police (e.g., as a result of a traffic accident) and the private prosecutions presented by citizens.

This also implies that the judge who is on call will be in charge of supervising all enquiries related to the facts of a criminal offense dealt with by the on-call service. It may include the adoption of precautionary measures for protecting victims (e.g., a restraining order), the adoption of particular court orders regarding the personal situation of a detainee, to hold immediate trials in those cases provided by the Criminal Law (e.g., as a result of driving without license), and carrying out other urgent procedures.

Apart from these general features, the on-call service is specially dedicated to the adoption of all the necessary court orders regarding the protection of female victims of domestic violence, and of minors.[16] Finally, the on-call service is entitled to act

---

[15] *Reglamento 1/2005, de los aspectos accesorios de las actuaciones judiciales.*

[16] Parts 1–4 of article 42, *Reglamento 1/2005, de los aspectos accesorios de las actuaciones judiciales.*

on civil issues in some special cases, though logically the on-call service usually only handles criminal offenses.

On the other hand, *all* judges—and the corresponding staff—in Courts of First Instance and Magistrate must accomplish on-call functions, but naturally the rotation recurrence for on-call will depend on the number of courts and judges within a single judicial district. Therefore those judges who are in Courts of First Instance and Magistrate with only 1 judge are continually on-call—though the law provides relief measures in those cases—, and those who are in judicial districts with, say, 4 judges have one on-call week per month.[17]

Most frequently, the on-call service consists of two different types of judicial activities (Rodrigo et al. 2004):

- Indoor activities (within the judicial facilities). Judges on call, in the presence of a public prosecutor, may hear detainees—who are assisted by a lawyer—, victims of a crime, witnesses, etc. They also may ask for a *habeas corpus* to the police in case of illegal restraint (more than 72 h in police premises), impose further imprisonment for detainees or decide over their conditional release; authorize protection to victims of domestic violence, impose measures of separation to aggressors, ask for judicial cooperation to another court, etc. As leaders of all criminal enquiries, judges also have to authorize police activities such as entering in a private building or intervening phone lines.
- Outdoor activities. These may consist of hearing a victim in a hospital, carrying out a corpse removal (though this act may be currently delegated to the forensic doctor), personally supervising the proper register of a house or of any other kind of building, or sealing an area so that the police may carry out the search for pieces of evidence for some case. Since clerks of the court are also entitled to assist judges performing most of these activities, judges may delegate the supervision to them.

In conclusion, the wide range of activities a judge has to endure while on call may entail paying attention over a number of parallel issues (raised by the police, lawyers, public prosecution, etc.). Usually, the need for quick decisions—e.g., deciding whether to apply preventive detention to a detainee at 4 a.m. as a result of a fight in a bar—seriously handicaps (or impedes) reviewing case law or jurisprudence. Therefore at the best of times inexperienced judges have to rely on uncertain consultation with peers or senior judges (if available, which is not very likely at 4 a.m.).

Thus when on-call, their decision-making process is very likely to take place in a context of special ambiguity, in sharp contrast with other routine and rule-based decisions that bind most legal proceedings in ordinary judicial decision-making.

[17] Junior judges are frequently appointed to courts of First Instance and Magistrate with only 1 judge (one-judge courts). Judges (and also other civil servants) who have been appointed to such courts tend to leave them as soon as possible. An illustrative example is given by the fact that despite only 59 out of the 528 Courts of First Instance and Magistrate to be filled with a junior judge are one-judge courts (CGPJ 2009), 33 of them (56 %) were available when the judges from the 52nd class of the Spanish Judicial School were to be appointed to a court in 2002.

4.3 Survey Data

The source of our data is survey on Spanish judges that focused exclusively upon junior judges and designed to gather deep information on junior judges' experiences during first appointments. The survey was carried out under the SEKT project[18] with the aim to use the information gathered to build a decision-support system for junior judges (Casanovas et al. 2006; Casellas 2011; Vallbé et al. 2010).

The survey covers 34 of the 52 Spanish provinces in 11 autonomous communities (regions). Access to the professionals was subjected to usual official procedures, so that before going to courts the presidents of the Superior Court of Justice of each Autonomous Community—its highest judicial authority—were officially contacted to inform them about the characteristics of the study. Credentials from the Judicial School were also obtained so that interviewers could be accepted as members of an official research program.

The population of the survey was composed by the total number of judges in their first appointment from the 52nd class of the Spanish Judicial School. This was a batch of 243 judges who passed the oral and written examinations in 2000, entered the Judicial School in September of that year and graduated in 2002 after having spent six months in judicial units as training judges. They took office by 2002. Therefore, when the researchers visited and interviewed them in 2005 they had already spent almost 2 years in office, were ready to move to another place and, eventually, to promote in the judicial career.

Judges of the 52nd class had been sent to fill vacancies of Courts of First Instance and Magistrate scattered throughout Spain. The Judicial School provided the official list with the destination and contact data of each of them. To create a relevant sample, 150 judges were randomly selected among the official list, preserving in the sample the proportion of judges in each Autonomous Community that appeared in the actual population.

However, due mainly to the high volume of work at Spanish lower courts and to the availalbility of judges when they are on call, not all planned interviews could be carried out in the first round of interviews. Access to judicial professionals is limited by a number of official constrains. Besides, many judges to be interviewed were located in judicial districts with one single court. This means, for instance, that they are virtually always on call and thus the actual celebration of appointed interviews were conditioned by unexpected situations in court. These unexpected situations took place in some cases and some interviews could not be performed at the predetermined moment and place.

This implied, therefore, a further delay in carrying out the remaining interviews, which resulted in the fact that when they were to be resumed, all 52nd-class judges had already promoted to other courts and new official contacts had to be started in 2006. Since our interest was to preserve the same conditions for all interviewed

[18] Semantically Enabled Knowledge Technologies, EU-IST Project IST-2003-506826 SEKT.

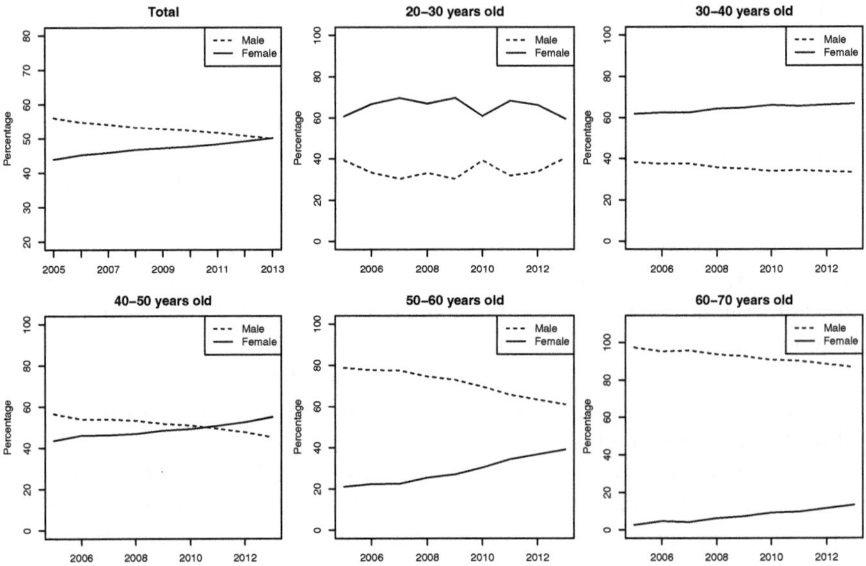

Fig. 4.4 Evolution of the gender distribution among judges in Spain, 2005–2013

judges as far as possible, at least 2 years were to be waited until judges with the same experience as the 52nd class ones could be interviewed. Besides, the geographical distribution imposed by the sample was to be preserved. Finally, all official requests were completed in 2008 and in the beginning of 2009 further interviews could be carried out.[19] All judges were interviewed when they were at least in their second year in court.

The questionnaire contains mostly multiple choice questions. Apart from these, though, a number of open-ended questions were asked requiring the judges to give expanded answers on their main professional problems as well as to identify specific problems encountered during their 1st year as judges on criminal issues, civil issues, and on-call situations. Further explanation on these answers will be given in the next chapter.

4.4 Who Are Spanish Junior Judges?

4.4.1 Demographics

If we randomly picked a judge from the set of junior judges of the 52nd class of the Spanish Judicial School, it is very likely that we would come up with a young woman with no children. Figure 4.4 shows that although at the moment of the survey

[19] Unfortunately, only 16 further interviews could be completed, making a total sample of 118.

Table 4.2 Distribution of the sample by civil status and gender

		Married	Single	Divorced	Partnership	Total
Male	Number	21	19	1	2	43
	Percent	48.84	44.19	2.32	4.65	100
Female	Number	39	33	1	1	74
	Percent	52.70	44.60	1.35	1.35	100
Total	Number	60	52	2	3	117
	Percent	51.28	44.44	1.71	2.57	100

most of Spanish judges were men, women were already an overwhelming majority among young judges (younger than 40) in 2004 and outnumbered men at middle age in 2011. For the time in Spanish history, in 2013 there were more female than male judges.

The average age at which our surveyed judges passed their examination was almost 30, with only 8 % of the sample having done so beyond 40. Once judges have passed their examinations they spend 1 year at the Spanish Judicial School, and another practical internship in a court guided by a senior judge, which means that the average judge will go at her first court being almost 32 years-old, over 8.5 years after obtaining their Law degree.

Although the years between Law graduation and their first appointment to court, which judges-to-be exclusively devote to prepare their examination, may have a toll on future judges' social life, data show that it does not seem to affect their chances to form a family.

In this regard, Table 4.2 shows that half of junior judges are married, which is only 6 points behind the percentage of marriages among the Spanish general population at the time.[20] Furthermore, no relevant difference is observed between males and females regarding civil status.

Table 4.3 gives us further information about judges' personal life regarding their chances to build a family. Among all judges, 77 % do not have offspring and only a very small percentage have more than one child, none of them having more than three children. If we look only at those who are married (who concentrate almost all children), over half of them have no offspring whatsoever, and 25 % have one child.

[20] Spanish civil law allows a *tertium genus* between being single and married, known as *de facto* partnership. This situation is fully legal and *de facto* partners (who have to register as such to be legally recognized) have almost the same rights and duties as married partners. Partnership among judges follows the general trend, too.

Table 4.3 Number of children by civil status

		Number of children				
		0	1	2	3	Total
Married	Number	34	15	9	2	60
	Percent	56.67	25.00	15.00	3.33	100
Single	Number	52	0	0	0	52
	Percent	100	0.00	0.00	0.00	100
Divorced	Number	1	1	0	0	2
	Percent	50.00	50.00	0.00	0.00	100
Partnership	Number	3	0	0	0	3
	Percent	100	0.00	0.00	0.00	100
Total	Number	90	16	9	2	117
	Percent	76.92	13.67	7.69	1.71	100

Table 4.4 Postgraduate studies and legal profession among junior judges

		Yes	No	Total
Postgraduate	Number	22	96	118
	Percent	18.6	81.4	100
Legal profession	Number	21	97	118
	Percent	17.8	82.2	100

4.4.2 *Education and Professional Experience*

Despite having obtained their Law degree in 37 different universities, our surveyed judges present a highly homogeneous educational profile. First and foremost, almost all the universities belong to the Spanish public system of higher education, which already sets a common educational ground.[21] Furthermore, a significant proportion of junior judges (81 %) do not have further postgraduate studies (Table 4.4), and almost the same percentage have not practiced any other legal profession before becoming judges.

Our data about junior judges' recent educational and professional experience seems to be consistent with the results obtained by Ayuso et al. (2002). In effect, in that survey 81.1 % of junior judges declared not to have practiced any profession before being a judge, while this percentage decreased among senior judges (65.9 %). This would suggest that the preparation for the judicial examination not only impedes enrolling in postgraduate studies, but it also prevents a high percentage of judges to perform any other legal work before becoming a judge.

[21] Only 15 respondents out of 118 affirmed to have studied in a private university.

Table 4.5 Crosstabulation between practicing legal profession and having postgraduate studies before becoming a judge

			Postgraduate		
			Yes	*No*	Total
Legal Profession	*Yes*	Number	12	9	21
		% row	57.14	42.86	100
		% col	54.54	9.38	
	No	Number	10	87	97
		% row	10.31	89.69	100
		% col	45.46	90.62	
	Total	Number	22	96	118
		Percent	18.64	81.36	100
			100	100	

Interestingly, though, having postgraduate studies and having practiced legal professions before seem not to be independent. Data in Table 4.5 show that over half of the judges who have postgraduate studies have also practiced legal professions before becoming judges. Inversely, 57 % of judges who have practiced some legal profession before becoming a judge have also postgraduate studies. Fisher's exact test for independence delivers evidence against the assumption of independence between having postgraduate studies and practicing other legal professions.[22]

This would mean that those judges who have postgraduate studies tend also to have practiced some other legal profession before becoming a judge. And inversely, it is reasonable to think that there is a high probability that those who do not have postgraduate studies have not practiced any other legal profession either. This correlation could be explained by at least two reasons. On one hand, future judges start the preparation of the examinations just after finishing the Law degree, leaving little room for other occupations. Judges tend to spend an average of 6.5 years between the obtention of their Law degree and passing their examination to enter the Judicial School. However, a few candidates pass their examinations in just 2 years, while others can wait more than 15 years to pass the exam.[23] Moreover, Toharia Cortés (1975, p. 40) found that 63.9 % of Spanish judges declared that the time between their Law degree and passing their judicial examination was exclusively dedicated to prepare that examination, while only 4.8 % declared to have practiced as a lawyer,

[22] FET estimate 95 % interval of $[0.025, 0.29]$, $p = 1.05 * 10^{-5}$. Due to the low frequency in some of the cells, a χ^2 test did not deliver reliable results, though consistent against the independence assumption.

[23] The standard deviation of the number of years passed between the Law degree and the examination is 11.7 years in the data.

Table 4.6 Legal professions practiced by junior judges before becoming a judge

Profession	Count	Percent (of the count)
Lawyer	10	34.48
Clerk[a]	4	13.79
Public prosecutor[a]	0	0
Public prosecutor (substitute)	1	3.45
Judge (substitute)	4	13.79
Public servant in Justice Adm.[b]	0	0
Others (legal consultant, etc.)	10	34.48
	29	99.99

[a] Examination required
[b] Examination sometimes required

and 5.3 % had combined the preparation of the examination and the practice of some other legal occupation.[24]

On the other hand, postgraduate studies might be only perceived perceived as useful when the intention is to practice those legal professions that do not require a full competitive examination of entrance. Table 4.6 shows the different legal professions practiced by junior judges before entering the judicial system.[25] Among those judges that had practiced other legal professions, 34.48 % worked as lawyers, 13.79 % worked as clerks, 1 worked as a substitute public prosecutor (3.45 %), and 4 as substitute judges (13.79 %). A significant high proportion of respondents (34.48 %) affirm to have practiced other professions than the ones specified in the questionnaire. These other professions mostly refer to legal consultancy, and legal audit in private firms. Note that those professions that—like the judicial career—require an examination (clerk, public prosecutor, and, in some cases, public servant in the Justice Administration, marked with * in the table) present a very low score (13.79 %). At the time of the survey there was no examination required to practice as a lawyer in Spain. Besides, every Spanish citizen with a Law degree may work as substitute judge or substitute public prosecutor, for which no further examination is required.[26]

[24] In this regard, the author also affirmed that a consequence of that fact was that "two out of three new judges lacked any experience of (or contact with) the judicial world before they entered the Judicial School" (Toharia Cortés 1975, p. 40).

[25] A total of 21 surveyed judges affirmed to have practiced other legal professions. Since the respondents could score for more than one legal profession if they had practiced more than one, the total score does not necessarily sum up 21.

[26] See, for instance, ACUERDO de 30 de enero de 2008, del Pleno del Consejo General del Poder Judicial, por el que se convocan plazas de Magistrado suplente y de Juez sustituto, para el año judicial 2008–2009, en el ámbito de los Tribunales Superiores de Justicia de Andalucía, Ceuta y Melilla, Aragón, Principado de Asturias, Las Islas Baleares, Canarias, Cantabria, Castilla

Table 4.7 Professional associations among judges with professional membership

Association	Number	Percent
Asociación Profesional de la Magistratura	16	40
Jueces por la Democracia	8	20
Asociación Francisco de Vitoria	7	17.5
Others	7	17.5
N/A	2	5
Total	40	100

4.4.3 *Professional Integration*

Due to the nature of their job, junior judges tend to present quite strong ties within their network of professional peers but high levels of isolation with respect to the outer social world. Besides, since they are by principle spread throughout the territory mostly in unfamiliar locations, junior judges are by definition physically isolated from relevant groups of social and professional peers.

Actually, half of the Spanish judicial districts gather 60,000 people or less, and one out of four are around 30,000. Due to this demographic structure, almost 20 % of the surveyed judges are located in small judicial districts with just one single court for the whole district, which undoubtedly hinders their interaction with other colleagues.

Data show that actually formal ties within the profession tend to be quite weak, as only one third of them (34 %) are members of any of the existing Spanish judicial associations.[27] Of those who do pertain to some association, 40 % are members of the conservative Asociación Profesional de la Magistratura, 20 % have joined the progressive Jueces por la Democracia, and 17.5 % the Asociación Francisco de Vitoria, which represent the three most important professional association among Spanish judges. Finally, 17.5 % are members of other associations, and 5 % did not name the association they were members of (Table 4.7).

In contrast, junior judges tend to have strong informal ties with their peers, as almost 94 % of them declare to have contact with the judges of their very same class—i.e., those with whom they shared a post-examination period at the Judicial School. Moreover, half of them affirms that the contact is either frequent or very frequent. The frequency of contact diminishes dramatically with respect to judges from other classes.

y León, Castilla-La Mancha, Cataluña, Comunidad Valenciana, Extremadura, Galicia, Comunidad de Madrid, Región de Murcia, Comunidad Foral de Navarra, País Vasco y La Rioja. (http://www.boe.es/boe/dias/2008/02/02/).

[27] This, on the other hand, is fully consistent with the findings in (Ayuso et al. 2002, pp. 22–23) who found that 35 % of junior judges affirmed to be members of any professional association, while among senior judges this percentage increased to 51.1 %.

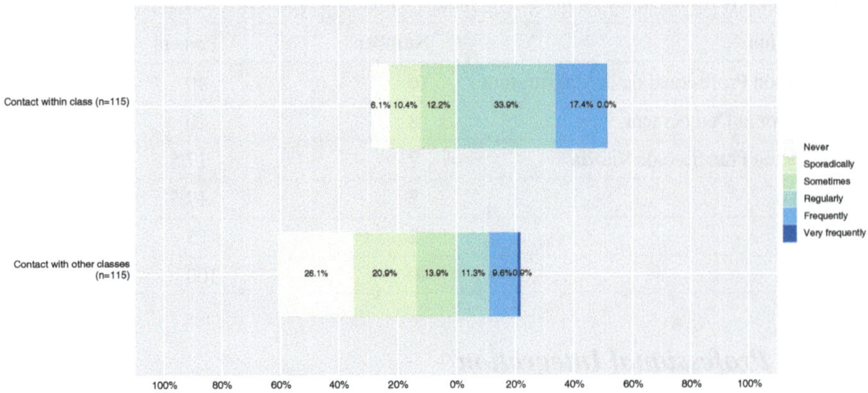

Fig. 4.5 Frequency at which junior judges declare to have contact with peer judges of their class and of other classes

Due to the nature of the Spanish judicial system, it is reasonable to think that as judges get older both the contact rate with judges from the same year and its frequency tends to diminish, while the contact with other judges increases. Actually, Ayuso et al. (2002, pp. 122–123) found that among senior judges the contact rate with judges from their year was 64.7 % while 85.5 % declared to have contact with professionals from other years.

4.4.4 Interprofessional Interaction

So far we have been concerned with the relationship judges have with other colleagues, i.e., other judges. In order to have a bigger picture of judges' professional environment, we now turn to the way judges relate to other professionals working in the judicial context. To that aim, different questions were directed to judges in order to assess the extent to which they interact with other professional groups, either within or without courts.

A first question asked judges to evaluate their relationship with those who work closer to them within courts: i.e., public prosecutors, lawyers, clerks, and the rest of the court staff. Figure 4.6 shows that the great majority of judges evaluate their relationship with these groups either as positive.

The group that receives more positive evaluation is the court staff, the relationship with whom 94 % of judges have evaluated as positive or very positive. None of the interviewed judges has evaluated his/her relationship with the court staff as negative or very negative. Note that the evaluation regarding lawyers, being lower, is by no means overall negative. In effect, almost 78 % of judges rate their relationship with lawyers as positive or very positive, while only 1.7 % affirms it is negative or very negative. These results, highly consistent with previous data on this matter either

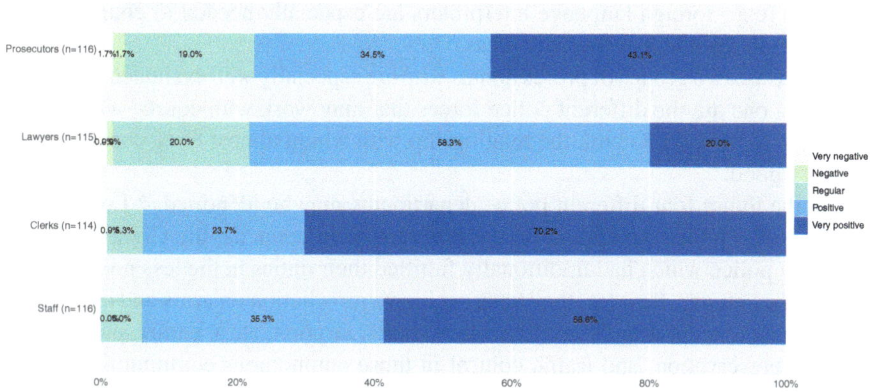

Fig. 4.6 Evaluation of judges' relationship with other professionals

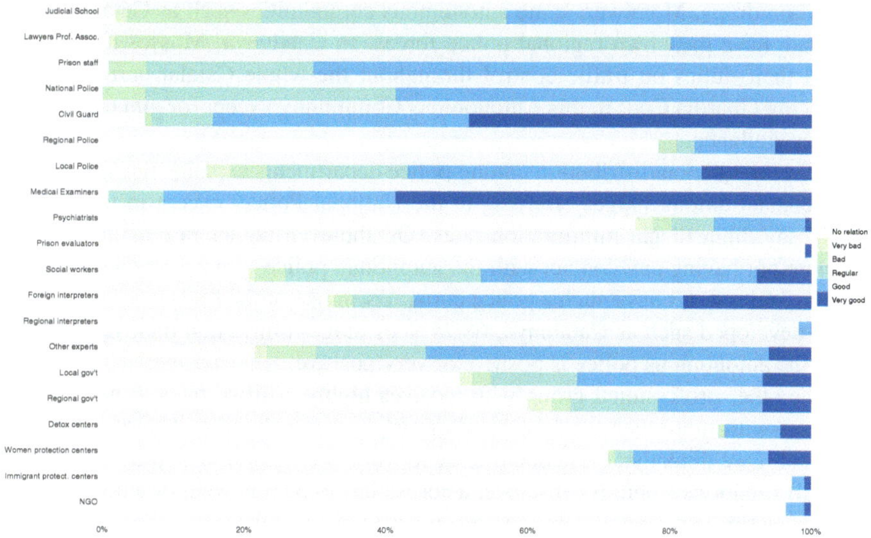

Fig. 4.7 Distribution of judges' evaluation of their relationship with other professional groups

with junior or senior judges (Ayuso et al. 2002, pp. 120–121), seem to indicate that the relationship with those professionals who work closer to junior judges at courts does not present drawbacks relevant enough to be mentioned, and that the overall evaluation that judges do of other professional groups within court is really positive.

A different pattern of relationships can be seen when judges rate their relationship (if any) with other groups of professionals who may have some participation in the courts daily work. As Fig. 4.7 shows, the relevance of some groups is more evident than others. For instance, the different police departments (that perform very different activities regarding judicial activity) tend to present higher rates of contact (first column of the table) than other groups that may be important only in particular settings (e.g., foreign language interpreters are especially needed in courts located near Spanish borders or touristic areas).

There are two groups of professionals who are especially well evaluated by judges. The first one are the different police forces that may work with courts, with special mention to the Civil Guard, the relationship with whom almost 85 % consider good or very good.

In the figure four different police departments may be identified.[28] Local police refers to the police depending on the different town councils, the Civil Guard is a military police which had traditionally fulfilled their duties in the less populated areas of the country. Besides, they have exclusive jurisdiction on arms and explosives, smuggling (except drugs), border control (ports, airports, etc.), nature and environmental preservation, and traffic control in those autonomous communities that do not have their own police department with that jurisdiction.

The National Police have exclusive jurisdiction on issuing passports and identity cards; immigration, refugee and asylum; control over game and gambling; and issues on drugs. Moreover, some autonomous communities such as Catalunya and Euskadi have their own regional police forces. In Catalunya, Mossos d'Esquadra fulfill their duties on traffic control throughout the whole Catalan territory, thus replacing Guardia Civil in this Autonomous Community except for gun control and border vigilance.

This jurisdiction distribution among police departments explains the high rate of non-contact among judges referring to the National Police, except in those areas with, say, high illegal immigration rates. Or, the even higher rate of judges who declare not having any contact with the autonomic police, since many autonomous communities don't have such a police corps. Yet in one of the few places where it is fully developed such as Catalunya, 68.75 % of judges affirm that their relationship with the autonomous police is positive or very positive.

The other professional group who receives highly positive rates in medical examiners with more than 90 % of good or very good evaluation. This is especially relevant if we think that these doctors use to work side by side with judges in urgent on-call situations when, for instance, a corpse has to be removed, or a domestic violence victim or a sexually abused person has to be examined. It is therefore highly significant that junior judges praise this group in such an enthusiastic manner.

Finally, a last measure of professional interaction is given by the professional shape of judges' inner friendship and parental circle. In Table 4.8 we can see that almost 20 % of friends are other judges, which is a bit lower than the results obtained by Ayuso et al. (2002, pp. 125–126) among junior judges (27.4 %) and even lower among senior judges.[29] Actually, these results are quite different to the ones encountered by Toharia Cortés (1975, p. 91) where 38.2 % of judges' friends were also judges.

[28] See the basic Spanish police regulation at Ley Orgánica 2/1986, de 13 de marzo, de Fuerzas y Cuerpos de Seguridad, http://noticias.juridicas.com/base_datos/Admin/lo2-1986.html.

[29] However, it's worth noting that regarding this question the questionnaire in (Ayuso et al. 2002) includes judges and clerks in the "judge" option. We include clerks as "other legal professions".

Table 4.8 Profession of junior judges' first three friends

	Friend 1		Friend 2		Friend 3		Total	
	Number	Percent	Number	Percent	Number	Percent	Number	Percent[a]
Judge	27	23.08	13	11.11	27	23.08	67	19.09
Other legal prof.	32	27.35	31	26.50	20	17.09	83	23.65
Liberal prof.	29	24.79	29	24.79	21	17.95	79	22.50
Military	2	1.71	–	–	1	0.85	3	0.85
Entrepreneur	1	0.85	5	4.27	–	–	6	1.71
Retailer	4	3.42	1	0.85	4	3.42	9	2.56
Public servant	8	6.84	11	9.40	6	5.13	25	7.12
Farmer	–	–	–	–	1	0.85	1	0.28
Worker	–	–	–	–	4	3.42	4	1.14
Employee	6	5.13	13	11.11	12	10.26	31	8.83
Housekeeper	4	3.42	9	7.69	14	11.97	27	7.69
Other	4	3.42	5	4.27	7	5.98	16	4.56
Total	117	100.01	117	99.99	117	100	351	99.98

[a]Percentages on the total number of answers, not on respondents.

Yet if we consider both judges and the other legal professions as one single response, in our case they represent almost 43 % of junior judges' friends, while they represented 32.55 % among junior judges in (Ayuso et al. 2002). In effect, Toharia Cortés (1975, p. 91) reported that almost 60 % of judges' responses regarding their top three friends referred either to judges or to other legal professionals, which the author interpreted as pointing to "a clear tendency, among judges, to have colleagues as their closest friends" Toharia Cortés (1975, p. 89).

Toharia Cortés (1975) concluded, on the one hand, that this bias toward other judges and legal professionals strengthened the traditional judges' isolation from Spanish society. Yet on the other hand, the author showed that this was not a particular phenomenon among Spanish judges *qua* specific group but a common feature among Spanish public servants. In Toharia's words, "strangely as it may sound (given the usual stereotypes on judges' isolation and closeness from the outer world), in general judges do not seem to have a stronger tendency to closeness than other social élites" (Toharia Cortés 1975, p. 90).[30]

If we look again to our data, we can see that apart from legal professionals, currently junior judges have a wide variety of friends in other professions. Consistently with a historical tendency, though, liberal professionals still have a relevant representation among judges' friends. In the mid 1970s (Toharia Cortés 1975, p. 91) 17.3 %

[30] The translation is ours.

of judges' responses referred to this professional group, while in our case it has even increased up to 22.50 %. Yet an increase is also perceived in other professions which were traditionally underrepresented. For instance, while in 1975 only 3.6 % of judges' responses referred to public servants (in non-legally related occupations), in our case this option represents 7.12 %. Other common professions are employee (administrative, service, etc.) (8.83 %) and housekeeper (7.69 %), while only 0.85 % of the responses referred to people from the military, 1.14 % to workers, and even less to farmers.[31]

Yet a final attempt to explain Spanish junior judges' professional context might be done through an analysis of Spanish judges' social origin. Common as it is in Civil Law systems, in Spain the recruitment process within the different levels of the public administration has been usually regarded as a family matter. Regarding this issue, Toharia Cortés (1975, pp. 64–74) reported that in the 1970s one out of four judges' father was a judge or a legal professional, while another 25 % of judges came from families linked to the public administration. These two typologies of self-recruitment were referred to, respectively, "specific" and "generic" self-recruitment, the former referring to judges who are sons of other judges, the latter meaning that judges come from families with members of the public administration (Toharia Cortés 1975, p. 65).

Besides, comparing these data to other Civil Law countries such as Italy and France, the author found that the "specific self-recruitment" among judges (judges who are sons of other judges) in Spain was significantly higher than in Italy and France (16 and 13 %, respectively), though he also conceded that data showed this "specific self-recruitment" pattern among Spanish judges was changing. In effect, recent figures on judges' social and economic origin confirm that now it is hardly possible to talk about neither specific nor generic self-recruitment among junior judges.

Table 4.9 shows that only a 5 % of judges' fathers were judges, while 9.4 % practice other legal professions. Of course, due to the traditional gender bias existing in Spanish civil service, mother judges are out of the question—an important percentage are housekeepers. Therefore, only 14.5 % of current junior judges come from families who are strongly related to the legal world. As for the generic self-recruitment, 10.26 % of judges' fathers are public servants, a significantly lower rate than 30 years ago (Toharia Cortés 1975, p. 65).

Regarding other professions, the table shows a high and almost equal representation of liberal professionals among both fathers and mothers (19.66 and 17.09 %, respectively). Yet other professions with no traditional social preeminence show

[31] Interestingly, although during Franco's authoritarian regime (1939–1975) the Spanish army was a relevant part of the social élite in Spain, Toharia Cortés (1975, p. 91) reports that only 3 % of the total judges' responses referred to people from the military among their closest friends. In our case, the proportion is even lower (0.85 %), to the extent that only 3 out of 117 judges chose that option. See (Martínez 2007, pp. 45–74) (especially pages 54–60) for an assessment of self-recruitment among the Spanish military.

Table 4.9 Profession of junior judges' father, mother, and partner

	Father		Mother		Partner	
	Number	Percent	Number	Percent	Number	Percent
Judge	6	5.13	–	–	11	13.75
Other legal prof.	11	9.40	2	1.71	19	23.75
Liberal prof.	23	19.66	20	17.09	25	31.25
Military	3	2.56	–	–	2	2.50
Entrepreneur	5	4.27	1	0.85	1	1.25
Retailer	11	9.40	9	7.69	–	–
Public servant	12	10.26	7	5.98	7	8.75
Farmer	2	1.71	–	–	–	–
Worker	10	8.55	2	1.71	–	–
Employee	21	17.95	12	10.26	6	7.50
Housekeeper	–	–	58	49.57	2	2.50
Other professions	10	8.55	4	3.42	7	8.75
Absent	3	2.56	2	1.71		
Total	117	100	117	99.99	80	99.99

also a significant role in the table. In effect, there are almost as liberal professionals as employees among fathers (17.95 % employees among fathers, while 10.26 % among mothers), and almost 10 % of judges' fathers (and 7.69 % of their mothers) are retailers. Among mothers, 49.57 % are dedicated to housekeeping.

Finally, data on those judges who have partners show that judges tend to marry other judges or other legal and liberal professionals. In particular, among male junior judges 52 % of their partners are either judges or practice other legal professions, but among female junior judges this percentage is notably lower (around 30 %), resulting in a high proportion of liberal professionals (almost 40 %).

In conclusion, the picture sketched by our data on judges at their first appointment is, first, that of a group of professionals who rely mainly on other professionals *within* the boundaries of their court. Secondly, judges' traditional social isolation due to their professional role does not seem to shape, at least at this early stage of their career, their most immediate friendship circle, which is consistent with the low levels of self-recruitment with respect to their family ties.

4.4.5 Quality of Life

Junior judges' reliance on the groups of professionals they mainly meet within the boundaries of the court contrasts with their lack of social life out of court. In particular, just 8 % of judges have joined some kind of association in their court's town. Furthermore, half of junior judges do not even live in the town that holds the court.

Table 4.10 Working at home and during weekends

Home			Weekend	
	Number	Percent	Number	Percent
Yes	109	93.16	97	82.91
No	8	6.84	20	17.09
Total	117	100	117	100

Table 4.11 Number of extra hours per week

Extra hours	Number	Percent
≤10	10	8.55
≥10≤20	45	38.46
≥20≤30	45	38.46
≥30≤40	14	11.97
≥40≤50	2	1.71
NA	1	0.85

Life during the first appointment as judges, then, seems to be mainly devoted to work, either in court or at home. This is apparent in different measures of quality of life. First, judges were asked (in two different questions) whether they used to bring work at home and whether they used to work during weekends. Table 4.10 presents the results for both questions.

It is worth noting that the vast majority of junior judges (93.16 %) affirm to bring work at home, and that almost 83 % declare to work during the weekends.[32] Having been asked to calculate how many extra hours per week they performed, only 8.55 % affirmed to work 10 extra hours or less per week, while a vast 76.92 % declare to work between 10 and 30 extra hours per week. According to Table 4.11, then, 38.46 % of junior judges work between 2 and 4 extra hours per day every week,[33] and another 38.46 % declare to work between 4 and 6 extra hours per day every week.

Besides, almost 12 % of judges affirmed to work between 30 and 40 extra hours per week, which would mean working between 6 and 8 extra hours every day, thus doubling the standard 8-h working day. Finally, 2 judges declared to work between 40 and 50 extra hours per week.

Considering these figures on extra working time, it is hardly surprising that 80 % of judges think that judges are not well-paid in comparison to other professionals of a similar level.[34] The current salary for judges was established in 2003 by law.[35]

[32] All judges must stay on-call a number of weekends per month. These weekends were not counted as extra work.

[33] For the sake of clarity, in order to calculate the extra hours per day we assume a Monday–Friday working week, 7 h a day.

[34] The answer of one of the interviewed junior judges seems illustrative: “I think judges are well-paid but bad remunerated.”

[35] Ley 15/2003, de 26 de mayo, reguladora del régimen retributivo de las carreras judicial y fiscal.

Table 4.12 Evaluation of pressure from working conditions

	Number	Percent
Very low	8	6.84
Low	13	11.11
Regular	23	19.66
High	40	34.19
Very high	33	28.21
Total	117	100.01

According to this law, the basic gross salary for newly recruited judges in 2003 was €3,152.21 per month.[36]

Referring to judges' low salary, Toharia Cortés (1975) commented that as long as judges in Spain are one of many types of public servants, their conditions regarding salary are also bound to public servants'—"which is an elliptical way of saying that their salary has always been very low" (Toharia Cortés 1975, p. 62). In that study, 77 % of judges perceived their salary was inferior than other public servants' and CEOs'. Besides, Ayuso et al. (2002) did not find significant differences between junior and senior judges in this regard, though the percentage among junior judges who felt judges were well-paid was even lower (7.4 %) than in our case.

This brings us to a couple of final, apparently contradictory statements of junior judges' evaluation of their feelings about their professional activity. First, Table 4.12 shows the results of a question in which judges had to evaluate the degree of pressure they received from their working conditions. Pressure here means the ratio between the amount of work to be done by judges (e.g., paper work, trials, on-call activities, etc.) and the time available to complete it. In this sense, a significant 62.4 % declares pressure is high or very high, which means that a majority of judges feel that the ratio between work and time is at least unbalanced in the negative direction—i.e., more work than time to carry it out.

This rate of high or very high pressure perception among junior judges is ten points higher than the one found in earlier studies with judges, junior and senior (Ayuso et al. 2003). Nevertheless—and here comes the apparent contradiction—once judges have evaluated the pressure they feel as high or very high; once they report to work a considerable number of extra hours per week; even though a vast majority of them work both at home and during weekends; and even they clearly declare they are under-paid, their final assessment regarding their overall satisfaction level with their work is clearly on the positive end of the scale, as shown in Table 4.13. Over 63 % of junior judges declare to be either satisfied or very satisfied with their work as they experience it, while only 8.54 % are on the negative (i.e., displeased or very displeased) end. Finally, almost 20 % feel that their level of satisfaction is just medium or regular.

[36] It does not include some complements regarding special situations such as, among others, being appointed to a court located in one of the Spanish islands.

Table 4.13 Evaluation of judges' level of satisfaction about their work as they experience it

	Number	Percent
Very displeased	3	2.56
Displeased	7	5.98
Medium	23	19.66
Satisfied	42	35.90
Very satisfied	38	32.48
NA	4	3.42
Total	117	100.00

4.5 Aggregated and Individual Sources of Uncertainty

Previous research (Ayuso et al. 2002, 2003) shows that there is ground to support the idea that junior judges perceive the on-call service as the source of most of their professional problems. However, no research so far has explored to what extent these problems dealt with when on-call are different from the ones raised during regular civil and criminal procedures. What is the main source of uncertainty on junior judges' decision making? Are the problems specific to on-call situations significantly special? Why do problems specifically related to on-call situations are more difficult to deal with than other problems equally related to judges' daily work?

As it will be explained in the next chapter, our hypothesis is that these sources of uncertainty are to be found at the organizational level. It could be the case, though, that doubts and uncertainty in lower courts were triggered by other factors, either at lower (individual) or higher (judicial district) levels than the organization. For instance, difficulties in decision-making might be explained by individual differences among judges: better educated judges should have less doubts when making decisions. This, though, is an implausible scenario, since as we have seen junior judges are highly homogeneous in almost all relevant demographic indicators. They share the same degree of education (by similar universities), they passed the same examination, and spent exactly the same amount of time in the Judicial School and in training.

However, it could also be possible that it is not their individual features that can affect their ability to make decisions but the features of the locations at which they first practice as judges. On the one hand, more populated and higly densed districts might also bring a higher volume and variety of situations to the on-call service, which in turn would increase the chances of finding hard cases. Yet on the other hand, more populated areas have judicial districts with more than one court to handle the volume of cases, and these courts are located in the same city, increasing the opportunity for communication among judges and thence the chances of helping each other when in doubt. On the contrary, judges in smaller and less densely populated districts use to be at single courts where no other judges are directly available, thus increasing solitude in decision making.

The fact is that when we ask junior judges whether they do comment doubts about decisions to their colleagues, 96 % say they do, half of them only occasionally, the other half frequently (Table 4.14).

Table 4.14 Frequency at which judges comment doubts with other peers on making decisions

	Percent
Frequently	50.00
Occasionally	45.69
Never	4.31

With the aim of testing these claims, we fit a logistic regression model on the need to comment on doubts. Due to the small number of respondents affirming that they actually never comment doubts with other peers, we have recoded this outcome variable as having only two categories, one where judges affirm they comment doubts frequently, the other where they only do so occasionally or never.

The models include a number of predictors, both aggregate and individual. On one hand, we have included both the population and the density of the judicial district (both in logarithmic scale), as well as whether the district of the respondent is a single- or multiple-court district. On the other hand, some individual features have also been included. Since the level of education is basically the same among all judges, we have included three different variables that try to capture potential individual differences in their ability to cope with decisions.

First, judges with postgraduate studies have in principle acquired a more specialized knowledge, and therefore they should be less prone to comment on doubts with others. Second, those judges with prior experience in other legal professions are likely to have less doubts when solving problems during their first appointments. Besides, we also include the gap (in years) between the year of judges' Law degree and the year they passed the exam to become judges.

Finally, two additional individual variables capture different ways through which judges interact with their daily work. First, we include their evaluation of the pressure they feel from their working conditions, expecting that those that perceive higher pressure are also more likely to comment frequently on doubts. And second, the amount of overtime they report should be an additional indicator of the difficulties judges face when dealing with their work.

However, when we test the effect of both individual and higher level factors on commenting about doubts, evidence does not give support to these arguments. Table 4.15 shows the results in two steps. The left column shows the coefficients of the logistic regression model using only the higher level predictors, while the column on the right includes these predictors and the individual-level ones.

As it turns out, none of the coefficients in the whole model is significant even at the minimum level of $p = 0.1$, giving little support to the idea that doubts and uncertainty may be raised by individual factors or features of the judicial districts.

Our general hypothesis is that the kind of problems junior judges encounter when on-call are of a special kind in so far they can be described as organizational demands that are practical and not theoretical in nature. That would explain why the on-call service in lower courts is the major source of uncertainty in the decision-making process of junior judges.

Table 4.15 Results of the logistic regression model of the frequency at which junior judges must ask other judges regarding doubts during their first appointment

	Aggregate factors	Individual factors
(Intercept)	−5.02	0.50
	(5.26)	(6.11)
log Population	0.58	0.14
	(0.52)	(0.59)
log Density	−0.26	−0.31
	(0.21)	(0.24)
Single court Yes/No	−0.82	−1.40
	(0.75)	(0.90)
Pressure at work (ref. Very low)		
Pressure: Low		−0.52
		(1.06)
Pressure: Regular		0.64
		(0.90)
Pressure: High		0.88
		(0.86)
Pressure: Very high		1.30
		(0.94)
Overtime (Ref. <= 10 h)		
Overtime: > 10 and <= 20		−0.33
		(0.81)
Overtime: > 20 and <= 30		−0.90
		(0.81)
Overtime: > 30 and <= 40		−1.45
		(1.03)
Overtime: > 40 and <= 50		14.33
		(1022.95)
Postgraduate studies: No		−0.32
		(0.62)
Legal profession before No		−0.83
		(0.65)
Years between graduation and exam		−0.04
		(0.05)
Likelihood-ratio	6.65	20.24
Log-likelihood	−77.08	−68.16

Table 4.15 (continued)

	Aggregate factors	Individual factors
AIC	162.16	166.33
BIC	173.17	207.24
N	116	113

Should the analysis carried out in the next chapter give support to this hypothesis, this phenomenon would represent both a professional and an organizational challenge to the whole Spanish judicial system. Professionally, the skills required to sort out the kind of problems during the on-call service would contrast sharply with the exclusively legal-theoretical education of Spanish judges. At the organizational level, the phenomenon would represent a suspension of the organization's role as a stable pattern of events, for ready-made solutions to most of these practical problems are not provided with at an organizational level (in contrast to, say, civil procedures), but judges must work them out by themselves. Hence the uncertainty.

References

Álvarez, R., M. Ayuso, and M. Bécue-Bertaut. 2005. Statistical study of judicial practices. In *Law and the semantic web. Legal ontologies, methodologies, legal information retrieval, and applications*, ed. V. R. Benjamins, P. Casanovas, J. Breuker, and A. Gangemi. vol. 3369 in Lecture Notes in Computer Science, pp. 25–35. Berlin: Springer.

Ayuso, M., M. Bécue-Bertaut, R. Álvarez, O. Valencia, M. Álvarez, M. Hernández, and M. Santolino. 2002. Jueces jóvenes en España, 2002. Análisis estadístico de las encuestas a los jueces en su primer destino (promociones 48/49 y 50). Internal report (project sec-2001-2581-c02-01/02), Consejo General del Poder Judicial [General Council of the Judiciary].

Ayuso, M., M. Bécue-Bertaut, R. Álvarez, O. Valencia, M. Álvarez, and M. Santolino. 2003. Análisis estadístico de las encuestas a los jueces en su primer destino. Internal Report SEC-2001-2581-C02-01/02, Consejo General del Poder Judicial [General Council of the Judiciary], Escuela Judicial (Barcelona).

Benjamins, V. R., J. Contreras, M. Blázquez, L. Rodrigo, P. Casanovas, and M. Poblet. 2004a. The SeKT use legal case components: Ontology and architecture. In *Legal knowledge and information systems. Jurix 2004*, ed. T. B. Gordon, pp. 69–77. Amsterdam: IOS Press.

Benjamins, V. R., J. Contreras, P. Casanovas, M. Ayuso, M. Bécue-Bertaut, M. Lemus, and C. Urios. 2004b. Ontologies of professional legal knowledge as the basis for intelligent it support for judges. *Artificial Intelligence and Law* 12 (4): 359–378.

Benjamins, V. R., P. Casanovas, J. Breuker, and A. Gangemi, eds. 2005. *Law and the semantic web. Legal ontologies, methodologies, legal information retrieval, and applications*. vol. 3369 in Lecture Notes in Computer Science. Berlin: Springer.

Calvet, J. 2005. *El govern de la Generalitat valenciana: 1983–1995*. PhD thesis, Departament de Dret Constitucional i Ciència Política, Universitat de Barcelona, Barcelona.

Capo, J. 1981. *Las Cortes del 15 de junio: estructura, composición y funciones*. PhD thesis, University of Barcelona, Barcelona.

Casanovas, P. 1995. Introducción al análisis científico-social de los procesos judiciales. In *Oñati Proceeding Series*, ed. R. Bergalli. vol. 19, 83–117. Gipuzkoa: Oñati.

Casanovas, P. 1997. Pragmática de las decisiones judiciales: diferencias de razonamiento y lenguaje ante el jurado. *Cuadernos de Derecho Judicial* XVI:111–142.

Casanovas, P. 2000. The culture of young legal professionals in spain: An interpretative hypothesis of some statistical and field research data. In *Law & society reader*, ed. P. Casanovas and P. Fabra, 101–112. Barcelona: UOC.

Casanovas, P. 2001. Los laberintos de H. A. Simon. In *El Derecho en la Teoría Social. Diálogo con catorce propuestas actuales*, ed. J. A. García-Amado, 185–224. Madrid: Dykinson.

Casanovas, P., V. R. Benjamins, J. Contreras, M. Lemus, and C. Urios. 2003. Iuriservice: un FAQ inteligente para los jueces en su primer destino. In *Internet y pluralismo jurídico: formas emergentes de regulación*, ed. P. Casanovas. Granada: Comares.

Casanovas, P., M. Poblet, N. Casellas, J. Contreras, V. R. Benjamins, and M. Blázquez. 2005. Supporting newly-appointed judges: A legal knowledge management case study. *Journal of Knowledge Management* 9 (5): 7–27.

Casanovas, P., N. Casellas, J.-J. Vallbé, M. Poblet, V. R. Benjamins, M. Blázquez, R. Peña-Ortiz, and J. Contreras. 2006. Semantic web: A legal case study. In *Semantic web technologies: Trends and research in ontology-based systems*, ed. J. Davies, R. Studer, and P. Warren, Chap. 12, 259–280. Chichester: Wiley.

Casellas, N. 2008. *Modelling legal knowledge through ontologies. OPJK: The Ontology of Professional Judicial Knowledge*. PhD thesis, Political Science and Public Law Department, Bellaterra, Catalonia, Spain.

Casellas, N. 2011. *Legal ontology engineering: Methodologies, trends, and the ontology of professional judicial knowledge*. Dordrecht: Springer.

Casellas, N., A. Jakulin, J.-J. Vallbé, and P. Casanovas. 2006. Acquiring an ontology from the text. In *Advances in applied artificial intelligence. 19th international conference on industrial, engineering and other applications of applied intelligent systems, IEA/AIE 2006*, ed. M. Ali and R. Dapoigny, vol. 4031 in Lecture Notes in Computer Science, 1000–1013. Berlin: Springer.

Cerviño Cuerva, E. 2003. *Políticas de representación sindical: UGT y CCOO ante el empleo temporal (1977–1997)*. PhD thesis, Departamento de Ciencia Política Universidad Autónoma de Madrid, Madrid, Spain.

CGPJ. 2009. Escalafón de la carrera judicial. Report, Consejo General del Poder Judicial [General Council of the Judiciary], Madrid, Spain.

CGPJ. 2013. *The Spanish Judiciary in Figures 2012*. CGPJ, Madrid.

CIS. 1984. *Primer barómetro interno de opinión. Encuesta realizada a una muestra estadísticamente representativa de Jueces y Magistrados*. Consejo General del Poder Judicial, Madrid, Spain.

Demoscopia. 1999. *Quinto Barómetro Interno de Opinión. Encuesta realizada a una muestra estadísticamente representativa de Jueces y Magistrados*. Consejo General del Poder Judicial, Madrid, Spain.

di Federico, G., ed. 2005. *Recruitment, Professional Evaluation and Career of Judges and Prosecutors in Europe: Austria, France, Germany, Italy, The Netherlands and Spain*. IRSIG-CNR, Unversity of Bologna, Ed. Lo Scarabeo, Bologna, Italy.

Estruch, J. 1993. *L'Opus Dei i les seves paradoxes*. Barcelona: Edicions 62.

García Herrando, J., ed. 1993. *Pluralismo religioso en España*. Madrid: Sociedad de Educación Atenas.

García-Valdés, C. 1987. La selección y formación de los jueces en españa: el centro de estudios judiciales. *Poder Judicial* Segunda época 1512 (7): 87–95.

Goldman, S. 2001. Judicial selection. In *International encyclopedia of the social & behavioral sciences*, ed. N. J. Smelser and P. B. Baltes, 8024–8027. New York: Elsevier.

González-Granda, P. 1993. *Independencia del juez y control de su actividad*. València: Tirant lo Blanch.

Gunther, R., J. R. Montero, and J. J. Linz, eds. 2002. *Political parties: Old concepts and new challenges*. Oxford: Oxford University Press.

Gunther, R., J. R., Montero, and J. Botella. 2004. *Democracy in modern Spain*. New Haven: Yale University Press.

Hermet, G. 1985. *Los católicos en la España franquista*. Madrid: Centro de Investigaciones Sociológicas.

Jiménez-Asensio, R., ed. 2001. *El acceso a la función judicial. Estudio comparado*. Manuales de formación continuada. Consejo General del Poder Judicial, Madrid, Spain.

Lancaster, T. D. 2002. Spain. In *Legal systems of the world*, ed. H. M. Kritzer. vol. IV, 1513–1520. Santa Barbara: ABC-CLIO.

Linz, J. J., and Montero J. R., eds. 1986. *Crisis y cambio: electores y partidos en la España de los años ochenta*. Madrid: Centro de Estudios Constitucionales.

Linz, J. J., and J. R. Montero. 1999. *The party systems of Spain: Old cleavages and new challenges*. Centro de Estudios Avanzados en Ciencias Sociales. Instituto Juan March de Estudios e Investigaciones, Madrid, Spain.

Magre, J. 1999. *L'alcalde a Catalunya*. Barcelona: Institut de Ciències Polítiques i Socials (ICPS).

Magre, J., ed. 2006. *Informe de l'Observatori de Govern Local*. Barcelona: Fundació Carles Pi i Sunyer.

Martínez, R. 2007. *Los mandos de las Fuerzas Armadas españolas del siglo XXI*. Madrid: Centro de Investigaciones Sociológicas.

Matas, J. 1995. *Els alts càrrecs: política i administració a la Generalitat de Catalunya*. Barcelona: Publicacions de la Universitat de Barcelona.

Montero, J. R. 1998. *Stablishing the democratic order: Electoral behaviour in Spain*. Centro de Estudios Avanzados en Ciencias Sociales. Instituto Juan March de Estudios e Investigaciones, Madrid, Spain.

Montero, J. R., J. Font, and M. Torcal, eds. 2006. *Ciudadanos, asociaciones y participación en España*. Madrid: Centro de Investigaciones Sociológicas.

Moreno Catena, V., ed. 2003. *Manual de organización judicial*. València: Tirant lo Blanch.

Muñoz-Mendoza, J. 2012. *La construcción política de la identidad española: Â¿del nacionalcatolicismo al patriotismo democrático?*. Madrid: CIS.

Pastor-Prieto, S. 1993. *Ah de la justicia! Política judicial y economía*. Madrid: Centro de Publicaciones del Ministerio de Justicia/Civitas.

Penella, M. 2005. *Los orígenes y la evolución del Partido Popular: una historia de AP*. Salamanca: Caja Duero.

Poblet, M., and Casanovas, P. 2005. Recruitment, professional evaluation and career of judges and prosecutors in Spain. In *Recruitment, Professional Evaluation and Career of Judges and Prosecutors in Europe: Austria, France, Germany, Italy, The Netherlands and Spain*, ed. G. di Federico, 185–213. Bologna: Lo Scarabeo.

Poblet, M., J.-J. Vallbé, N. Casellas, and P. Casanovas. 2008. Judges as IT users: The IURISERVICE example. In *E-justice, using information communication in the court system*, ed. A. Cerrillo and P. Fabra. Hershey: IGI Books.

Reniu, J. M. 2001. *Las teorías de las coaliciones políticas revisadas: la formación de gobiernos minoritarios en España, 1977–1996*. PhD thesis, Constitutional Law and Political Science Department, Barcelona.

Rodrigo, L., M. Blázquez, P. Casanovas, and M. Poblet. 2004. D10.1.1 legal case study before analysis, semantically enabled knowledge technologies. Technical report, EU-IST Project IST-2003-506826 SEKT.

Tezanos, J. F., R. Cotarelo, and A. de Blas, eds. 1989. *La transición democrática española*. Madrid: Sistema.

Toharia Cortés, J. J. 1975. *El juez español: un análisis sociológico*. Madrid: Tecnos.

Toharia Cortés, J. J. 1987. *Pleitos tengas! Introducción a la cultura legal española*. Madrid: Centro de Investigaciones Sociológicas/Siglo XXI.

Toharia Cortés, J. J. 1989. El juez español: quince años después. *Revista del Centro de Estudios Constitucionales* 3:345–364.

Toharia Cortés, J. J. 2001. Judges. In *International encyclopedia of the social & behavioral sciences*, ed. N. J. Smelser and P. B. Baltes, 8014–0020. New York: Elsevier.

Toharia Cortés, J. J. 2003. Sistema judicial y cultura jurídica en españa (1975–2000). In *Culturas jurídicas latinas de Europa y América en tiempos de globalización*, ed. H. Fix-Fierro, L. M.

Friedman, and R. Pérez-Perdomo, 305–358. México: Instituto de Investigaciones Jurídicas-UNAM.
Toharia Cortés, J. J. 2006. Qué esperan los ciudadanos de la justicia? *Estudios de Derecho Judicial* 109:34–42.
Toharia Cortés, J. J., and J. J. García de la Cruz Herrero. 2005. *La Justicia ante el espejo: 25 años de estudios de opinión del CGPJ*. Consejo General del Poder Judicial, Madrid, Spain.
Vallbé, J.-J., N. Casellas, P. Casanovas, and J.-M. López-Cobo. 2010. A decision-support system to manage legal organizational memories. In *SubTech 2010. 11th international conference on substantive technology in legal education and practice*, Zaragoza, Spain. SubTech.

Chapter 5
Representing Organizational Uncertainty

Abstract This chapter presents the main data analysis of the book. First, the hypotheses are presented. Second, the framework for treating text as data is discussed, and textual data are described. Third, the data analysis itself is performed. The analysis begins exploring the extent to which the problems raised during the on-call service are indeed different from the other problematic situations judges deal with in their work. After that, we test whether the problems faced when on call are not related to theoretical doubts but mainly practical doubts, i.e., they are identifiable demands from the outer environment whose solution is not specifically contained in the legal knowledge they acquire either in the law degree or preparing the entrance examination.

5.1 Introduction

Our general hypothesis is that the kind of problems junior judges encounter when on-call are of a special kind in so far they can be described as organizational demands that are practical and not theoretical in nature. That is why the on-call service in lower courts is the major source of uncertainty in the decision-making process of junior judges.

Should our analyses give support to this hypothesis, this phenomenon would represent both a professional and an organizational challenge to the whole Spanish judicial system. Professionally, the skills required to sort out the kind of problems during the on-call service would contrast sharply with the exclusively legal-theoretical education of Spanish judges. At the organizational level, the phenomenon would represent a suspension of the organization's role as a stable pattern of events, for ready-made solutions to most of these practical problems are not provided with at an organizational level (in contrast to, say, civil procedures), but judges must work them out by themselves. Hence the uncertainty.

A first hypothesis can be thus stated:

Hypothesis 1 The types of problems raised during the on-call service are significantly different from those raised by ordinary civil and criminal procedures.

J.-J. Vallbé, *Frameworks for Modeling Cognition and Decisions in Institutional Environments*, Law, Governance and Technology Series 21, DOI 10.1007/978-94-017-9427-5_5

As we have explained earlier, the features of the on-call service make us expect that there are sharp differences between the problems encountered in on-call situations and the ones raised by civil procedures, because civil procedures are rarely started through the on-call service in lower courts. A major challenge to our first hypothesis, though, is expected to come from the relationship between the on-call problems and other ordinary criminal procedures. In particular, as we know, most of the problems dealt with by the on-call service are of criminal nature. The key question here is whether the issues dealt with during on-call situations and ordinary procedures, albeit both criminal in nature, are significantly different from each other.

Should this difference exist, we would then be able to explore the nature of the problems raised during on-call situations. In particular, we want to explore the role of the organizational environment in junior judges' working problems—i.e., the extent to which these problems and doubts raised during the on-call service are demands from the outer, organizational environment. The practical, organizational nature of the on-call problems would then contrast with a more theoretical-based nature of the problems raised during ordinary criminal procedures, and therefore their solution should not be specifically contained in the legal knowledge judges acquire either in the law degree or preparing the entrance examination: theoretical *legal* knowledge.

Our second hypothesis can now be thus stated:

Hypothesis 2 The problems faced when on call are not related to theoretical doubts but mainly practical doubts, i.e., they are identifiable demands from the outer environment whose solution is not specifically contained in the legal knowledge they acquire either in the law degree or preparing the entrance examination.

Before our general hypothesis can be tested, though, some exploratory analysis should first be carried out. In particular, we should explore the extent to which the problems raised during the on-call service are indeed different from the other problematic situations judges deal with in their work. As we have just explained above, previous research (Ayuso et al. 2002, 2003) shows that there is ground to support the idea that junior judges perceive the on-call service as the source of most of their professional problems. However, no research so far has explored to what extent these problems dealt with when on-call are different from the ones raised during regular civil and criminal procedures.

5.2 Data

The first attempt to carry out an empirical assessment of the difficulties and problems encountered by judges during their first years in the career (Ayuso et al. 2002; Benjamins et al. 2004) presented an added value compared to similar studies: it contained an open-ended question in which junior judges could explain what were their major problems encountered during their daily work.

The textual data from the answers to this question were analyzed with textual statistics methods to extract the domains where the difficulties lied. In order to identify these domains, Ayuso et al. (2003) separated the answers given by junior judges (subcorpus JJ) from those given by experienced judges (EJ), and sought what nouns were significantly overrepresented in junior judges' answers.

The research problem consisted in that for each word i the researchers had to assess a statistical conclusion about the significance of the count k_{ij}, the frequency of the word i in part j of the corpus of answers. For example, 18 occurrences of the noun *guardia* (on-call) were used by the judges, which was used by the research team to see whether junior judges referred to problems related to the on-call service significantly more than to other issues.

The count k_{ij} had to be compared to the other counts obtained with all the possible samples comprised of $k : j$ occurrences extracted from the whole corpus without replacement. The probability distribution for a sampling without replacement under the hypothesis of independence is the hypergeometric distribution (Ayuso et al. 2002), which contrasts with the binomial distribution (with replacement). Or in other words, the "probability of obtaining k items, of one out of two categories, in a sample of n items extracted without replacement from a population of N items that has $D = pN$ items of that category (and $(1-p)N = qN$ items from the other category)" (Marques de Sá 2007).

Results showed that the word *guardia* [on-call] turned out to be over-represented in the subcorpus JJ, the one from junior judges. Furthermore, this over-representation was found to be significant (Ayuso et al. 2003).

The data available in that survey, though, were limited. Questions were general, not specific, and answers were too short to allow any further text exploration. This led to our current survey on Spanish junior judges, which, on one hand, was specifically focused on junior judges, and on the other was designed to gather the types of problems that sprang from on-call situations.

Having rich textual data—part of it specifically focused on on-call problems—permits a variety of research strategies in order to both gather relevant data for modelling a knowledge base, and advance in our understanding of the problems faced by judges at courts when on-call.

5.2.1 Corpora

In order to carry out our analysis, we use three different textual corpora. These are composed by the set of responses to the open-ended questions contained in our survey. In particular, these questions were:

- A question about the main types of problems regarding *civil* issues during the first appointment.
- A question about the main types of problems regarding *criminal* issues during the first appointment.
- A question about the main types of problems during *on-call* periods.

Table 5.1 Number of respondents and non respondents for each corpus

Corpus	Responses			
	Expected	*No record*	*No answer*	*Actual*
Civil	118	4	3	111
Criminal	118	4	5	109
On-call	118	4	4	110
Total	354	12	12	330

Since interviews were recorded, each answer was literally transcribed and saved in a different text file. Thus we have three different corpora (i.e., sets of responses) that contain a number of text files, each of which representing a single answer to a particular question. The three corpora are thus named and described:

- `civil`: The collection of all responses regarding problems about civil issues, each document representing one single answer. It contains 111 responses out of 118 interviewed judges. Out of the 7 lacking respondents, 4 did not accept a recording, while 3 were not able to recall a single civil problem during the interview.
- `criminal`: The collection of all responses regarding problems about criminal issues, each document representing one single answer. It contains 109 responses out of 118 possible responses. Out of the 9 lacking responses, 4 were due to non recorded interview, while 5 respondents were not able to recall any problem specifically related to criminal issues.
- `on-call`: The collection of all responses regarding problems about on-call issues, each document representing one single answer. It contains 110 responses out of 118. As already noted, half of them were not recorded, while the other half were not able to recall any on-call problem at that moment.

Finally, Table 5.1 summarizes the state of each corpus regarding respondents and non-respondents.

5.2.2 *Text as Data*

Our hypotheses involve, on one hand, testing whether our textual corpora (civil, criminal, and on-call problems) are significantly different from each other, and on the other exploring the content of these corpora in a systematic way. Note that in both cases we treat text as data. We assume that the significant differences among documents can be reduced to differences in the use of language in the documents. Specifically, if two documents refer to different topics (e.g. they refer to different kinds of problems), these differences can appear in both the types of words they contain, and the frequency of these words. We apply statistical methods to these textual data in order to account for these differences in meaningful ways.

Table 5.2 Descriptive statistics of the textual corpora used in the analysis

Corpora	N docs	Min.	Mean	Median	Max.	Std. Dev.	Tokens	Types
On call	110	21	664.1	459	3692	742.7	73,048	3290
Civil	111	5	380.5	115	5027	782.4	36,147	2685
Criminal	109	11	454.8	192.5	3339	634.3	42,748	2925

Using text as data to extract relevant social or political information in systematic ways is an old practice in political science (e.g. Lasswell et al. 1949). Compared to classical content analysis, computer-assisted text analysis (CATA) has peaked recently due to the ease of access to massive amounts of textual data (Grimmer and Stewart 2013), with applications in the analysis of party manifestos (e.g. Klingemann et al. 2006), media political content (e.g., Sementko and Valkenburg 2000), actor influence in policy dynamics (Klüver 2009), or the analyisis of coalition dynamics (Falcó-Gimeno and Vallbé 2013).

A number of reasons support the use of computerized methods for textual data analysis over semi-automated or even manual methods. On one hand, CATA-based research strategies are less time- and resource consuming than classical content analysis, the latter being highly dependent upon human or semi-automatic codification of units of text (Budge et al. 2001; Klingemann et al. 2006; Jones and Baumgartner 2012), which in times of large amounts of available textual information turns out to be a serious shortcoming. On the other hand, CATA techniques are better equipped to deal with potential measurement problems that typically affect classical content analysis projects (Neuendorf 2002; Krippendorff 2004; Benoit and Laver 2007; Budge and Pennings 2007a, b; Benoit et al. 2009).

Text may be analysed automatically at different levels responding to the research purpose at hand. Lower units such as words, sentences or text chunks are often used to account for the identification of semantic features within relatively extensive corpora, while whole documents (be they simple queries, court decisions or party manifestos) are usually taken for classification and scaling. In particular, Natural Language Processing (NLP), Machine Learning, and Text Mining techniques (e.g., multiple correspondence analysis, principal components analysis, multidimensional scaling and hierarchical clustering) have been widely used for topic identification (Lebart and Salem 1988), semantic extraction (Reinert 2000; Schonhardt-Bailey 2005, 2008), semi-automated dictionary construction (Young and Soroka 2012), and document scaling and classification (Srivastava and Sahami 2009; Falcó-Gimeno and Vallbé 2013).

Regardless of the method applied, though, we must begin with a basic description of our textual data. To this effect, Table 5.2 presents basic descriptive statistics based on the word frequency of each document of the three corpora. We observe, first, that the On-call corpus is by far the larger of the three, with just above 73,000 word occurrences (tokens) and 3290 different words (types). Accordingly, the documents within the On-call corpus present a higher average frequency. Nevertheless, the three corpora have some similarities. First, all three present large differences regarding the word count of their documents. Note that in three cases there are documents with a very low word count (e.g., there is a document with just five words in the Civil corpus), and documents with a very large number of words (the larger document in the Civil corpus has 5027 words). The fourth and fifth columns of the table present measures of concentration. The fact that the median number of words is larger than the mean indicates a larger number of low-frequency documents in all three corpora. The standard deviation indicates the average distance between document frequencies and the mean frequency.

In order to compare the content of the documents through statistical methods to textual data we adopt the Bag of Words (or Vector Space) Model, that represents documents as vectors in a common vector space and is widely used in text mining and information retrieval (Salton et al. 1975; Baeza-Yates and Ribeiro-Neto 1999; Manning and Schütze 1999; Jakulin and Buntine 2004; Manning et al. 2008; Fortuna et al. 2009). Consider a corpus D that contains a number n of documents d:

$$D = \{d_1, d_2, d_3, \ldots, d_n\}$$

In turn, each document d has a number m of terms t:

$$d = \{t_1, t_2, t_3 \ldots, t_m\}$$

Each term t occurs with frequency $tf_{t,d} > 0$, which denotes the frequency of term t in document d. The frequency of all m terms in a document d will then be:

$$tf_d = \sum_{i=1}^{m} (tf_1, tf_2, tf_3, \ldots tf_m)$$

This way, each document d can then be represented as a a "bag of words" with repeated elements (each one repeated as many times as its frequency), or as a vector $\vec{d}$ of m weighted terms (Huang 2008):

$$\vec{d} = (tf_{1,d}, tf_{2,d}, tf_{3,d}, \ldots, tf_{m,d}),$$

where weights are term frequencies.

In this approach, the order in which terms occur in documents is ignored, and a corpus D is represented as a matrix X_D in which rows are the document vectors $d_1, d_2, \ldots d_n$, and terms are columns—a so-called document-term matrix. Each cell of the matrix will denote $tf_{t,d}$—the frequency in which each term t occurs in each document d. Typically document-term matrices are highly sparse (large number of zeroes) and highly dimensional (large number of columns).

Intuitively, content similarity between two documents is understood as the two document vectors having similar vector representations (Manning et al. 2008).

5.2.3 Data Preparation

Before textual data can be used for statistical or analytical purposes, they typically undergo a process of preparation and cleaning, which is intended to reduce the amount of unnecessary data and, therefore, to reduce computational burden and improve the quality of the analysis. In particular, data preparation eventually leads to term reduction, which may be understood both as a reduction (or standardization) of terms themselves and as a reduction of the corpus size (number of terms), and which eventually leads to the reduction of matrix sparsity.

On one hand, reduction of words to their roots has been usually referred to as a necessary step before performing statistical treatment to any textual corpus with the aim of extracting reliable information from it (e.g. Guérin-Pace 1998; Korenius et al. 2004; Bécue-Bertaut et al. 2005; Proksch and Slapin 2009).[1] The main reason for that operation is that having word roots instead of original tokens reduces drastically the noise of a corpus and enables having a more reliable count of word frequency. However, there are two different and widely used methods for word reduction, but these methods do not perform equally well for all languages. The first method is known as stemming, while the second is lemmatization.

Stemming implies the application of a set of rules to transform a word into its stem usually by cutting-off that word's suffix. For instance, elsewhere Vallbé et al. (2007) pointed out that a stemmer would put all the variants of *love* (verb and noun), *loving* (verb), *lover* (noun), *lovely* (adjective), etc., behind the reduced form "lov+". A lemmatizer, on the other hand, would assign the above words to three different lemmas: *love, lover*, and *lovely*, based on their grammatical form.

Poorly inflected languages such as English present only four possible forms for verbs (infinitive [to rul*e*], third person *–s* in the singular [rul*es*], gerund [rul*ing*], and participle [rul*ed*]). Note that future and conditional tenses are performed with the use of *will* and *would*. Therefore, variation is rare.

On the contrary, Roman languages such as Spanish and Catalan have a very rich inflection rate.[2] Therefore, if stemming is used for word reduction in any of these languages, a lot of information remains hidden and the stemming process will perform roughly. Furthermore, a lot of nominal, verbal and/or adjectival forms are identical, for instance *hammer* (can be verb and noun and can form adjectival forms through the adjunction of some other particles, as in *hammer-shaped*) (Vallbé et al. 2007).

In effect, stemming may put many different forms behind the same stem. For instance, in Spanish it may put *estafa* [fraud] and *estafeta* [post office] behind the root *estaf+*, while these two forms are obviously not even related. Lemmatization would give both different forms as they represent two different types.

---

[1] Unless the information we want to extract be directly related to any form of language inflection.

[2] Both languages can have up to 60 different forms for verbs, not counting the composed forms (Vallbé and Martí 2009). The case is also applied to other languages such as Slovenian (Vallbé et al. 2007).

Moreover, in some cases stemming gives different stems when there should be the same stem. As an example, in irregular verbal forms such as *absolver* [to absolve] and *absuelto* [absolved], a stemming algorithm is very likely to deliver two stems: *absol+* and *resuel+*, though it would be wrong as long as they are two different forms of the same verb, and the only valid lemma would be its infinitive form *absolver*.[3] As a consequence, lemmatization proves a more suitable word reduction strategy for our textual corpora. To obtain the lemmatized version of our corpora we use MACO (Carmona et al. 1998), a Morphological Analyser for Spanish (and Catalan) developed by public Spanish universities.[4]

However, despite having reduced the noise in our data through an effective reduction to term lemmas, our data still suffer from a relevant problem: our documents still contain a number of words that do not contribute to shaping documents' semantic meaning—i.e. "certain terms have little or no discriminating power in determining relevance" (Manning et al. 2008). We want our vector representations (i.e., documents) to be as semantically relevant as possible.

On one hand, typically the most frequent words in a corpus are function words—i.e., prepositions, articles and other grammatical words. These are commonly known as stopwords—they also may include a few auxiliary verbs—, words that generally do not add any content or information to text (as also happens with numbers in this case) and occur with high frequency in all texts.

These words may be really important for some research purposes such as author identification through some stylistic features (Murtagh 2005; Feinerer et al. 2008). Besides, discourse analysis and pragmatics have also made an extensive use of these linguistic particles. But as semantic content retrieval is concerned, they are thought of as rarely adding information (Manning and Schütze 1999). For instance, in the legal text retrieval field, Moens (2001) asserts that a stop list typically "contains terms in the subject domain that are insuficiently specific to represent content", and they have been systematically removed in research involving building conceptual structures that represent specific knowledge domains (Casellas 2011). The fact is that they are too common to tell us anything relevant about our texts, and removing them can reduce a corpus to half of its tokens (Manning and Schütze 1999, p. 534). A most effective way to remove all the functional terms from a corpus is filtering the text through a list of stopwords.

On the other hand, in our collection of documents it is very likely that a number of terms that are not merely functional occur in almost if not all the documents. These may be terms referring to the Civil Law itself (*Ley de Enjuiciamiento*

[3] Of course, different stemming algorithms yield different results depending on the set of rules upon which they operate (e.g., Porter 1980). See also http://snowball.tartarus.org/texts/introduction.html for an excellent introduction.

[4] I would like to give special thanks here to Toni Martí and Montse Nofre from CLiC—Centre de Llenguatge i Computació at the University of Barcelona—for granting my free access to the analyzer during the completion of this work. There are other open source tools available that include lemmatization among other features, such as FreeLing, available at http://nlp.lsi.upc.edu/freeling/.

Table 5.3 Descriptive statistics of the final, clean corpora

Corpora	N docs	Mean	Median	Std. Dev.	Tokens	Original lemmas	Lemmas TFIDF	Reduction
On call	110	85.6	74	71.8	9414	3290	1535	−0.53
Civil	111	94.4	42	142.9	10,483	2685	1259	−0.53
Criminal	109	80.4	48	84.6	8762	2925	1318	−0.55
Whole								
corpus	330	50.7	33	50.7	16,722	5150	1896	−0.63

Criminal (LEC)), or other generic terms referring to legal procedures such as process (*proceso*) or notification (*notification*). Since they tend to occur many times in all documents, these terms do not discriminate the specific topics present in each document.

In order to identify the most irrelevant terms from a collection of texts, text mining and textual statistics usually make use of the *Term Frequency - Inverse Document Frequency* (TF-IDF) criterium (Manning and Schütze 1999; Manning et al. 2008; Srivastava and Sahami 2009), with the objective of giving lower weight to those terms that occur in most documents in a corpus, since they do not bear relevant content to the corpus (Basu and Davidson 2009).

Term-Frequency (tf_t) of a term t is the number of occurrences of a particular term in a document. df_t is the number of documents in which t appears. If we have N documents in the corpus, the Inverse Document Frequency (IDF) of t is:

$$idf_t = ln\frac{N}{df_t}$$

When we combine the frequency of each term in a document (tf_i) with that term's inverse document frequency (idf_t), we obtain a score of the relevance of each term with respect to each document, that typically will be high when a term occurs many times in just a few documents, and low when a term occurs in all documents or has a very low frequency in a document (Manning et al. 2008):

$$tfidf_t = tf_t * idf_t$$

For each corpus, we select the terms that have a mean TFIDF score over the documents just over the median (Grün and Hornik 2011), so that we keep the really relevant terms.

Once we lemmatize all three corpora and remove stopwords and non-relevant terms, the dimensions and sparsity of the document-term matrices is critically reduced, as observed in Table 5.3.[5] The column called *Original lemmas* indicates the

[5] Numbers and punctuation have also been removed from the documents, as is common practice. Also, a small of other terms was also removed from the corpus for other reasons. First, a full commitment regarding full respect for respondent's identity was specifically signed in an agreement between the General Council of the Judiciary and the research group under which this project was

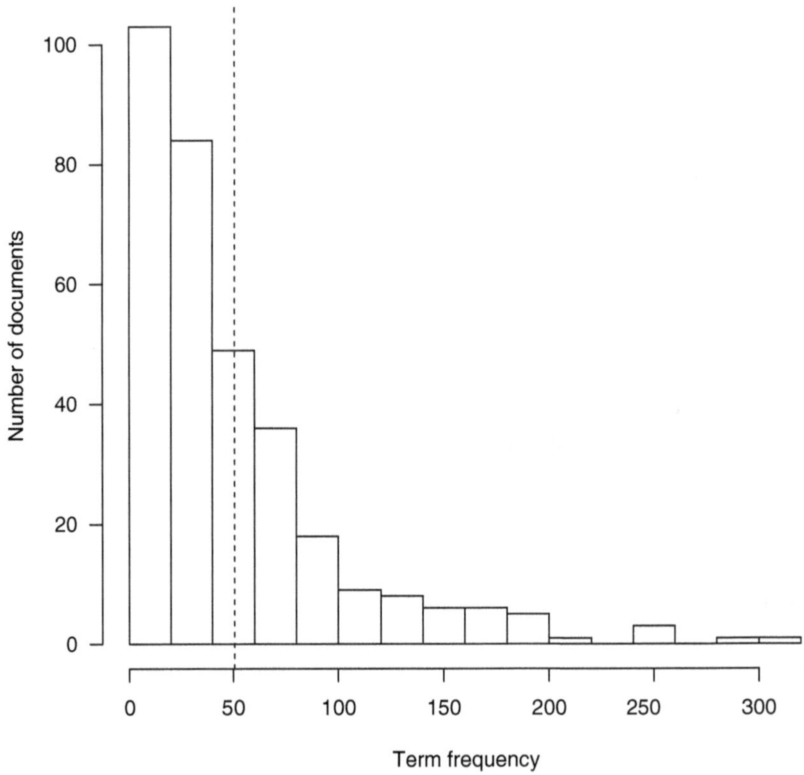

Fig. 5.1 Distribution of term frequency among all the documents in the whole corpus

number of different terms of the lemmatized corpora, while *Lemmas TFIDF* shows the number of relevant terms selected considering TFIDF. In all three corpora, the number of terms is reduced to its half. Table 5.3 also shows the results of data reduction when we carry it out to a textual corpus containing all three previous corpora altogether. Note that the implementation of the TFIDF criterium in the "Whole" corpus produces a higher level of lemma reduction. The inclusion of the responses on all three issues (civil, on-call, and criminal) has an effect on the heterogeneity of the "Whole" corpus, which in turn reduces the number of discriminating terms within the documents. As shown in Fig. 5.1, now most documents have on average a small

carried out (Institute of Law and Technology) before interviews were carried out. Besides, each interviewed judge was informed that this agreement existed before the interview was recorded. When requested, a copy of the agreement was also handed. Due to this, all information that might be interpreted as revealing either personal names or toponyms that could lead to the identification of a judge has been removed from the data. And also due to this agreement, full records of the interviews are not openly delivered in an on-line appendix to this book. Finally, the term *guardia* [on-call] was also removed from the corpus so as not to produce a clear bias the automatic classification of judges' responses when applying cluster analysis or any other classification method.

number of very relevant terms (the dotted vertical line marks the mean number of terms per document). We now have clean data ready to be analyzed in the rest of the chapter.

5.3 On-Call Service as a Professional Problem (Hypothesis 1)

As explained above, judges who have recently finished their courses at the Judicial School start their professional career in Courts of First Instance and Magistrate. Findings in organizational decision theory and behavioral decision making suggest that the decision-maker adapts to a problem environment shaped by a number of organizational constraints.

Empirical findings related to Spanish junior judges suggested that on-call periods are specially problematic to junior judges during their 1st years. Regarding our first hypothesis, we aim at testing whether the differences betweeen civil, criminal, and on-call problems are significantly different from each other. These differences should arise because when asked about their main problems during civil procedures, criminal procedures, and on-call situations, judges refer to different things in each case. To carry out a systematic comparison of documents, we adopt a double strategy of analysis that involves both a classification and a scaling procedure.

On one hand, the hypothesis involves a simple classification problem—the identification of homogeneous groups of documents. In particular, we aim at testing whether the three different textual corpora constitute three different, homogeneous sets of textual data, different from each other. On the other hand, we also aim at representing and explaining any structure or pattern in the (dis)similarities between (groups of) documents, in a way that the proximity between clusters and documents can be analyzed.

To do so, first, in order to obtain similar groups of documents based on the similarity of their vector representations, we will implement a hierarchical clustering algorithm and the results will be discussed. Second, a Multidimensional Scaling (MDS) algorithm will be used to scale the documents so that similarity between documents and clusters can be tested.

5.3.1 Method: Document Clustering and Scaling

The unprecedented growth of available textual data, either on the World Wide Web or in digital archives from publishers, governments or companies, has made of text mining a basic toolkit to "help people better understand and make use of the information in document repositories" (Srivastava and Sahami 2009). Among text mining techniques, Cluster analysis and Multidimensional scaling are now key methods for data grouping and classification, widely used in all kinds of data-intense scientific endeavors, such as market segmentation (Mooi and Sarstedt 2011), population cluster identification through genetic similarity (Witherspoon et al. 2007), analysis of political and legal data (Jakulin 2007), and information retrieval (Srivastava and Sahami 2009).

On one hand, a clustering algorithm divides a collection of documents into a set of similar documents, or clusters, so that "documents within a cluster should be as similar as possible; and documents in one cluster should be as dissimilar as possible from documents in other clusters" (Manning et al. 2008). This allows not only reducing large amounts of information to a small set of coherent elements, but its output can also be further used to train machine learning algorithms with various purposes such as automatic information retrieval or information extraction (Huang 2008). On the other hand, Multidimensional scaling (MDS) is an effective exploratory data analysis tool—used in various domains such as psychology (Jaworska and Chupetlovska-Anastasova 2009), political science (Lauderdale and Clark 2012), or text visualization (Fortuna et al. 2005)—to handle and visualize multidimensional data into a lower dimensional space, so that inferences can be drawn from the representation of the similarities between objects.

Note that both methods require a definition of what is for two documents (vector representation) to be "similar". Instead of the commonly used Euclidean distance metric, we use the Bray-Curtis dissimilarity measure (Bray and Curtis 1957). Although Euclidean distance is very common in all kinds of clustering applications due to its more "natural" flavour (it can be conceptualized as "distance", Greenacre 2005), it works well with ratio or interval data (Mooi and Sarstedt 2011) but not with count data. For count data (term frequencies), the Bray–Curtis dissimilartiy measure (Bray and Curtis 1957) is most adequate and is often used in ecological studies to account for clustering species based on species abundance in different sites (Greenacre 2005), although it has been also used and recommended in some NLP applications under certain conditions (Paukkeri 2012).

The Bray–Curtis distance metric between documents X and Y is

$$d(X,Y) = \frac{\sum_{i=1}^{n} |x_i - y_i|}{\sum_{i=1}^{n} (x_i + y_i)},$$

where x_i and y_i are the frequencies of the ith term in documents X and Y, respectively. Note that dividing the absolute value of the differences between frequencies by their sum, we always obtain a value between 0 and 1, which is a nice feature for a dissimilarity measure. A dissimilarity matrix is created for the 330 documents of our whole corpus using the `vegan` R package (Oksanen et al. 2013).

The clustering method that best suits our objectives is Hierarchical Agglomerative Clustering (HAC) (Manning et al. 2008). First, compared to other clustering methods (e.g., flat clustering methods such as k-means), hierarchical clustering does not require the previous specification of a desired number of clusters. Second, the output of the hierarchical method is highly informative in so far it delivers a hierarchy of high-quality clustered elements (Sandhya and Govardhan 2012). Typically, HAC starts out considering each document as one single cluster "and then successively merges pairs of clusters until all clusters have been merged into a single cluster that contains all documents" (Manning et al. 2008). This "nested sequence of partitions" (Sandhya and Govardhan 2012) is carried out on the dissimilarity matrix of all the documents. In order to minimize the within-cluster variance we use Ward's minimum variance method (Ward 1963).[6] On the other hand, the Multidimensional scaling (MDS) will handle the dissimilarity matrix of pairs of documents and reduce it to a low-dimensional representation so that dissimilarities among documents is preserved. Therefore MDS will deliver the relative positioning of our documents according to their similarity.[7] Note that we use the tool here both as an exploratory data analysis method to observe structural patterns within our data, and as a check to the clustering analysis output. In order to achieve a precise understanding of the underlying structure of the data, only two embedding dimensions are specified (Borg and Groenen 2005).[8]

5.3.2 Results

Figure 5.2 shows the results of the hierarchical clustering with a dendrogram of the whole corpus of judges' descriptions of the main problems encountered during civil and criminal procedures, and on-call situations. Starting at the upper level of the tree, the method subdivides the documents into two main branches, each of which is in turn subdivided into two subbranches. Therefore, it is advisable to look at the clusters in a middle level of partition (i.e., at a proximity or height of between 2 and 3), since further down the tree the method starts creating too small clusters.

Moreover, given the source of our documents (three different questions in the questionnaire), we would expect to have three different clusters within which documents should be most similar to each other and most dissimilar with respect the documents in the other clusters. Therefore, we cut the tree so that we have three different clusters—that is, at a level of proximity (height) of 3 in the dendrogram.

In order to further explore the clustering results, we cross the content of each cluster against the actual source of each document (civil, criminal, or on-call). Table 5.4 shows the share of clusters within each type of document, while Table 5.5 accounts for the distribution of each type of document within each cluster. We observe two distinct phenomena. First, more than 90 % of the documents regarding

[6] The analysis is carried out using the `hclust` function from the R basic `stats` package (R Core Team 2013).

[7] Quinn and Keough (2002) point out that using the Bray–Curtis dissimilarity measure in scaling methods such as classical Multidimensional Scaling may pose a number of problems because "principal coordinates represent only part of the variation in the original dissimilarities". The problem is minimized, though, when we use such techniques as a data reduction strategy and therefore only the few first components are used.

[8] The classic Multidimensional scaling (MDS) model is fit using the `cmdscale` function (with $k = 2$) of the `stats` R package(R Core Team 2013).

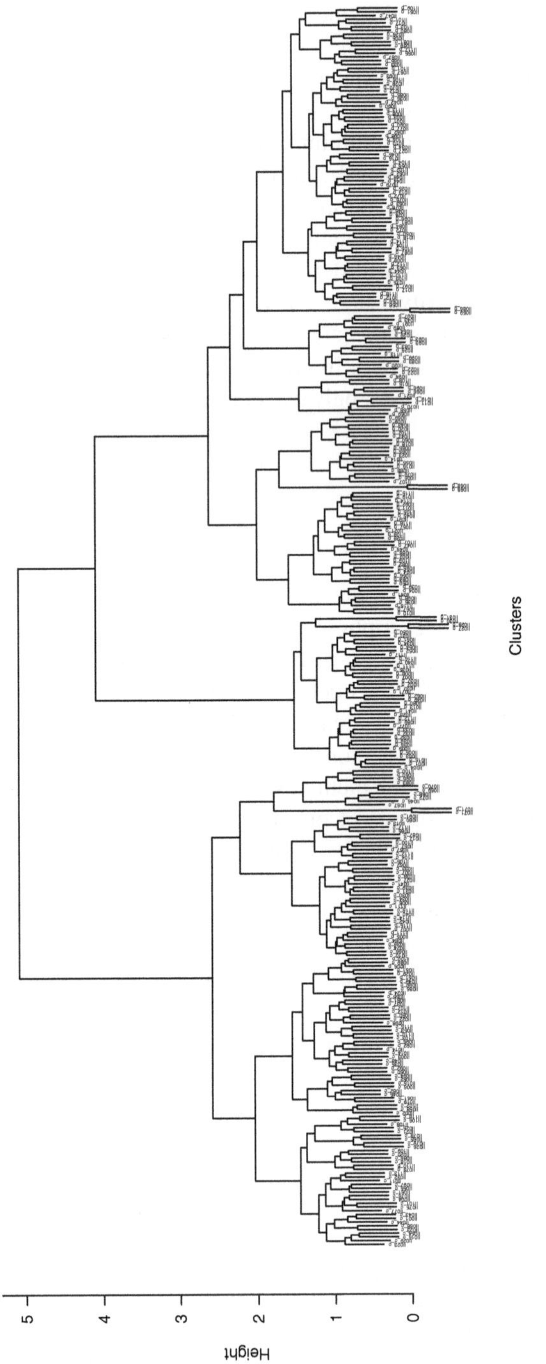

Fig. 5.2 Dendrogram representing the results of the hierarchical clustering algorithm on all documents

Table 5.4 Distribution of the clusters within each type of documents. The results should be read as row percentages of documents

	Cluster 1	Cluster 2	Cluster 3	Total
Civil	92.79	0.00	7.21	100
On-call	2.73	33.64	63.64	100
Criminal	19.27	3.67	77.06	100

Table 5.5 Distribution of each type of document in each cluster. The table should be read as column percentages of documents

	Cluster 1	Cluster 2	Cluster 3
Civil	81.10	0.00	4.94
On-call	2.36	90.24	43.21
Criminal	16.54	9.76	51.85
Total	100	100	100

civil problems have been classified into the first cluster, which points to the fact that problems related to civil procedures are highly specific and distinct from any other kind of problem. On the other hand, problems during on-call situations and problems regarding criminal procedures are less easily distinguishable. Although cluster number 3 contains a large share of both types of documents, the second cluster also contains one third of the on-call problems.

This would point to the idea that while civil procedures raise doubts and problems of a very specific nature, there are commonalities between some of the problems related to criminal procedures and the ones raised during on-call situations. According to what we explained before in this chapter, this is hardly surprising, since most of the issues dealt with during on-call situations are regarding criminal matters. Table 5.5 helps depicting this relationship between these two types of documents. From the distribution of each type of document within each cluster we observe that the first two clusters seem to be distinctively thematic, the first one containing mostly civil issues, and the second one being overwhelmingly restricted to problems raised during on-call situations. The third cluster contains a fair share of both on-call and criminal issues, which would point to the overlapping areas in which problems during on-call situations could also be described as problems regarding criminal procedures.

The extent to which, as clustering suggests, on one hand, civil procedures pose significantly different kinds of problems, and, on the other hand, criminal procedures and on-call situations trigger problems that occupy both overlapping and non-ambiguous areas of expertise, can be further tested when we apply a scaling method (MDS) to our set of documents so that we can both better visualize the results *and* use the method output to carry out further analyses.

Figure 5.3 represents the relations of similarity among all documents in just two dimensions. To ensure visualization we plot each type of document (civil, on-call and criminal) using different symbols. Note that documents lay nicely along the axis representing the first dimension showing a clear scale pattern. Substantive interpretation of the dimensions provided by scaling methods is fraught with dangers (Buntine and Jakulin 2006). In particular, when data are reduced into just a few latent variables (as we do with any scaling method by definition), we have no straightforward way to substantively interpret the components.

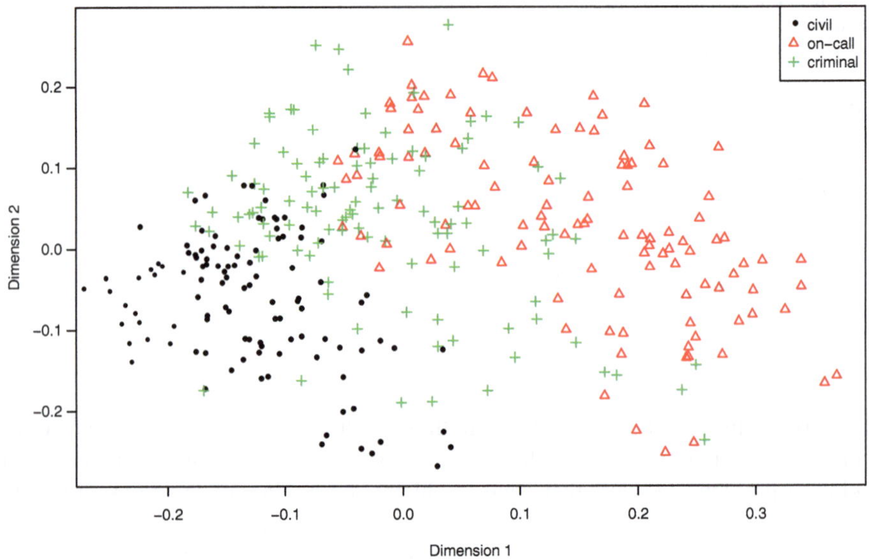

Fig. 5.3 Representation of the positions of all the documents through multidimensional scaling. Different *symbols* account for the three different types of documents

However, the results show a continuous scale—which we may safely call "dissimilarity scale"—from documents relating problems during civil procedures (far left) up to documents depicting specifically on-call problems, where documents on each extreme point of the scale are most dissimilar. Problems relating criminal issues lay in the mid section of the scale.

Although there is some overlapping between the documents from the criminal corpus with the other two types of documents, MDS provides us with a quite clear distinction between each type of document. This is still more apparent in Fig. 5.4, in which we have added ellipses representing the clusters previously obtained.

As we expected, clusters 1 and 2 mostly contain documents of just one type (civil and on-call, respectively), while cluster 3 represents an overlapping area between problems during on-call situations and criminal procedures, that is, the intersection between both sets of problems. Additionally, Fig. 5.5 shows the distribution per cluster of the values of each document in the first dimension provided by the Multidimensional scaling algorithm, showing a sharp separation between positions of documents in clusters 1 and 2, while documents in cluster 3 are move spread along the dimension, with the median position very close to zero (0.02).

Finally, we test the effect of the type of problem and the membership of a document in a cluster on that document's position in the scale. To do so we fit an Ordinary Least Squares regression model using the position of the document in the first dimension of MDS as outcome and the type of document and the clustering category as predictors. Note that the outcome variable (the position of the documents on the MDS first dimension) has both positive and negative values, denoting positions more to the right (positive) and left (negative), respectively. Results are shown in Table 5.6.

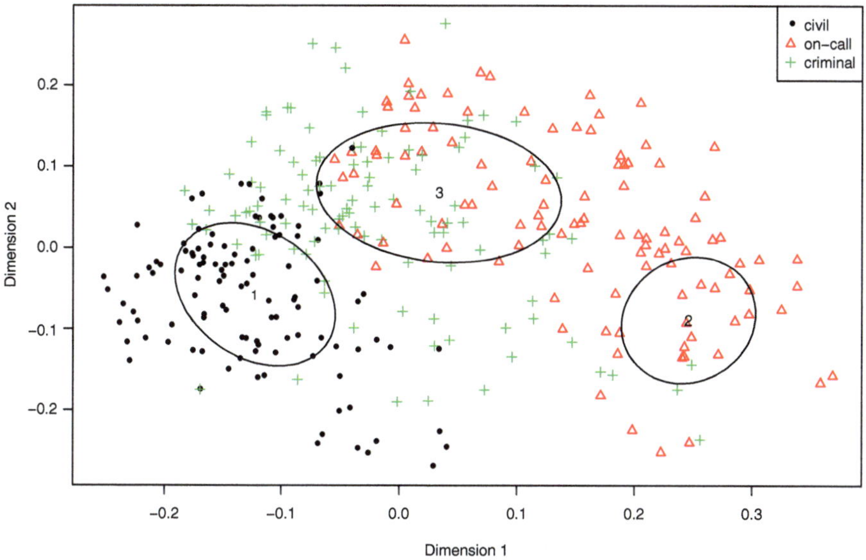

Fig. 5.4 Representation of the positions of all the documents through multidimensional scaling and clustering results. Different *symbols* account for the three different kind of documents, and *ellipses* represent the three clusters

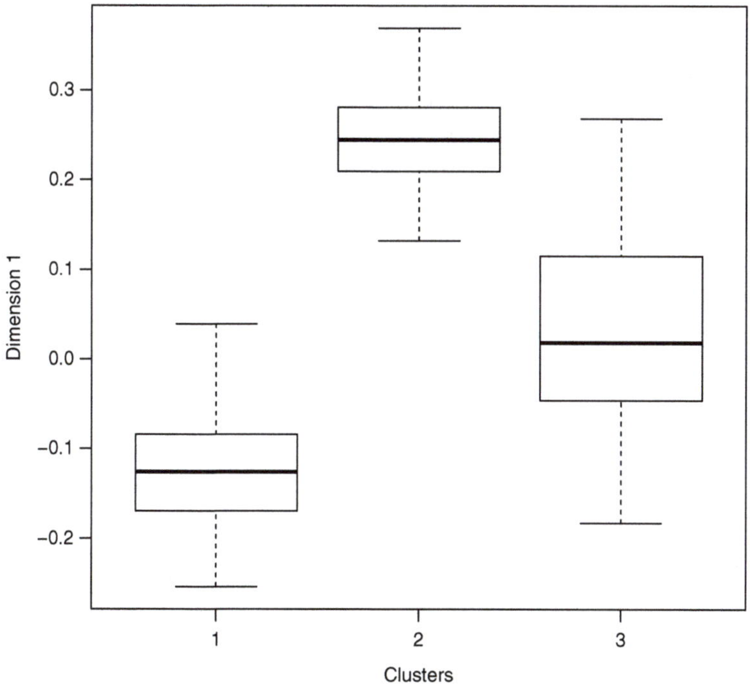

Fig. 5.5 Boxplot representing the distribution of the scores of the first dimension of MDS for each of the four clusters

Table 5.6 Ordinary least squares regression results of the multidimensional scaling method on the results of hierarchical clustering

	Model 1	Model 2	Model 3
(Intercept)	−0.13*	−0.12*	−0.13*
	(0.01)	(0.01)	(0.01)
[Ref. Civil corpus]			
On-call corpus	0.28*		0.15*
	(0.01)		(0.02)
Criminal corpus	0.11*		0.05*
	(0.01)		(0.01)
[Ref. Cluster 1]			
Cluster 2		0.37*	0.24*
		(0.02)	(0.02)
Cluster 3		0.16*	0.08*
		(0.01)	(0.01)
N	330	330	330
R^2	0.60	0.65	0.74
Resid. sd	0.09	0.09	0.08

Standard errors in parentheses
*indicates significance at $p < 0.001$

Model 1 in the table shows only the effect of the type of document on the position in the scale, using the civil type of document as the reference category. Note that the model predicts that both the on-call and criminal types of documents will have positive and significantly different positions in the scale than the documents depicting problems raised during civil procedures. Moreover, documents pertaining in the on-call corpus show higher positive values than those in the criminal corpus, indicating that, on average, these will be farther on the right side of the scale, while the coefficient for the criminal documents is smaller.

In a similar way, Model 2 shows the effect of a document being in a specific cluster on the posistion it occupies on the scale, with cluster 1 (the "civil cluster") as the reference category. The results are similar in both the coefficients and their significance. Again, for a document being in cluster 2 (the "on-call cluster") the model predicts a significantly different and positive position on the scale compared to documents within the "civil cluster", while documents in corpus 3 will present on average smaller coefficients, though positive.

The two predictors are brought together in Model 3, where the same conclusions largely hold. On one hand, despite a potential collinearity problem caused by the inclusion of both predictors, all coefficients preserve reasonable values and remain significant. On the other, the fit of the model overall improves. While the models including the type of document and the cluster category separately were able to explain between 60 and 65 % of the variation in the data, the inclusion of both

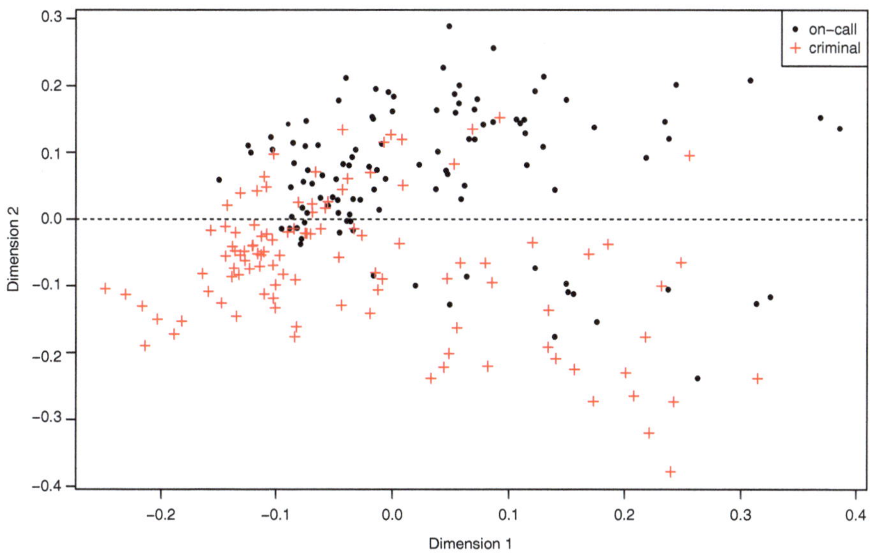

Fig. 5.6 Representation of the positions of all the documents through multidimensional scaling. Different *symbols* account for the three different types of documents

predictors raises the model's goodness of fit to 75 % and lowers its residual standard deviation.[9]

The models, therefore, seem to provide evidence of the significant differences among documents, although these differences are only clear between problems triggered by civil procedures and the rest of the documents, while the distinction between criminal and on-call documents deserves a separate analysis.

In order to explore the relationship between problems from criminal procedures and from on-call situations, we replicate the Clustering analysis and the Multidimensional scaling with only those documents. The results of the Multidimensional scaling in this separate analysis are shown in Fig. 5.6, that plots the results of Multidimensional scaling only on documents from the on-call and criminal corpora.

While differences here are not as apparent in one single dimension as those shown by documents pertaining to the civil corpus when the three corpora were taken into the analysis, here differences between the two types of documents seem to be in both dimensions. On the first dimension, documents depicting problems from ordinary criminal procedures tend to lay on the left side, while problems triggered by on-call situations are more on the right. On the other hand, most documents from the criminal corpus tend to be below zero in the second dimension (marked with a dotted

[9] However, due to potential collinearity problems, the R^2 coefficient of Model 3 should be taken with care. Additionally, ANOVA tests on all models not reported here yield significant differences in scale positions.

Table 5.7 Ordinary least squares regression results of the multidimensional scaling method on the results of hierarchical clustering of the documents coming from the criminal and on-call corpora

	Type of document		*Cluster*		*Both predictors*	
	Dim. 1	Dim. 2	Dim. 1	Dim. 2	Dim. 1	Dim. 2
(Intercept)	0.03*	0.07*	0.14*	−0.03*	0.17*	0.03*
	(0.01)	(0.01)	(0.01)	(0.01)	(0.01)	(0.01)
[Ref. On-call corpus]						
Criminal corpus	−0.06*	−0.13*			−0.05*	−0.14*
	(0.02)	(0.01)			(0.01)	(0.01)
[Ref. Cluster 1]						
Cluster 2			−0.20*	0.05*	−0.20*	0.06*
			(0.01)	(0.02)	(0.01)	(0.01)
N	219	219	219	219	219	219
R^2	0.07	0.30	0.55	0.03	0.59	0.34
Resid. sd	0.12	0.10	0.08	0.12	0.08	0.10

Standard errors in parentheses
*indicates significance at $p < 0.05$

line in Fig. 5.6), while most of the documents from the on-call corpus have positive coordinates on the second dimension.

In order to test the differences between both types of documents in both dimensions, we fit an OLS regression model to predict the position of documents in each of the two dimensions delivered by the scaling algorithm. Again, we use the type of document and the clustering results as predictors, although each of them now has only two categories.

Results in Table 5.7 show that differences between documents from criminal procedures and on-call situations are significantly different in *both* dimensions, although these differences are smaller on average than what we found in the model including the three corpora.

An interesting feature of the model, though, is that each predictor seems to perform well in one dimension but not on the other. In particular, the first two columns show the effect for a document from the criminal corpus on its position on each dimension compared to the position of the documents from the on-call corpus. We may observe that the average difference in position between documents of both corpora are larger when taking into account the second dimension. On the contrary, when the predictors are the clusters (columns 3 and 4 of Table 5.7), the coefficient is larger when the outcome variable is the position in the first dimension.

Moreover, the model including the first dimension shows a much better goodness of fit with the clusters as predictors (both in R^2 and standard error of the model), while the one with the second dimension as outcome is better fitted when predicted by the type of document.

Results, therefore, give support to our first hypothesis in two different aspects. On one hand, when all the documents are considered, the specific and distinct features of the problems triggered by civil procedures stand out in a significant way, while the classification methods used are not able to clearly distinguish documents containing problems of criminal nature and raised during on-call situations. On the other hand, when only these latter two types of documents are taken into account, smaller but still signficant differences between the criminal and on-call problems are identified.

We now turn to our second hypothesis—the exploration of the distinctive problems raised during the operation of the on-call service.

5.4 Mapping Problems Through Topic Modeling (Hypothesis 2)

In our second hypothesis we aim at exploring the role of the outer environment (the organization) into the decision-making process of junior judges. In particular, we address the extent to which most problems and doubts faced when judges are on-call constitute demands from their organizational environment, and therefore merely procedural and behavioral, in contrast with a more theoretical-based nature of the problems raised during ordinary criminal, and specially civil, procedures. Should this be the case, solutions to these problems would not be contained in the corpus of legal knowledge judges acquire either in the law degree or preparing the entrance examination: theoretical legal knowledge.

To test our hypothesis, we carry out two different analyses. On one hand, we need to retrieve the issues and problems that judges refer to in their responses. On the other, we need to explore whether the kinds of problems they identify as specific of on-call situations are of a different kind than those raised during ordinary civil and criminal procedures.

In order to extract the issues referred to by judges in their responses in a systematic way, we use Latent Dirichlet Allocation (LDA), a generative probabilistic topic model for the identification and representation of the content of collections of documents (Blei et al. 2003; Blei 2012). Once topics have been identified and interpreted, they will be used as outcomes to test the practical nature of the problems raised during on-call situations.

5.4.1 Probabilistic Topic Models

Behind the development of topic models lies the challenge to handle an ever growing bulk of textual information. In particular, topic models address the need to explore the semantic structure underlying a collection of documents by finding semantically similar documents and "exploring the collection through the underlying topics that run through it" (Blei and Lafferty 2009).

The notion of semantic similarity is based upon the general assumption that "semantically similar words behave similarly' (Manning and Schütze 1999, p. 295) a basic approach to understand, for instance, the way query systems or search engines—with a variable level of sophistication—are able to retrieve documents related to the words used in a simple and brief query.

A number of techniques have been traditionally used to uncover the semantic structure of (a collection of) documents. For instance, Reinert (1985, 1987, 2000) and Lapalut (1995) proposed a statistical classification method with the aim of finding "semantic contexts" within a textual corpus. It is based on the top-down hierarchical classification method proposed by Bénzecri (1982) that makes use of correspondence analysis (CA) (Escofier and Pagès 1992; Murtagh 2005; Blasius and Greenacre 2006; Greenacre 2006; Morin 2006 Greenacre and Nenadić 2007). Correspondence analysis allows for description and analysis of contingency tables, and enables low dimensional graphical representation of the correspondence among rows, among columns, or both. A very close relationship exists between correspondence analysis and principal components analysis (PCA), although each method's suitability depends on the kind of data at hand (Murtagh 2005).

Originally designed to handle real valued data (Buntine and Jakulin 2004), these and other methods for information retrieval have usually relied on word frequency (i.e. discrete) data normalization, such as binary conversion (in Correspondence analysis) or the common "term frequency–inverse document frequency" (*tf-idf*). Despite the advantages of these methods in providing efficient low-dimension spatial representations of the data, though, their ability to provide "inter- or intra-document statistical structure" (Blei et al. 2003) and directly interpretable topics (Steyvers and Griffiths 2007) is quite limited. Equivalent methods specifically designed to deal with discrete data have been proposed (Buntine and Jakulin 2004), such as latent semantic analysis (Deerwester et al. 1990), its probabilistic variant for latent semantic indexing (pLSI) (Hofmann 1999), and various kinds of topic models such as Latent Dirichlet Allocation (LDA) (Blei et al. 2003). LDA and other topic model extensions, therefore, are regarded as "a discrete analogue to principal component analysis (PCA) and independent component analysis (ICA)" (Buntine 2009), and have been characterized under a unified theoretical "discrete component analysis" framework (Buntine and Jakulin 2006). LDA has been successfully used in exploring and retrieving topics in large collections of documents in various fields such as science papers (Blei and Lafferty 2009) and computational historiography (Mimno 2012a, b).

5.4.1.1 The Latent Dirichlet Allocation (LDA) Model

Latent Dirichlet Allocation (LDA) is a *generative* Bayesian mixture model for discrete data (Grün and Hornik 2011).[10] The idea behing LDA is that documents have a

---

[10] The following explanation on LDA draws mainly on Blei et al. (2003), Blei and Lafferty (2009), Blei (2012), Buntine and Jakulin (2004, 2006), Buntine (2009), Grün and Hornik (2011), Steyvers and Griffiths (2007), Mimno (2012a).

certain number of topics, where a topic is conceptualized as a probability distribution over a set of terms (a vocabulary V). In particular, LDA is based on the assumption that a collection of documents is associated to a number of topics, and that each document will present a certain proportion of these topics. Then each document can be seen as representing a particular combination of those topics. Thence the *generative* model behind LDA (Steyvers and Griffiths 2007):

> it specifies a simple probabilistic procedure by which documents can be generated. To make a new document, one chooses a distribution over topics. Then, for each word in that document, one chooses a topic at random according to this distribution, and draws a word from that topic.

Since the only observed data are words within documents, LDA is usually formally described as a *hidden variable model* (Blei and Lafferty 2009), in which the topic structure of the document collection and of each document is unknown and must be discovered using posterior probabilistic inference given the observed documents (Blei and Lafferty 2009). Following the bag-of-words model LDA therefore assumes a generative process for the data in three general steps (Blei 2012; Grün and Hornik 2011):

1. For each topic, a term distribution β is drawn:

$$\beta \sim Dirichlet(\delta)$$

2. For each document d, a distribution θ of topics is chosen:

$$\theta \sim Dirichlet(\alpha)$$

3. For each of the N terms t_i in each document d
   a. a topic z_i is randomly chosen over the distribution θ of topics: $z_i \sim Multinomial(\theta)$, and $P(z)$ is the probability distribution over topics z in a document
   b. a term t_i is chosen from the multinomial probability distribution conditioned on the topic z_i: $p(t_i|z_i, \beta) = \phi$ is the probability of term t_i given topic z_i, and given the term distribution β for topics.

Blei et al. (2003), Blei and Lafferty (2009), Blei (2012), Steyvers and Griffiths (2007) have provided (slightly different versions of) a probabilistic graphic model for Latent Dirichlet Allocation, represented in Fig. 5.7. The shaded color of variable t points to the only observable data—the terms in each document—while ϕ (the sampling of term distributions over topics for each document), θ (the topic proportions for each document d), and z (topic assignments per word) rest unobserved.

The rectangular plates in the graphic model represent the different sampling processes of the generative model.[11] The smaller, inner plate over z and t represents the generative process within each document by which a repeated sampling of topics

[11] The explanation of the graphic model draws on (Steyvers and Griffiths 2007), but some of the notation has been adapted.

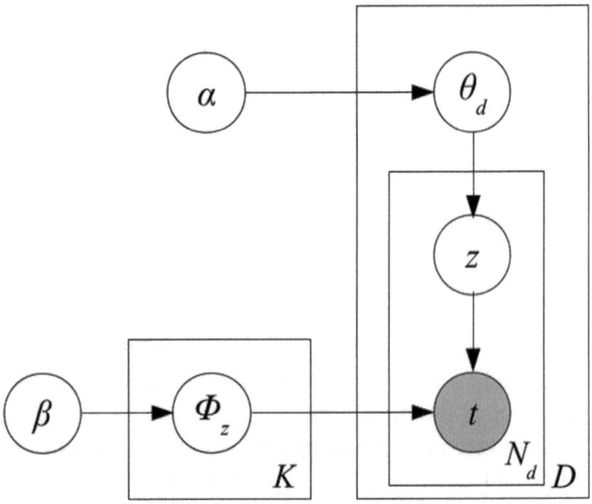

Fig. 5.7 Probabilistic graphic model for Latent Dirichlet Allocation (LDA). Based on Blei et al. (2003), Blei and Lafferty (2009), Blei (2012), Steyvers and Griffiths (2007)

and terms is carried out until N_d terms (the total number of terms in document d) have been generated. The inner plate over θ_d represents the sampling over topics for each document d until D documents. Finally, the plate surrounding ϕ_z represents the sampling of word distributions for each topic z until K topics have been generated. The corpus-level hyperparameters α and β are constants in the model, introduced for smoothing purposes (Blei et al. 2003).

The main goal of LDA is to reverse the process depicted in the data generation model: given the set of observed terms in our collection of documents, we infer the underlying topic structure Blei (2012) through the posterior distribution of the latent variables, as if the data were generated by the model.[12] This way we obtain probabilities at the different levels of analysis: topic distribution for documents, and term distribution for each topic.

5.4.2 *Input Data*

Our input data for the LDA topic model is the same as in the previous analysis— a corpus of 330 documents containing the clean text of the responses of judges regarding their main problems during the operation of the on-call service, civil procedures, and criminal procedures.

[12] Estimation is made through maximum likelihood estimation (MLE), where the log-likelihood of the data is maximized with respect to the hyperparameters α and β. Different methods have been proposed to the computational problem of approximating the posterior distribution of the topic decomposition of a corpus, including mean field vaiational inference and Gibbs sampling. See Blei et al. (2003), Buntine and Jakulin (2006) and Steyvers and Griffiths (2007) for discussions.

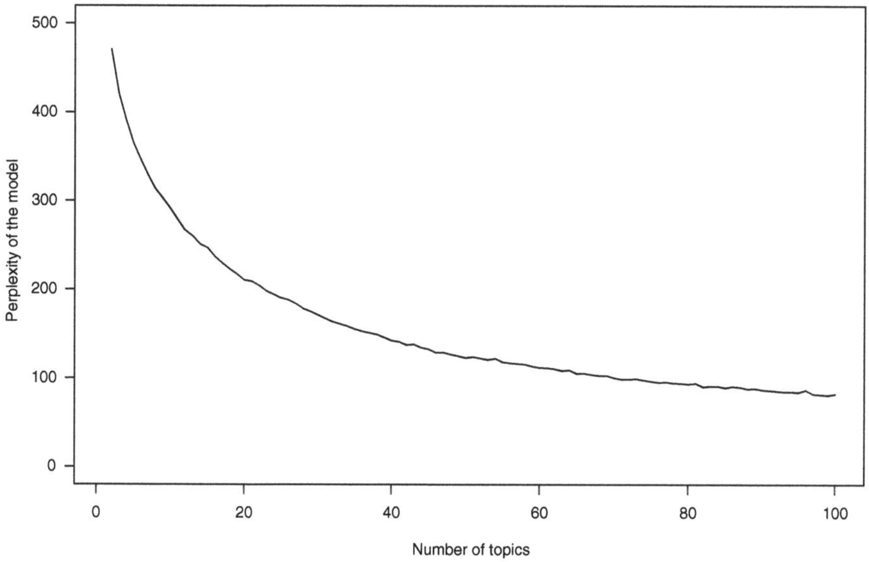

Fig. 5.8 Perplexity of the LDA topic model between 2 and 100 topics

The LDA algorithm requires that the researcher sets a number of topics, a problem for which a universal recommendation does not exist (Blei and Lafferty 2009), since it may depend entirely upon the problem that is addressed in the analysis. At first glance, we do not expect our texts to present a very high number of topics, for various reasons. First, the collection is rather small in number of documents. Second, the population from which data have been generated is not a random sample from the general population but a random sample within a very specific group of respondents with a high level of similarity (judges with little experience). Finally, the documents themselves are generated as responses to only three very specific questions: professional problems (on-call, civil, criminal) raised during the operation of lower courts during a span of 2 years.

However, in order to set a number of topics, the performance of successive LDA models including from 2 to 100 topics has been evaluated. To do so, we compare the perplexity of the successive LDA models with different number of topics. Perplexity is "an intrinsic evaluation metric [...] which measures the quality of a model" (Jurafsky and Martin 2008) often used for evaluating fitted language models (Jurafsky and Martin 2008) topic models (Blei et al. 2003; Grün and Hornik 2011), for it helps measuring improvements on model fit (likelihood).[13]

Figure 5.8 shows the evolution of the perplexity of all the LDA models from 2 to 100 topics. Notice that lower perplexity indicates better fit of the model. As expected,

[13] The perplexity of the models is computed with the `topicmodels` R package (Grün and Hornik 2011).

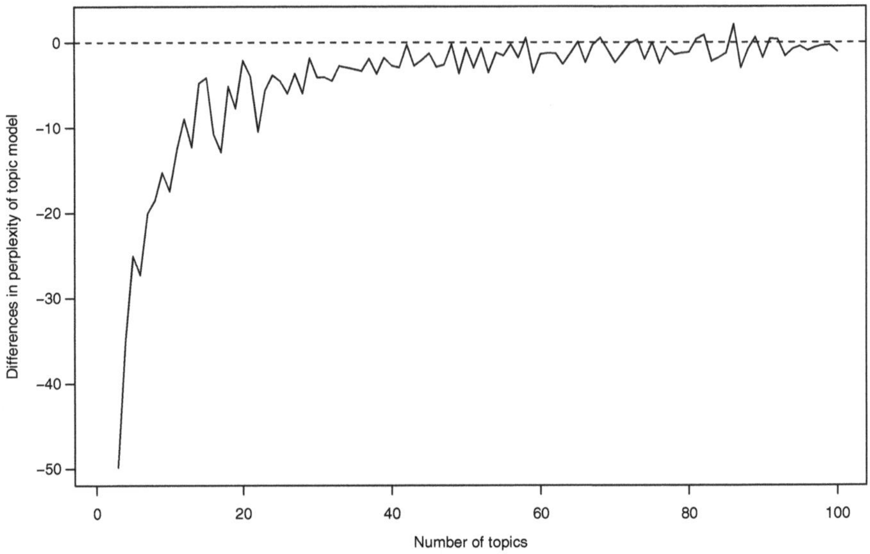

Fig. 5.9 Differences in perplexity of the LDA topic model at different number of topics. Differences tend to zero with higher number of topics

models with a higher number of topics are better fitted than models with just a few topics. Intuitively, a higher number of topics increases the probability assignment of each term to one topic. Yet, note that the improvement in model perplexity—the rate at which it decreases—starts to fall pretty soon, at around 20 topics, indicating that the improvement of the fitted model with an additional topic is marginally decreasing.

Figure 5.9 presents the differences in the evolution of perplexity of each model with an additional topic. Notice that these differences in effect approach to zero at around 20 topics, although they already cease to decrease in steady form at around 10 topics. Actually, Fig. 5.10 presents the rate of change in perplexity of the models and shows that well before the 20th topic the percentage differences in perplexity start a new pattern of change, indicating that a relative low number of topics is sufficient for our data. We set our number of topics at ten.

5.4.3 Results

Table 5.8 shows the results of LDA in terms of the distribution of documents in each of the ten topics. We observe that the overall distribution is quite balanced, with topic 2 having the higher number of documents and topics 6 and 9 being the smaller ones. At first glance, the results look normal, since neither topic is extremely over- nor under-populated.

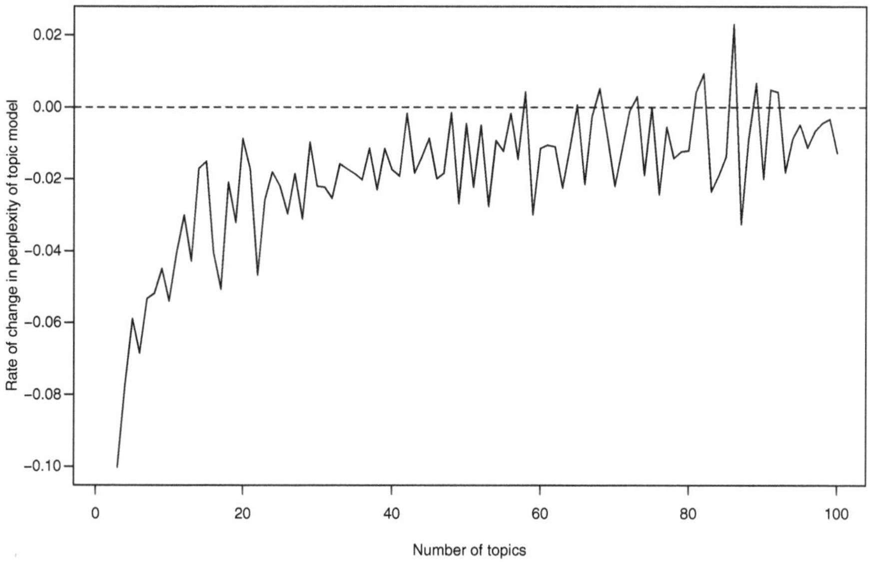

Fig. 5.10 Rate of change in perplexity of the LDA topic model at different number of topics. Decrease of perplexity is smaller when the number of topics grows

Table 5.8 Distribution of documents in each topic resulting from the LDA model

Topic	Documents	Percent
1	30	9.09
2	53	16.06
3	43	13.03
4	32	9.70
5	29	8.79
6	19	5.76
7	40	12.12
8	29	8.79
9	23	6.97
10	32	9.70
Total	330	100

Another feature of the LDA algorithm may be observed in Fig. 5.11, which presents the distribution of topics and their probabilities per document for a sample of 20 documents. We see that the model favors the assignment of significant probabilities of each document in one or just a small number of topics. Notice that while some documents have a maximum of three topics with significant proportions, (e.g., document # 12), most of them have just one topic associated to a high probability.

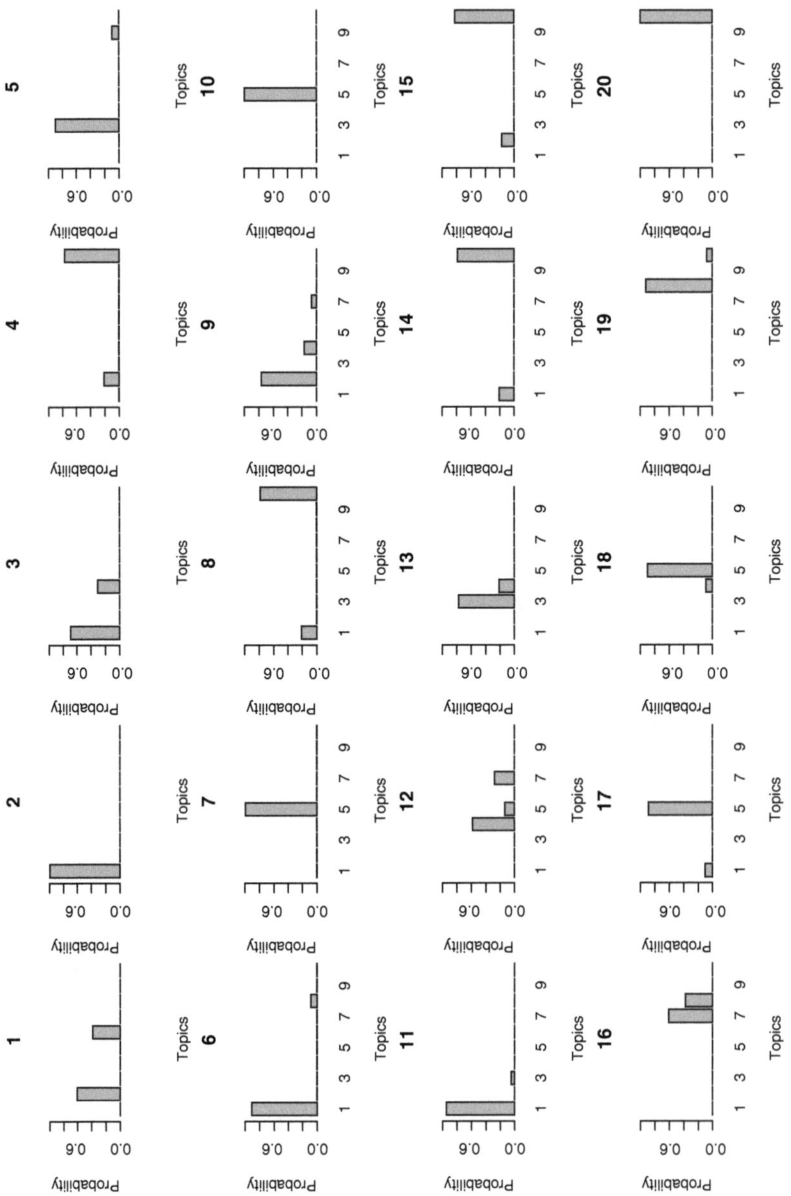

Fig. 5.11 Distribution of topics per document for a sample of 20 documents in the collection

Apart from that, the existence of a few significant topics might also indicate that some judges simply point out a higher number of different problems than others. Should this be the case, we could expect that topic distribution could be related to the length of the documents—the higher the number of words, the higher the number of topics. When we test this computing a diversity index that measures the probability, for each document, that two terms randomly selected belong to two different topics,[14] results show that longer documents tend to be topically more homogeneous.[15]

5.4.3.1 The Topics and Their Meaning

Let's now turn to the contents of the topics. It is worth noting here that our first interest is not focused on the thorough analysis of the problems encountered by each junior judge—we do not want to measure what specific problems each judge has encountered and assess how many judges have each kind of problem. Instead, our intention is to identify different domains within the whole set of problems pointed out by judges.

Table 5.9 lists the 20 more relevant terms of each of the ten topics generated by our topic model. Note that there are terms that appear in more than one topic, although the probability these terms are assigned to each topic by the model differ in each case. Therefore, both the presence and the order in which terms appear ranked within topics are relevant to their interpretation.

Of these sets of terms, roughly three different groups of topics can be identified based upon their content. The first set of topics (2, 5 and 8) is composed mainly by legal technical terms of both civil and criminal procedures. On the other hand, topics 1, 3, 7, 9 and 10 refer to behavioral problems. Topics 4 and 6 are hard to classify in either of the previous two sets.

Technical Topics

If we take a look at the terms with highest probability to belong on topics 2, 5, and 8 we shall observe that most of them refer to technical, theoretical legal typologies. For instance, the highly ranked presence of terms such as *servidumbre* [right of way], *obra* [construction], and *derecho* and *real* (for *derechos reales*) [tax on the conveyance of land or property, *jus in rem*] indicates that Topic 2 gathers terms belonging to problems on technical issues of civil procedures, especially regarding ancient civil figure such as the *jus in rem*. This is not surprising given that, recalling the previous chapter, first appointments for junior judges are mainly small to medium cities that cover vast rural areas of Spain (Vallbé 2012), where civil cases are usually issued by disputes on ancient rights and taxes on paths and property lines.

---

[14] We computed the Gini-Simpson index from the Simpson index, $\lambda = \sum_{i=1}^{m} p^2$, where p is the proportion of each topic for the m topics represented in each document. The Gini-Simpson index is $1 - \lambda$.

[15] The effect is small, though. An OLS regression model of the Gini-Simpson diversity index of the documents on the log of their term size yields a (significant) coefficient of 0.05. This means that to an increase in 10 % in the length of the document produces on average an increase of 0.002 in that document's diversity index.

Table 5.9 List of the most relevant terms in each topic, with their assigned probability (p)

Topic 1	Topic 2	Topic 3	Topic 4	Topic 5	
term	p term	p term	p term	p term	p
1 médico	0.07 tema	0.04 duda	0.05 fiscal	0.08 asunto	0.02
2 fiscal	0.04 derecho	0.03 fiscal	0.03 delito	0.04 año	0.02
3 violencia	0.04 complicado	0.02 levantamiento	0.02 instrucción	0.03 fuerza	0.01
4 doméstico	0.03 servidumbre	0.02 violencia	0.01 causa	0.02 tema	0.01
5 internamiento	0.03 asunto	0.02 prisión	0.01 sumario	0.01 propiedad	0.01
6 protección	0.02 escuela	0.01 ley	0.01 procedimiento	0.01 sentencia	0.01
7 tema	0.02 sentencia	0.01 medida	0.01 responsabilidad	0.01 cuestión	0.01
8 urgente	0.02 tierra	0.01 social	0.01 prisión	0.01 letrado	0.01
9 nunca	0.02 real	0.01 dónde	0.01 complicado	0.01 duda	0.01
10 asunto	0.01 estudiar	0.01 dificultad	0.01 droga	0.01 quiebra	0.01
11 testigo	0.01 obra	0.01 extranjero	0.01 jurado	0.01 complicado	0.01
12 prisión	0.01 libro	0.01 detención	0.01 asunto	0.01 testigo	0.01
13 muerte	0.01 aplicar	0.01 tema	0.01 tema	0.01 reivindicatorio	0.01
14 levantamiento	0.01 cuestión	0.01 práctico	0.01 difícil	0.01 finca	0.01
15 ley	0.01 jurisprudencia	0.01 delito	0.01 estafa	0.01 muchísimo	0.01
16 cuestión	0.01 procedimiento	0.01 protección	0.01 dificultad	0.01 complejo	0.01
17 preso	0.01 quiebra	0.01 actuación	0.01 lesión	0.01 mesa	0.01
18 lesión	0.01 práctico	0.01 procedimiento	0.01 hacienda	0.01 comunidad	0.01
19 muchísimo	0.01 año	0.01 comparecencia	0.01 preso	0.01 situación	0.01
20 ingresar	0.01 cantidad	0.01 género	0.01 criterio	0.01 ley	0.01

Table 5.9 (continued)

Topic 6	Topic 7	Topic 8	Topic 9	Topic 10	
term	*p* term	*p* term	*p* term	*p* term	*p*
1 audiencia	0.03 tema	0.03 ejecución	0.06 prisión	0.05 tío	0.04
2 tema	0.03 perito	0.03 ley	0.03 ley	0.02 tema	0.03
3 fiscal	0.02 asunto	0.02 sentencia	0.02 médico	0.02 prisión	0.02
4 sentencia	0.02 niño	0.02 procedimiento	0.02 cuestión	0.02 duda	0.02
5 procedimiento	0.02 realmente	0.02 embargo	0.02 año	0.02 medida	0.01
6 nacional	0.01 protección	0.02 pleito	0.02 causa	0.02 fiscal	0.01
7 libertad	0.01 medida	0.02 resolución	0.02 fiscal	0.02 niño	0.01
8 prisión	0.01 malos	0.02 pericial	0.02 violencia	0.01 acordar	0.01
9 asunto	0.01 tratos	0.02 año	0.01 protección	0.01 asunto	0.01
10 escuela	0.01 alejamiento	0.01 antiguo	0.01 asunto	0.01 concreto	0.01
11 complicado	0.01 violencia	0.01 derecho	0.01 registro	0.01 detención	0.01
12 detención	0.01 doméstico	0.01 finca	0.01 nunca	0.01 delito	0.01
13 resolución	0.01 tráfico	0.01 familia	0.01 chico	0.01 personal	0.01
14 dónde	0.01 dificultad	0.01 duda	0.01 doméstico	0.01 oficina	0.01
15 instrucción	0.01 daño	0.01 muchísimo	0.01 modificar	0.01 situación	0.01
16 ejecución	0.01 maltratar	0.01 asunto	0.01 vender	0.01 menor	0.01
17 complicar	0.01 procedimiento	0.01 menor	0.01 derecho	0.01 registro	0.01
18 delito	0.01 querella	0.01 mayor	0.01 internamiento	0.01 surgir	0.01
19 medida	0.01 separación	0.01 embargar	0.01 duda	0.01 muchísimo	0.01
20 realmente	0.01 importante	0.01 cuestión	0.01 afortunadamente	0.01 mossos	0.01

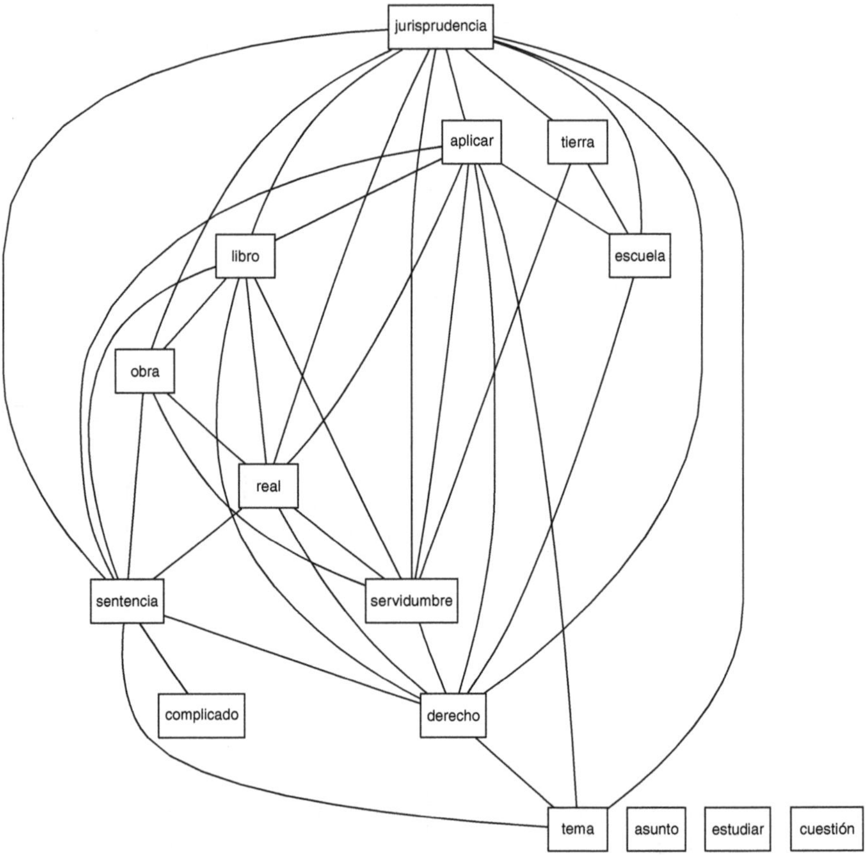

Fig. 5.12 Representation of the correlation network of the 15 most relevant terms of Topic 2

A better assessment of these results is achieved when we plot the relationships between the terms within each topic, as in Fig. 5.12.[16]

These plots reflect the way judges express their main problems, so the presence or absence of particular terms, on one hand, and the association among terms that

[16] The visualization of correlated terms in a DocumentTerm matrix has been carried out using the R `tm` package (Feinerer 2008). This search for correlations is carried out in the vector space computing the cosine between vectors interpreted as the *normalized correlation coefficient* (Manning and Schütze 1999, p. 300)—with values between 0 and 1. That is, the cosine of the angle between vectors representing the documents, which is a similarity measure rather than a distance measure (Solka 2008). Due to the sparsity of the original matrix, we use here relatively low correlation thresholds ($r \sim 0.25$) in order to increase the density of the correlation networks. I would like to warmly thank Dr. Ingo Feinerer, the creator of the `tm` R package, at the Vienna University of Technology, for delivering a quick and detailed account and explanation of the code behind the `tm` library.

do significantly appear in a topic, on the other, may be interpreted as a quite reliable representation of this particular portion of discourse related to their problems *as they describe them*. At the same time, terms (nodes) with a higher degree in the network (number of edges) may be interpreted as gravitational centers of the topic from which a data-driven interpretation of the results of the topic models can be made.[17] This representation will be able to stress out, first, those aspects of particular situations which seem problematic by judges, and second, whether these situations are related to doubts regarding particular actors and their actions (behavioral interpretation) or to doubts regarding theoretical interpretation.

In Fig. 5.12 we see that technical terms such as *servidumbre* [right of way] and *derecho* and *real* have have a prominent position in the correlation network. Moreover, the term *sentencia* [sentence, judicial decision] is correlated to this civil vocabulary, to other procedural legal terms such as *procedimiento* [procedure] and *ejecución* [enforcement of a judicial decision], and also to the key term *jurisprudencia* [precedent].

Problems with the enforcement of judicial decisions, in fact, seem to be the central point of all topics relating to civil procedures, although the topic model seems to separate different kinds of procedures. If Topic 2 was focused on problems of enforcement in issues dealing with *jus in rem*, Topic 8 seems to be of a more procedural type but with references to family law (*familia*), having the term *ejecución* as its top term Fig. 5.13.

In turn, Topic 5 is highly focused on technical problems regarding civil cases involving disputes over property. If we look at Fig. 5.14, the (civil) technical nature of this topic is quite evident. Along with a term such as *sentencia* [sentence, decision], that was also to be found in the other technical topics, terms such as *propiedad* [real estate] and *reivindicatorio* [from action of recovery of possession] and *quiebra* [bankruptcy] indicate that judges are here referring to problems in the enforcement of decisions that involve legal issues on real estate.

Behavioral Topics

Topics 1, 3, 7, 9 and 10 seem to clearly belong to an entirely different semantic context than the ones just interpreted, mainly because the terms and their pattern of relationships refer to behavioral problems, usually raised during on-call situations.

For instance, Topic 1 contains highly significant terms that relate to three different but typical on-call situations. On one hand, terms such as *internamiento* [confinement] and *urgente* [urgent, urgently] do point to those cases involving the request of confining mentally disturbed people into mental institutions, a usual critical situation

[17] Terms with no edges such as *asunto* and *año* in Fig. 5.12 point to a lower coefficient of correlation with any other term in the plot.

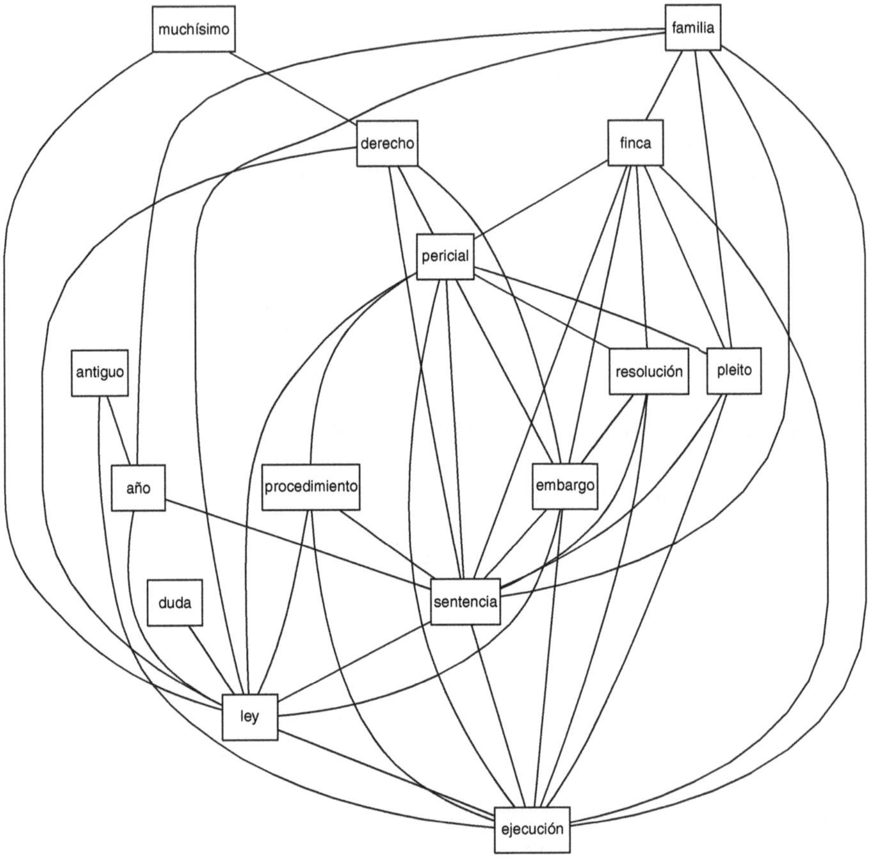

Fig. 5.13 Correlations among the most relevant terms of Topic 8

dealt with by the on-call service in lower courts.[18] On the other hand, terms such as *muerte* [death] and *levantamiento* [removal, for corpse removal] point to on-call situations related to the death of a person and the subsequent removal of the corpse. Finally, words such as *violencia* and *doméstico*, and *protección* (as in *medida de protección*, injunction of protection) refer to cases of domestic violence (*violencia doméstica*).

Note that in this topic, the two most relevant terms are *fiscal* [public prosecutor] and *médico* [doctor, medical examiner], who are two very relevant actors in the operation of the on-call service. First, the intervention of the medical examiner (ME) is required in all the cases: to certify the state of a corpse, to evaluate a victim

[18] The term mostly used by judges and legal experts for these situations is *internamiento urgente*, which is a very common issue raised during the operation of the on-call service (Percellar-Giménez 2000).

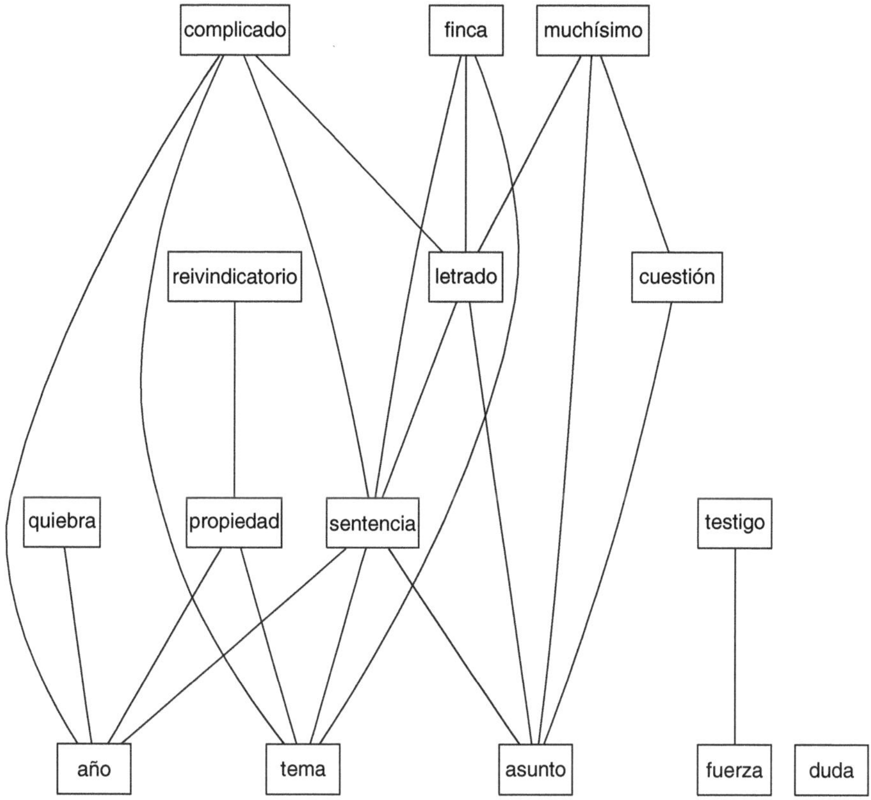

Fig. 5.14 Correlation network of the most relevant terms in Topic 5

in domestic violence situations, or to carry out an urgent examination of a mentally disturbed person in a critical situation. On the other hand, any case involving criminal charges on a detainee (e.g., provisional imprisonment as a result of domestic violence) must involve the appearance of the public prosecutor on-call (*fiscal*).

The presence and relevance of these terms in this topic, then, can bring us to the conclusion that some problems exist regarding the role of both medical examiners (forensic doctors) and public prosecutors in these situations, including the corpse removal itself or even the certification regarding the circumstances of the death, the management of domestic violence cases, or problems triggered by the need to institutionalize mentally ill persons.

Figure 5.15 shows the correlation between the first 15 terms in Topic 1 in the DocumentTerm matrix used to generate the topic model. If we observe it as an undirected network of terms (correlation goes both ways), it reveals that, although both the ME and the public prosecutor are in principle relevant to the topic (they both have high probabilities attached), the medical examiner has a relevant role as a node in the description of the on-call problems made by judges. As expected, other

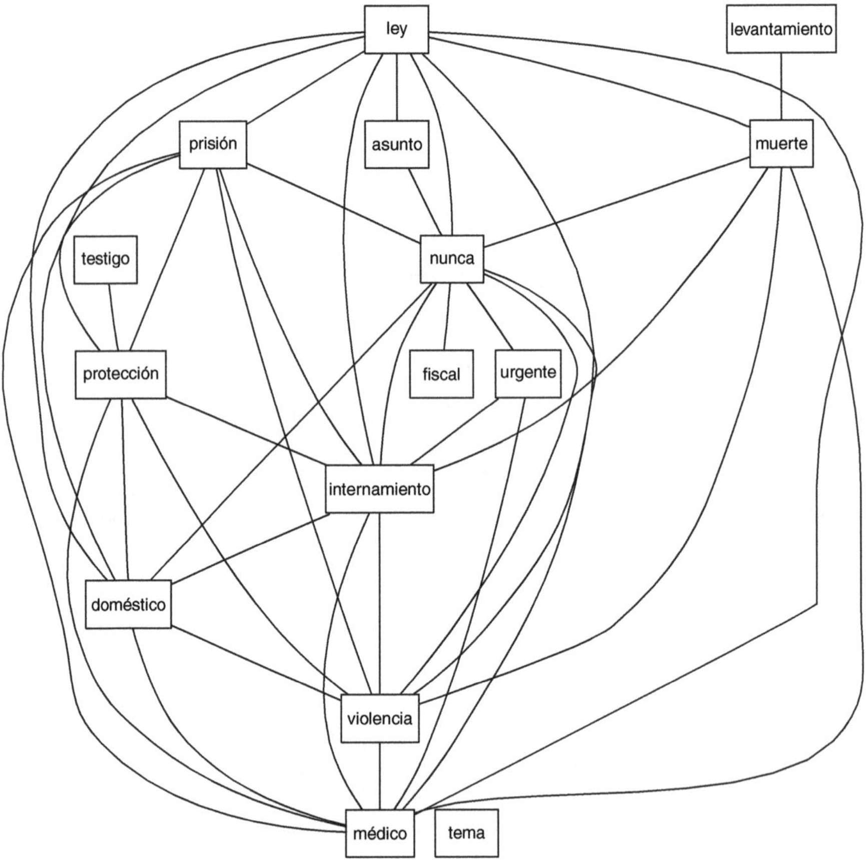

Fig. 5.15 Correlations among terms within Topic 1 in the DocumentTerm matrix, which refer to three different kinds of problems during on-call situations

terms that present a high number of edges in the correlation network are *violencia, doméstico, protección, internamiento, muerte* and *prisión*. In contrast, Figs. 5.16 and 5.17 reveals a context of problems (Topics 3 and 10) in which the public prosecutor has a more relevant role during on-call situations, specifically related to decisions related to imprisonment (*detención* [detention], *prisión* [imprisonment]).

Topics 7 and 9 point to problems related to domestic violence at different levels and from different perspectives. Figure 5.18 shows that Topic 7 relates specifically to the management of problems around domestic violence during on-call situations. First, terms such as *violencia, doméstico, tratos* and *malos* (from *malos tratos* [abusive treatment]), refer to the violent act itself in various forms. Second, terms such as *medida, alejamiento*, and *protección* point directly to different ways by judges refer to the basic legal procedure in these cases: *medida de alejamiento*, *orden de protección*, and *orden de alejamiento* are different ways of naming an injunction of protection

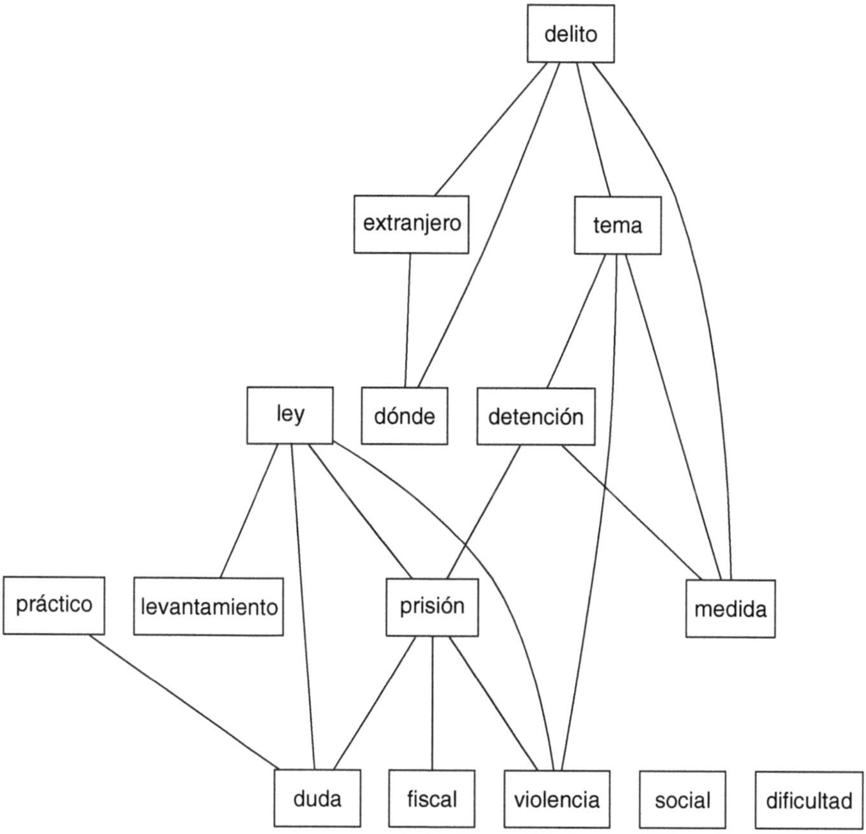

Fig. 5.16 Correlation of terms in Topic 3 within the DocumentTerm matrix

issued to protect a victim of domestic violence. In turn, in Topic 9 (Fig. 5.19), while still referring to the problems with injunctions of protection (*protección*), the focus is centered on the legal and physical status of the agressor (*chico*) such as imprisonment (*prisión*). Note also that both the public prosecutor (*fiscal*) and the medical examiner (*médico*) seem to be relevant actors in both the imprisonment (of the agressor) and the protection (of the victim).

Hard Cases

Topics 4 and 6 are difficult to interpret. These topics seem to be devoted to legal procedural issues, specifically on difficulties encountered during the preliminary proceedings (*instrucción del sumario*) that junior judges must initiate in their courts. Figure 5.20 shows that these difficulties are most related to the constitution of a jury (*formación del jurado*), and lawsuits (*causa*), involving drugs (*droga*), fraud

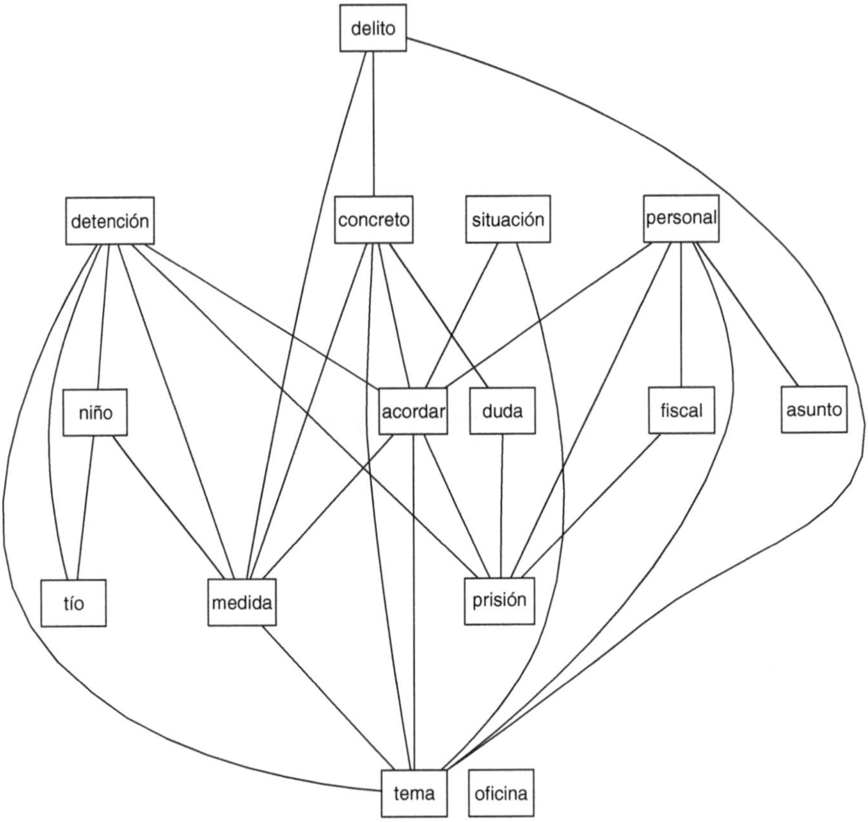

Fig. 5.17 Correlation of terms in Topic 10 within the DocumentTerm matrix

(*estafa*), and issues over liability (*responsabilidad*). The reference to these issues might make us classify this topic as a technical one, but at the same time, the central role played by the public prosecution (*fiscal*) strongly correlated with both the preliminary proceedings and actions such as imprisonment (*prisión*) indicate that the problems may be referring on practical or behavioral matters during the proceedings. Therefore, due to their purely procedural nature they might contain technical terms on procedural law and behavioral vocabulary on legal actors and actions at the same time.

5.4.4 The Behavioral/Technical Divide

The figures above look like incomplete maps of which we only see some relevant milestones, terms that may be seen as representing the main features of junior judges' problem spaces regarding a number of situations of their professional activity

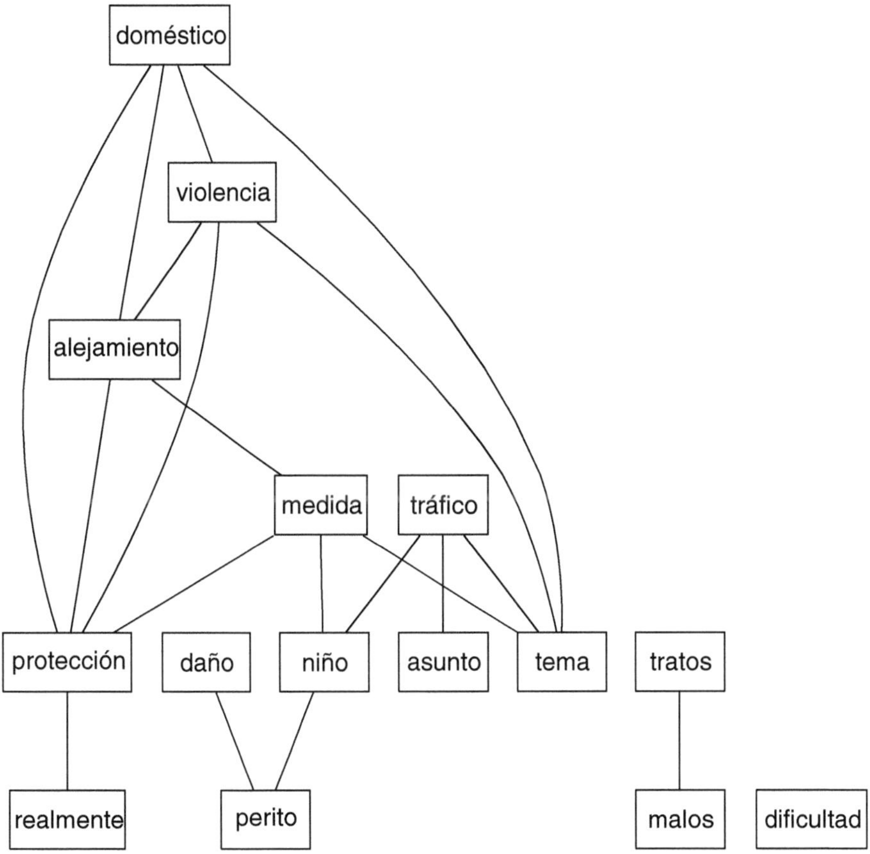

Fig. 5.18 Correlation between the 15 most relevant terms in Topic 7 within the DocumentTerm matrix

(be it the removal of a corpse or starting preliminary proceedings for fraud). Moreover, the results from the topic model have helped us classify the topics in two broad categories: some topics are clearly legal technical, others refer more to behavioral situations.

On one hand, the graphical display of topics show that problem spaces represented by what I call "technical topics" are centered mostly upon technical terms from the development and management of legal procedures. They are typical abstract legal typologies (*servidumbre*, *fraude*, *delito*, *ejecución*), somehow revealing the boundaries of technical legal problems. Note that in the technical topics the terms pointing to actual actors in the procedings (e.g., *fiscal* [prosecutor]) are rare, and when present they have a secondary role.

In contrast, the problem spaces of the "behavioral topics" are mainly built around a set of very important actors: prosecutors (*fiscal*), medical examiners (*médico forense*), victims and agressors, and people with critical mental issues. These topics

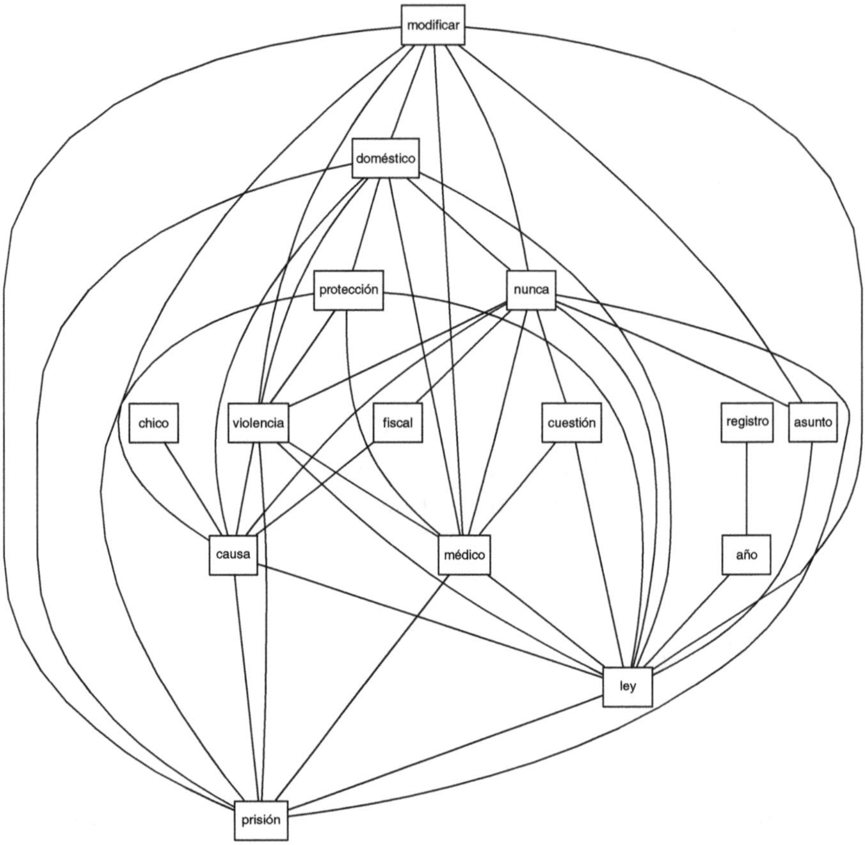

Fig. 5.19 Correlation between the 15 most relevant terms of Topic 9 within the DocumentTerm matrix

do not point to legal theoretical problems but to the practical difficulties produced by the need to cope, manage and deal with these actors' behavior in critical situations that usually combine urgency and highly consequential decisions such as imprisonment, detention or the examination of victims.

Moreover, our theoretical classification between technical and behavioral topics receives support in the data. To test our classification we have performed a Principal Components Analysis on the posterior probability attached to each document within each topic, in a matrix where rows are the 330 documents from the civil, criminal, and on-call corpus, while columns are the probabilities attached to each of the ten topics.

Principal components analysis (PCA) is a method designed to produce synthetic (latent) variables from data in order to summarize linear relationships both between individuals and between variables.[19] Since we want to check whether the divide

[19] The basic model for PCA is similar to that of latent semantic analysis and the other methods we briefly discussed in Sect. 5.4.1. See (Buntine and Jakulin 2006) for a unified theoretical framework.

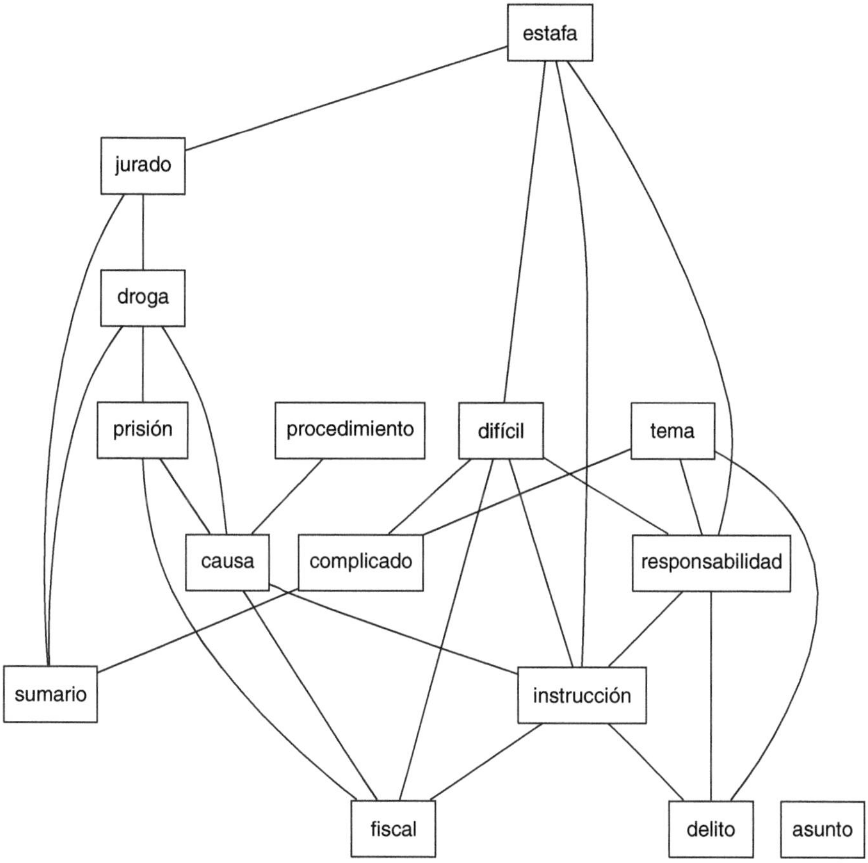

Fig. 5.20 Correlation network of the most relevant terms in Topic 4. The presence of both technical and behavioral terms makes this topic hard to classify

between theoretical and behavioral topics is supported by the data, our interest lies in the variables (topics) and in the extent to which our theoretical expectations are supported by a latent variable in the data. Due to the nature of the input data—the results of the topic model—the components produced through PCA explain a similar proportion of variance in the data, as Table 5.10 shows. Recall that Latent Dirichlet Allocation is designed to attach as few topics as possible to each document, so each document tends to present a high probability of belonging to just one topic and very low probability with respect to the other topics.

Still, if we use the component that explains the highest percentage of variation in the data, it supports our theoretical model. Table 5.11 shows the correlation of each topic with the first component produced by PCA, revealing that our behavioral topics 1, 3, 7 and 9 are significantly and positively correlated with the latent variable, while topics 2, 5, 8 (the theoretical ones) present significantly negative correlations, while topics 4, 6, and 10 (that we interpreted to be behavioral) have no significant correlations.

Table 5.10 Distribution of eigenvalues and percentages of variance for each component of the Principal Components Analysis on the topics

Components	Eigenvalue	Percentage of variance	Cumulative % of variance
comp 1	1.24	12.36	12.36
comp 2	1.17	11.74	24.11
comp 3	1.13	11.34	35.45
comp 4	1.13	11.27	46.72
comp 5	1.11	11.07	57.78
comp 6	1.07	10.68	68.47
comp 7	1.06	10.58	79.04
comp 8	1.05	10.50	89.54
comp 9	1.05	10.46	100.00
comp 10	0.00	0.00	100.00

Table 5.11 Correlation of each topic to the first component of the Principal Component Analysis

Topic	Correlation	*p-value*
3	0.55	0.00
9	0.31	0.00
1	0.27	0.00
7	0.18	0.00
4	0.08	0.16
10	0.07	0.18
6	−0.02	0.78
5	−0.24	0.00
8	−0.34	0.00
2	−0.74	0.00

Figure 5.21 presents the visualization of the position of each topic along this first PCA component, that we interpret as the Technical-Behavioral scale. The pattern in the data supports our theoretical expectations: the technical topics are aligned on the left-hand side of the scale, while the behavioral ones tend to be aligned on the right. Topics 4, 6 and 10 (which we misclassified) are too close to the zero position so as to fall clearly on either category—which we shall call Neutral. With this new three-category classification we can now classify each document in one single category using the document's highest posterior probability to a particular topic.[20] The general correspondence between our theory and the structure of the data may be finally seen in Table 5.12, that crosstabulates the result of classifying all the documents following both our theoretical model and the criterium offered by

[20] Again, it is convenient that in Latent Dirichlet Allocation documents tend to be strongly associated with one single topic.

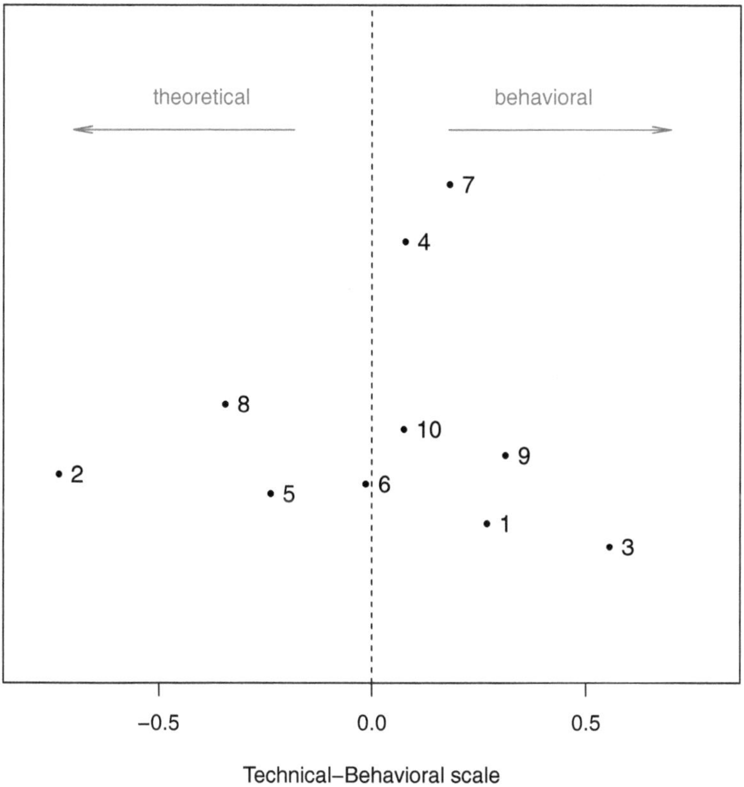

Fig. 5.21 Classification of the topics along the first component of the Principal Components Analysis on the posterior probability of each document on each topic. The first component captures the technical-behavioral divide

Table 5.12 Crosstabulation of the document classification results of our theoretical model against the results of PCA

		Data driven model		
		Technical	Neutral	Behavioral
Theoretical model	Technical	111	0	0
	Neutral	0	51	0
	Behavioral	0	32	136

Principal Components Analysis. The table shows that the only mismatching between both criteria is to be found between the Neutral and Behavioral categories.

Table 5.13 Percentage of each type of document in each category for our two classification models

	Theoretical model				*Data driven model*			
	Technical	Neutral	Behavioral	*Total*	Technical	Neutral	Behavioral	*Total*
Civil	81.08	3.60	15.32	100	81.08	8.11	10.81	100
Criminal	11.93	31.19	56.88	100	11.93	44.04	44.04	100
On-call	7.27	11.82	80.91	100	7.27	23.64	69.09	100

5.4.5 On-Call Problems as Practical Problems

We are now ready to put our main hypothesis to test—whether problems faced by junior judges when on-call are distinctively practical in nature compared to the problems raised during ordinary procedures (civil and criminal), which are more theoretical. In particular, we expect to find that most judges' responses regarding civil procedures are technical while most problems during on-call situations fall into the behavioral category. We also expect that problems about on-call situations are more behavioral than the ones during criminal procedures, and that the latter are more neutral or behavioral than problems on civil procedures.

Table 5.13 shows the distribution of each type of document (civil, criminal and on-call) in each problem category (technical, neutral, behavioral) for the two classification criteria explained in the previous section. These first results show that a wide majority of civil problems fall into the technical category in both classification models, while most of the on-call problems seem to be of a behavioral nature. However, the data driven model classifies more on-call problems into the neutral category than our theoretical model. Finally, in both models problems during criminal procedures fall almost equally either in the neutral or behavioral category.

In order to further test our hypothesis we fit an unordered multinomial logit model of the Technical-Neutral-Behavioral classification on the type of problem depicted by junior judges. In particular, we fit two separate multinomial logistic regression models, one for the classification we inferred directly from the topic model (theoretical model), and another one for the classification delivered by Principal Components Analysis (data driven model), with the Technical category as reference in both models. Our predictor for the type of problem is whether junior judges are explaining problems encountered during civil procedures, criminal procedures, or on-call situations. The model can be represented as a set of two independent logistic regressions with binary outcomes:

- $ln\left(\frac{P(problem=Behavioral)}{P(problem=Technical)}\right) = \beta_0 + \beta_1(corpus = criminal) + \beta_2(corpus = on - call)$
- $ln\left(\frac{P(problem=Neutral)}{P(problem=Technical)}\right) = \beta_0 + \beta_1(corpus = criminal) + \beta_2(corpus = on - call)$

Table 5.14 Results of the multinomial logistic regression model of the Technical/Behavioral classification on the type of problems (civil, criminal, on-call). The hypothesis is tested using two different outcome variables (theoretical and data driven)

	Theoretical model		*Data driven model*	
	Neutral	Behavioral	Neutral	Behavioral
(Intercept)	−3.11***	−1.67***	−2.30***	−2.01***
	(0.51)	(0.26)	(0.35)	(0.31)
Corpus: Criminal/Civil	4.08***	3.23***	3.61***	3.32***
	(0.61)	(0.40)	(0.47)	(0.44)
Corpus: On-call/Civil	3.60***	4.08***	3.48***	4.27***
	(0.68)	(0.45)	(0.53)	(0.48)
Deviance	467.77		522.26	
Log-likelihood	−233.88		−261.13	
AIC	479.77		534.26	
BIC	502.56		557.05	
N	330		330	

*** indicates significance at $p < 0.001$

Table 5.14 presents the results of the multinomial logit models. The first two columns present the results when we use the outcome variable drawn from our theoretical model, while the last two columns show the ones using the data driven classification. In both cases, the reference predictor is the civil type of document. Since there are not sharp differences between the effect of the type of document on the nature of the problem for the two models, our interpretation applies for both.

Results support our hypothesis regardless of the classification used as outcome variable. In particular, first, the log odds of being a behavioral *versus* a technical type of problem increase by 4 if moving from a document containing problems of civil nature to a document on problems about on-call situations. Moreover, on-call problems present also a higher likelihood to be neutral than technical, compared to documents on civil problems. On the other hand, when we compare problems on civil and criminal procedures, our expectations are also met. In effect, the log odds of being neutral or behavioral compared to being technical increase by 4 and 3, respectively when we move from a document on civil problems to a document depicting problems encountered during criminal procedures.

To ease interpretation, Table 5.15 shows the predicted probabilities of each type of document to belong to each category. As it can be observed, the difference between civil and on-call problems is sharp again regardless the classification model. In particular, problems on civil procedures have a 80 % chance to be of technical nature, while on-call problems present a change between 70 and 80 % of being behavioral, and only a 7 % chance of being technical. Finally, Fig. 5.22 plots these predicted probabilities graphically with confidence intervals. As we see, problems during criminal procedures present roughly a 50 % chance to be either behavioral or

Table 5.15 Predicted probabilities for the documents within each type of corpus of being technical, neutral, and behavioral. Predicted values from both the theoretical and the data driven model

	Theoretical model			*Data driven model*		
	Technical	Neutral	Behavioral	Technical	Neutral	Behavioral
Civil	0.81	0.04	0.15	0.81	0.08	0.11
Criminal	0.12	0.31	0.57	0.12	0.44	0.44
On call	0.07	0.12	0.81	0.07	0.24	0.69

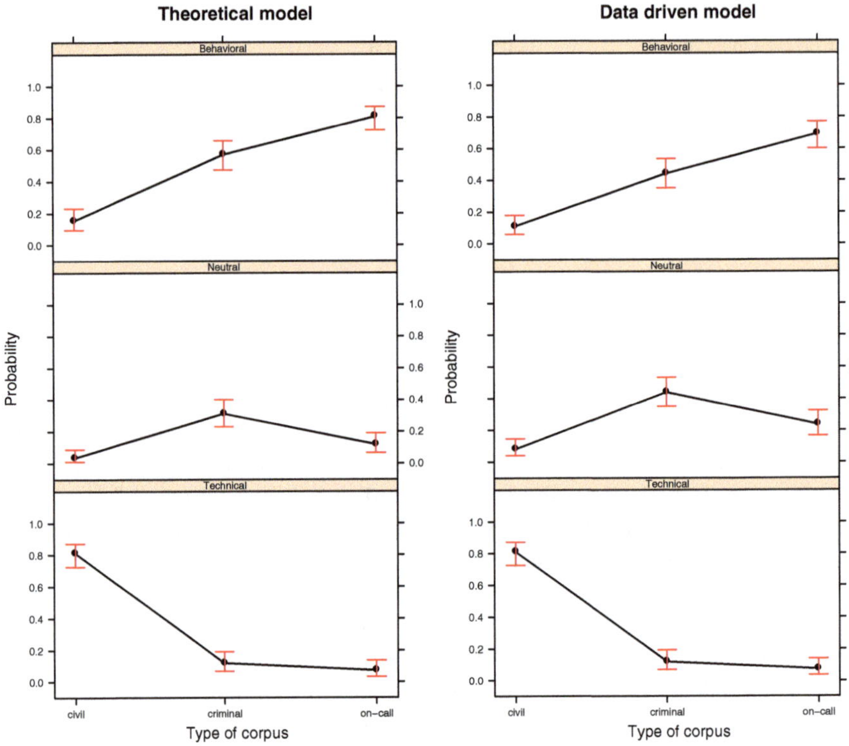

Fig. 5.22 Predicted probabilities of belonging to either category for the documents by our three corpora and in the four multionmial logistic models

neutral, while both civil and on-call problems present a very specific profile in the technical and behavioral categories, respectively.

These results give support to the idea that problems junior judges do face when on call may be regarded as being of a behavioral, practical nature. In effect, the terms that shaped semantic contexts pointed to actual references in the judicial world, in the sense that these terms did not point to abstract legal concepts but to instances that have a representation in the world, whether they be particular actors (e.g., medical examiner) or actions (e.g., arresting a person).

The fact that the problems explained refer mostly to actions triggered by (legal or non-legal) actors whose behavior requires a solution by the judge is essential for our interpretation of these problems as organizational demands—according to what we commented in Chap. 3—which ask for organizational decisions.

Our contention is that these organizational demands are not abstract instances but actual situations triggered by real agents who bring the problems into the judges' area of action. Yet these problems usually require satisfactory solutions that junior judges do not have in their knowledge storage, since their legal education is based exclusively on theoretical knowledge.

In particular, when we access individual problems reported by judges regarding on-call situations, we observe that they report two broad kinds of problems regardless of the specific context in which they occur (say, domestic violence or urgent confinement). The first kind are situations for which legal procedures exist that establish how each actor should behave, though we see that not all actors do behave as they should. The second kind are situations for which simply there is established protocol to the knowledge of junior judges.

The fact, though, is that regardless of the specific kind of practical problem they face, judges do need solutions which are likely to become routines. This is quite obvious when situations imply coordinating some actors' behavior, especially public prosecutors. In particular, as shall be observed below, a number of on-call problems imply that the public prosecutor should attend the court but actually does not:

> ¿Qué hacer cuando el fiscal no quiere venir a una comparecencia para una orden de protección? ¿Qué hacer cuando el fiscal considera que no viene porque no quiere pedir la prisión y ni siquiera quiere escuchar al imputado cuando tú crees que está más claro que el agua? ¿Qué haces, vas a buscarlo? Yo entiendo que la ley es muy tajante en muchas cosas, orden de protección, comparecencia y al fiscal, y te salen diciendo que no, que adoptes una medida cautelar de oficio. Eso no lo leo en la ley, la ley habla de comparecencia.
> [What can I do when the public prosecutor doesn't agree to come to an appearance necessary for issuing a restraining order? What can I do when the public prosecutor decides not to come because he won't request a prison sentence and he doesn't even want to hear the accused when you think it is the clearest thing? What can I do, do I make him come? I understand the law is really unequivocal in many things and it states: restraining orders, appearance and to the public prosecutor, and they tell you no, that you should take an *ex-officio* precautionary measure. I don't see that within the law, the law says an appearance should be carried out.]

Yet in other situations implying the non-appearance of the public prosecutor, junior judges do not blame it on the professionals' own behavior but on their actual impossibility to attend many things at the same time, since a number of judicial districts actually share the same public prosecutor (and sometimes the same medical examiner). Then the fax or the phone seems to be a solution, though an unsatisfactory one:

> # Claro, en partidos grandes en que está el fiscal ahí, pues llamas. Que no hablamos ya de prisión, que la ley te permite meterlo en prisión y después volver a convocar, y demás, pero son decisiones, a lo mejor, en los que la nueva legislación te prevé al fiscal, casi para todo! ¡Y no tienes! Y tú dices, ¿qué hago? ¿Voy a dejar de resolver?
> [Of course, when you're in a big judicial district you have your own public prosecutor and you just call him. The problem is not sending someone into prison because the law allows doing that before summoning again, and so forth, but these are decisions in which the new

legislation requires the public prosecutor to attend almost in every single situation. But you don't have him here! And you say: What can I do? Must I stop deciding?]

Problema de la guardia es que tienes una orden de protección y tienes que ponerte con el fiscal para que venga ya. Y te dice: mejor me viene venir por la tarde. Y yo: no, que tengo que tener a un funcionario y no le quiero hacer comer aquí, ni quedarse aquí. Porque la mayoría viven fuera y no los quiero tener aquí todo el día tirados.
[A problem when on call is that you must issue a restraining order and you must contact the public prosecutor in order him to come. Yet he tells you: I'd better come in the afternoon. And I say: no, because then I should make some civil servant have lunch here and remain in court and I don't want that. Because most of them live out of town and I don't want them be waiting all day here.]

El fiscal, si no aparece, pues bueno, le mandamos el fax; si él nos comunica que no viene por X motivos, pues bueno, yo hago constar que no viene el fiscal, y sigo adelante, a ver cómo lo hacemos.
[If the public prosecutor does not appear we send him a fax; if he informs that he does not come due to X reasons, well, I state that he doesn't come and then I just go on to see how to work it out.]

Hay un fiscal de guardia para todos los pueblos, que a la vez hace las faltas y los juicios rápidos. Los fiscales no se pueden desdoblar. Entonces tú, por mucho que tú estés dispuesto a pasar detenidos un domingo, un sábado por la tarde, cuando sea, pues no tienes el fiscal allí. No tienes al forense aquí.
[There is only one public prosecutor on call for all towns, who is also responsible for dealing with misdemeanours and quick trials. Public prosecutors cannot attend all things at once. Then, even though you would agree with hearing a detainee on Sunday or Saturday evening, you won't have a public prosecutor there. You don't even have a medical examiner.]

Notice that in cases where judges report that public prosecutors do not appear in court when they should, the use of the phone or the fax is perceived by most judges as a solution, either satisfactory or not, but a solution indeed. This type of solution is precisely an "embodiment of 'once and for all' decisions" (Simon 1997, p. 89) to implement responses to organizational stimuli, as we showed in Chap. 3, and it is very likely that it becomes a routine action.

The difficulties for reaching these solutions are expressed by judges in a clear manner specially when faced to delicate situations such as having to remove a corpse and cases involving domestic or gender-based violence. Regarding corpse removal, some junior judges give detailed examples of very specific tasks to be carried out in these situations—such as the corpse identification or the decision on what to do with the dead person's belongings—which illustrate quite clearly the nature of the problems encountered when details are pointed out. A first example is given by cases which involve further medical and scientific tests such as DNA tests (or other acts for corpse identification) or autopsies, in which judges seem to lack specific, established protocols on the steps to be followed:

Hombre, hemos tenido algún asunto de varios muertos en un solo siniestro, el último que yo recuerde fue un helicóptero y murieron cuatro personas, y en fin, y luego puedes tener alguna cosilla, tienes pruebas de identificación, tienes que esperar o coordinar muchos equipos que están afectados, pero vamos fuera de equipos de la policía, de la policía judicial, de médicos forenses, en fin, todos están pendientes de ti, todos te llaman: ¿qué hacemos con estas muestras? ¿Con aquellas otras? ¿Adónde llevamos los cadáveres? ¿Hay espacio

en el tanatorio? ¿No hay espacio en el tanatorio, los llevamos al hospital, no los llevamos? ¿Qué hacemos mientras que vienen los las pruebas de ADN? ¿Extraemos pruebas? ¿No hace falta? Tienes que organizar un poco todo para que no haya trabajo duplicado inútilmente. Para que todo esté un poco organizado.
[Well, we've had some cases involving various dead men in one single accident, the last one being a helicopter, and four people got killed. And then you have some small things such as the identification tests, you must wait for or to coordinate a great deal of different teams involved, but well, except teams from the police, the judicial police, or medical examiners, all the rest are always calling you: what may we do with these samples? Where are we taking the corpses? Is there enough space in the morgue? There is not enough space in the morgue, do we take them to the hospital or not? What must we do while the DNA-tests team is coming? Do we carry out our own tests? Is that necessary? One must organize everything a bit in order double work is not unfruitfully performed. In order everything is a little bit organized.]

Identificación de cadáveres, a veces durante la guardia tienes un muerto, a ver quién identifica el cadáver, especialmente cuando se encuentre en un estado especialmente malo.
[Corpse identification, sometimes when on-call you have a corpse, and then who is to identify the corpse, specially when it is in a very bad condition.]

Por ejemplo, en los casos en que va el forense en lugar del juez, la ley lo permite y sí, no pasa nada, se hace, pero luego después el forense no presenta nada. Entonces claro, yo aquí he tenido que luchar contra eso. Yo preguntaba, pero entonces si va el forense y no, el forense hace la autopsia y la autopsia llega más tarde. Claro, en [. . .] la autopsia era inmediata. Aquí tardan una semana. Claro, entonces, qué haces en una semana, entierras, no entierras. ¿Qué haces? Bueno, te puede avanzar la causa de la muerte, ya pero es que lo veo muy leve, eso. Entonces yo ya hablé con el forense y si vas tú al levantamiento por favor hazme un informe de lo que ves aquí. Luego con la policía también tardan días a traerte el atestado. No, por favor, traiganmelo al día siguiente y entonces yo ya firmo, pero todo un poco por sentido común y que no te lo enseñan, esto.
[For instance, in those cases when it is the medical examiner who attends instead of the judge—as allowed by the law—and then nothing happens, it is done, but later on the ME doesn't deliver any report. Well, I've had to fight against this. I used to ask for it, but then if the ME attends, he performs the autopsy and the results arrive later. Well, in [. . .] the results came immediately. Here they last a week. Then, what can you do during a week, do you bury the corpse or not? What can you do? Well, he may give you an idea of the cause of death prior to the definite report, but this is too weak. Then I spoke to the medical examiner and asked him to please write down a report (containing his observations in situ) whenever he attended a corpse removal. Then the police also take some days to bring their report. No, please, bring it here just the day after so that I can sign it, but all this is a matter of commonsense and that you have not been taught about it.]

Y problemas prácticos que te quedabas así con la duda, como yo qué sé: la familia quiere que la autopsia se practique en determinado sitio y por tal médico. Evidentemente la autopsia la va a practicar el médico forense pero bueno, accedí a que designaran un médico para que estuviera presente que fuera de su confianza. Preguntas tales como: ¿el médico se puede llevar algún órgano? Ya. Tienes que decidirlo ya. No te voy a decir lo que resolví. Prefiero no decir lo que resolví. Es que tienes que tomar una decisión pero ya y es una cosa que te pilla completamente de nuevas. Porque dices: ¿sí? ¿No? ¿Por qué sí? ¿Por qué no? Sí: puede ser útil. No: puede ser complejo o complicado, puede dar lugar a problemas. Tienes que decidirlo.
[And then practical problems which make you doubt, for instance: the dead person's family wants the autopsy to be done in a particular place and by a particular doctor. Obviously the autopsy is to be done by our medical examiner, but well, I accepted a doctor they trusted be designated in order him to also attend the autopsy. Questions such as: may the doctor take any organ away? I know. You must decide now. I won't tell you what I decided. I prefer not to tell you that. The fact is that you must make a decision in a second but you don't have

any idea about that. You ask yourself: yes? No? Why yes? Why not? Yes: it may be useful. No: it may be complex or complicated, it can bring trouble. You must decide.]

These are very intensive examples showing the need by judges to access to specific protocols or determined patterns of behavior that ease their decision making in situations they perceive as critical. In cases such as domestic violence, though, their focus shifts to the efficiency of the legal measures to be taken to either protect the victims or prosecute the aggressors. The fact, though, is that judges find difficulties in dealing with the actual behavior of both men and women involved in domestic violence situations. For these actors' behavior is what specifically affects the enforcement of those legal measures and thus their efficiency. Both aspects usually appear mixed up in a single response, as in the following examples.

Y luego otra cosa que se planteó, fue una señora que puso denuncia de malos tratos, pero había dicho expresamente que no quería que se acordara ninguna medida de alejamiento. Pero luego empezó a llamar a la Guardia Civil, que estaba muy asustada, porque el marido estaba en el pueblo, estaba rondando por ahí, ¿pues qué se hace? Â¡Cuando ella ha dicho que no quería medida de alejamiento, cuando todo lo que consta es que no la quiere! Pero tampoco quiere que se le acerque.
[And yet another thing was a woman who reported ill-treatment, but she had expressly said that she wished no restraining order was enforced whatsoever. But later on she started calling the police saying she was frightened because her husband was in town, he was wandering around, so what do we do? She had told us she didn't want any restraining order, and the official record tells she doesn't want any! But she doesn't want him nearby either.]

¿En violencia doméstica debe acordarse el alejamiento del agresor en caso de lesiones de poca entidad o amenazas si la mujer se niega a él?
[Must I confirm a restraining order in domestic violence when injuries are slight, or there is only a threaten, when the woman doesn't want the order?]

A mí me ha pasado un caso que viene una señora y te lo cuenta. Que realmente tienes que darle una orden de protección y ves que no la pide. Entonces que los presionas para que te la pidan. Y les dices tú: "señora que esto es mejor". Hay que orientar a la gente. Y la típica orden de alejamiento que se dicta respecto del marido, y luego vienen y te dicen: es que le hice el caldo, ¿y ahora qué hago? "Porque tiene que venir a comer el caldo" me lo dijo la señora al salir de un juicio. Y yo le dije: "mire señora, lo que hagan a partir de aquí es su problema, pero sepa que su marido no se pueda acercar a usted".
[Once it happened that a woman came and told me it all. You must give her a restraining order but you see that she doesn't ask for it. Then you somehow push her to ask for it. And you tell her: lady, that's the best for you. You must advise them. And the typical restraining order announced against the husband, and then she comes and tells you: I cooked a soup for him and what am I going to do now? Because he must come and eat the soup—the woman told me that on leaving the court trial. And I told her: look, lady, what you do from now is none of my business, but be aware that your husband can't stay close to you.]

A órdenes de alejamiento vienen a menudo a pedir que las revoques. Hubo uno que el problema que tenía el señor es que era alcohólico y cuando bebía, pues había problemas en casa. Mientras estuvieron viviendo los hijos en casa, los hijos mayores pararon al padre, pero cuando se fueron los hijos la madre se quedó sola. La madre lloraba como una descosida, porque ella sabía que si su marido no bebía, su marido estaba bien. Pues hubo un día que dictamos una órden de protección. Y tenían una explotación ganadera y la señora decía que con las vacas ella sola no podía entonces que también necesitaba a su marido.
[They usually come and ask you to revoke a restraining order. There was a man who was alcoholic and when he drank he caused trouble at home. While their sons were living with

them they kept their father under control, but when when they left their mother was left alone with the father. The mother used to cry inconsolably, because she knew if her husband didn't drink it was all right. Well, one day we announced a restraining order against him. But they ran a farm and the woman said that she could not manage the cows on her own and that she needed her husband with her.]

A veces estás trabajando, dictando órdenes de alejamiento y te viene al día siguiente la persona, la mujer, que quiere volver a vivir con él. Mi compañera no sé si te habrá contado se quedó hace poco hasta las cinco de la tarde y al notificarle el auto de alejamiento a él, le dijo ella que quería retirarla. Y a mi me han llegado casos de decirme el abogado: estos vuelven.
[Sometimes you're working, signing restraining orders and then the day after the person comes back and tells you she wants him back. I don't know whether my colleague told you she had to be working here until 5 o'clock in the evening in order to notify a restraining order to a man and the woman said she wished it to be revoked. And a lawyer told me once: they'll be back together soon.]

Violencia familiar y órdenes de protección. Aquí hay bastante porque hay mucho alcohólico y yo he puesto muchas órdenes de protección, medidas de alejamiento. Lo que pasa es que puse muchas pero el 90 % duran 7 días, 15 días, a que venga la persona, la mujer generalmente, que la saques, que se lleva de nuevo a su marido para casa. Que ya está, que fue una tontería, que fue nosequé. Claro, la medida pierde todo sentido porque dices tú: claro, si va a meterlo en casa, para qué vas tú a poner tú un alejamiento. Pues bueno: le quito el alejamiento. Pero el procedimiento sigue, ¿eh señora? Usted verá y dicen: sí, sí, sí.
[Domestic violence and restraining orders. We've' had several cases here because here we have several alcoholics and I've announced a number of restraining orders, injunctions of protection. I've announced a great deal of them but they last 7 days, 15 days, and then the person comes back, generally the woman, who wants you to revoke it, that she is bringing her husband back home. They tell you that was just a silly thing. But then the order becomes nonsense because if she is taking him in, why should you sign a restraining order? All right: I revoke the order. But lady, note that the legal procedure goes on, be aware of that. And they tell you: yes, yes, yes.]

5.5 The Lack of Routines and Its Behavioral Consequences

The absence of particular organizational routines in the operation of the on-call service of those courts filled with junior judges is coherent with the theoretical literature upon which we based this whole work, specially conclusions drawn in Chap. 3 regarding the outer environment of decisions. In particular, in Sect. 3.3.4 we saw that bureaucratic organizations counted largely on routines to implement responses to organizational stimuli, and in general as a method for ensuring the role of organization as a stable pattern of events.

Yet in our analysis we have seen that while mechanisms for dealing with bottlenecks of attention—such as specialization of work—are surely at work in Courts of First Instance and Magistrate, a mechanism such as organizational routines are not only lacking during on-call services, but they are perceived as needed by most junior judges in their responses. Note that these were reported by judges when asked specifically for *problems* during on-call services.

The practical or procedural nature of the problems identified for on-call services would in fact emphasize the need for sets of routinized responses to similar problems, which would be also coherent with recent accounts of organizational routines seen more as patterned processes emphasizing their procedural nature (Royer and Langley 2008) instead of the substantive flavor that somehow covers Herbert Simon's classical definition, though we already noted that this distinction is more apparent than actual.

We saw that behavioral data show that a relevant proportion of organizational behavior is based on following rules rather than on calculating consequences of that behavior (Cyert et al. 1959), and that then routine behavior occurs when choice is simplified by de development of a script of a fixed response (March and Simon 1958, p. 143) by "the application of standard operating procedures or rules to appropriate situations" (March 1981).

In addition, the observation of actual decision-making situations (Klein and Calderwood 1991) has brought many scholars to think organization members usually do face situations that may require either content-based or procedural solutions, in which cases they may search first in their "repertory of response programs" (March and Simon 1958, p. 140)—for which an analysis of ready-made, full-content solutions would seem most adequate—and then, if these programs are not adequate, they may search for other alternatives, in which case the adoption of a 'procedural' view of routines (Royer and Langley 2008) would be worth undertaking (see Sect. 3.2.2.2 above). In these uncertain situations, judges will carry out "purposeful human behavior which seems to be ruled at the same time by intuition, competence, design and chance" (Ciborra 1999). In other words, they improvise (Lanzara 1999).

Yet it will be the specific nature of the problems faced what will determine whether the decision-maker will search for new alternatives in order to find solutions to doubts. In our case, problems expressed by judges have been interpreted as practical ones as they express the need for procedural and not substantive (theoretical) solutions.

Moreover, according to our elaborations in Sect. 3.3.5, we feel ready now to conclude that junior judges' practical problems are a function of a certain degree of uncertainty about means, i.e., lack of knowledge about the procedural means to solve specific problems that produce doubts. Thus viewed, the kind of routines junior judges lack can now be interpreted in a procedural way in the sense that procedural problems expressed by judges may be dealt with by the application of 'procedural' routines (Royer and Langley 2008) as they were overviewed in Sect. 3.3.4. In our case the lack of these "repertory of response programs" seems quite apparent, and this would explain that judges on call must search for new alternatives when doubts arise.

In our second chapter we observed that one of the main benefits of adopting routinized adaptive responses to organizational stimuli is that routines tend to increase the *predictability* of individual activities within an organization, which is by definition a highly predictable pattern of events itself. Yet our description of the outer environment of junior judges' decision making has brought us to the conclusion that judges cannot count on such a relevant mechanism for organizational predictability.

On the contrary, the on-call service can be defined as a moment in junior judges' professional activity where they lack specific routines that enable them to find out quick solutions when urgent decisions are needed. Given that outer environment and a particular problem space, junior judges may be understood as decision-makers who must adapt to a procedurally uncertain environment searching heuristically for solutions which their organizational environment has not provided them with.

This is the way we understand our central contention that the on-call service embodies a moment in which an organization such as the Court of First Instance and Magistrate—within the Spanish judicial system—*suspends its role as a reliable pattern of events*.

References

Ayuso, M., M. Bécue-Bertaut, R. Álvarez, O. Valencia, M. Álvarez, M. Hernández, and M. Santolino. 2002. Jueces jóvenes en España, 2002. Análisis estadístico de las encuestas a los jueces en su primer destino (promociones 48/49 y 50). Internal report (project sec-2001-2581-c02-01/02), Consejo General del Poder Judicial [General Council of the Judiciary].

Ayuso, M., M. Bécue-Bertaut, R. Álvarez, O. Valencia, M. Álvarez, and M. Santolino. 2003. Análisis estadístico de las encuestas a los jueces en su primer destino. Internal Report SEC-2001-2581-C02-01/02, Consejo General del Poder Judicial [General Council of the Judiciary], Escuela Judicial (Barcelona).

Baeza-Yates, R., and B. Ribeiro-Neto. 1999. *Modern information retrieval*. New York: ACM.

Basu, S., and I. Davidson. 2009. Constrained partitional clustering of text data: An overview. In *Text mining. Classification, clustering, and applications*, ed. A. N. Srivastava and M. Sahami, 155–184. Boca Raton: Chapman and Hall.

Bécue-Bertaut, M., M. Rajman, L. Lebart, and E. Gaussier. 2005. Extraction of the useful words from a decisional corpus. Contribution of correspondence analysis. *StudFuzz* 185:159–179.

Benjamins, V. R., J. Contreras, P. Casanovas, M. Ayuso, M. Bécue-Bertaut, M. Lemus, and C. Urios. 2004. Ontologies of professional legal knowledge as the basis for intelligent it support for judges. *Artificial Intelligence and Law* 12 (4): 359–378.

Benoit, K., and M. Laver. 2007. Benchmarks for text analysis: A response to budge and pennings. *Electoral Studies* 26:130–135.

Benoit, K., M. Laver, and S. Mikhailov. 2009. Treating words as data with error: Uncertainty in text statements of policy positions. *American Journal of Political Science* 53 (2): 495–513.

Bénzecri, J.-P. 1982. *L'analyse des données*. Paris: Dunod.

Blasius, J., and M. Greenacre. 2006. Correspondence analysis and related methods in practice. In *Multiple correspondence analysis and related methods*, ed. M. Greenacre and J. Blasius, 3–40. Boca Raton: Chapman and Hall.

Blei, D. 2012. Probabilistic topic models. *Communications of the ACM* 55:77–84.

Blei, D., and J. D. Lafferty. 2009. Topic models. In *Text mining. Classification, clustering, and applications*, ed. A. N. Srivastava and M. Sahami, 71–94. Boca Raton: CRC Press.

Blei, D., A. Y. Ng, and M. I. Jordan. 2003. Latent dirichlet allocation. *Journal of Machine Learning Research* 3:993–1022.

Borg, I., and P. J. F. Groenen. 2005. *Modern multidimensional scaling. Theory and applications*. 2nd ed. New York: Springer.

Bray, J. R., and J. T. Curtis. 1957. An ordination of upland forest communities of southern wisconsin. *Ecological Monographs* 27:325–349.

Budge, I., and P. Pennings. 2007a. Do they work? Validating computerised word frequency estimates against policy series. *Electoral Studies* 26:121–129.

Budge, I., and P. Pennings. 2007b. Missing the message and shooting the messenger: Benoit and laver's 'response'. *Electoral Studies* 26:136–141.
Budge, I., H.-D. Klingemann, A. Volkens, and J. Bara. eds. 2001. *Mapping policy preferences. Estimates for parties, electors, and governments 1945–1998*. Oxford: Oxford University Press.
Buntine, W. 2009. Estimating likelihoods for topic models. NICTA Technical Report NICTA-SML-09-001, NICTA, Canberra (AU).
Buntine, W., and A. Jakulin. 2004. Applying discrete PCA in data analysis. In *Proceedings of the 20th conference on Uncertainty in Artificial Intelligence (UAI 2004)*, ed. C. Meek and J. Halpern, Banff, Canada.
Buntine, W., and A. Jakulin. 2006. Discrete component analysis. In *Subspace, latent structure and feature selection techniques*, ed. C. J. Saunders, S. R. Gunn, M. Grobelnik, and J. Shawe-Taylor. Berlin: Springer-Verlag.
Carmona, J., S. Cervell, L. Márquez, M. A. Martí, L. Padró, R. Placer, H. Rodríguez, M. Taulé, and J. Turmo. 1998. An environment for morphosyntactic processing of unrestricted Spanish text. In *Proceedings of the first conference on language resources and evaluation*, 915–922, Granada, Spain.
Casellas, N. 2011. *Legal ontology engineering: Methodologies, trends, and the ontology of professional judicial knowledge*. Dordrecht: Springer.
Ciborra, C. 1999. Notes on improvisation and time in organizations. *Accounting, Management and Information Technologies* 9:77–94.
Cyert, R. M., E. A. Feigenbaum, and J. G. March. 1959. Models in a behavioral theory of the firm. *Behavioral Science* 4 (2): 81–95.
Deerwester, S., S. T. Dumais, G. W. Furnas, and T. K. L. R. Harshman. 1990. Indexing by latent semantic analysis. *Journal of the American Society for Information Science* 41 (6): 391–407.
Escofier, B., and J. Pagès. 1992. *Análisis factoriales simples y múltiples: objetivos, métodos e interpretación*. Euskal Herriko Unibertsitateko Argitarapen-Zerbitzua, Bilbao.
Falcó-Gimeno, A., and J.-J. Vallbé. 2013. Coalition agreements and party preferences: A principal components analysis approach. In *3rd annual general conference of the European Association of Political Science (EPSA)*, Barcelona.
Feinerer, I. 2008. *tm: Text Mining Package*, R package version 0.3-3 edition.
Feinerer, I., K. Hornik, and D. Meyer 2008. Text mining infrastructure in R. *Journal of Statistical Software* 25 (5): 1–54.
Fortuna, B., M. Grobelnik, and D. Mladenič. 2005. Visualization of text document corpus. *Informatica* 29:497–502.
Fortuna, B., C. Galleguillos, and N. Cristianini 2009. Detection of bias in media outlets with statistical learning methods. In *Text mining. Classification, clustering, and applications*, ed. A. N. Srivastava and M. Sahami, 27–50. Boca Raton: CRC Press.
Greenacre, M. 2005. Weighted metric multidimensional scaling. In *New developments in classification and data analysis*, ed. M. Vichi, P. Monari, S. Mignani, and A. Montanari, 141–150. Berlin: Springer.
Greenacre, M. 2006. From simple to multiple correspondence analysis. In *Multiple correspondence analysis and related methods*, ed. M. Greenacre and J. Blasius, 41–76. Boca Raton: Chapman and Hall.
Greenacre, M., and O. Nenadić. 2007. *ca: Simple, multiple and joint correspondence analysis*. http://www.carme-n.org/. R package version 0.21.
Grimmer, J., and B. M. Stewart. 2013. Text as data: The promise and pitfalls of automatic content analysis methods for political texts. *Political Analysis* 21 (3): 298–313.
Grün, B., and K. Hornik. 2011. `topicmodels`: An R package for fitting topic models. *Journal of Statistical Software* 40 (13): 1–30.
Guérin-Pace, F. 1998. Textual statistics: An exploratory tool for the social sciences. *Population: An English selection* 10 (1): 73–95.
Hofmann, T. 1999. Probabilistic latent semantic indexing. *Proceedings of the twenty-second annual international SIGIR conference on research and development in information retrieval.*

Huang, A. 2008. Similarity measures for text document clustering. In *New Zealand Computer Science Research Student Conference (NZCSRSC)*, ed. J. Holland, A. Nicholas, and D. Brignoli, Christchurch (NZ).

Jakulin, A. 2007. Analysis of legal and political data. In *Trends in legal knowledge—the semantic web and the regulation of electronic social systems*, ed. P. Casanovas, P. Noriega, D. Bourcier, and F. Galindo, 213–226. Granada: European Press Academic Publishing.

Jakulin, A., and W. Buntine. 2004. Applying discrete PCA in data analysis. In *Proceedings of the twentieth conference on uncertainty in artificial intelligence*, ed. C. Meek and J. Halpern. Arlington: AUAI Press.

Jaworska, N., and A. Chupetlovska-Anastasova. 2009. A review of multidimensional scaling (MDS) and its utility in various psychological domains. *Tutorials in Quantitative Methods for Psychology* 5 (1): 1–10.

Jones, B. D., and F. R. Baumgartner. 2012. From there to here: Punctuated equilibrium to the general punctuation thesis to a theory of government information processing. *Policy Studies Journal* 40:1–19.

Jurafsky, D., and J. H. Martin. 2008. *Speech and language processing: An introduction to natural language processing, computational linguistics, and speech recognition*. 2nd ed. Englewood Cliffs: Pearson Prentice Hall.

Klein, G. A., and R. Calderwood. 1991. Decision models: Some lessons from the field. *IEEE Transactions on Systems, Man, and Cybernetics* 21 (5): 1018–1026.

Klingemann, H.-D., A. Volkens, J. L. Bara, I. Budge, and M. McDonald. 2006. *Mapping policy preferences II: Estimates for parties, electors, and governments in Eastern Europe, European Union, and OECD 1990–2003*. Oxford: Oxford University Press.

Klüver, H. 2009. Measuring interest group influence using quantitative text analysis. *European Union Politics* 10:535–549.

Korenius, T., J. Laurikkala, K. Järvelin, and M. Juhola. 2004. Stemming and lemmatization in the clustering of Finnish text documents. In *Proceedings of the thirteenth ACM conference on information and knowledge management*, ed. D. A. Evans, L. Gravano, O. Herzog, C.-X. Zhai, and M. Ronthaler, 625–633. New York: ACM Press.

Krippendorff, K. 2004. *Content analysis: An introduction to its methodology*. 2nd ed. Thousand Oaks: Sage.

Lanzara, G. F. 1999. Between transient constructs and persistent structures: Designing systems in action. *Journal of Strategic Information Systems* 8:331–349.

Lapalut, S. 1995. Text clustering to support knowledge acquisition from documents. Rapport de recherche 2639, Institut National de Recherche en Informatique et en Automatique, Sophia Antipolis (France).

Lasswell, H., N. Leites, R. Fadner, J. M. Goldsen, A. Grey, I. L. Janis, A. Kaplan, D. Kaplan, A. Mintz, I. De Sola Pool, and S. Yakobson. 1949. *Language of politics: Studies of quantitative semantics*. Cambridge: MIT Press.

Lauderdale, B. E., and T. S. Clark. 2012. Scaling politically meaningful dimensions using texts and votes. In *7th annual conference on empirical legal studies*.

Lebart, L., and A. Salem. 1988. *Analyse statistique des données textuelles*. Paris: Dunod.

Manning, C. D., and H. Schütze. 1999. *Foundations of statistical natural language processing*. Cambridge: MIT Press.

Manning, C. D., P. Raghavan, and H. Schütze 2008. *Introduction to information retrieval*. Cambridge: Cambridge University Press.

March, J. G. 1981. Footnotes to organizational change. *Administrative Science Quarterly* 26:563–577.

March, J. G., and H. A. Simon. 1958. *Organizations*. New york: Wiley.

Marques de Sá, J. P. 2007. *Applied statistics using SPSS, STATISTICA, MATLAB, and R*. 2nd ed. Berlin: Springer.

Mimno, D. 2012a. Computational historiography: Data mining in a century of classics journals. *Journal on Computing and Cultural Heritage* 5 (1): Article 3.

Mimno, D. 2012b. Reconstructing pompeian households. *Computing Research Repository* abs/1202.3747.

Moens, M.-F. 2001. Innovative techniques for legal text retrieval. *Artificial Intelligence and Law* 9:29–57.

Mooi, E., and M. Sarstedt. 2011. Cluster analysis. In *A concise guide to market research*, eds. M. Sarstedt and E. Mooi, 237–284. Berlin: Springer-Verlag.

Morin, A. 2006. Intensive use of factorial correspondence analysis for text mining: Application with statistical education publications. *Proceedings of the 7th international conference on teaching statistics*, ICOTS, Salvador, Bahia, Brazil.

Murtagh, F. 2005. *Correspondence analysis and data coding with Java and R*. Boca Raton: Chapman and Hall.

Neuendorf, K. A. 2002. *The content analysis guidebook*. Thousand Oaks: Sage.

Oksanen, J., F. Guillaume-Blanchet, R. Kindt, P. Legendre, P. R. Minchin, R. B. O'Hara, G. L. Simpson, P. Solymos, M. H. H. Stevens, and H. Wagner. 2013. *vegan: Community ecology package*. R package version 2.0-8.

Paukkeri, M. S. 2012. Language- and domain-independent text mining. PhD dissertation, Department of Information and Computer Science, Aalto University, Finland.

Percellar-Giménez, E. 2000. El procedimiento de internamiento por razón de trastorno psíquico. *Noticias Jurídicas*.

Porter, M. F. 1980. An algorithm for suffix stripping. *Program* 14 (3): 130–137.

Proksch, S.-O., and J. B. Slapin. 2009. *WORDFISH: Scaling software for estimating political positions from Text (version 1.3)*. http://www.wordfish.org. Accessed 10 August 2014.

Quinn, G. P., and M. J. Keough. 2002. *Experimental design and data analysis for biologists*. Cambridge: Cambridge University Press.

R Core Team. 2013. *R: A language and environment for statistical computing*. Vienna: R Foundation for Statistical Computing.

Reinert, M. 1985. *Classification descendante hierarchique: un algorithme pour le traitement des tableaux logiques de grandes dimensions*. Paris: INRIA.

Reinert, M. 1987. *Un logiciel d'analyse de données textuelles ALCESTE*. Paris: INRIA.

Reinert, M. 2000. La tresse du sens et la méthode alceste: Application aux "rêveries du promeneur solitaire". In *JADT 2000. 5es Journées Internationales d'Analyse Statistique des Données Textuelles*.

Royer, I., and A. Langley. 2008. Linking rationality, politics, and routines in organizational decision making. In *The Oxford handbook of organizational decision making*, ed. G. P. Hodgkinson and W. H. Starbuck, 250–270. New York: Oxford University Press.

Salton, G., A. Wong, and C. S. Yang. 1975. A vector space model for automatic indexing. *Communications of the Association for Computing Machinery* 18 (11): 613–620.

Sandhya, N., and A. Govardhan. 2012. Analysis of similarity measures with wordnet based text document clustering. In *Proceedings of the InConINDIA 2012*, ed. S. C. Satapahy, P. S. Avadhani, and A. Abraham. Berlin: AISC.

Schonhardt-Bailey, C. 2005. Measuring ideas more effectively : An analysis of bush and kerry's national security speeches. *PS: Political Science and Politics* 38 (4): 701–711.

Schonhardt-Bailey, C. 2008. The congressional debate on partial-birth abortion: Constitutional gravitas and moral passion. *British Journal of Political Science* 38:383–410.

Sementko, H. A., and P. M. Valkenburg. 2000. Framing european politics: A content analysis of press and television news. *Journal of Communication* Spring:93–109.

Simon, H. A. 1997. *Administrative behavior: A study of decision-making processes in administrative organizations*. 4th ed. New York: The Free Press.

Solka, J. L. 2008. Text data mining: Theory and methods. *Statistics Surveys* 2:94–112.

Srivastava, A. N., and M. Sahami, eds. 2009. *Text mining. Classification, clustering, and application*. Boca Raton: CRC Press.

Steyvers, M., and T. Griffiths. 2007. Probabilistic topic models. In *Latent semantic analysis: A road to meaning*, ed. T. Landauer, D McNamara, S. Dennis and W. Kintsch, Mahwah: Laurence Erlbaum.

Vallbé, J.-J. 2012. Autonomía y organización en el sistema judicial español. In *Sistema político español*, ed. Josep M. Reniu, Huygens Editorial.

Vallbé, J.-J., and M. A. Martí. 2009. *Stemming* y lematización: técnicas de procesamiento del lenguaje para el análisis del discurso del conocimineto profesional del juez. In *Web Semántica y ontologías jurídicas. Aplicaciones para el derecho en la nueva generación de la red*, ed. P. Casanovas, J.-J. Vallbé, M. Fernández-Barrera, and V. R. Benjamins. Comares, Forthcoming.

Vallbé, J.-J., Martí, M. A., Fortuna, B., Jakulin, A., Mladenič, D., and P. Casanovas. 2007. Stemming and lemmatisation: Improving knowledge management through language processing techniques. In *Trends in legal knowledge—the semantic web and the regulation of electronic social systems*, ed. P. Casanovas, P. Noriega, D. Bourcier, and F. Galindo, pp. 227–242. Granada: European Press Academic Publishing.

Ward, J. H. 1963. Hierarchical grouping to optimize an objective function. *Journal of the American Statistical Association* 58:236–244.

Witherspoon, D. J., S. Wooding, A. Rogers, E. Marchani, W. Watkins, M. Batzer, and L. Jorde. 2007. Genetic similarities within and between human populations. *Genetics* 176 (1): 351–359.

Young, L., and S. Soroka. 2012. Affective news: The automated coding of sentiment in political texts. *Political Communication* 29:205–231.

Chapter 6
Conclusions and Further Work

Abstract In this chapter we present, first, general conclusions to the book. Afterward, we discuss three different sets of issues regarding the results presented in this book. First, we outline the need for a general framework that combines statistical programming and natural language processing. Second, we discuss the challenges that our results pose to the design of bureaucratic organizations and how improvised solutions should be integrated into organizational memories. Third, we relate our results with further paths of research about procedural rationality and expertise.

6.1 Conclusions

This work has presented the results of a research about the implications of bounded rationality in the operation of an institution such as the Spanish Court of First Instance and Magistrate. In particular, the work has focused on the environment within which decision-making under uncertainty is possible.

The main contribution of this book has been to identify the on-call service as an organizational challenge both to judges' decision-making activity and to the classical view of this institution as a source for behavioral predictability. In particular, we have shown that the on-call service implies a suspension of that institution's role as a stable pattern of events.

Our approach has emphasized the role of procedural rationality delivering also a procedural notion of uncertainty—in contrast to a substantive notion—understood as lack of procedural knowledge in problem solving situations. These problematic situations have been retrieved from junior judges' own textual accounts of problems faced during the on-call service at Spanish Courts of First Instance and Magistrate. Our hypotheses have been tested through the intensive use of textual statistics and text mining techniques, but our approach has deep roots in behavioral traditions of organizational and decision analysis.

As a matter of fact, our behavioral approach has elaborated upon the analysis of the main contributions made within research fields such as organization theory, behavioral decision making analysis, and cognitive science.

In particular, the first part of the book (the two first chapters) was devoted to carry out a critical analysis of the main features of human rationality—i.e., the

J.-J. Vallbé, *Frameworks for Modeling Cognition and Decisions in Institutional Environments*, Law, Governance and Technology Series 21, DOI 10.1007/978-94-017-9427-5_6

human capacity to make rational decisions—and the role of organizations in decision making.

In Chap. 2 a simple model has been presented in order to classify and briefly review different approaches to decision-making within organizations in political science. To this end, two variables have guided the critical account: the theory of rationality underlying each perspective, and the organizational influence on decision-making, dividing this last factor into two sub-variables (nature of influence and direction of influence).

One of the many criticisms our model may deserve is that of being too simple, for it depicts a world of research programs that are neatly separated and that seldom communicate or debate with each other. Certainly, in the chapter we have noted that debate has taken place around a number of issues, though the impression was that interventions from one perspective into the other's matters were rather sparse. However, certain debate can be identified along at least three different dimensions:

- Empirical, which affects the assumptions on human rationality upon which each perspective rests.
- Methodological, which refers to the possibility of building general models of rational decision making.
- Research agenda, which refers to the need and adequacy of either descriptive or prescriptive models of human decision making.

We have assumed that the aim of a behavioral model of decision making is not to bring out the biases in judgment by people, but to "attempt to arrive at a descriptive model of human judgment" (Shapira 2008, p. 291). Therefore, our first conclusion has been that a descriptive, behavioral assessment of some aspects of actual judicial decision making was worth undertaking, at least before any prescriptive work on decision making was tackled.

Regarding the behavioral approach, we have also commented that while the early works on behavioral decision making contributed a group of ideas that were mainly intuitions about organizational decision processes, there was actually a set of topics that built on these intuitions and that have received most attention from behavioral researchers on decision-making (March 1990), including the problem of preferences, the problem of optimality, and the need for allocating attention.

We have concluded affirming that these problems refer to the general duty of drawing a realistic picture of rational behavior in order to understand decisions made both by individuals and by organizations. Which, in fact, directly points to a discussion on the differences between the normative, descriptive, and prescriptive role of the social sciences, in particular of political science.

A theoretical framework to guide our descriptive analysis of decision making has been attempted in Chap. 3. Following the main behavioral decision analysis tradition both in cognitive sciences and organizational analysis, we have explored the implications of adopting the model of bounded rationality to organizational decision making. In particular, we have explored the implications of separating the inner and outer environments of decisions in our analysis.

Regarding the inner environment, we saw that decisions are made with respect to a simplified model of the world (according to that classical view of the "definition of the situation" (March and Simon 1958, p. 139)) required by the limits of human rationality. In this direction, three different dimensions have been presented that explain the limits that shape human rationality.

The first one refers to the cognitive limits humans have to process information, which are mostly viewed as limits in our capacity for attaining and learning concepts, storing and processing information, and processing natural language.

The second dimension accounts for the notion of *satisficing* (Simon 1996) as a mechanism of human bounded rationality. First, we have reviewed the criticism to different unrealistic—in terms of human rationality—approaches. Second, we have seen that a satisficing policy can also be seen as a trigger for search for better alternatives.

The third dimension tackled the difference between procedural rationality and substantive rationality and briefly outlined a problem-solving theoretical framework that helped understanding the mechanisms individuals use in order to adapt to the constraints imposed by the outer environment. In particular, a theory of problem-solving was overviewed that accounts for the way human beings selectively (heuristically) search for solutions in a 'space' provided by the problem to be solved.

Regarding the external environment, our starting premise was that the elements of this simplified model of the world are neither fixed nor given but are the outcomes of the interaction between the individual and his social and organizational environment (including his psychological outcomes) (Simon and Stern 1955; Cyert and Simon 1956). This is especially important in information-rich domains as the one we are involved in.

We argued that, as a consequence, only the analysis of the individual's adaptive problem-solving behavior would give us access to the characteristics and complexity of this external environment through the problems that spring from it (and that are perceived by the individual). This has had methodological consequences in the development of our own work, as shall be seen.

Nevertheless, a preliminary overview of the potential elements to be accounted for in our own study has been carried out. Our presentation was based upon our and others' previous observation of incomplete data pertaining to our case.

In our approach, we have started focusing on the organization as the most relevant part of the outer environment in the context of our work. First two major general factors have been identified that make rationality possible in an organizational environment:

- The organization's structure is a rather stable pattern of events enabling both predictability and stability of the behavior of the people that surrounds the decision-maker.
- The organizational frame reinforces the human tendency to split problems, tasks, and goals into smaller subparts, achieving a rather simplified model of the objective situation.

Later on, we have seen that there may be a number of problems that may challenge rationality in decision-making within organizations, and some mechanisms that typically counteract these phenomena have been briefly presented as they appear in the mainstream specialized literature on organizational decision analysis.

Among these mechanisms we have focused upon (a) bottlenecks of attention—tasks and subtasks division, selective perception, and communication biases—that show that attention is a scarce resource; (b) mutually inconsistent preferences within the organization—departmentalization, time as a scarce resource, organizational slack; and (c) the production and institutionalization of effective adaptive responses—routines, organizational memory—to particular situations.

Finally, two sections have been devoted to relate the former elements to two further phenomena that are potentially critical in our case. Firstly we tackled the notion of uncertainty, mainly understood as lack of knowledge about the processes to be followed in order to solve a problem. Secondly we noted that some recent accounts of decision-making processes in real settings may point to establish a connection between the notion of expertise and our former notion of uncertainty.

This relation becomes clear when both uncertainty and expertise are understood as functions of procedural rationality, i.e., as functions of the process of search for alternatives by the decision-maker.

Globally, these and other features are seen as mechanisms that make organizations adaptive systems that are able to achieve goals and make decisions that otherwise (e.g. at an individual level) would have been very difficult. We ended up this chapter commenting on two different concluding issues that affected the development of our work in the second part. On one hand, we observed that the main behavioral literature on decision-making we had reviewed so far rarely presented cases in which decisions were made under conditions of absolute certainty, and in this respect we suggested that the amount of uncertainty surrounding a decision might be viewed as a function of the efficiency in which mechanisms for organizational bounded rationality succeed in that particular situation.

Regarding the second observation—a methodological one—we noted that coherently with our approach to the definition of the outer environment, we emphasized the relevance of considering this environment's demands as they are perceived by the decision-makers themselves. This commitment therefore implied that our analysis would not be based upon neither objective nor fixed definitions of problems but rather on data gathering the decision-makers' perceptions of those problems.

Chapter 4 has provided us the chance to begin such an analysis. To begin with, and based upon our own data from a survey, we have provided a profile for Spanish junior judges, with the aim of better understanding their professional integration. In particular, the chapter had two main purposes. First, to outline the main characteristics of our decision-makers (junior judges) and their organizational context (Spanish judicial system). Second, to explore whether their main difficulties in decision-making might be explained by differences in individual or contextual factors.

Though in the first section a brief overview of the Spanish judicial system has been carried out, our first objective was to give an account of the context in which junior judges start working, and so we have seen that the first appointment locations of

Spanish junior judges are the actual entry—as for citizens—to the Spanish judicial system: Courts of First Instance and Magistrate scattered throughout the Spanish territory.

Further commenting on this organizational unit, we have identified the court office as the basic structural unit within Courts of First Instance and Magistrate. Regarding its members, different administrative levels have been identified which outline official and actual authority lines within the court office itself. Thus a preliminary conclusion was that a lack of clear hierarchical lines might be observed among the constituents of the court office. However, we have also noted that no relevant conflict within the court office has been observed in our data resulting from this situation, since judges actually *are* the highest authority within the court office.

The second main purpose of this chapter was to present the main individual features of Spanish junior judges. As for judges' educational and professional experience, three different variables have been analyzed: (a) whether judges had studied postgraduate studies before their examination, (b) whether they had practiced other legal professions before their examination, and (c) the time passed between their Law degree and their passing the examination. In this sense, the results show that those who had practiced other legal professions tended also to have postgraduate studies. And, inversely, those who had postgraduate studies tended also to have practiced other legal professions.

We have then related having practiced other legal professions with the time spent before passing the examination, and we have found that a very high percentage of those who have not practiced any legal profession before have actually passed their examination within 7 years, while nearly 40 % of those who have spent more than 7 years in passing the examination had practiced some legal profession. We thus concluded that judges who spend more than 7 years between their Law degree and the judicial examination have actually dedicated those extra years working in other legal occupations and/or attending to postgraduate studies.

With regard to professional integration, we have observed that Spanish junior judges present a quite low level of formal professional integration but fairly high levels of informal ties with other colleagues. In particular, we observed that consistently with previous studies, junior judges present a low rate of membership in professional associations, while a very high percentage of junior judges affirmed to have contact with their Judicial School mates, and this contact was mostly frequent or very frequent. A high percentage also declared to keep contact with judges from other classes.

In addition, we also observed that the assessment judges make regarding their relationship with other professionals within their working environment is seen as mainly positive. In particular, the professional groups that work both within (clerks, public prosecutors, office staff, and lawyers) and outside (the police) the boundaries of the judicial office receive very high evaluation scores from judges. However, junior judges report to have very little contact with members of institutions out of the court's daily work.

On the other hand, judges' answers on their three best friends have been used as an indicator for measuring judges' traditional (or stereotypical) isolation from the society. We have seen that although historical studies showed that a high percentage of judges' friends were other judges or legal professionals, this percentage is now lower, with a very rich distribution of friends in other diverse professions.

Finally, the profession of junior judges' parents and partner has been used to show the extent to which the historical self-recruitment pattern among Spanish judiciary has changed compared to the first studies made in the 1970s. In this respect we have also seen that while a high proportion of male junior judges have partners linked to the judicial world, female judges do not present such a clear pattern but tend to have liberal professionals rather than legal professionals as partners.

And finally we have explored some quality of life indicators, along with an assessment of their overall satisfaction. It is worth commenting that despite junior judges vastly present low scores in all indicators of quality of life (such as the number of extra hours or the fact of working at home and during weekends), they deliver fairly high levels of satisfaction regarding their work.

In general, according to our data Spanish junior judges present a high degree of *homogeneity* in all basic aspects of their social and professional life. Most of them, first, have no previous experience—either postgraduate or professional—before they pass the examination for becoming judges. Second, homogeneity has been also identified regarding their vastly shared low membership rate to the various existing judicial professional organizations. Thirdly, no special differences among them can be observed as regards their relationship with other groups of professionals with whom they usually work. A vast majority of them even share a lower consideration of those professionals with whom they hardly have any contact. Finally, a final argument for homogeneity was found the various indicators of quality of life presented. Almost all junior judges assure they work at home and during weekends, which gives us an idea of the pressure under which they work. Yet we have seen that a majority of them affirm that they feel satisfied or very satisfied with their work.

However, data also show that most junior judges have difficulties in making decisions to the point of having to comment their doubts to other peers with varied frequency. We have observed, though, that neither the (small) differences among judges in their individual features nor the variation in the demographical composition in their judicial districts were able to explain the frequency at which judges need to comment on these decision-making doubts. We have hypothesized that their main source of uncertainty is to be found in the nature of the problems they face. In particular, our general hypothesis was that "the problems junior judges encounter when on-call are of a special kind in so far they can be described as organizational demands that are practical and not theoretical in nature. That would explain why the on-call service in lower courts is the major source of uncertainty in the decision-making process of junior judges".

In particular, Chap. 5 has been devoted to present and test two different but related hypotheses: first, that the types of problems raised during the on-call service are significantly different from those raised by ordinary civil and criminal procedures; second, that the problems faced when on call are not related to theoretical doubts but mainly practical doubts, i.e., they are identifiable demands from the outer environment whose solution is not specifically contained in the legal knowledge they acquire either in the law degree or preparing the entrance examination.

In order to test our hypotheses we have adopted a textual analysis strategy—text as data. To begin with, three different corpora were used:

- `civil`: the collection of all responses regarding problems about civil issues, each document representing one single answer.
- `criminal`: the collection of all responses regarding problems about criminal issues, each document representing one single answer.
- `on-call`: the collection of all responses regarding problems about on-call issues, each document representing one single answer.

We have treated our first hypothesis both as a classification problem to test whether the three types of corpora are significantly different from each other, and as a representation problem in order to identify patterns in the textual data that allow the identification of clusters of documents. To do so, we have used a hierarchical clustering method and multidimensional scaling, which have provided evidence of the existence of clusters of documents based upon their content similarity in the Vector Space Model. In addition, an Ordinary Least Squares regression model provides further support to the existence fo significant differences among documents depicting problems of civil, criminal, and on-call nature.

In our second hypothesis we aimed at exploring the role of the organizational environment into the decision-making process of junior judges. In particular, the hypothesis addressed the extent to which most problems and doubts faced when judges are on-call constitute demands from their organizational environment, and therefore merely procedural and behavioral, in contrast with a more theoretical-based nature of the problems raised during ordinary criminal, and specially civil, procedures.

Following our textual analysis strategy, to test our hypothesis we carried out two different analyses. On one hand, we automatically retrieved the issues and problems that judges refer to in their responses. On the other, we explored whether the kinds of problems they identify as specific of on-call situations are of a different kind than those raised during ordinary civil and criminal procedures.

In order to extract the issues referred to by judges in their responses in a systematic way, we used Latent Dirichlet Allocation (LDA), a generative probabilistic topic model for the identification and representation of the content of collections of documents. Once topics have been identified and interpreted, they were be used as outcome variables to feed a model to test the practical nature of the problems raised during on-call situations.

Based on the twenty first terms of each of the ten topics generated by our probabilistic topic model, two main kinds of topics were identified: some topics referred mainly to technical, theoretical legal problems, especially through legal terms related to civil procedures such as *jus in rem* and to civil procedures themselves. On the other hand, another set of topics were classified as behavioral given their reference to actors and behavioral situations. Instead of presenting technical legal terms, these topics contain mainly actors (prosecutor, medical examiner) and terms referring to practical actions (detention, domestic violence).

Moreover, results give support to our hypothesis that on-call problems are mainly behavioral while civil and criminal problems depicted by junior judges are mainly theoretical. In particular, according to our results problems on civil procedures have a 80 % chance to be of technical nature, while problems depicting on-call situations present a chance between 70 and 80 % of being behavioral, and less than 10 % chance of being technical. Finally, judges' explanations on problems during criminal procedures have a 50–50 chance of being either technical or behavioral.

These results point to a first methodological conclusion regarding the use of textual analysis techniques in this and other similar endeavors. On one hand, our strategy of assessing judges' problems through different textual statistics and text mining techniques has proved successful in helping us simplifying and delivering the basic elements that constitute these judges' different problem spaces through which they must search for solutions. Regarding this question, there is room for optimism, because through these basic elements we have been able to assess the presence or absence of particular terms and their association to other terms, which in turn enabled us drawing preliminary conclusions on the practical nature of the problems.

But on the other hand, we must accept that these techniques have perceivable limits that affect both on the richness of the data they deliver and thus on the interpretation they allow for. In effect, even though information simplification may be regarded as a benefit for our analytic purposes, it certainly may also be a drawback, since a notable information loss is produced when textual data results are necessarily reduced to a manageable size.

In particular, certain amount of domain knowledge has proved absolutely necessary in order to give a first interpretation of the textual statistical results. Yet we do not regard this need as a real drawback but as a feature to be taken into account in any attempt to represent domain knowledge. This finding is actually coherent with specific studies on this field (e.g., Casellas 2011).

In addition, we have also observed that when semantic spaces are reduced to small sets of vocabulary, a great deal of information is lost regarding the particular problems represented by these terms. In other words, although we count on the valuable possibility to give empirically grounded reasons to the association of both the relevance and the association of particular terms so that they enable a semantic interpretation, the final assessment of the actual content of these associations—their details—requires accessing the textual corpora.

Yet while these boundaries are unquestionable and unavoidable, our opinion is that some of our objectives were achieved through statistical means (plus some domain knowledge). In particular, the combination of clustering and scaling algorithms and multivariate techniques (and some visualization tools) have given us the opportunity to (a) outline the basic elements that constitute every relevant problem environment, and to (b) test whether these elements referred to behavioral or theoretical problems, so that despite reading the actual responses has been needed in order to test the validity of our insights, their representation had been previously possible.

These results connect to the need for solutions in the form of organizational routines which would enable a more efficient management of these problems and, ultimately, to reduce the unpredictability of typical on-call situations.

In particular, our analysis brings us to the assessment that the lack of these "repertory of response programs" has been apparent during on-call services. These routines have been widely studied by many behavioral scholars as adaptive responses to organizational stimuli, so that they ensure the role of organizations as predictable and stable patters of events, which is one of the is that routines tend to increase the *predictability* of individual activities within an organization, which has been one of the columns upon which behavioral organization analysis has traditionally evolved since Herbert Simon's and James March's seminal contributions in the field (Simon 1947; March and Simon 1958).

Based on our findings in this chapter, we have finally proposed a description of the on-call service as a "well-defined organizational element in junior judges' professional activity where they lack specific routines that enable them to find out quick solutions when urgent decisions are needed". Moreover, this description proved coherent with our research regarding uncertainty about means and the heuristic nature of human problem solving.

Finally, we have reached our final conclusion using the terms of our central hypothesis: the on-call service, under certain conditions, embodies a moment in which an institution such as the Court of First Instance and Magistrate—within the Spanish judicial system—*suspends its role as a reliable pattern of events.*

6.2 Further Work

The work we have presented should not be viewed as an end in itself but as an opportunity to either start new lines of research, or to strengthen lines in which we have already been involved through research projects. Three different lines of discussion will be briefly outlined here, one methodological, and two substantial.

The methodological one refers to the need of an integrated framework for carrying out different kinds of textual analysis (e.g., text statistics and text mining).

As for the substantial issues for discussion, the suspension of an organization's role as a stable and predictable pattern of events seems to have at least two interpretations for future research that seem worth briefly exposing here. The first one refers to our work as a contribution in organizational or institutional design. The second one points out its potential usefulness in studies on decision-making proper.

6.2.1 Textual Methods

As for the methodological comment, this work might be viewed not only as a contribution to the reliable application of textual analysis to the study of decision-making and institutions, but also as a contribution to the use of R as a general and reliable tool for textual analysis.

To our knowledge, while some research is being developed using R as such a framework for content analysis with potential political application (e.g., Benoit and Laver 2002; Laver et al. 2003; Lowe 2008; Hopkins and King 2007) our use of it for organizational decision-making analysis has not been common so far.

Nevertheless, this book has also shown that, on the one hand, when text is presented in languages with rich inflection rates, default word reduction tools included in this general framework and others may pose some problems for ulterior analyses on text. On the other hand, we have seen that in order to meet our goals a multi-stage strategy had to be developed so that the outcomes delivered by some tools could be used as inputs for other ones. Though the overall result has been evaluated as satisfactory, these operations, in particular those of converting natural language text files into lemmatized text files, can be very time-consuming for users.

Therefore, an integration of most needed textual analytic tasks such as lemmatization or producing term frequency lists and term-document matrices would seem highly useful. In particular, while a library such as `tm` (Feinerer 2008) has proved excellent to convert textual data into statistically treatable data, no other tool has been found to quickly convert natural language corpora into its lemmatized (not just stemmed) form within the same programming framework.

6.2.2 *Organization Design*

Regarding the first non-methodological issue for discussion, we may outline the suspension of an organization's role as a stable and predictable pattern of events as a typical matter of organizational or institutional design. Certainly, some reasons may be argued for defending that the current way in which the on-call service is designed for Spanish judicial settings could leave room for some improvements.

A first and general one would be related to the fact that a necessarily formalized and predictable institution such as any justice administration should be able to assure stable and predictable decisions at all its organizational units and during all decision situations.

A second one deals with the fact the professionals who work within this organization express doubts that in their purely procedural nature sharply contrast with the purely theoretical and substantial content of judges' educational experience. This perspective would entail, in our opinion, a reflection on the match between current methods for judicial recruitment (i.e., a merely theoretical-based entrance examination) and the actual kind of situations judges must face in their two first years as judges. Let us recall here that Courts of First Instance and Magistrate—junior judges' working settings—are Spanish citizens' actual entry to the Spanish judicial system.

We have seen that discussions around this issue have actually been carried out (e.g., Jiménez-Asensio 2001; Poblet and Casanovas 2005). These discussions, as we saw, focus on the method through which judges are recruited.

However, in our opinion one of the main objectives of a new organizational design for the on-call service should also be to provide judges with the kind of procedural information they need to make urgent decisions when they are required. And this task would not be impossible, either through modifications in the entrance system, or through *a posteriori* interventions.

As a matter of fact, we have seen that judges do generally find solutions to their procedural problems. These solutions may be achieved through their own search or through the consultation with other judges or whoever they feel confident with. Yet when these solutions have been found, they may be used in the future as adaptive rules of behavior, or routines.

The design and implementation of knowledge management tools in the legal domain has been triggered by the need to cope with the volume and complexity of knowledge and information produced by current legal organizations.

Applied to judicial administration, these systems typically help with storing, managing, and keeping track of documents used in or related to legal proceedings. Obviously these documents include judicial decisions (and templates and protocols to produce them), but they are specially designed to enable an efficient management of secondary but highly relevant documents issued by the court personnel—such as court orders, decrees, notifications, and transcripts of declarations. These systems help judicial units maintain the information and knowledge that their members need in order to work effectively on every stage of the procedure.

Yet, legal organizations (and organizations in general) prove less efficient in storing and routinize informal knowledge or knowledge produced while managing improvisation-prone situations.

In this sense, technological advances have been made that enable formalizing, interpreting and storing knowledge so that it can be retrieved when needed. In particular, the construction of a knowledge-based decision-support system for judges such as Iuriservice (Casanovas et al. 2006a, b; Casellas et al. 2006, 2007; Poblet et al. 2008), is to be seen as an excellent research line to explore the unequivocal benefits knowledge technologies can bring to organizational design.

Moreover, Casellas (2011) has recently pointed out the necessity of judges' participation (as experts) in such technological projects, providing precise guidelines in order to acquire their knowledge, and proposing a data-grounded formalization. Elsewhere Bösser et al. (2005) have provided also examples of judges' participation in building such a decision-support system. And finally Casanovas et al. (2006a) have presented an empirical assessment of judges' evaluation of the benefits provided by such a tool when user satisfaction tests have been carried out with a prototype. In addition, relevant contributions have been made during the last decade in Europe on the role of knowledge and information technologies aiding information and knowledge management in courts (Fabri and Contini 2001; Fabri et al. 2003; Langbroek and Fabri 2004; Fabri 2007; Poblet et al. 2008).

Therefore, with regard to this first research field, our contribution in this book seems quite adequate for identifying knowledge-intensive areas when outlining the elements that constitute judges' problem space in several decision situations. In addition, our use of various text analysis techniques could also help knowledge acquisition processes for the construction of knowledge-based systems aimed at helping decision-makers.

6.2.3 Procedural Rationality, Expertise, and Heuristics

Finally, a third broad line of further research may focus upon the relationship between procedural rationality and expertise, as it was commented in Sect. 3.3.6. Our assertion was that routines as we understood them are relevant in our analysis so far they are not only devices for solving immediate problems, but, most important, they are devices for learning and for turning inexperienced professionals into experts. Besides, we therefore regard them as mechanisms for making better decisions.

In this work we have observed that the relationship between adaptive rules of behavior and learning from experience has been related to different aspects of organizational behavior, change, and evolution. In addition, we have also seen that many scholars (e.g., Levitt and March 1988; March 1990) have analyzed routines as containers of expert knowledge from which inferences may be made in order to guide both individual and organizational behavior. Yet while this knowledge can be recorded in the organization's collective memory, it can also be lost. We may thus interpret the phenomenon we have studied as a loss of judges' expert knowledge, coherently with previous attempts to approach it (e.g., Benjamins et al. 2005; Blázquez et al. 2005; Casanovas et al. 2005).

In our theoretical contextualization of uncertainty in the behavioral decision analysis tradition, we have observed that according to our perspective, problem solving (both by human beings and organizations) occurs through information processing. We also contended that "the process of solving the problem has at least two different moments. In the first one, the decision-maker will search for solutions in his long-term memory (LTM) in the form of patterns related to past problems and solutions attached to those problems. The second one is that when this search fails, the decision-maker will initiate the search for new alternatives or solutions".

Finally, we also linked expert knowledge to uncertainty by stating that the extent to which an individual is able to recognize, associate, and retrieve information stored in his long-term memory and, thus, to propose a quick solution makes the difference between a layman and an expert. In these terms, our notion of uncertainty is related to procedural rationality, but also to expertise.

Regarding expertise, we explored empirical assessments of decision-making situations which show that decisions may be better understood as a "matching process between situations and actions instead of the generation of, and choice from, the set of possible actions" (Rosen et al. 2008, p. 214), in clear contrast with other model-based approaches.

Drawing on (Rosen et al. 2008) we have reviewed the two basic levels in which expertise has been approached. The first refers to expertise as "a function of extensive domain specific knowledge", represented by classical studies on expert performance such as de Groot (1978) and Chase and Simon (1973). The second refers to the fact that the decision-maker's adaptation to the task demands enable expertise (Ericsson and Chi 1996), which brought us to the problem of uncertainty about the means to reach a solution to a problem.

Our final statement regarding this issue was that according to this framework there seems to be a direct link between the path followed by the decision maker and the structure of the problem to be decided upon (i.e., solved). Therefore, this has brought us to the necessity of gathering the description of the problems related to a set of decision-making situations in order to better understand the environment demands these problems are an expression of.

In our case, being professional problems mainly related to on-call situations, and understanding routines junior judges lack of as mainly procedural in nature—due to the on-call environmental demands—the process by which they search for solutions might be approached as a process by which they turn from professionals to experts.

Moreover, this book could be seen as an empirically grounded framework for further research on heuristic strategies used in real working environments. Recent developments on so-called naturalistic decision making analysis (Todd and Gigerenzer 2001; Salas and Klein 2001; Currey and Botti 2003; Hoffman 2007; Koehler and Harvey 2007; Rosen et al. 2008) and heuristics (Gigerenzer and Selten 2001; Gigerenzer and Engel 2006; Schraagen et al. 2008; Gigerenzer and ABC-Research-Group 2008) let us regard our contribution as potentially fruitful.

In conclusion, the work we have just presented is to be seen as an opportunity to carry out further research on uncertainty as a function of the efficiency with which mechanisms for organizational bounded rationality succeed in particular problem-solving situations. In this sense, the relationship between procedural rationality and uncertainty (Royer and Langley 2008), and then the relationship of both with expertise seem critical to an empirical approach to decision-making in professional environments.

References

Benjamins, V. R., P. Casanovas, J. Contreras, J. López-Cobo, and M. Lemus. 2005. Iuriservice: An intelligent frequent asked questions system to assist newly appointed judges. In *Law and the semantic web: Legal ontologies, methodologies, legal information retrieval, and applications*. Lecture notes in computer science, ed. V. Benjamins, P. Casanovas, J. Breuker, and A. Gangemi. vol. 3369, 205–222. Berlin: Springer.

Benoit, K., and M. Laver. 2002. Estimating Irish party policy positions using computer wordscoring: the 2002 election. Research note, Trinity College Dublin, Dublin, Ireland.

Blázquez, M., R. Peña-Ortiz, J. Contreras, V. R. Benjamins, P. Casanovas, J.-J. Vallbé, and N. Casellas. 2005. D10.3.1 legal case study: Prototype. Technical report, SEKT, EU-IST Project IST-2003-506826, Intelligent Software Components S.A. (iSOCO) and Universitat Autonoma de Barcelona (UAB).

Bösser, T., E.-M. Melchior, I. Thurlow, S. Close, D. Alsmeyer, J. Contreras, J.-J. Vallbé, and R. Zeilbeck. 2005. User needs and opportunities for business improvement with knowledge technology. Deliverable D8.2.1 WP8 Usability and business benchmarking, SEKT Project (EU-IST Project IST-2003-506826 SEKT), Springer, Switzerland.

Casanovas, P., N. Casellas, J.-J. Vallbé, M. Poblet, F. Ramos, J. Gorroñogoitia, J. Contreras, M. Blázquez, and V. R. Benjamins. 2005. Iuriservice II: Ontology development and architectural design. Proceedings of the international conference on artificial intelligence and law, ICAIL-05,AAAI-ACM, 188–195, Bologna, Italy.

Casanovas, P., N. Casellas, J.-J. Vallbé, M. Poblet, V. R. Benjamins, M. Blázquez, R. Peña-Ortiz, and J. Contreras. 2006a. Semantic web: A legal case study. In *Semantic web technologies: Trends and research in ontology-based systems*, ed. J. Davies, R. Studer, and P. Warren, Chap. 12, 259–280. Chichester: Wiley.

Casanovas, P., J.-J. Vallbé, N. Casellas, M. Poblet, M. Blázquez, J. Contreras, V. R. Benjamins, and J. López-Cobo. 2006b. Legal case study after analysis D10.4.1. case study: Intelligent integrated decision suppot for legal professionals. Technical Report D10.4.1, SEKT Project (EU-IST Project IST-2003-506826 SEKT), Barcelona.

Casellas, N. 2011. *Legal ontology engineering: Methodologies, trends, and the ontology of professional judicial knowledge*. Dordrecht: Springer.

Casellas, N., A. Jakulin, J.-J. Vallbé, and P. Casanovas. 2006. Acquiring an ontology from the text. In *Advances in applied artificial intelligence. 19th international conference on industrial, engineering and other applications of applied intelligent systems, IEA/AIE 2006*. Lecture notes in computer science, ed. M. Ali and R. Dapoigny, vol. 4031, 1000–1013. Berlin: Springer.

Casellas, N., P. Casanovas, J.-J. Vallbé, M. Poblet, M. Blázquez, J. Contreras, J. López-Cobo, and V. R. Benjamins. 2007. Semantic enhancement for legal information retrieval: IURISERVICE performance. In *Proceedings of the 11th international conference on artificial intelligence and law (ICAIL)*, 49–57. ACM: Stanford.

Chase, W. G., and H. A. Simon. 1973. Perception in chess. *Cognitive Psychology* 4 (1): 55–81.

Currey, J., and M. Botti. 2003. *Naturalistic decision making: A model to overcome methodological challenges in the study of critical care nurses' decision making about patients' hemodynamic status. American Journal of Critical Care* 12 (3): 206–211.

Cyert, R. M., and H. A. Simon. 1956. Observation of a business decision. *The Journal of Business* 29 (4): 237–248.

de Groot, A. 1978. *Thought and choice in chess*. 2nd edn. The Hague: Mouton de Gruyter.

Ericsson, K. A., and M. T. H. Chi. 1996. Expert and exceptional performance: Evidence of maximal adaptation to task constraints. *Annual Review of Psychology* 47:273–305.

Fabri, M., ed. 2007. *Information and communication technology for the public prosecutor's office*. Bologna: CLUEB.

Fabri, M., and F. Contini, ed. 2001. *Justice and technology in Europe: How ICT is changing the judicial business*. The Hague: Kluwer Law International.

Fabri, M., P. M. Langbroek, and H. Pauliat, ed. 2003. *The administration of justice in Europe: Towards the development of quality standards*. IRSIG-CNR, Unversity of Bologna. Bologna: Lo Scarabeo.

Feinerer, I. 2008. *tm: Text Mining Package*, R package version 0.3-3 edition.

Gigerenzer, G., and ABC-Research-Group, ed. 2008. *Simple heuristics that make us smart*. New York: Oxford University Press.

Gigerenzer, G., and E. Engel, ed. 2006. *Heuristics and the Law*. Cambridge: MIT Press.

Gigerenzer, G., and R. Selten, ed. 2001. *Bounded rationality: The adaptive toolbox*. Dahlem Workshop Reports. Cambridge: MIT Press.

Hoffman, R., ed. 2007. *Expertise out of context: Proceedings of the sixth international conference on naturalistic decision making*. New York: Lawrence Erlbaum Associates.

Hopkins, D., and G. King. 2007. Extracting systematic social science meaning from text. Technical report, Institute for Quantitative Social Science, Harvard University, Cambridge, MA.

Jiménez-Asensio, R., ed. 2001. *El acceso a la función judicial. Estudio comparado*. Manuales de formación continuada. Consejo General del Poder Judicial, Madrid, Spain.

Koehler, D. J., and N. Harvey, ed. 2007. *Blackwell handbook of judgment and decision making*. Oxford: Blackwell.

Langbroek, P. M., and M. Fabri, ed. 2004. *Case assignment to courts and within courts: A comparative study in seven countries*. Maastricht: Shaker.

Laver, M., K. Benoit, and J. Garry. 2003. Extracting policy positions from political texts using words as data. *The American Political Science Review* 97 (2): 311–331.

Levitt, B., and J. G. March. 1988. Organizational learning. *Annual Review of Sociology* 14:319–340.

Lowe, W. 2008. Understanding wordscores. *Political Analysis* 16:356–371.

March, J. G. 1990. Introduction: A chronicle of speculations about decision-making in organizations. In *Decisions and organizations*, ed. J. G. March, 1–21. Oxford: Blackwell.

March, J. G., and H. A. Simon. 1958. *Organizations*. New York: Wiley.

Poblet, M., and P. Casanovas. 2005. Recruitment, professional evaluation and career of judges and prosecutors in Spain. In *Recruitment, professional evaluation and career of judges and prosecutors in Europe: Austria, France, Germany, Italy, The Netherlands and Spain*, ed. G. Di Federico, 185–213. Bologna: Lo scarabeo. (IR).

Poblet, M., J.-J. Vallbé, N. Casellas, and P. Casanovas. 2008. Judges as IT users: The IURISERVICE example. In *E-justice, using information communication in the court system*, ed. A. Cerrillo and P. Fabra. Hershey: IGI Books.

Rosen, M. A., E. Salas, R. Lyons, and S. M. Fiore. 2008. Experts and naturalistic decision making in organizations: mechanisms of effective decision making. In *The Oxford handbook of organizational decision making*, ed. G. P. Hodgkinson and W. H. Starbuck, 211–230. Oxford: Oxford University Press

Royer, I., and A. Langley. 2008. Linking rationality, politics, and routines in organizational decision making. In *The Oxford handbook of organizational decision making*, ed. G. P. Hodgkinson and W. H. Starbuck, 250–270. New York: Oxford University Press.

Salas, E., and G. A. Klein, ed. 2001. *Linking expertise and naturalistic decision making*. New York: Lawrence Erlbaum Associates.

Schraagen, J., L. Militello, T. Ormerod, and R. Lipshitz, ed. 2008. *Naturalistic decision making and macrocognition*. Aldershot: Ashgate.

Shapira, Z. 2008. On the implications of behavioral decision theory for managerial decision making: Contributions and challenges. In *The Oxford handbook of organizational decision making*, ed. G. P. Hodgkinson and W. H. Starbuck, 287–304. New York: Oxford University Press.

Simon, H. A. 1947. *Administrative behavior: A study of decision-making processes in administrative organizations*. 1st edn. New York: Macmillan.

Simon, H. A. 1996. *The sciences of the artificial*. 3rd edn. Cambridge: MIT Press.

Simon, H. A., and F. Stern. 1955. The effect of television upon voting behavior in Iowa in the 1952 presidential election. *The American Political Science Review* 49 (2): 470–477.

Todd, P., and G. Gigerenzer. 2001. Putting naturalistic decision making into the adaptive toolbox. *Journal of Behavioral Decision Making* 14 (5): 381–382.

Index

J.-J. Vallbé, *Frameworks for Modeling Cognition and Decisions in Institutional Environments*,
Law, Governance and Technology Series 21, DOI 10.1007/978-94-017-9427-5

MIX
Papier aus verantwortungsvollen Quellen
Paper from responsible sources
FSC® C105338

If you have any concerns about our products,
you can contact us on
ProductSafety@springernature.com

In case Publisher is established outside the EU,
the EU authorized representative is:
Springer Nature Customer Service Center GmbH
Europaplatz 3, 69115 Heidelberg, Germany

Printed by Libri Plureos GmbH
in Hamburg, Germany